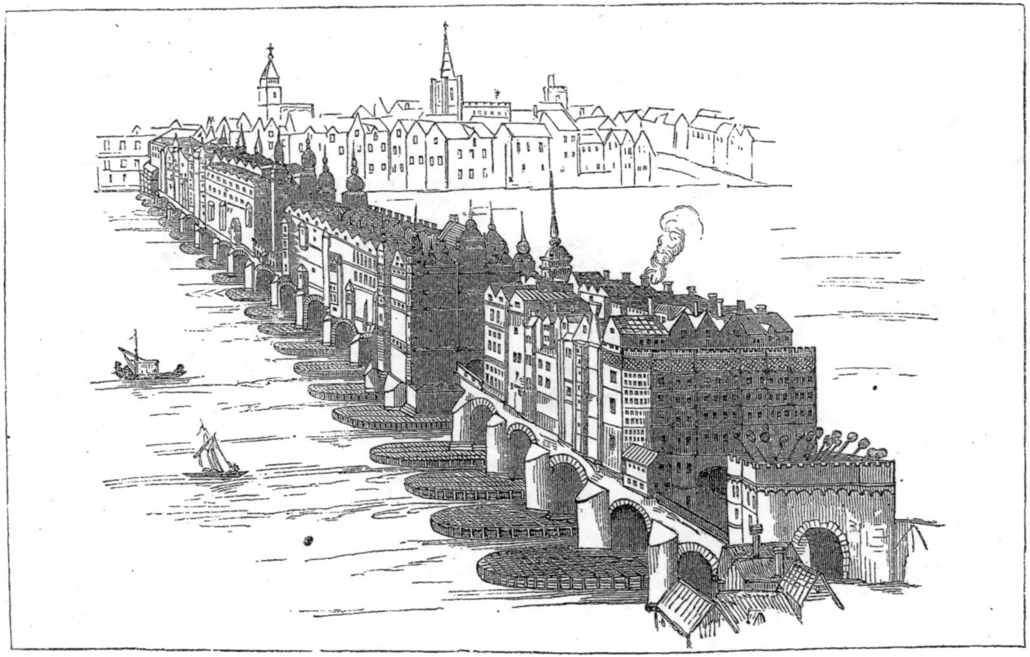

LONDON BRIDGE, 1616.

A

SMALLER HISTORY OF ENGLAND,

FROM THE EARLIEST TIMES TO THE YEAR 1862.

EDITED BY

WILLIAM SMITH, LL.D.

Illustrated by Engravings on Wood.

NEW YORK:
HARPER & BROTHERS, PUBLISHERS,
FRANKLIN SQUARE.
1868.

NOTICE.

The present History has been drawn up by Mr. Philip Smith, under the superintendence and direction of Dr. William Smith, with whose smaller Histories of Greece and Rome it is intended to range.

The most recent authorities have been consulted, and it is confidently believed that the work will be found to present a careful and trust-worthy account of English History for the lower forms in schools, for whose use it is chiefly intended.

The Table of Contents gives a full analysis of the work, and has been so arranged that the teacher can frame from it questions for the examination of his class, the answers to which will be found in the corresponding pages of the volume.

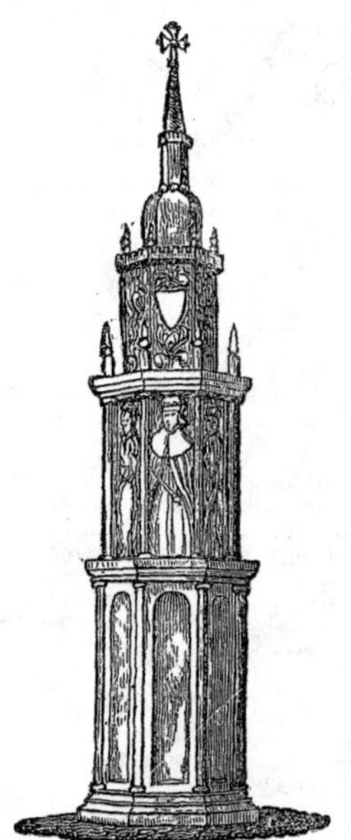

Charing Cross.

The earliest figure of Britannia on a Roman Coin.

CHRONOLOGICAL TABLE OF CONTENTS.

CHAPTER I.

THE BRITONS AND ROMANS. B C. 55—A.D. 446.

CHAPTER II.

THE ANGLO-SAXONS TO THE REIGN OF EGBERT.—THE HEPTARCHY. A.D. 450–827.

CHAPTER III.

THE ANGLO-SAXONS, FROM THE UNION OF ENGLAND UNDER EGBERT TO CANUTE THE DANE. A.D. 827–1016.

CHAPTER IV.

THE DANES AND ANGLO-SAXONS FROM CANUTE TO THE NORMAN CONQUEST. A.D. 1016–1066.

CHAPTER V.

THE ANGLO-NORMAN KINGS.—WILLIAM I. A.D. 1066–1087.

CHAPTER VI.

THE ANGLO-NORMAN KINGS (*continued*).—WILLIAM II., HENRY I., STEPHEN. A.D. 1087–1154.

CHAPTER VII.

THE HOUSE OF PLANTAGENET.—HENRY II. A.D. 1154–1189.

CHAPTER VIII.

THE HOUSE OF PLANTAGENET (*continued*).—RICHARD I., JOHN. A.D. 1189–1216.

CHAPTER IX.

THE HOUSE OF PLANTAGENET (*continued*).—HENRY III. A.D. 1216–1272.

CHAPTER X.

THE HOUSE OF PLANTAGENET (*continued*).—EDWARD I., EDWARD II. A.D. 1272–1327.

CHAPTER XI.

THE HOUSE OF PLANTAGENET (*continued*).—EDWARD III., RICHARD II. A.D. 1327–1399.

CHAPTER XII.

THE HOUSE OF LANCASTER.—HENRY IV. AND HENRY V. A.D. 1399–1422.

CHAPTER XIII.

THE HOUSE OF LANCASTER (*continued*).—HENRY VI. A.D. 1422–1461.

CHAPTER XIV.

THE HOUSE OF YORK.—EDWARD IV., EDWARD V., RICHARD III. A.D. 1461–1485.

CHAPTER XV.

THE HOUSE OF TUDOR.—HENRY VII. A.D. 1485–1509.

CHAPTER XVI.

THE HOUSE OF TUDOR (*continued*).—HENRY VIII. PERIOD I. TO THE FALL OF WOLSEY. A.D. 1509–1530.

CHAPTER XVII.

THE HOUSE OF TUDOR (*continued*).—HENRY VIII. PERIOD II. A.D. 1529–1536.
THE FIRST ENGLISH REFORMATION.

CHAPTER XVIII.

THE HOUSE OF TUDOR (*continued*).—HENRY VIII. PERIOD III. FROM THE EXECUTION OF ANNE BOLEYN TO THE DEATH OF THE KING. A.D. 1536–1547.

CHAPTER XIX.

THE HOUSE OF TUDOR (*continued*).—EDWARD VI. A.D. 1547–1553.

CHAPTER XX.

THE HOUSE OF TUDOR (*continued*).—LADY JANE GREY AND QUEEN MARY I. A.D. 1553–1558.

CHAPTER XXI.

THE HOUSE OF TUDOR (*continued*).—ELIZABETH. A.D. 1558–1603.
SECTION I.—PROGRESS OF THE REFORMATION.

CHAPTER XXII.

THE HOUSE OF TUDOR (*continued*).—ELIZABETH. SECTION II.—MARY STUART AND THE CATHOLICS. A.D. 1558–1587.

CHAPTER XXIII.

THE HOUSE OF TUDOR (*continued*).—ELIZABETH. SECTION III.—THE SPANISH ARMADA. THE QUEEN'S DEATH. A.D. 1587–1603.

CHAPTER XXIV.

THE HOUSE OF STUART.—JAMES I. A.D. 1603–1625.

CHAPTER XXV.

THE HOUSE OF STUART (*continued*).—CHARLES I. FROM HIS ACCESSION TO THE MEETING OF THE LONG PARLIAMENT. A.D. 1625–1640.

CHAPTER XXVI.

THE HOUSE OF STUART (*continued*).—CHARLES I. FROM THE MEETING OF THE LONG PARLIAMENT TO THE EXECUTION OF THE KING. A.D. 1640–1649.

CHAPTER XXVII.

THE COMMONWEALTH. A.D. 1649–1660.

CHAPTER XXVIII.

THE HOUSE OF STUART (*continued*).—CHARLES II. A.D. 1660–1685.

CHAPTER XXIX.

THE HOUSE OF STUART (*continued*).—JAMES II. A.D. 1685–1688.

CHAPTER XXX.

THE REVOLUTION DYNASTY.—WILLIAM AND MARY. A.D. 1689–1694.
WILLIAM III. ALONE. A.D. 1694–1702.

CHAPTER XXXI.

THE REVOLUTION DYNASTY (*continued*).—ANNE. A.D. 1702–1714.

CHAPTER XXXII.

THE HOUSE OF BRUNSWICK, OR HANOVER.—GEORGE I. A.D. 1714–1727.

CHAPTER XXXIII.

THE HOUSE OF BRUNSWICK (*continued*).—GEORGE II. A.D. 1727–1760.

CHAPTER XXXIV.

THE HOUSE OF BRUNSWICK (*continued*).—GEORGE III. FROM HIS ACCESSION TO THE BREAKING OUT OF THE FRENCH REVOLUTION. A.D. 1760–1789.

CHAPTER XXXV.

THE HOUSE OF BRUNSWICK (*continued*).—GEORGE III. FROM THE BEGINNING OF THE FRENCH REVOLUTION TO THE DEATH OF THE KING.

CHAPTER XXXVI.

THE HOUSE OF BRUNSWICK (*continued*).—GEORGE IV. A.D. 1820–1830.

CHAPTER XXXVII.

THE HOUSE OF BRUNSWICK (*continued*).—WILLIAM IV. A.D. 1830–1837.

CHAPTER XXXVIII.

THE HOUSE OF BRUNSWICK (*continued*).—VICTORIA I. A.D. 1837–1862.

LIST OF ILLUSTRATIONS.

HISTORY OF ENGLAND.

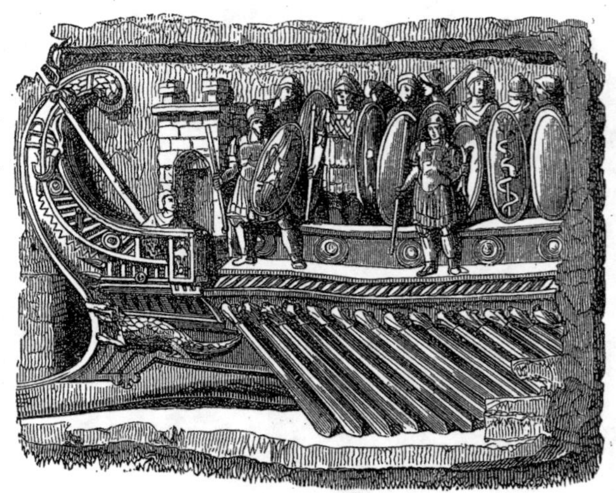

Prow of a Roman Galley.

CHAPTER I.

THE BRITONS AND ROMANS. B.C. 55—A.D. 446.

For the earliest history of Britain we must look to the Greek and Roman writers. Long before Virgil spoke of the Britons as "cut off afar from all the world," the Phœnicians had traded on her shores and obtained tin from the Scilly Isles, which were hence called *Cassiterides* (*Tin Islands*). The British Islands are first mentioned by name by Aristotle, in the fourth century before Christ. He calls England and Scotland *Albion* (probably from the native word for *white*), and Ireland *Iërne.*

The Greek colonists of Massilia (*Marseille*) and Narbo (*Narbonne*) also traded with Britain through Gaul. The chief British exports were tin, lead, skins, hunting-dogs, and slaves; and as the natives became more civilized they exported corn and cattle, gold, silver, and iron, and an inferior sort of pearl.

The Romans had begun to talk of Britain in the second century before Christ; but the real history of her islands begins with their invasion by Julius Cæsar, B.C. 55. His pretext was to avenge the aid which the Britons had given to one of the Gallic tribes; a most interesting testimony to the maritime habits of the people even thus early, as well as to their close relations with the Gauls.

Cæsar reached the coast, probably near Deal, Aug. 26, B.C. 55. The Roman soldiers were intimidated for a moment by the wild enemy, who crowded to defend the beach; but the standard-bearer of the 10th legion dashed through the waves, and the army, following his example, made good their landing. The approach of winter, and pressing affairs, soon caused Cæsar to withdraw to Gaul, having made the Britons only feel his power, and taken hostages for their obedience. His absence relieved them from the fear of the as yet unknown might of Rome. In the following year, however (B.C. 54), he returned, and advancing beyond the Thames he took and burned Verulamium (*St. Alban's*), the fortress of Cassivelaunus, or Caswallon, chief of the Trinobantes, in whose place he set up his own ally Mandubratius, and then returned to Gaul.

The people who inhabited the island at the time of Cæsar were a tribe of the great *Celtic* family who had passed over to Britain from the opposite continent. This is proved by the identity of their language and the resemblance in their manners, government, and religion.

The Celts were divided into two great branches, the *Gael* and the *Cymry*, of whom the former now inhabit Ireland and the highlands of Scotland, and the latter Wales. The Britons almost certainly belonged to the Cymry, and the Celtic words still found in English are of the Cymric, or Welsh, dialect.

The religion of the Britons, which formed one of the most considerable parts of their government, was a terrible form of idolatry called Druidism. The Druids, who were the priests, directed all religious duties, and presided over the education of the youth; they enjoyed an immunity from war and taxes; they possessed both the civil and criminal jurisdiction; they decided all controversies, among states as well as among private persons, and whoever refused to submit to their decrees was exposed to the most severe penalties; the sentence of excommunication was pronounced against him; he was forbidden access to the sacrifices or public worship; he was debarred all intercourse with his fellow-citizens; and was refused the protection of the law. The Druids inculcated piety toward the gods (for they worshiped a plurality of gods), charity toward man, and fortitude in suffering; they taught their disciples astronomy, or rather, perhaps, astrology, and magic, and trained them to acuteness in legal distinctions. Their rites were mysterious and terrible; but we know little of these rights, except their veneration for the oak and mistletoe, and that human sacrifices formed one of the great features of their worship, which was celebrated in the recesses of their forests. Gigantic ruins in different parts of England are supposed to be the remains of Druidical temples, of which the most remarkable are those of Stonehenge on Salisbury Plain, and those at Abury in Wiltshire.

The equestrian order were the next in authority to the Druids. The bards also were closely connected with the Druids. They sang the genealogy of their princes, and accompanied their songs with an instrument called the *chrotta*.

The inhabitants of the southeastern parts of Britain had become somewhat civilized before the time of Cæsar, while the other tribes led the wild and roaming life of shepherds and herdsmen. The Britons tattooed their bodies and stained them with woad. They wore checkered mantles like the Scotch highlanders, girdles round their waists, and metal chains on their breasts; the hair and mustache were suffered to grow, and a ring was worn on the middle finger. Their arms were a small shield, javelins, and a pointless sword. They fought from chariots (*esseda, covini*) having scythes affixed to the axles. They had no regular fortresses, and their towns were mere clusters of huts in the midst of forests, surrounded by a ditch and a rampart of felled trees.

The Britons were divided into several tribes, the government of which was monarchical, but free. The chief tribes known to the Romans were the *Cantii* (in Kent), the *Trinobantes* (in Middlesex and Essex), with the capital *Londinium* (London), the *Cenimagni* or *Iceni* (in Norfolk, Suffolk, and Cambridgeshire), the *Segontiaci* (in Hants and Berks), and the *Ancalites* and *Bibroci* (in Berks and Wilts).

For nearly a century Roman conquest ceased in Britain, but Roman civilization continued to spread, chiefly through intercourse with Gaul. To this period belongs the Prince Cunobelin, a successor of Caswallon, immortalized by Shakspeare under the name of *Cymbeline*. The mad Emperor Caligula only talked of invading Britain, as his soldiers gathered shells on the opposite beach for trophies of his conquest of the ocean, A.D. 40; but his successor, Claudius, in A.D. 43, sent Aulus Plautius, with four legions, to conquer the island. The emperor himself followed, and the southeastern part, from Essex to Hampshire, became a Roman province. The other tribes, however, held out under their heroic leader Caradoc, or CARACTACUS, against whom the emperor sent Ostorius Scapula in A.D. 47. After a brave resistance all the tribes south of the Tyne were defeated, except those of Wales, whither Caractacus had retreated. At length his strong-hold, *Caer Caradoc*, was taken, together with his wife and family, and he himself was soon afterward surrendered to the Romans by his step-mother, Cartismandua, queen of the Brigantes, with whom he had taken refuge. Carried as a prisoner to Rome, he asserted in chains before the throne of Claudius his free-born rights as boldly as he had defended them in arms; and he was treated with the respect due to his courage.

His valor was soon emulated by "the British warrior queen," BOADICEA, princess of the *Iceni*, whose daughters had been outraged and herself scourged by the Roman tribunes. Suetonius Paulinus, whom Nero sent as governor in A.D. 59, attacked the island of Mona (*Anglesey*), which was at once the retreat of those who still resisted, and the chief seat of the worship of the Druids. He burned them in the fires which they had prepared for their captive enemies, and cut down their sacred groves. But his absence was used by the subject Britons as an opportunity for insurrection. Boadicea inflamed their fury by the recital of her cruel wrongs and the exhibition of her outraged daughters with her in her war-chariot. London (*Londinium*), already one of the chief Roman colonies, was reduced to ashes, and 70,000 Romans and other strangers were massacred. But Suetonius avenged this cruelty in a great battle (A.D. 62), in which 80,000 Britons perished, and Boadicea only saved herself from captivity by poison. Suetonius was recalled by Nero; and after the successive administrations of Cerealis (A.D. 71) and Julius Frontinus, Vespasian intrusted the government to JULIUS AGRICOLA, who completed the conquest of the island, and whose campaigns are recorded by his son-in-law, the great historian Tacitus. His government lasted seven years (78–85). In 81 he drew a line of fortresses across the island, between the Firths of Clyde and Forth. In 84 and 85 he advanced into Caledonia (*Scotland*), and in the latter year he defeated the Caledonians, under Galgacus, at the foot of the Grampians. His fleet also circumnavigated the island.

Thus was the country subdued by the Romans as far north as the feet of the Scottish highlands, in which the Caledonians kept their ground. The frontier on this side was not well defined till the reign of Hadrian, who visited the island in person, and fixed the limit of the empire with his characteristic moderation. He raised an earthen rampart across from the Solway Firth to the Tyne, the remains of which are known as the *Picts' Wall*. The frontier was extended under his successor Antoninus Pius, so as to embrace the southern part of what is now Scotland; and a new rampart was drawn by the governor, Lollius Urbicus, along the line of Agricola's forts, between the Firths of Forth and Clyde, A.D. 140, which was called the WALL OF ANTONINUS, and is now known as *Graham's Dyke*.

This more advanced line, however, was not maintained. The great Emperor Severus was summoned in his old age to repel the Caledonians. Though so ill with the gout that he had to be borne in a litter, he penetrated to the extremity of the island, but with the loss of 50,000 men. On his return to York (where he died in A.D. 211) he caused the WALL OF HADRIAN to be repaired; and that wall may be regarded henceforth as the true frontier of the empire.

Thus limited on the north, the Roman province of Britain was governed by a consular legate and a procurator down to A.D. 197, after which it was divided into two provinces, *Britannia Superior* and *Inferior;* and at a later period (under Diocletian or Constantine) into four; namely—(1) *Britannia Prima*, south of the *Severn* and *Thames;* (2) *Britannia Secunda*, containing *Wales* and the border counties, or all to the west of the *Severn* and the *Dee;* (3) *Flavia Cæsariensis*, the whole middle portion from the *Humber* to the *Thames*, except *Wales;* (4) *Maxima Cæsariensis*, embracing all to the north of the estuaries of the *Mersey* and the *Humber*. To these was added in A.D. 369 a fifth province, called (5) *Valentia*, north of the Wall of Severus; and the writers of the Middle Ages divide this into *Valentia*, between the Walls of Severus and Antoninus; and *Vespasiana*, north of the latter. The whole island was subject to the *Vicarius Britanniæ*, whose residence was at *Eboracum* (*York*). The next city in importance was *Londinium* or *Augusta* (*London*); and there were numerous other Roman cities, including several colonies. The chief ports connecting the island with the continent were *Portus Dubris* (*Dover*) and *Rutupiæ* (*Richborough*), the ruins of which are still to be seen near *Sandwich*.

On the death of Severus his son Caracalla hastened back to Rome, after concluding a peace with the wild tribes on the northern frontier. But a new enemy soon appeared in an opposite quarter, namely, the Saxon pirates, whose descents on the eastern coast from the opposite shores of Germany, in the third century, caused the appointment of an officer for the protection of that coast, called Count of the Saxon shore (*Comes littoris Saxonici*). The first two of these officers, Carausius (A.D. 286) and Allectus (293), used their power to seize the purple; but Allectus was subdued by Constantius (296), and the island remained quiet till the end of the Roman sway over it. Constantius himself was the last emperor who resided in Britain. He died at York (306), where his son, Constantine the Great, assumed the title of Cæsar. Constantine is believed to have had a share of British blood through his mother Helena.

Soon after this the province was again disturbed on the north by the PICTS and SCOTS, savage tribes, who had now supplanted the earlier Caledonians and Meatæ in Scotland. The Scots had crossed over from Ireland, which was for centuries called Scotia. The Picts are thought to have been a remnant of the Caledonians. In 368, under Valentinian I., the Picts and Scots penetrated to London, but were repulsed by Theodosius, who recovered the district between the walls of Severus and Antoninus, and named it *Valentia.*

Under his son, the Emperor Theodosius, a Briton named Maximus, who had fought gloriously against the Picts and Scots, set up a western empire at Trèves, but was defeated at Aquileia, and put to death A.D. 388. Under Maximus Britain was further weakened by the establishment of a colony of its warriors in Armorica (*Brittany*). The great General Stilicho gave the province temporary aid in 396, but the growing pressure of the Alani, Suevi, and Vandals on the empire at length compelled Honorius to withdraw his legions from Britain. They returned in 418, at the prayer of the Britons, on a new inroad of the Picts and Scots; but after repulsing the enemy, repairing the fortresses, and trying to teach the use of arms to the enervated people, they took their final leave. The Britons now made one last effort in their own defense, and under the Gaulish bishop, St. Germain of Auxerre, they gained the victory over the Picts and Scots which was called, from their battle-cry, the HALLELUJAH VICTORY, A.D. 429. In 446 they made their last appeal to Rome, by a letter to the great patrician Aëtius, inscribed *The Groans of the Britons.* Aëtius was "not deaf to their cry of anguish," but, pressed by the terrible Attila, he had no help to give them. In their despair, and guided by the advice of Vortigern, a prince in the south of Britain, they invoked the aid of the Saxons to repel the Picts and Scots—a remedy more fatal than the disease.

The state in which the Romans had left Britain was one of great prosperity in agriculture and the arts of life. The province was traversed by four great roads, parts of which are still used; namely, *Watling Street*, the high-road from the continent to the northwest, beginning at Rutupiæ (*Richborough*) on the coast of Kent, passing through London, and ending at Caernarvon; *Ikenild* or *Rikenild Street*, from Tynemouth, through York, Derby, and Birmingham, to St. David's; *Irmin* or *Hermin Street*, from St. David's to Southampton; and the *Foss*, between Cornwall and Lincoln. Other great works of civilization, though vanished from the face of the country, are continually disinterred from beneath its soil. There were cities with great walls, temples, theatres, baths, and circuses, the remains of which are still seen at remote stations, such as Caerleon (*Isca Silurum*) in Wales, and in bare sites, such as Silchester, as well as at London, York, Chester, and other still flourishing cities and towns. Westminster Abbey stands on the site of a temple of Apollo, and the hill on which Wren built the basilica of St. Paul was occupied by the temple of the goddess whose servants resisted the apostle at Ephesus. The irruption of the Saxons was made on no wild country, but on a province adorned with all the arts of civilization. Still, this was chiefly external. The Roman occupation of Britain was military; the people retained their own language; the peasantry were not Romanized; and they were easily excited to revolt.

Christianity was introduced into Britain at an early period of the Roman rule, though probably not through Rome, but from the East. An old tradition makes Lucius or Lever Maur (the *Great Light*), in the second century, the first Christian prince. It is certain that Britain had martyrs under Diocletian (as St. Alban at Verulam, which was called after him St. Alban's); it sent bishops, in 314, to the Council of Arles; had the Bible in the native tongue, and possessed learned ecclesiastics. Pelagius, the opponent of St. Augustine, was a Briton, whose real name is said to have been Morgan; and his disciple, Celestius, was an Irishman. The expulsion of the Pelagians by Severus, bishop of Trèves, and by St. Germain of Auxerre, in 446, was one of the last acts of Roman power in the island.

Two Druids. Bas-relief found at Autun.

Abbot Elfnoth and St. Augustine, Archbishop of Canterbury.

CHAPTER II.

THE ANGLO-SAXONS TO THE REIGN OF EGBERT. THE HEPTARCHY. A.D. 450–827.

THE people now called in by the Britons to their aid were of the German race. Their homes were on the northwestern coast of Germany—from the peninsula of Denmark to the mouths of the Rhine. They consisted of three principal tribes—the *Saxons*, the *Angles*, and the *Jutes*. These names were merged, in their new country, into that of *Anglo-Saxons*—that is, *the Saxons of England* (not the Angles and Saxons), when the Saxons of Wessex acquired the supremacy over the other races. But the name of the country itself, *Engle-land*, was derived from the *Angles* or *Engle*.

All these tribes belonged to that branch of the race called *Low Germans* (the Germans of the plains near the coast), in distinction to the *High Germans* (the Germans of the higher land in the interior). Hence the English language, which was founded on theirs, is a dialect of Low German.

The *Saxons*, who at first dwelt on the narrow neck of the peninsula of Denmark and some islands at the mouth of the Elbe, had now spread to the mouths of the Rhine. Subject to them were the *Friesians*, whose language is, in many respects, the nearest of the German dialects to the English. These probably formed the majority of the Saxon invaders, though their name was lost in that of the dominant race. The Saxons and Friesians occupied the southern parts of the island in three kingdoms, namely, *Es-sex* (the *East* Saxons), *Sus-sex* (the *South* Saxons), and *Wes-sex* (the *West* Saxons). Their western boundary corresponded nearly to a line drawn across the narrowest part of the country, between the Bristol and English channels, from Bridgewater to Lyme Regis.

The *Angles* or *Engle* were a more powerful tribe, and occupied a larger portion of the island; namely, all the eastern coasts, from *Essex* to the *Firth of Forth*, and the midland counties, in three kingdoms—*East Anglia*, *Mercia*, and *Northumbria*. The Angles came from the part of the Danish peninsula which lay north of the Saxons, and between them and the Jutes. They had formerly lived near the mouth of the Elbe, in the neighborhood of High German tribes, which accounts for certain traces of High German in the Anglo-Saxon tongue.

The *Jutes* were a race of *Goths* from the peninsula of *Jutland*, which afterward became Danish. They were the fewest of the invaders, and occupied only *Kent* and the *Isle of Wight*, with part of Hampshire; but they have a fame beyond their numbers from having been the first of the German invaders of Britain.

All these people were Pagan barbarians, who worshiped the heavenly bodies and deified heroes. Hence were derived the names of the week, which we still use:

Sunday,	i. e.	*Sunnundæg*,	from the	*Sun*;
Monday,	"	*Monundæg*,	"	*Moon*;
Tuesday,	"	*Tiuesdæg*,	"	*Tiue* or *Tuisco* (a hero);
Wednesday,	"	*Wodnesdæg*,	"	*Woden* or *Odin* (god);
Thursday,	"	*Thorsdæg*,	"	*Thor* (chief god);
Friday,	"	*Freyadæg*,	"	*Freya* (goddess);
Saturday,	"	*Sætesdæg*,	"	*Sætes* (god).

Of these deities Woden was the god of war; Thor, the thunderer, had a resemblance to the Greek and Roman Jove, and wielded a mighty hammer in place of a thunder-bolt; Freya was not unlike Venus; and Sætes was a water-god. They believed in a future state, where the brave, admitted to the hall of Woden, would quaff ale from the skulls of their slain enemies. Thus, by a ferocious contempt for the lives of their enemies and for their own, they hoped to indulge forever their ruling passion of intemperance. Such were the terrible allies who now crossed to Britain in their rude ships or keels (*ceolas*), made of planks and wattled osiers, and covered with skins, in which they learned to despise the constant danger of shipwreck. The following are the traditions about their successive settlements, the historic certainty of which is as yet undecided:

1. The *First* invaders were *Jutes*, under two chieftains, Hengist and Horsa, who had been banished, and were in search of a new home, when Vortigern, a British prince, called in their aid against the Picts and Scots (A.D. 450). Their reward was the isle of *Thanet*, then separated from Kent by an estuary. The *British* legend goes on to relate how Vortigern, for the love of Rowena, Hengist's daughter, ceded the rest of Kent to Hengist, and himself renounced Christianity; how his son Vortimer, taking up the British cause, drove out Hengist; how Rowena poisoned Vortimer; and how the restored Vortigern recalled Hengist, who soon afterward, at a conference held at Stonehenge between 300 chiefs of each nation, bade his followers massacre the Britons, of whom 299 fell; Vortigern alone being spared, at the cost of Essex, Sussex, and Middlesex, as his ransom, and these counties formed the kingdom of Hengist and of his son Ochta. It is certain, however, that these three provinces did not become Saxon till much later; and the whole story seems to be an invention of the Welsh bards to palliate the weak resistance of their countrymen.

According to the more trust-worthy story of the *Saxon* writers, Hengist and Horsa landed in Kent, at Vortigern's invitation (in A.D. 450), to oppose the Picts and Scots, who had advanced to Lincolnshire, and whom they easily defeated. They invited others of their countrymen to the fertile island, and formed a settlement in Kent, which was given them in consideration of their past and future services. But war soon broke out between the Britons and their strange allies. In 455 Horsa was killed in battle at *Ægelesford* (Aylesford). In 457 Hengist and his son Eric completely routed the Britons at *Creccanford* (Crayford), and drove them out of Kent, over which Hengist and his son reigned, the former for 40 years, and the latter for 24. From the surname of Eric, *Æsc* (the Ash-tree), the succeeding kings of Kent were called *Æsc-ings* or *Ash-ings* (sons of the Ash-tree). The most powerful of them was *Ethelbert*, the fourth after Eric, who began to reign A.D. 568, and was the first Christian king of the Saxon race in England. After him but little is heard of the kingdom of KENT.

2. The *Second* Settlement of the German invaders is said to have been made A.D. 477, when Ella and his three sons landed in Sussex with a body of Saxons in three ships. In 490 they took the fortress of *Andredes-ceaster* (the Roman Anderida, *Pevensey*), and Ella assumed the title of King of the SOUTH SAXONS (*South-sexe*) or *Sussex*, to which he added *Surrey*. His capital was *Chichester*, named after his son Cissa, who succeeded him some time between 514 and 519. His descendants reigned long; their names are lost; but their division of Sussex into *rapes* is still preserved.

3. The *Third* Settlement was effected in 495 by a body of Saxons who landed on the eastern side of Southampton Water, under Cerdic and his son Cynric. They met with firm resistance, and held their ground with great valor till 514, when they were reinforced by Cerdic's two nephews, *Stuf* and *Wightgar*, who are called Jutes. They were rewarded with the *Isle of Wight*, which was now conquered, with many other districts. At last, in 519, a great victory over the Britons at *Cerdices-ford* (Charford), in Hampshire, gave Cerdic the right to assume the royal title, and he founded the great kingdom of the West Saxons (*West-sexe*) or *Wessex*.

Cerdic's further progress to the west was checked by the heroic Arthur, prince of Damnonia or Cornwall, whose name, with those of his queen and his "Knights of the Round Table," in association with the enchanter Merlin, has formed the theme of the earliest and latest British poetry, from the lays of the Cambrian bards to the "Idyls of the King"—a most curious example of a mythical period interposed between two ages of certain history. But all these fables scarcely justify a doubt of Arthur's real existence, or of his defense of the British cause.

Cynric, the son of Cerdic (534–560), added to the kingdom, and fixed its capital at *Winton-ceaster* (Winchester), the Venta Belgarum of the Romans.

4. The *Fourth* body of the invaders, in A.D. 527, founded the kingdom of the East Saxons (*East-sexe*) or *Essex*, including *Middlesex*. Its first king was Æscevine or Ercemvine. His son Sleda having married a daughter of Ethelbert, the kingdom became subject to Kent.

5. The *Fifth* Settlement was made by the *Angles*, who founded the kingdom of East Anglia about the middle or end of the sixth century. Besides parts of *Cambridgeshire* and *Huntingdon*, it included the counties named after the two tribes of the *North-folk* (Norfolk) and the *South-folk* (Suffolk). Its first king was Uffa, from whom his successors were named *Uffingas* (sons of Uffa). The further history of East Anglia is little known.

6. The *Sixth* kingdom was that of Northumbria, also founded by the Angles, A.D. 547, in the country between the Humber and the Forth. In this region there were two British states, *Deira* (Deifyr), between the Humber and the Tyne, and *Bernicia* (Berneich), between the Tyne and the Forth. In 547 Ida landed, with a body of Angles, at Flamborough Head, and became king of Bernicia, while Ella founded another kingdom in Deira. After some years of hostility the two kingdoms were united, and on the accession of Edwin, the son of Ella, they received the name of Northumbria, A.D. 617.

7. A *Seventh* kingdom was formed in the March—that is, the

border-land west of East Anglia and Deira, and hence called MERCIA, under Penda, about 626; and it was afterward extended to the Severn, so as to embrace all the midland counties. It was divided by the Trent into North and South Mercia.

Map of Britain, showing the Settlements of the Anglo-Saxons.

These seven kingdoms, founded in about a century and a half from the first Saxon invasion, formed what is called the HEPTARCHY. But they were not, at any one time, all independent of each other.

There were also states still belonging to the Britons. These were, first, DAMNONIA, or West Wales (Welsh, *Walsch*, being the German for Foreigners), which included Cornwall and *Devonshire;* CAMBRIA, or *Wales;* CUMBRIA, or *Cumberland*, with *Westmoreland* and *Lancashire*, and part of *Yorkshire;* and the two kingdoms of REGED and STRATHCLYDE, between the two Roman walls, in the southwest of what is now Scotland. The fact that the population of the Scotch lowlands was chiefly Saxon is important in the subsequent history of the country. The British kingdoms were at times united under one chief, called PENDRAGON, who claimed to represent the Roman emperors. Other bodies of Britons crossed the Channel into *Armorica*, in the northwest of Gaul, which was thence called BRITTANY. With these exceptions the Britons were so completely subdued that even their language was replaced by that of their conquerors. But the Celtic words in English confirm the Welsh traditions that many of the Britons were left as slaves among the Saxons.

Among the Saxon kingdoms there were continual conflicts, and each chieftain aspired to the dignity of BRETWALDA or supreme king. This rank seems to have arisen out of the need for a common leader against the Britons, Picts, and Scots; and it was probably elective. The first Bretwalda was *Ella* king of Sussex; the second *Ceawlin*, grandson of Cerdic, of Wessex; the third was *Ethelbert* king of Kent, in whose reign Christianity was introduced among the Anglo-Saxons.

Three Anglo-Saxon youths were exposed for sale in the market-place at Rome when Gregory (afterward Pope Gregory the Great) was passing by. Struck by their fair and open countenances, he asked of what nation they were. "Angles," was the answer. "Say rather, *Angels*," replied he, "if they were only Christians. But of what province?" "*Deira.*" "De ira!" said he; "yes, they are called from the wrath of God to his mercy. And who is their king?" "His name is *Ella* or *Alla.*" "Allelujah!" he exclaimed; "the praises of God must be sung in their country." He at once undertook the mission, but the Romans retained him at home; and on his accession to the Papacy he sent to Britain a Roman monk, AUGUSTINE, at the head of forty missionaries. After some delay in Gaul, from the dread of danger among the fierce Saxon heathens, Augustine landed in Kent in 597. He found Ethelbert favorably disposed, owing to his marriage with the Christian princess Bertha, daughter of Caribert king of Paris. The king assigned him a residence in the Isle of Thanet, and received him to a conference; and in a short time Ethelbert and many of his subjects were baptized. Augustine was made by Gregory archbishop of Canterbury and Metropolitan of all the British churches. Augustine also founded the see of Rochester. Soon after, Sebert king of Essex, the nephew of Ethelbert, received the faith from MELLITUS, who became the first bishop of London. The cathedral of St. Paul's was erected, as already mentioned (p. 7), on the site of a temple to Diana, and another church was dedicated to St. Peter on Thorney Island, an islet formed by a small tributary of the Thames, now the site of Westminster Abbey. In 627 Edwin king of Northumbria was converted by PAULINUS, a bishop who was introduced by his queen, Ethelburga, the daughter of Ethelbert. He was baptized in a temporary church dedicated to St. Peter, soon replaced by a cathedral, which became the seat of the archbishopric of York, and the centre whence Christianity spread over the north.

The name of Ethelbert is famous also in the civil history of England, for his enactment of the first written laws made by any of the Saxon kings. He cultivated intercourse with the continent, and his reign forms a bright epoch in the history of English civilization. He died in 616, after a reign of fifty years.

The fourth Bretwalda was REDWALD king of East Anglia, who defeated and killed Ædefrid, the usurping king of Northumbria, and restored Edwin the son of Ella to his kingdom, about 617. EDWIN became the fifth and greatest of the Bretwaldas; and his authority was acknowledged by all the Anglo-Saxons except in Kent. He reclaimed his subjects from their licentious lives; and it was said that a woman or child might openly carry about a purse of gold without fear of violence or robbery. The affection of his servants was unbounded. He fell in battle with Penda king of Mercia in 633, and Northumbria relapsed into a state of disorder, which lasted, with some bright exceptions, till it was united to the other kingdoms under Egbert.

It was reserved for Wessex to give the first Saxon king to all England. This kingdom had reached to great prosperity under Ina, who began to reign in 688, and was famed for his justice, policy, and prudence, especially toward his subjects of the British race. From his brother Ingild was descended, in the fourth generation, the prince who first united England under one sceptre. EGBERT'S great natural gifts received a fine culture in the courts and armies of Charles the Great; and, in the same year in which the German Empire of the West was founded by that monarch's coronation, Egbert was called by the nobles of Wessex to the throne, A.D. 800. The gradual extinction of all the original royal houses in the other six kingdoms left him the sole direct descendant of the first conquerors, who claimed their descent from Woden. Of the other kingdoms Mercia alone was powerful, but it was now declining. Its king, *Penda*, has already been mentioned as the successful enemy of Edwin of Northumbria. He was defeated and slain in his turn by the Northumbrian *Oswy*, who was the sixth

Bretwalda, A.D. 656. Mercia became even more powerful under *Ethelbald* (716–755), who, in his wars against the Britons, united under his standard the kingdoms of East Anglia, Kent, Essex, and, for a while, also Wessex. At one time his power extended over all England south of the Humber, and he signs himself "King of Britain" in a charter of the year 736. His still greater successor, *Offa*, curbed the Britons of Cambria by a rampart drawn from the Dee to the Wye, called Offa's Dyke; and he enjoyed the friendship and alliance of Charlemagne. But he brought a stain upon his fame by treacherously murdering Ethelbert king of East Anglia in 792, and seizing his kingdom—a crime for which he sought to atone by liberality to the Church and the institution of "*Peter's pence.*" After his death, in 796, the kingdom declined; but in 823 Beornwulf invaded Wessex, hoping to strike a fatal blow at the rising power of Egbert, who had till now been engaged in regulating his kingdom and making war upon the Britons in Cornwall and Wales. Egbert defeated the invaders, and wrested from Mercia the tributary kingdoms of Kent and Sussex. The East Angles revolted from Mercia, and placed themselves under Egbert's protection. Both to them and Mercia he granted the power of electing kings subject and tributary to himself; and he soon afterward received the submission of Northumbria, which he placed on the same footing. Thus England was virtually united in 827 under Egbert as the eighth Bretwalda; but the title of "King of the English" was first adopted by Edward the Elder, son of Alfred the Great.

Anglo-Saxon Females.

Saxon Church. From Cotton MS.

CHAPTER III.

THE ANGLO-SAXONS, FROM THE UNION OF ENGLAND UNDER EGBERT TO CANUTE THE DANE. A.D. 827–1016.

SCARCELY had the first-fruits of the union of Saxon England been shown by a successful expedition made by Egbert into Northumbria, when the kingdom was threatened by a new enemy of kindred race, and from regions bordering on the old homes of the Angles and Saxons. The people known by the name of NORTHMEN came from Norway, Sweden, and Denmark, which were then included under the general name of *Scandinavia*. They retained, with the worship of Odin, the savage character and piratical habits which the Saxons had brought into Britain four centuries earlier; and their blood-red flag, bearing a black raven, which they used in divination, was the signal of fire and bloodshed. These *Vikings* (that is, in Danish, *pirates*) wasted all the coasts of the Baltic and North Sea. They had already begun to take up winter-quarters on the coasts of England, when Egbert died in A.D. 836.

His son ETHELWULF (836–858), a feeble devotee, divided his kingdom with his eldest son Athelstane, who reigned over Essex, Kent, and Sussex. Athelstane having died before his father, the kingdom was divided, on the death of Ethelwulf, between his next two sons, ETHELBALD and ETHELBERT (A.D. 858–866), but reunited under his fourth son ETHELRED (A.D. 866–871). The last year of Ethelred was signalized by the martyrdom of ST. EDMUND, king of East Anglia, by the Danes. The place of his burial is still marked by the town of *Bury St. Edmund's*, in Suffolk, with the ruins of the splendid monastery dedicated to the royal saint and martyr. But the same year witnessed the accession of Alfred, to save his country then, and to be honored by her forever:

"The pious Alfred, king to justice dear,
Lord of the harp and liberating spear."

ALFRED THE GREAT (A.D. 871–901) was the fifth son of Ethelwulf, and the grandson of Egbert. He was born at *Wantage*, in Berkshire, in 849. To his devoted mother, Osburga, he owed, besides a training in every virtue, the excitement of a spirit of patriotism and the love of learning through the knowledge of the Anglo-Saxon poems. When only six years old he was taken by his father to Rome; and he was not too young to receive lasting impressions from the visit. Amidst his studies he obeyed the call to arms; and at the age of twenty he shared in his brother's victory over the Danes at *Ashdune* (probably Ashton), in Berkshire. He succeeded to the crown of Wessex in 871 under his father's will, and by the public voice, in preference to Ethelred's children. For seven years he fought against the Danes, who had penetrated as far as Wiltshire; often defeating them, and then again reduced to extremity by the swarms of fresh invaders.

On such an occasion he had dismissed his followers, and taken refuge in the cottage of his own neat-herd, whose wife, not knowing the king, desired him to mind some cakes that were baking on the hearth. While busying himself with his weapons Alfred neglected to turn the cakes, and bore the reproof of the dame, when she saw them burnt, with the same grace with which he forgave her when she learned his dignity.

In 876 Alfred made a peace with Guthrum and his Danes, who

swore on their holy ring to leave the island; but they instantly broke the oath, and surprised Exeter. In 877 Alfred drove them into Mercia, but in 878 they returned, and compelled him to take refuge in *Æthelingay* (*i. e.*, the *Isle of Nobles*, now Athelney), an island amidst morasses in Somerset. Here he maintained and exercised his followers by frequent sallies till he judged that the time had come for a new effort. He then ventured himself into the Danish camp, disguised as a harper, and gained by his music and wit the hospitality of Guthrum. Finding the Danes sunk in security, he secretly gathered an army, surprised their camp near Westbury, and defeated them with great slaughter. Guthrum, closely besieged with the remnant of his army, accepted peace on the condition that he should embrace Christianity and receive the kingdom of East Anglia, to which a large part of Mercia was soon added. The Danes were thus finally established in the East and centre of England, their western boundary being the line of *Watling Street.* They had already possessed themselves of the part of Mercia north of the Wash and of Northumbria.

Alfred now devoted himself to the military organization of his remaining dominions, and to every means of improving the condition of his subjects. He rebuilt the ruined cities, and among them London; established a militia; and gathered a fleet of 120 ships, built even better than the Danish. In 893 he had to meet a new invasion of the Danes under Hasting, whom he finally repulsed in 897. He died October 26, 901, at the age of 52, and in the 30th year of his reign.

Few, if any kings, have so well deserved the epithet of GREAT. He possessed and cultivated every virtue, public and private, belonging to a man, a Christian, and a king, and suited to the times in which he lived and the work he had to do. He saved his people in war; ruled them firmly in peace; and gave them just laws and the light of learning. And all this he did chiefly by first training and governing himself. His time was divided into three equal portions: one for sleep and bodily exercise; one for business; and one for study and devotion. To measure his time, he invented the plan of burning candles of certain lengths in lanterns. By such self-discipline, the same man who gained, in 56 battles, the fame of Founder of the English Monarchy, became also the Founder of English Literature. He himself translated the Histories of Orosius and Bede, Boethius's "Consolation of Philosophy," and many other works; and he invited celebrated scholars from the Continent. He founded schools, and enjoined their use; but there is no sufficient authority for the tradition which makes him the founder, or restorer, of the University of

Oxford. The arts of wealth and common life were equally promoted by him. He encouraged commerce and manufactures; devoted a seventh of his revenue to public works; and invited ingenious foreigners to settle in the country.

Alfred's fame as a civil governor has caused the institutions of other Anglo-Saxon legislators to be ascribed to him. But, at all events, his reign is the most convenient epoch for a brief review of the institutions of the early Saxons, of which the English still retain the essential spirit, together with many of the forms.

These institutions were derived from those of the Old Germans. Their leading principle was that of personal liberty, regulated for the common good by a discipline chiefly military. The form of government was an elective monarchy, which was generally retained in one family, but not in strict lineal succession. The *chieftain* (*Heretoga*, *i. e.*, army-leader) became afterward *king* (*Cyning*, probably *son of the nation*, from *cyn*, race, and *ing*, the patronymic suffix), and his sons and kindred were *nobles* (*athelings*, from *Aethel* or *Ethel*, i. e., *noble*). The rest of the people were divided into *earls* (*eorls*) and *churls* (*ceorls*)—that is, *gentle* and *simple*. The *Ealdormen* (*aldermen*, i. e., *elder-men*) were originally the chief nobles, but afterward persons of official rank, such as governors of shires. Next came the *thanes* (*theyn*, from *thegnian*, to *serve*), a kind of *knights*, whose rank depended on the possession of a certain estate, and who were liable to serve in war as cavalry. The *churls* (*ceorls*) were the rest of the freemen; and the *serfs* (*theowas* or *esnas*) were slaves, chiefly of the conquered Celtic race. The *clergy* shared with the nobles in the government. There was a national council, called *Witena-gemôt*—that is, assembly of the *witans*, or wise men, whose assent was necessary before the king could enact a law. It was composed of bishops, abbots, aldermen, and perhaps the superior thanes.

The *land* was divided between the state (*folcland*) and individuals who held their property as freeholds in perpetuity (*boc-land*, from *boc*, the *book* or *charter* by which the title was conveyed); the latter was granted by the king, with consent of the *witan*. The division into *Shires* is much more ancient than Alfred: it arose in part from the smaller kingdoms and their subdivisions, as *Kent*, *Sussex*, *Surrey*, *Essex*, *Suffolk*, and *Norfolk*; but the more general distribution is not explained. Yorkshire and Lincolnshire were subdivided into *thirds* (*tredings*, now corrupted into *ridings*). Each county held its court of justice twice a year, under the alderman and bishop; and the executive officer was the *scir-gerefa* (shire-reeve, or sheriff).

The subdivision of counties into *hundreds* arose out of a very ancient German institution, but it is uncertain whether the number refers to *families* or quantities of land.

Justice was administered in the courts of the hundred and the county, with an appeal from the latter to the king in council. The county court being too large, it became the custom to intrust the finding of a verdict to a committee of 12 or 24 or 36 of the principal thanes, which was thus somewhat like the later jury. But, instead of the verdict depending on the evidence, the accused was permitted to clear himself by his own oath and those of neighbors, as *compurgators*. Another mode of trial was the *ordeal*, which was conducted in church by the clergy. It consisted in the exposure of the accused to some dangerous or painful experiment, such as plunging the hand in boiling water (the ordeal by *water*), or carrying a bar of hot iron (the ordeal by *fire*). Such trials are open to the suspicion of collusion, without which few could have escaped. The general *punishment* was a *fine*, or compensation to the injured man, or, in cases of murder, to his relatives (*wergild*); but *capital punishment* was inflicted in atrocious cases, as was also *banishment*. The exile was said to bear a wolf's head; and, as such, he might be hunted down and killed with impunity. In the Anglo-Saxon *gilds*, or associations of persons of different ranks, may be seen the origin of municipal corporations.

The *Anglo-Saxon Literature* reached its highest point in the reign of Alfred. The earliest works are metrical; the oldest extant being the *Gleeman's Song*, written about A.D. 400, before the Saxons came over to England. To about the same time belong the *Battle of Finsburgh* and the *Tale of Beowulf*. The oldest Anglo-Saxon poems written in England are those of CÆDMON, a monk of Whitby, in the latter part of the 7th century. There are other poems, coming down to the 11th century, the noblest of which is the *Version of the Psalms*. In *prose literature*, besides the writings of Alfred, the chief works are translations of portions of the Holy Scriptures, and the Saxon Chronicle. The latter is composed of several different historical narratives, by ecclesiastics, beginning with the reign of Alfred and ending with the year 1154. There were also Latin works by learned Anglo-Saxons, of which the chief was the *Ecclesiastical History of England*, by Beda, a monk of Jarrow (A.D. 672–735), surnamed the "Venerable Bede," which is still a work of high authority.

Alfred was succeeded by his son, EDWARD THE ELDER (901–925), notwithstanding the opposition of the partisans of his cousin Ethelwold, son of Ethelred, aided by the Danes. He first used the title of KING OF ENGLAND. His children being very young when he died, the crown passed on to his natural son, ATHELSTANE

(925–940), who enacted laws in favor of commerce, and maintained a close intercourse with the Continent.

He was succeeded by his brother, EDMUND THE ELDER (940–946), who took Cumberland from the Britons, and gave it to Malcolm king of Scotland, on his undertaking to do homage for it, and to protect the North from the Danes. Edmund was murdered, when at table in his own hall, by a robber named Leofu, whom he had banished; and, as his children were young, the *witan* elected as king his brother EDRED (A.D. 946–955), who curbed the rebellious Danes by placing garrisons in their chief towns, and setting over them an English governor.

His reign is marked in English annals by the advance of ecclesiastical power, through the ascendency gained over the king by ST. DUNSTAN, abbot of Glastonbury. By extreme austerities, and reports of his personal conflicts with the evil one, Dunstan obtained a high reputation for sanctity. He adopted in his conduct the rigid discipline of the new sect of the Benedictines, who, among other tenets, enforced the celibacy of the clergy. His ambitious designs were interrupted by the death of Edred, who was succeeded by his nephew EDWY, son of Edmund, a beautiful and amiable youth of sixteen (A.D. 955–958).

Against the advice of his counselors, Edwy married the Princess Elgiva, who was within the prohibited degrees of affinity. On his coronation-day, Dunstan, with Odo archbishop of Canterbury, tore the king from his wife's arms, and dragged him like a truant into the banqueting-hall. Edwy avenged the insult by calling Dunstan to account for his administration of the treasury, and Dunstan fled to Ghent. He soon gathered a party in the Danish provinces; and, having caused Edgar, the younger brother of Edwy, to be proclaimed king in Mercia, East Anglia, and Northumbria, Dunstan returned to England, and, with the consent of a witena-gemôt, received from Edgar the sees of London and Worcester. Next, Odo dragged Elgiva from the palace, branded her in the face, forced Edwy to consent to her divorce, and carried her off to Ireland. The queen recovered from her wounds, and was returning to Edwy, when she was most brutally murdered at Gloucester by the emissaries of Odo. Edwy, who had been excommunicated, died soon after at the same place.

EDGAR (958–975) now made Dunstan archbishop of Canterbury, and favored the monks in every way; thus earning the highest praise from them, though he was most arrogant and licentious. But he was signally fortunate in his government. The Danes being no longer formidable, perhaps through having obtained settlements in France, he used his great armaments to enforce submission from the king of Scotland, the princes of Wales, Man, and the Orkneys, and the Northmen of Ireland.

Upon his death, in the 33d year of his age, his second wife, Elfrida, tried to obtain the kingdom for her son Ethelred, who was only 7 years old; but the influence of Dunstan secured it to Edgar's elder son, EDWARD II., who was only 13 (A.D. 975–979). He was surnamed the MARTYR, from the manner of his death. As he was hunting one day in Dorsetshire he was led by the chase near Corfe Castle, the residence of his step-mother, Elfrida, whom he visited without attendants. While drinking a parting cup, after he had mounted his horse, he was stabbed from behind by a servant of Elfrida. He put spurs to his horse, but soon dropped from the saddle and was dragged by the stirrup till he died.

Elfrida's son, ETHELRED II., THE UNREADY (979–1016), was crowned at Kingston by Dunstan, who is said to have pronounced over him a curse instead of the blessing. Henceforth we hear little of the ambitious prelate, who lived ten years longer. But the Northmen renewed their attacks, which were only the more encouraged by Ethelred's attempts to buy them off. The tribute raised for this purpose, and continued afterward, became odious under the name of *Danegelt* (Dane-money). Ethelred tried also to propitiate his enemies by a marriage with Emma, sister of Richard II., duke of Normandy, A.D. 1001. But shortly after his fears prompted him to contrive a massacre of the Danes, which began on the festival of St. Brice, November 13, 1002. It can not have been universal, as the Danes formed by far the majority in some parts of the kingdom; but, in the south, the rage of the Saxon populace spared neither age nor sex. Among the victims was Gunilda, sister of the king of Denmark, who, put to death by Ethelred's own command, prophesied with her latest breath the speedy ruin of the English. Her brother, SWEYN, soon appeared off the western coast to fulfill her prophecy. In 1013 he had conquered the kingdom, and Ethelred fled to Normandy. But in a few weeks Sweyn's death opened the way for his return, early in 1014. CANÚTE (properly Knut), Sweyn's son and appointed successor, retired to Denmark; but he returned in 1015, and found an easy prey in the kingdom, reduced to confusion by Ethelred's indolence. Ethelred shut himself up in London, where he died, leaving only the name of king to his son EDMUND, who was surnamed IRONSIDE, from the valor he had already displayed in battle with the Danes, against whom he now made a stand in the west. But the nobles of both nations forced their kings to an agreement for the division of the kingdom. Scarcely, however, was the peace concluded, when Edmund was murdered by the contrivance of Edric duke of Mercia, on November 30, 1016. Thus ended, for a time, the Saxon kingdom of England. It was revived in the person of Edmund's brother, Edward the Confessor (1042–1066), only to be again extinguished by the Norman Conquest. But the Saxon and Norman dynasties were again united by the marriage of Henry I. with Matilda, the daughter of Malcolm king of Scotland, and of Margaret, the grand-daughter of Edmund Ironside. In the person of Henry's daughter Matilda, the mother of Henry II., both royal families became one. (See Genealogical Table A, at the end of the volume.)

Shrine of St. Ethelreda, Ely.

Hall of Castle of Lillebonn in Normandy, where William the Conqueror decided upon the invasion of England.

CHAPTER IV.

THE DANES AND ANGLO-SAXONS FROM CANUTE TO THE NORMAN CONQUEST. A.D. 1016–1066.

CANUTE THE DANE (1016–1035) secured the crown by a vote of the states of the kingdom convened at London, setting aside the brothers and the young children of Edmund Ironside. To gain over the nobles, and to reward his Danes, he imposed heavy taxes on the people; but he governed them justly, and made life and property secure. He restored the Saxon customs, and made no open distinction between the two nations in the administration of justice. He formed an alliance with Richard duke of Normandy, by marrying his sister Emma, the widow of Ethelred the Unready. He strove to atone for his many crimes of violence and deceit by exercises of devotion. His admiration of church music is recorded in the rhymes which tell of his staying his boat on the Nene to hear the songs of the monks of Ely:

> "Merrily sang the monks within Ely
> When that Cnute, king, rowed thereby;
> Row, my knights, row near the land,
> And hear we these monkys song."

Still more celebrated is his reproof of his courtiers, who one day thought to flatter him by telling him that his power was without bounds. He ordered his chair to be set on the beach when the tide was rising, and commanded the waves to retire. Affecting to expect their obedience, he sat till the water was around him, and then, leaving his chair to be washed away, he reminded the flatterers that he himself was powerless before Him who alone could say to the ocean, "*Thus far shalt thou go and no further.*"

In the same pious spirit he made a pilgrimage to Rome, whence he addressed a letter to the clergy of England, expressing the desire to atone for his youthful excesses by promoting the welfare and union of his people, A.D. 1027. In fact, the time had now come when, in spite of some invidious privileges still possessed by the Danes, the two kindred races were so far blended that they may be regarded as one people.

After his return from Rome Canute made war upon Malcolm king of Scotland, and his nephew Duncan king of Cumberland, whom he reduced to subjection A.D. 1030. He died in 1035, leaving two sons, Sweyn and Harold, by his first wife, and Hardicanute by his marriage with Emma. He left Norway to Sweyn, and Denmark to Hardicanute, to whom the crown of England also belonged by the conditions of Canute's marriage with Emma; but, in his absence, Harold claimed the kingdom, and the danger of civil war was only averted by a compromise, under which Harold received all England north of the Thames, with London for his capital, while the south was held by Emma, at Winchester, as regent for her son.

The reign of HAROLD I., surnamed HAREFOOT from his fleetness (1035–1040), contains no memorable event, except the murder of Alfred the son of Ethelred, by the treachery of Godwin earl of Kent, of whose power more will be said presently. Harold died in 1040.

HARDICANUTE (1040–1042) was now welcomed back to England; but he proved a drunken and cruel despot. He fell a victim to his intemperance, in the very act of raising the cup to his lips at a feast, A.D. 1042. With him ended the brief dynasty of Canute; the English recovered their liberty; and the crown was restored to the house of Cerdic.

At the time of Canute's usurpation Edmund Ironside had left behind two infant sons, *Edmund* and *Edward*, whom Canute sent to Olave king of Sweden, it is said with a murderous intent, but Olave sent them to Stephen king of Hungary. They were brought up at his court; and Edward became afterward the ancestor of King Henry II. Edmund had also left a brother, *Edwy*, whom

Canute put to death in 1017, and two half-brothers, *Alfred* and *Edward*, sons of Ethelred and Emma. These two princes kept alive their claims to the throne, and it was in attempting to assert them that Alfred perished, as we have seen. When Hardicanute died Edward was in England; and his succession was secured by the support of Earl Godwin, who married him to his daughter Editha, though Edward is said to have been reluctant to accept either the crown or the bride.

EDWARD THE CONFESSOR (1042-1066) was received with joy by the Saxons, and his gentle character soon conciliated the Danes. But he was weak as well as gentle; more of the priest than the king; and his education in Normandy had left him only half an Englishman. He spoke the Norman-French. His court was filled with Normans, whose greater refinement, while it seemed to justify their advancement, especially in the church, excited the jealousy of the people, and at the same time prepared the way for the Norman conquest.

The Saxon party found a leader in GODWIN, the great earl of Kent, whose authority extended over Kent, Sussex, and the south of Wessex; while his eldest son, *Sweyn*, governed the rest of Wessex; and his second son, *Harold*, was duke of East Anglia and governor of Essex. An accidental encounter between the people of Dover and the retainers of Eustace count of Boulogne, caused Godwin to raise the standard of rebellion. But the king was aided by Leofric earl of Mercia, and Siward duke of Northumberland, and Godwin and his sons were driven out of the kingdom, A.D. 1051. He returned the next year with two fleets, gathered by himself in Flanders and by Harold in Ireland; and Edward was obliged to make terms with him; and a witena-gemôt restored Godwin and his sons to all their honors. Godwin soon afterward died, while sitting at table with the king, and was succeeded by Harold, who by his address gained the good-will of Edward.

Harold's power was increased by an event connected with the noblest memorials of English literature. The kingdom of Scotland had been usurped by MACBETH, a powerful thane, who had murdered "the gracious Duncan," and driven his son and heir, Malcolm Kenmore, into England. By Edward's command, SIWARD duke of Northumberland marched into Scotland, defeated and slew Macbeth, and restored Malcolm. Siward died soon after, and Harold obtained the dukedom for his brother Tosti.

Edward, becoming anxious about the succession, invited home from Hungary his nephew, *Edward the Outlaw*, the sole heir of the Saxon line. But he died soon after his arrival, A.D. 1057, and his son, *Edgar Atheling* (surnamed from his princely birth), was too young for the hard task of ruling the turbulent and divided realm. As a last resource, Edward turned to his kinsman, WILLIAM duke of Normandy, the illegitimate son of Robert the Devil, who was the son of Richard II., brother of Edward's mother, Emma. Whether Edward employed Harold on this business is uncertain; but Harold did pay a visit to William, who entrapped him into a most solemn oath to espouse his cause, and to deliver up to him the castle of Dover. The duke also gave his daughter Adeliza in marriage to Harold.

In the last year of Edward's reign, 1065, Harold, who had meanwhile subdued Wales, was called into Northumberland to put down a rebellion against his brother Tosti. But such was the case made out by the insurgents, that Harold advised Edward to confirm their choice of Morcar, grandson of the great Duke Leofric, for their duke. He also procured the election of Morcar's brother, Edwin, as governor of Mercia, and married their sister. Tosti fled, vowing vengeance, to return at a moment fatal for Harold's fortunes.

Meanwhile Edward died on the 5th of January, 1066, and was buried in Westminster Abbey, then just consecrated, where his successors are still crowned in his chair. He was canonized, with the surname of Confessor, a century after his death. He compiled a body of laws from the codes of Ethelbert, Ina, and Alfred, which is now lost.

HAROLD II. (1066) had now so extended his power over England that he mounted the throne without any opposition within the kingdom. But the Duke of Normandy was also ready to assert his claims, under color of the declared wishes of the late king and the broken oath of Harold. On this ground the pope, Alexander II., declared for William, gave him a relic and a consecrated banner, and excommunicated Harold and his partisans. He collected a fleet of nearly 1000 vessels and an army of 60,000 men for the invasion of England.

At this crisis Harold was called into the north to meet the invasion of his brother Tosti, leagued with Harold Hardrada, king of Norway. He defeated them in a bloody battle, in which both the invading chiefs fell, at Stanford Bridge, thence called Battle Bridge, Sept. 25.

Only two days after (Sept. 27) William sailed from St. Valéry on the Somme, and landed next day, the eve of St. Michael, at Pevensey, in Sussex. Falling to the ground as he stepped ashore, he cried that he was seizing the land as his own, and so turned the accident into an omen.

Harold flew to meet him, but it was too late. His army melted away on the march, and his resolution to give battle without sparing his own person was the last effort of a courageous despair. The stories of revelry in his camp and prayer in that of William during the night before the battle come from a suspicious source. Both leaders proved their skill in marshaling their hosts. Harold occupied an eminence and secured his flank by trenches; and having placed his own Kentishmen in the van, and the Londoners round the royal standard, he himself took his post on foot with his two brothers at the head of the infantry, resolved to perish if he could not conquer. William advanced in three lines, the last of which, formed of the cavalry, under his own command, was extended so as to cover the flanks of the main body. His attack made no impression on the English, till a feigned retreat enticed them into the plain, where the Norman cavalry wheeled round upon their flanks. Twice was this stratagem successful; and, though Harold twice rallied his diminished forces, his army was now reduced to a small but compact body around his banner. William directed upon them the whole force of his infantry, while his archers galled them from a distance. The charge succeeded; Harold fell, pierced by an arrow through the eye; his two brothers shared his fate; and the English fled. Thus ended, after a long day's fight, on the 14th of October, 1066, the decisive *Battle of Hastings.* The true site of the field of battle was at Senlac, about nine miles from Hastings. The body of Harold, discovered among the heaps of the slain of both armies, was buried, by William's permission, at Waltham Abbey, which he had founded, and where a stone is said to have been till lately visible, with the inscription, HAROLD INFELIX. If the stone be not genuine, the epitaph is too true.

William afterward erected *Battle Abbey*, near Hastings, enjoining the monks to pray for the soul of Harold and his own.

A most interesting memorial of the battle, and the events that preceded it, still exists in the tapestry of Bayeux, which tradition ascribes to the hands of Matilda, wife of William, though it is probably of later date. It is an invaluable witness to the costume, arms, and standards of the period.

William I. and Toustain bearing the Consecrated Banner at the Battle of Hastings. Bayeux Tapestry.

CHAPTER V.

THE ANGLO-NORMAN KINGS.—WILLIAM I. A.D. 1066–1087.

WILLIAM I., surnamed the CONQUEROR, was himself the representative of a line of northern chieftains, like the ancestors of those whom he had subdued. Rollo, or Rolf, the founder of his house, was a Norwegian sea-king, who landed in *Neustria* in 876. In 912 Charles the Simple, king of France, granted him a large part of Neustria, and he embraced the Christian faith. His turbulence extorted new territory from the French king; and his successors advanced their power, sometimes by alliances with the sovereign, sometimes by rebellion against him, till their authority was firmly established over one of the fairest provinces of France, called from their original home *Normandy* (the province of the Northmen). Meanwhile they had adopted the civilization and language of their new country; and nowhere was the *langue d'oil*, or Northern French, spoken with greater purity. Thus, though Gothic in race and physical characters, they were French in all else; and the Norman conquest was, in reality, the imposition of a French dynasty, with a French nobility, on England. The dynasty remained French for more than a hundred years; French phrases, then introduced, are still used in English courts of law; and the French element was permanently grafted on the English language.

After the battle of Hastings the Saxons made one last effort by the proclamation of EDGAR ATHELING, the son of Edward the Outlaw; but the rapid advance of William struck terror into the bravest, and Edgar himself came into his camp and made submission. William was crowned in Westminster Abbey on Christmas-day, by Aldred archbishop of York. The ceremony was attended by the Saxon as well as Norman nobles, and both peoples accepted the new king with acclamations. But the cry alarmed the Norman soldiers without, and a tumult, which was hardly appeased by William's own exertions, threw a fearful augury over the concord of the day.

The first acts of William's reign, however, increased the confidence of his subjects, while they secured his own power. Justice was impartially administered. No suspicion was shown even toward the Saxon prince who had claimed the throne; and, except the estates of Harold and his most conspicuous adherents, most of the property of the Saxons remained undisturbed. London and the other cities had their liberties confirmed, while they were disarmed and citadels were built to overawe them, of which the "Tower of London" is an example.

It seemed that all would have gone well if William had continued to watch with his own eye over the change that was taking place. But in 1067 he ventured on a visit to Normandy, and his absence was fatal. As a measure of precaution he took with him Edgar Atheling and others of the chief Saxons, leaving the government in the hands of his half-brother Odo, bishop of Bayeux, and William Fitz-Osborne, earl of Hereford. They began to build great castles, and showed other marks of distrust, which the Saxons were not slow to return. Open hostilities soon broke out; and William hastened back in alarm and anger. Henceforth he treated the Saxons as conquered and implacable enemies. His active movements quelled a powerful conspiracy between the sons of Harold, the earls Edwin and Morcar, and Cospatric earl of Northumberland, who were encouraged by the kings of North Wales, Scotland, and Denmark. William took York, and drove Cospatric, with Edgar Atheling, into Scotland; and he received the homage of Malcolm king of Scotland, for Cumberland (A.D. 1068).

Next year, 1069, the Danes landed in the Humber, and Edgar Atheling returned from Scotland. York was taken by assault, and the garrison of 3000 Normans put to the sword; and the insurrection became more determined than the last. But William's activity again prevailed. The Danes were bought off. Waltheof, a leading

Saxon, submitted to William, who rewarded him richly. Malcolm was too late in the field; and Edgar Atheling fled back to Scotland. William now laid waste the land between the Humber and the Tees, at a sacrifice of 100,000 lives—a barbarity which was perhaps designed as a defense against the Scots and Danes quite as much as for revenge.

Then followed unsparing confiscations, which enlarged the domains of the crown, enriched the Norman nobles, and drove many of the noblest Saxons from their country. Some of these exiles, entering into the service of the Greek emperor at Constantinople, formed, with Danes and other Northmen, the celebrated body-guard called the Varangians. Those who remained at home were deprived of all offices in the state and in the church. The zeal of William in filling up ecclesiastical dignities with Normans was seconded by the pope, whose legate assembled a council at Winchester, in 1070, by which the primate Stigand was deposed, with all the other Anglo-Saxon prelates except Wulstan of Worcester, while the plunder of the Saxon monasteries enriched the royal coffers. *Lanfranc*, the successor to the see of Canterbury, has gained high renown for his piety and learning, as well as for his success in compelling the Archbishop of York to acknowledge the primacy of Canterbury.

Meanwhile the Anglo-Saxon cause was maintained by its last defender, HEREWARD, in his "Camp of Refuge" amidst the fens that protected the *Isle of Ely*. Here he was joined by his brothers and Harold's old comrades, the earls Morcar and Edwin. William gathered a fleet of flat-bottomed boats, and at the same time made a causeway across the fens, and so forced the Saxons to surrender. Hereward alone cut his way through the enemy, and, after further exploits, inspired William with such respect that he restored his estate and received him into favor. Morcar died in prison; Edwin was killed; and Edgar Atheling himself submitted to the conqueror, and retired with a pension to Rouen.

The conquest of England was now complete; but discontents arose among the Norman nobles, and a formidable conspiracy was headed by Roger, earl of Hereford, son of William's trusted comrade Fitz-Osborne, with the concurrence of the Saxon earl Waltheof, whose services to William had been rewarded with the hand of his niece Judith, as well as with the earldoms of Huntingdon, Northampton, and Northumberland. Under a feeling of misgiving Waltheof revealed the plot to Judith, who betrayed it to William. The result was a premature attempt, which was easily put down. Hereford was imprisoned, and lost his estate; while Waltheof, the Englishman, though far less guilty, suffered death (1075). The traitress Judith soon had her reward in contempt and misery.

Meanwhile William's power in Normandy was threatened by the rebellion of his eldest son Robert, who levied open war against him, and on one occasion almost killed his father with his own hand. The sound of William's voice, under his closed helmet, calling for help, revealed him to his son, who was struck with remorse, and asked for pardon. William not only forgave him, but intrusted him with a command against Malcolm king of Scotland (1079).

The peace of England was no further disturbed during William's reign except by forays of the Welsh, who were compelled to pay compensation, and a more serious inroad of the Danes, which led to the revival of the odious *Danegelt*, 1085.

In 1086 a grand ceremony was held at Salisbury, which has left a lasting record to our own day. All the freeholders of the kingdom took the oath of fealty to William as their feudal lord; and the great record of the landed estates of the kingdom was finished, which bears the name of *Domesday Book*. It describes the divisions and products of the various properties in the land. It registers 283,000 persons, from which basis the whole population is reckoned at about a million.

This crowning act of William's government was his last. Incensed by the inroads of certain French barons upon Normandy, and offended by some personal sarcasms of the French king Philip, he led an army into l'Isle de France, burning and destroying on every side. His rage brought its own retribution. As he was viewing the ruins of Mantes, which his followers had just burnt, his horse, stepping on some hot ashes, plunged violently, and bruised him against the pommel of his saddle. His advanced age and his state of body rendered the hurt mortal. On his death-bed he testified his remorse for his acts of violence and tyranny by gifts to the church and pardons to prisoners; and so he died, in the monastery of St. Gervas, in the 61st year of his age, the 54th of his reign over Normandy, and the 21st from his conquest of England, A.D. 1087. He was buried in the church of St. Stephen at Caen.

The character of William the Conqueror is best seen in the work he achieved. To conquer a kingdom, and to establish in it a foreign dynasty, amidst the resentment of the natives and the jealousies of his own subjects, was a task requiring great military ability, capacity for government, and ascendency over the minds of men. To such qualities William united a determined will and an unscrupulous conscience. He could, however, treat his enemies with generosity, and he attempted to govern at first without those acts of tyranny and cruelty which made the Norman Conquest so disastrous to the English. But, when once he began this course, he pursued it in a spirit of wanton insult, as well as unrelenting injury, till the Saxons became as despised as they were miserable.

There were two outward signs of their degradation, which were perhaps more keenly felt than their exclusion from all posts of power and honor. The one was ever before their eyes in the castles of the Norman barons. The other consisted in the new

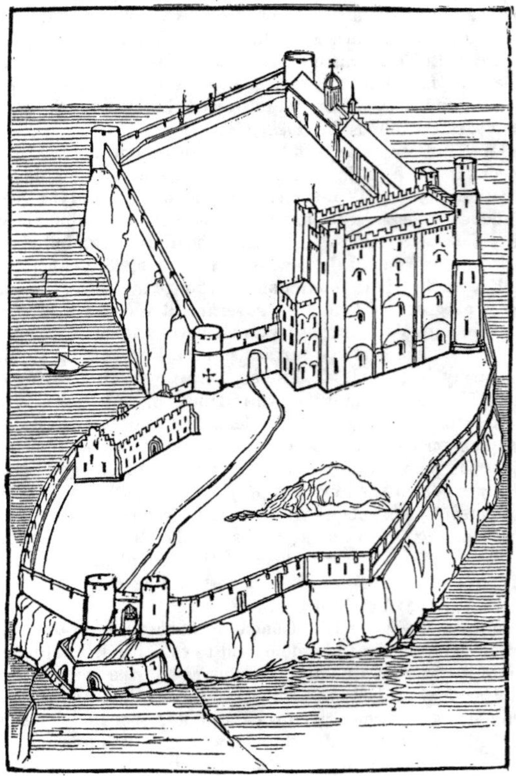

A Norman Castle.

and severe forest laws, which deprived them of all share in the sport, for the sake of which their lands were laid waste. The most memorable instance was that of the "New Forest," which William formed in the neighborhood of his palace at Winchester, at the cost of numerous villages and churches. Mutilation was the penalty for killing game; while that of homicide was a moderate fine.

The curfew (i. e., *couvre feu*) bell, on the ringing of which fires had to be extinguished at sunset in summer, and about eight o'clock in winter, is often mentioned as a badge of servitude. It was a Norman custom, as a precaution against fire.

But, in its lasting results, the Norman Conquest was an incalculable benefit to England. It gave her a strong government in place of the effete Saxon dynasty. It placed around the throne a body of nobles whose very pride and jealousy were soon to prove the means of extorting the people's liberties; and it brought England into a relation with the Continent, which, in spite of long and desolating wars, raised her at length to the rank of a European power.

William left three sons, Robert, William, and Henry, his second son, Richard, having been killed while hunting in the New Forest. He left to Robert his duchy of Normandy and Maine; to Henry he gave 5000 pounds of silver; bequeathing the crown of England to William.

The Traitor's Gate of the Tower.

Mount St. Michael in Normandy.

CHAPTER VI.

THE ANGLO-NORMAN KINGS (*continued*).—WILLIAM II., HENRY I., STEPHEN. A.D. 1087–1154.

William II., surnamed Rufus from his red hair (1087–1100) hastened to England, bearing his father's letter to Archbishop Lanfranc, which directed the prelate to crown him. He seized the fortresses of Dover, Pevensey, and Hastings, and the royal treasure of £60,000 at Winchester. His coronation took place on the 26th of September; and he easily crushed a rebellion of the partisans of Robert. But no sooner was he securely seated on the throne than he disregarded the promises by which he had gained the good-will of the English; and the death of Lanfranc, in 1089, removed the only check upon his tyranny. Both Saxons and Normans lived under a government of fear.

William next invaded Normandy (1090), but the war was stopped by the nobles, on the terms that, in case of either of the two brothers dying without issue, the dominions of both should be inherited by the survivor. Henry, who had been left out of the treaty, threw himself into the fortress of St. Michael's Mount, whence he made incursions upon Normandy. After a siege, attended by some romantic incidents, he was forced to capitulate, and was sent away in poverty and exile.

Robert returned to England with William, and joined him in an expedition against Scotland, which resulted in Malcolm's ceding Cumberland to England (1091), and in the submission of Edgar Atheling to William. Edgar accompanied Robert to Normandy. Two years later Malcolm again invaded England, and was killed in Northumberland. He was succeeded by his brother, Donald Bane.

About the same time William was at variance with the new Archbishop of Canterbury, Anselm, about the temporalities of the church; and such was the king's violence that Anselm at last retired from the kingdom (1097).

Meanwhile the preaching of Peter the Hermit had enkindled the zeal of Christendom for the recovery of the Holy Sepulchre from the Saracens; and the FIRST CRUSADE was undertaken in 1095. Robert of Normandy joined in the enterprise; and, to raise the needful funds, he mortgaged to William his duchies of Normandy and Maine for 10,000 marks, which were raised by violent extortion from the English, 1096. The example of Robert was followed by William, duke of Guienne and count of Poitiers, in 1099; but before William Rufus could prepare his army to take possession of those provinces his reign was closed by a violent death. As he was hunting in the New Forest, with a French gentleman named Walter Tyrrel, an arrow shot by Tyrrel glanced from a tree full into the king's breast, and killed him. Tyrrel fled to France. William's body was found by peasants and carried to Winchester, where he was buried. The manner of his death led to the suspicion of assassination; while the place of it was regarded as a divine judgment on the family of the Conqueror, two of whose sons had now perished in the forest which he had so tyrannically inclosed.

William Rufus died on the 2d of August, 1100, in the 13th year of his reign, and about the 40th of his age. The success of his government proves that he possessed much of his father's ability; but there were none of his father's better qualities in his fierce and unscrupulous character. Even that noble monument of his reign, the great hall of the royal palace of Westminster (*Westminster Hall*), as well as the bridge which he built over the Thames, and his wall round the Tower of London, are said to have been reared by great oppression.

HENRY I., surnamed BEAUCLERC, from his education and literary tastes (A.D. 1100–1135), was on the spot when William died, and hastened to secure the crown, to the exclusion of Robert, who was absent in Palestine. He was proclaimed at Winchester on the 3d of August, and crowned at London on the 5th. His first act was to grant a charter, in which he made fair promises to the church, the barons, and the English. To the latter he pledged himself to observe the laws of Edward the Confessor. In this charter the *barons* are for the first time named, in place of the *witan*, as concurring with the king. The confidence of his English subjects was completely gained by the marriage of Henry with *Matilda*, the niece of Edgar Atheling, and lineal representative of the house of Cerdic, who is known in English history as "the good Queen Maud." (See Genealogical Table A.) By this marriage Henry also allied himself to the royal family of Scotland.

But he had now to meet the hostility of his brother Robert, who claimed the English crown by the double right of birth and of his treaty with William Rufus; while on Henry's side there were the choice of his subjects, and the plea that his interests had never been consulted by his brothers. Robert landed at Portsmouth, (July 19, 1101), but war was averted on terms like those of the former treaty between Robert and William, that is, the succession of the survivor.

Henry soon found, in the discontent of Robert's Norman subjects, a pretext for setting aside the treaty. Landing in Normandy in 1105, he defeated his brother in the great battle of Tenchebray. Robert himself was taken prisoner, and after a captivity of twenty-eight years, died in the castle of Cardiff; a prince whose many generous impulses were rendered fruitless by passion and imprudence. Edgar Atheling was also taken at Tenchebray; liberated and pensioned by Henry, he lived in obscurity in England to a good old age, and with him expired the male line of Cerdic.

Henry next settled an important controversy with the pope. When a bishop was appointed the king claimed the right of *investiture* into the benefice, and at the same time he received the new prelate's *homage* for the temporal possessions of the see. By refusing these ceremonies the king virtually reserved the appointment to himself. These claims were resisted by the papal see, which was now aiming at entire independence; and the archbishop, Anselm, had refused homage to the king. The controversy was ended by Henry's giving up the right of *investiture*, but retaining the claim to the *homage*.

Much of Henry's time was spent in Normandy, where the cause of Robert's son, William, was espoused by the French king. His English subjects were oppressed by the cost of continual wars, which were only ended by the death of William in a skirmish in 1128. But another Prince William, the only legitimate son of Henry, had already met with a lamentable fate.

It was in the year 1120 that Henry, having made a peace with the king of France, set sail from Barfleur for England. Prince William remained behind for a short time; and the captain and crew of his ship drank so freely that, soon after setting sail, they drove the vessel on a rock. The prince was escaping in the long-boat, when, hearing the cries of his natural sister, the Countess of Perche, he put back to save her. A rush was made to the boat, which sank with all on board; while only two survivors still clung to the ship. The one was the captain, Fitz-Stephens, who threw himself into the sea when he heard that the prince was dead; the other was a butcher of Rouen, who alone escaped to tell the tale. When, after three days' suspense, the king received certain news of his loss, he fainted away, and it is recorded that "he never smiled again." The loss to the nation was of a doubtful character; for, though William's death caused the civil wars that followed, he is said to have expressed the most hostile intentions toward the English.

Henry was now left without a male heir. "The good Queen Maud" had died in 1118, leaving but one daughter, Matilda, who was married to Henry V., emperor of Germany. Henry now married Adelais of Louvain, February 2, 1121, but she had no children. In 1125 the Emperor Henry V. died; and the Empress Maud came over with her father, on his return from Normandy to England, in 1126. On the Christmas-day of that year the king caused all his nobles to swear fealty to Maud as his heir; the first to take the oath being her uncle, the king of Scotland, and the next after him being Stephen, the future king, who was related by marriage to the royal family. In the following year Henry married Maud to Geoffrey Plantagenet, the son of Fulk earl of Anjou, who had hitherto supported William's claims in Normandy; and in 1133 a son was born of this marriage, who afterward, as Henry II., became the first lineal descendant of both lines, the Saxon and the Norman, who was king of England. The oath of fealty to Maud was repeated on this occasion.

In the same year Henry went to Normandy, where he died from eating too freely of lampreys, in the night of the 1st of December, 1135, the same year in which his brother Robert had died in prison. He was buried in the abbey of St. Mary's, at Reading, which he had founded.

Henry inherited his father's ability, with graces of mind and person which the Conqueror wanted, and a far greater spirit of moderation. Though equally determined and unscrupulous, he was less violent, and his cruelties arose more from policy than passion. In his character we see the old Norman spirit tempered by the literary culture which he maintained throughout his life;

and, above all, he set the first example of justice to his Saxon subjects.

Stephen, A.D. 1135-1154.—All Henry's cares for his daughter's succession were frustrated by the treason of a relative, who had professed to be one of her warmest supporters. William the Conqueror had married his daughter to Stephen count of Blois; and the two youngest of their sons, Stephen and Henry, had been invited to England by Henry I., who made Henry bishop of Winchester, and gave Stephen immense estates. In spite of these benefits and his own oath Stephen now hastened to London, where he was saluted king by the populace; and the Archbishop of Canterbury, misled by a false statement of the late king's feelings toward his daughter, crowned Stephen on the 26th of December, 1135. This more than doubtful title was sanctioned by a papal bull, and recommended to the English by a new charter; while Stephen strengthened himself by mercenary soldiers from Flanders. The great barons, perhaps distrustful of a female sovereign, gave their support to Stephen, on terms which made them almost independent of his authority, especially stipulating for the right of fortifying their castles. Even Robert earl of Gloucester, the late king's natural son, found it prudent to submit to Stephen, on condition that his own dignities should be respected. The Norman barons followed the example of the English by deserting the cause of Matilda.

But, in 1138, Earl Robert fled from England, and openly defied Stephen, whom he accused of violating their agreement. The cause of Matilda was also espoused by David king of Scotland, who devastated the north of England, till he was stopped by an army gathered at Northallerton. The Scots were entirely defeated in the "Battle of the Standard," so called from the crucifix which was carried in a wagon in the midst of the English army.

Stephen now thought himself strong enough to curb the power of the nobles. But he committed the mistake of beginning with the clergy. The bishops of Salisbury and Lincoln, who had erected castles, like their lay peers, were thrown into prison, and compelled to yield up their fortresses. This act roused the whole church against Stephen, headed by his own brother Henry bishop of Winchester, who was now the papal legate, and who condemned the king's violence in a synod assembled at Westminster. The occasion was seized by Matilda, who landed in England with her brother Robert, and established herself at Arundel Castle, in Sussex, 1139.

The country now suffered the worst horrors of civil war. The land was left untilled, and famine was added to bloodshed. The newly built castles became robbers' dens, whence their owners issued forth to extort plunder even by torture. At length Stephen was taken prisoner by Earl Robert, and conducted to Gloucester, where he was closely confined in irons, A.D. 1141.

But Matilda's triumph was short. Her imperious rejection of the petition which Stephen's queen presented for his liberty, on condition of his renouncing the crown and retiring to a convent, turned the popular feeling against her. The legate, Henry, incited the Londoners to revolt, and besieged the empress in Winchester. Matilda escaped, but her brother Robert was taken prisoner. In exchange for his release she consented to set Stephen at liberty. The civil war became fiercer than ever; and so it raged for five years, till the retirement of Matilda into Normandy, and the death of her brother Robert in 1148.

But her son Henry now began to take an active part in the contest. In 1148 he went to Scotland, whence he made incursions into England, and gave promise of the abilities which he afterward displayed as king. In 1150 he became, by his mother's consent, Duke of Normandy, to which Maine was added in the following year, by the death of his father Geoffrey. Anjou was bequeathed to his younger brother, Geoffrey, from whom he afterward took it by force. His marriage with Eleanor, the divorced wife of Louis VII. of France, brought him Guienne, Poitou, and other provinces in the south of France, of which she was the heiress, 1152; and thus was laid the foundation of those interests in France which his successors fought so hard to maintain.

Henry now seemed powerful enough to reclaim his mother's crown; and he landed in England in 1153. His hopes were encouraged by a slight advantage gained over Stephen at Malmesbury. But once more, as in the contests between the sons of William I., the nobles of both sides arranged a treaty, by which the crown was left to Stephen for his life, and Henry was designated his successor. In less than a year Stephen died, October 25, 1154; and Henry, who had only returned to Normandy in the spring, landed in England on the 6th of December, to found that famous dynasty in which the Saxon and Norman blood were mingled, and which reigned over England for three centuries, from Henry II. to Richard III. The house received the surname of PLANTAGENET, from the sprig of Spanish broom (*planta genista*) which their founder Geoffrey used to wear in his hat.

Marriage of the Father and Mother of Becket. (From the Royal MS. 2 B. vii.)

CHAPTER VII.

THE HOUSE OF PLANTAGENET.—HENRY II. A.D. 1154–1189.

HENRY II. ascended the throne of England amidst the acclamations of all classes; and was crowned on the 19th of December, 1154. His first acts fully justified the hopes formed of him. He confirmed the charter of Henry I.; reversed the illegal acts of the late reign; demolished all newly erected castles; reformed the debased coin; suppressed robbery and violence; and executed the laws with firm impartiality (1155). He sent the mercenaries of Stephen to render useful service to the kingdom on the Welsh border, where he himself made a campaign in 1157, and nearly lost his life. He drove the Scots out of the north of England, at the same time confirming Malcolm IV., king of Scotland, in the earldom of Huntingdon. On the Christmas-day of this year, 1157, Henry was again crowned at Worcester.

In 1158 the death of his brother Geoffrey gave occasion to new relations with France. Henry had already (1156) despoiled Geoffrey of Anjou and certain castles which his father had bequeathed to him; and Geoffrey fled to Nantes, in Brittany, the people of which received him as their count. On his death Nantes was seized by Conan duke of Brittany, and Henry sailed to Normandy to recover it. In the war which followed Henry laid siege to Toulouse (1159); but Louis VII. of France supported the Count of Toulouse. Henry, however, paid Louis a visit, and so won him over by his attentions that a peace was made (1160), and ratified by the betrothal of Prince Henry, the heir to the English crown, who was only five years old, to the Princess Margaret of France, who was in her cradle. Nantes presently submitted to Henry, and another marriage of infants was arranged between Conan's daughter and only child, and the king's third son, Geoffrey. Henry was now the real master of Brittany; and on the death of the duke, seven years later, he entered into the full possession of the province as its *suzerain*. At this epoch his dominions on the Continent comprised about one-third of the whole French monarchy of later days, while the provinces under the immediate authority of the king of France were inferior to his both in extent and opulence. The time seemed at hand when both crowns might be united on Henry's head.

But in the mean time events of the deepest interest had occurred in England, where Henry's attempt to limit the power of the clergy had involved him in his celebrated conflict with THOMAS À BECKET. This remarkable man was the first Englishman who emerged from the obscurity to which his race were consigned when the Normans seized upon all the higher offices of church and state. He was born of respectable parents in London. He began life in the household of Archbishop Theobald, who rewarded his talents and industry with preferment. He employed the emoluments thus obtained in a journey to Italy, where he studied civil law in the then most famous University of Bologna. The learning thus acquired obtained for him, on his return, the archdeaconry of Canterbury; and Theobald employed him also in a mission to Rome. On Henry's accession the archbishop obtained Becket's appointment to the high office of chancellor. The king enriched him with several forfeited baronies, and intrusted to him the education of his son and heir, Prince Henry. Becket now assumed a state in which no English subject had lived before. A large retinue of knights waited upon him; the highest barons crowded his halls to pay their court, and placed their sons in his household for education; and the king himself was frequently his guest.

On the death of Theobald, Henry at once fixed on Becket as his successor, relying on his support in his contemplated measures against the encroachments of the clergy. Becket accepted the dignity with very different intentions; and was installed as Archbishop of Canterbury on Whitsunday, May 24, 1162. He at once resigned the office of chancellor, thereby intimating to the king, who was deeply offended, his resolution to free himself from all ties of dependence on the crown. He maintained the pomp of his household on a scale proportioned to his new dignity, while in his own person he practiced extreme austerity. He lived on bread and water; and not only wore sackcloth next his skin, but kept it unchanged till it was full of vermin, and scarred his back with frequent discipline. In professed imitation of Christ, he daily washed the feet of thirteen beggars, dismissing them with presents. How much of this was ostentation, or how little of it genuine piety, it is not for the historian to decide; but at all events, no course could have been better suited to gain over the minds of the people, and so to prepare the way for schemes of ambition.

But Becket chose a strange case for a trial of strength. A clergyman in Worcestershire, after debauching a gentleman's daughter, murdered her father; and, when the king claimed the offender for condign punishment, Becket interposed the authority of the church. He kept him safe, in the bishop's prison, from the king's officers; declared that his degradation was an adequate punishment; and denied that the clerk, when degraded, could then be seized by the civil power, as it would be trying him twice for the same offense.

Henry gladly availed himself of so flagrant a case to decide the whole question of the relative authority of church and state. He called a council at Westminster, 1163, and demanded of the prelates whether they would observe the "customs" of the kingdom, as settled under Henry I. They professed their willingness "saving the rights of their order;" thus evading the whole question.

But Henry was not to be so duped. Resolved to have a clear decision as to what these ancient customs were, and then to enforce compliance with them, he assembled a council of the nobles and clergy, under the presidency of John bishop of Oxford, at Clarendon, near Salisbury, January 25, 1164. This assembly, overawed, according to the writers of the clerical party, by threats of violence, passed the sixteen articles known as the CONSTITUTIONS OF CLARENDON. Their chief provisions were: that every clerk accused of crime should appear before the secular courts—that no clerk should absent himself from the realm without permission of the king—that vacant bishoprics and other high benefices should be in the keeping of the king, who should receive their revenues; and that they should be filled up by the higher clergy, convened under the king's direction, subject to his approval of their choice—that no officers of the royal household, or tenants-in-chief under the crown, should be excommunicated without the king's consent—

primate's ruin. Becket, however, made his escape, and fled to France (Nov. 1164). During the six years that he lived in exile his cause was espoused by Louis VII., and less vigorously by the pope Alexander III., while Henry treated his adherents in England with great severity. Louis's protection of Becket caused a war with France (1167), in which Henry gained some advantages, but peace was made on January 6, 1169; and in the following year Louis effected a reconciliation between the king and the archbishop, who had an interview at Fretville, in Touraine, July 22, 1170.

But even before Becket returned to England he found a new cause for quarrel. Henry, fearing that his kingdom might be placed under a papal interdict, had thought it prudent to associate his son Henry in the kingdom, and had caused him to be crowned by the Archbishop of York, June 15, 1170. Becket held that the primate alone could perform the ceremony of a coronation; and Henry had promised its repetition. But Becket could not wait for the fulfillment of this promise. On his return to England in December he met the Archbishop of York, on his way to join the king in Normandy, and pronounced against him a sentence of deprivation, which he had previously obtained from the pope. By the same authority he excommunicated the bishops of London and Salisbury, who accompanied the Archbishop of York. But this was his last act of arrogant authority.

While Becket continued his journey in state, welcomed with acclamations and hymns by the people, who came out in procession to meet him, the prelates just named arrived at Bayeux, and informed the king of the sentence pronounced against them. "What!" cried the king, "this man, who has eaten my bread, who came to my court on a lame horse, insults me to my face, and there is none of the servants who eat at my table that will avenge me!" These words were probably but the vague expression of unbridled anger; but they found only too willing hearers. Four gentlemen of the king's household, Reginald Fitz-Urse, William de Tracy, Hugh de Moreville, and Richard Brito (the Breton), agreed with each other to execute his supposed wishes. They departed secretly, but not until they had dropped some expressions which induced the king to send after them a messenger, charging them to do nothing against the primate's person; but this messenger arrived too late.

Meanwhile Becket had found himself surrounded, at Canterbury, with danger, even to his life; but, maintaining his haughty bearing, he preached in the cathedral on Christmas-day, and afterward excommunicated Ranulf and Robert de Broc, who had been the sequestrators of the see during his absence.

It was at the house of this same Ranulf, at Saltwood, that the conspirators met three days later (December 28), having traveled from Normandy by different routes. The day after they proceeded to Canterbury, and, being joined by certain assassins, they went to the palace, and, with many threats, required Becket to absolve the prelates. His alarmed attendants hurried him into the church, whither the assassins followed, after arming themselves. Becket met them at the door of the chapel of St. Benedict. Fitz-Urse approached him, battle-axe in hand, exclaiming, "Where is the traitor?" and Becket replied, "Reginald, here I am; no traitor, but the archbishop and priest of God; what do you wish?" They again demanded that he should revoke the excommunication, which he still steadfastly refused. Then began the scene of violence: they tried to drag him out to unconsecrated ground; he resisted, and flung Tracy on the pavement. Fitz-Urse struck off his cap with his sword: then Tracy aimed at him a blow which was intercepted by the arm of Grim, a monk of Cambridge, but still it grazed Becket's head and wounded his shoulder. Wiping away the trickling blood, he said, "Into thy hands, O Lord, I commend my spirit." Another stroke from Tracy brought him to his knees; and, having gently murmured, "For the name of Jesus and the defense of the church I am willing to die," he fell motionless on his face; and one more tremendous blow from Richard the Breton cleft his skull and finished the deed of murder. This fearful crime was perpetrated on Tuesday, the 29th of December, 1170, and the mangled corpse was buried hastily in the crypt on the 31st. Becket was canonized, as a saint and martyr, by pope Alexander III., March 3, 1173; and the anniversary of his death became a marked day in the Anglican calendar. His body was removed, in 1220, to a magnificent shrine behind the high altar, which was enriched with presents from all Christendom, and visited by troops of pilgrims, the number of whom amounted in one year to 100,000. The shrine was destroyed, and the celebration of the martyrdom of St. Thomas was abolished, by Henry VIII., but his story still forms one of the most interesting "Memorials of Canterbury;" his name is borne by sixty-four English churches; and the genius of Chaucer has given to the "Canterbury Pilgrims" another immortality than that which they sought at Becket's shrine.

Never could a name attain such eminence by party prejudice or mere fanaticism: there must have been real greatness to command such fame. Becket was an intrepid champion of what he deemed a sacred cause; and neither the object he pursued nor the means he employed should be judged by the notions of our age. Neither Becket nor his adversaries thought of the cause of the church as spiritual, or of worldly power and ambition as opposed to it; and doubtless the feelings of the Englishman against the Norman inflamed the opposition of the prelate to the king. But in no age can violence and perjury be excused; and both Becket and his murderers must bear their burden—the former of reproach, but the latter of execration. Nor can Henry's memory be cleared of the blame of extreme harshness in what was mainly the cause of good government, even if he could be acquitted of all share in the final deed of blood.

The storm of indignation which might have been expected to burst forth from Rome was averted, for the present, by Henry's excusing himself from participation in the deed, and by the pope's sense of the impolicy of breaking with England; and Henry was left at liberty to carry on the schemes which he had already commenced for subjugating Ireland.

The four knights who had slain Becket were suffered to expiate their crime by a pilgrimage to Jerusalem, where they all died.

Ireland, the Ierne of the Greeks and Hibernia of the Romans, and the Erin of its own musical tongue, was probably peopled from Britain, but by a different branch of the Celtic race from that which inhabited the greater part of the island, and more akin to those of Scotland; the Britons being *Cymry*, the Scotch and Irish *Gael*. The tribes nearest to Scotland maintained close relations with that country, sharing in their wars and festivals. The island received Christianity through the preaching of Palladius in the 4th century, and of St. Patrick about the middle of the 5th; and while Britain was plunged back into heathen barbarism by the Saxon conquest, Ireland was celebrated as the seat of learning and religion, and was called the *Island of the Saints*. Foreigners resorted to her schools; and she sent forth missionaries, of whom the most celebrated was St. Columban, the apostle of the Hebrides (540-615). The Northmen extended their ravages to Ireland; but from this evil she had begun to recover; and the cities and kingdoms of Dublin, Waterford, and Limerick, founded by these invaders on the coast, were now rising into importance. The country was divided into five principal kingdoms—Munster, Leinster, Meath, Ulster, and Connaught; and one of the five chieftains (*riaghs*) generally held a sort of supremacy over the rest (*ard-riagh*). This dignity was now held by Roderick O'Connor, king of Connaught, but he had little real power beyond his own province.

In fact, thus early in their history, the Irish seem to have displayed those generous infirmities, in which the virtues and vices of the Celtic character were both exaggerated; and their brave enthusiasm was neutralized by the want of power to apply themselves steadfastly to one object. The division into clans combined with the law of *tanistry*—that is, the succession of an elective instead of an hereditary chieftain—to create endless broils and petty wars. The tenure of property was rendered uncertain by the law of *gavelkind*, under which each estate returned, on its owner's death, into a common stock, and was redistributed among the clansmen—a custom incompatible with any advance in agriculture.

Henry had early formed the design of adding Ireland to his dominions; and he had recourse to the convenient doctrine that, under an alleged donation of Constantine, the pope could dispose of outlying countries, and especially of islands. Adrian IV. (Breakspear), the only English pope of the whole line of pontiffs, was equally disposed to aggrandize his country, and to subject the Irish church to the authority of Rome, which she had always resisted. He issued a bull in 1156, granting the sovereignty over the island to the king of England, but it was some years before Henry was prepared to make the acquisition.

The desired occasion at length arose out of a quarrel among the Irish chieftains. Dermot Macmorrogh, king of Leinster, being expelled from his kingdom for an outrage he had committed, sought the aid of Henry, whose vassal he offered to become (1167). Henry, who was fully engaged, as above related, in France, granted Dermot letters patent, empowering any English subjects to give him aid. In the southwest of Wales Dermot found certain Norman adventurers willing to undertake his cause, among whom were Robert Fitz-Stephens, Maurice Fitz-Gerald, and especially Richard de Clare, of Chepstow, surnamed Strongbow, son of the Earl of Pembroke. In 1169 Fitz-Stephens crossed the Channel and took Waterford, and Fitz-Gerald followed him. In the next year Strongbow took Dublin, and having married Eva, the daughter of Dermot, he inherited the kingdom of Leinster (1170). The native princes, headed by Roderick, now leagued against him, and besieged Dublin with 30,000 men; but a charge of ninety Norman knights, on their war-horses, and in their full armor, routed the whole army of wild *kernes* with immense slaughter; and the terror of the English name spread over the whole island.

It was now time for Henry to interfere, unless he wished to see Ireland an independent kingdom. He recalled to England all his subjects in Ireland. But on full submission made to his authority by Strongbow and the other adventurers, who gave up to him the principal cities, he suffered them to retain their possessions as fiefs of the crown; and he appointed Strongbow as *Seneschal of Ireland*. He visited the island in person, and received the homage of the people of the south, who offered no resistance; but Roderick of

Connaught and the king of Ulster refused submission. The English power in Ireland was long bounded by a line drawn from the mouth of the Boyne to that of the Shannon. A synod assembled at Cashel united the church of Ireland to the see of Rome.

With this acceptable offering Henry met the papal legates on his return to Normandy in 1172; and having sworn on sacred relics that he had neither compassed nor desired the death of Becket, he received full absolution from the pope.

But now began the worst troubles of Henry's life and reign, in the unnatural rebellion of his children. His wife, Eleanor of Poitou, was a disgraced woman when he married her; and he had offended her, in turn, by his infidelities. She now incited his children to defy his authority, notwithstanding his having given all of them splendid establishments. Henry, the eldest (since the death of his brother William), had, besides the inheritance of the English crown, Normandy, Maine, Anjou, and Touraine; his second surviving son, Richard, was Duke of Guienne and Count of Poitou; Geoffrey, the fourth son, possessed the duchy of Brittany in right of his wife; and for John, the youngest, the king destined the splendid appanage of Ireland. But, instigated by their mother, and encouraged, at least in part, by the French king, the three eldest fled to the court of France, and announced to Henry their claim to be invested with full sovereignty in their respective appanages. They were supported by many of the Norman, Breton, and Gascon nobility, but these Henry easily defeated. The great danger was in England, where revolts broke out, while William king of Scotland invaded the northern counties, and the Flemings made a descent on Suffolk.

Aware that the murder of Becket still rankled in the minds of his people, Henry resolved to conciliate them, and the clergy at the same time, by a full and public penance. He came over from Normandy, and reached Canterbury on the 12th of July, 1174. He entered the city barefoot, worshiped at the shrine of St. Thomas, and, assembling a chapter of the monks, submitted to be scourged by them at the martyr's tomb. The next day he received full absolution from the clergy of Canterbury.

On his return to London he was greeted by news which seemed to add the sanction of Heaven to his penance; for on the very day of his absolution his generals had gained a great victory over the Scots at Alnwick, in which King William (the Lion) himself was taken prisoner. The Scotch king only regained his liberty by ceding Berwick and Roxburgh to Henry, doing homage to him, with all the Scottish barons and prelates, in the cathedral of York, and placing the castle of Edinburgh in his hands for a limited time

(1175). Meanwhile the French king made peace with Henry; the English rebels submitted to him; and his sons returned to their obedience, and did homage for their possessions.

The following years were occupied in the internal administration of the kingdom; the constitution of which, as a Norman sovereignty, was now definitively settled, before it received those new elements of freedom which were added under the later Plantagenets.

The Norman constitution had this one point in common with the Saxon, that both were based on a military organization. The state was modeled on the camp. But this organization assumed very different forms among the Germans in their native homes, and among the hordes that overran the provinces of the Roman empire. The former cherished greater loyalty to their chiefs, and greater respect for the rights of individual citizens; the latter, banded together as brethren in arms, made a boast of personal independence and equality among themselves, while the people subdued by them formed a lower class, looked upon as having no political and scarcely any social rights. When Charles the Simple inquired of the Northmen what title their leader bore, the reply was, "None; we are all equally free." When they began to form settled states they found it necessary to frame institutions based upon, but modifying, these principles; and hence arose that celebrated constitution, of which many traces are still preserved, called the FEUDAL SYSTEM.

The essential idea of this system was, that among the gentlemen of equal birth, and equally entitled to bear arms, such voluntary service should be rendered to those whom fortune and ability had raised above the rest, as might be honorable in itself and consistent with personal independence; and that this service should be rewarded in the like spirit. It was on these terms only that the king was raised over his *peers* (i. e., *pares*, as the nobles were emphatically called, to assert their *equality*), and they above their retainers who were of gentle blood. The relation may be compared to that which still exists in the English naval and military services, where the officers are equal as gentlemen, but have their allotted ranks for the purposes of the service; only the bond of *discipline* was almost wanting. The *persons* being in this position, their claim on the *property* acquired in the countries they overran was also equal in theory; but its distribution was regulated as follows: The king was the supreme lord of the land, with exceptions to be mentioned presently. The public land was the fund for rewarding the military service which his peers and others were bound to render to the king, while its possession formed a new obligation to such service. The possessions so held were called *fiefs* (in Latin, *beneficia*); and the possessor became the *vassal* of the king, who was the *feudal lord* or *suzerain.* The vassal was bound to follow the banner of his lord with a force proportioned to the extent of his tenure, to assist him with his counsel, and to attend as an assessor in his courts of justice, besides other minor services. The lord was bound to protect the vassal in the secure enjoyment of his fief; and both owed to one another the protection of each other's person.

Such being the relation between the king and great vassals, who held immediately under him, these were, in their turn, surrounded by a class of retainers, who owned them as their feudal lords. To such vassals the lord parceled out his estate by a process called *sub-infeudation,* and he administered justice to them in his own courts. The few lands that remained free, that is, which were not bound to render service to a suzerain, though liable to burdens for the public defense, were called *alodial* in contradistinction to *feudal.*

The vassals received their fiefs from the feudal lord by *investiture,* taking an oath of *fealty* and doing *homage* to him for the fief. This homage was either *liege* or *simple,* the former being the more binding.

This system tended to increase the power of the great feudatories at the expense of the crown. Their service to the sovereign was only occasional; but they themselves were constantly surrounded by their retainers, who feasted in their halls, shared their sports, and lived under their protection. Their castles were for the most part fortified; and they kept their retainers exercised in constant petty wars among themselves. Hence the feudal system tended to that *military aristocracy,* which only yielded to the progress of commerce and the rise of cities, the true strong-holds of freedom.

The feudal system was introduced into England by the Norman Conquest. Its pressure on the common people was aggravated by the completeness of the subjection of the Saxon race. *All* the land was held by feudal tenure, and there was no *allodium.* The few Saxons who were permitted to retain their lands were brought under the feudal system; and the thanes were reduced to the condition of *franklins,* or simple freeholders. The Normans, who held most of the manors from the king, were called *tenants-in-chief (in capite)*; and they were bound to *knight service*—that is, to maintain in the field, for forty days at a time, a certain force of their subtenants. This service extended to religious foundations and monasteries. Exclusive of these, 1400 tenants-in-chief and about 8000 mesne lords (holding fiefs not directly from the crown) are enumerated in Domesday Book.

There were some peculiarities in the Anglo-Norman feudal system which gave greater power to the king than he had in other countries—for instance, France. Generally the oath of the vassal was taken to his immediate lord; but William made all the vassals, *mesne* as well as *chief*, take the oath to himself. Again, as the conquered lands were distributed to his followers at his pleasure, he took care not to make the estates so large as to be dangerous to himself, and he distributed them over different counties. Hence the nobles of England seldom defied the crown, or carried on private wars, as they did in other countries.

The legislative power was vested in the king, together with the *Great Council of the Realm, or Royal Court*, afterward called THE PARLIAMENT.

This council was composed of the archbishops, bishops, and principal abbots, with the *Greater Barons*, that is, the superior class (for there were two classes) of tenants under the crown. The lesser barons were also summoned, especially when taxes were to be imposed; but the commons, that is, the representatives of counties and boroughs, had no place in the council before the reign of Henry III. The functions of the Great Council were to grant money to the king, and to assist him in making new laws. For the former purpose the consent of the lesser as well as the greater barons was required; and the Norman kings bound themselves not to levy money from their tenants without their consent being given in a great council of the realm. The council used to be summoned at the great festivals of Christmas, Easter, and Whitsuntide, and at other times as occasion required. How far its assent was necessary to the making of laws does not appear. Indeed, the whole process of legislation under the Norman kings was in a very unsettled state. The royal charters were confirmations of old privileges, rather than new enactments; and in the practical administration of justice there seems to have been a conflict between the will of the sovereign and the Anglo-Saxon laws, in which the latter constantly gained more and more force. Some even regard the Norman Code, called the *Grand Coutumier* (or great customary), as of Anglo-Saxon origin. It was not till the reign of Henry II. that the Norman kings began to be real legislators, and to this reign belong most of the changes which are commonly ascribed to the Conqueror.

Justice was administered by the king, in his select council (*Curia* or *Aula Regis*), which always attended his person. It was composed of the great officers of state, who were also the king's political advisers and executive servants. A branch of this council, called the *Court of Exchequer*, which can be traced back to the reign of Henry I., decided all questions connected with the revenue. Afterward another branch was made for private suitors, who had been compelled previously to follow the royal court, called the *Court of Common Pleas*. It originated early in the reign of

Richard I., and was fully established by Magna Charta. Thus arose the three great courts of common law, which continue to the present day.

The old Saxon courts of the County and the Hundred still continued; and they formed a great check on the courts of the barons, as all freeholders, up to the greatest barons, were bound to assist the sheriff in these courts. An appeal lay from both the county and the baronial courts to the court of the king; and, to save suitors the trouble and expense of following the king's court, itinerant judges (*Justices in Eyre*) were appointed under Henry II. (A.D. 1176) to visit the six districts into which the kingdom was divided for this purpose, and which very nearly corresponded to the present circuits of the judges.

The modes of deciding cases by *compurgation* and by the *ordeal* were continued for a time; but the former was abolished by Henry II., except in London and the other boroughs, and the latter by the Fourth Lateran Council at the beginning of the reign of Henry III. The ordeal was superseded by the *trial by combat*, in which the accused might maintain his cause by his body in single combat with his accuser, in the faith that "God would defend the right." In suits for the recovery of land, Henry II. enacted that a tenant, who was unwilling to risk the combat, might put himself on the *assize*, consisting of four knights chosen by the sheriff, who chose twelve more, and the verdict of the sixteen decided the case. But this was only in the king's court, and in those of the itinerant justices.

The Norman kings derived a fixed and independent revenue from their vast crown lands; but they also levied taxes, called *tallages*, on all who lived within their demesne. There was also the *escuage* or *scutage*, a composition paid by the chief tenants who neglected to furnish the number of soldiers corresponding to their estate. The *Danegeld* was also continued; the last instance of its levy being in the 20th year of Henry II., A.D. 1174. There were other important sources of revenue arising out of the feudal system. (1) A *Relief* was a fine paid to the lord by a new heir when succeeding to his fief. (2) A *Fine upon alienation* was paid when a tenant transferred his fief to another. (3) An *Escheat* was when a fief reverted to the lord in consequence of the death of a tenant without heirs. (4) A *Forfeiture* arose from the tenant failing to perform his duties to the lord or to the state. (5) *Aids* were contributions demanded from the vassals under special circumstances. (6) *Wardship* was the right of the lord to the care of his tenant's person, and to receive the profits of his estate, during his minority. (7) The *Marriage* of female wards was a source of revenue, by the forfeiture of the sum which the guardian could have obtained for a marriage alliance, in case of the ward (during her minority) refusing the husband proposed by her guardian.

The *Church* was advanced in power by the Conqueror, in return for the support which Rome gave to his claim to the crown. He separated the civil and ecclesiastical jurisdictions, which had been united under the Anglo-Saxon kings. He prohibited the bishops from sitting in the county courts, and allowed ecclesiastical causes to be tried in spiritual courts only. He assigned to the church one-third of the knights' fees into which he divided England.

From all the benefits of the political system thus described, one class, the lowest, of the people were excluded. These were the *villeins,* who were in fact *slaves,* like the *serfs* of the Anglo-Saxons. But, at the Conquest, most of the *ceorls,* or freedmen in the rank above the serfs, lost their liberty, and were degraded into *villeins.* This class was more and more oppressed, till under Henry II. the villein was incapable of holding property, and was at the mercy of his lord's arbitrary will, except that the law protected him from the worst forms of personal injury. Villeins were of two classes. The *villeins regardant* (in Latin *adscripti glebæ*) changed owners with the lands to which they were attached; while the *villeins in gross* (or *at large*) were not attached to particular lands, and might be sold in the open market to any purchaser. Of all the steps in the progress of English liberty none is more interesting than the process by which *villenage* was abolished and its degraded victims became the noble peasantry of England. Their recovery of their liberty was not only the removal of the stain of slavery, but the revival of the old Anglo-Saxon race of freemen.

The years in which Henry was chiefly occupied with internal administration (1175-1181) present no important events, except Prince John's appointment as Lord of Ireland (1177); in which office he so enraged the native chieftains by his petulance and incapacity that it was necessary to recall him. In 1180 Louis VII., king of France, was succeeded by Philip Augustus.

But in 1182 the king's sons were again in open rebellion. Henry had claimed for Prince Henry, his eldest son, the homage of his brothers for their continental possessions. They all refused, and Richard was especially violent and insolent. Even Prince Henry, alarmed by an alliance between Richard and the French king, took part with his brothers; but he was seized with a fatal illness, and died in bitter remorse at the age of 28, June 11, 1183. Three years later Geoffrey was killed at a tournament at Paris, August 19, 1186. It was after his death that his widow, Constance, gave birth to the unfortunate Prince Arthur.

In the following year the capture of Jerusalem by Saladin roused the wrath of all Christendom, and the kings of England and France, with the Emperor Frederick Barbarossa, pledged themselves to a new crusade, 1188. The funds were raised by an oppressive tax, called "the tithe of Saladin." But a quarrel arose between Henry and Philip Augustus about Prince Richard's claims to be declared heir to all his father's dominions; and Richard, even to his father's face, professed his allegiance to the French king, and did him homage for the English provinces in France, Nov. 18, 1188. The war which ensued was ended by a peace disadvantageous to Henry, 1189; but the last drop in his cup of bitterness was added by the discovery that his favorite son, John, had been in the league against him. The broken-hearted father cursed his children and the day of his own birth. His health yielded to his sorrows, and he died of a lingering fever at the castle of Chinon, near Saumur, in the 58th year of his age and the 34th of his reign. His natural son, Geoffrey, attended his corpse to the abbey of Fontevraud, and, as it lay there in state, Richard came to gaze upon his father's remains. The old chronicler Matthew of Paris tells how a flow of blood from the nostrils of the corpse was taken as a sign of indignation by Richard, who expressed the deepest remorse for the undutiful conduct which had brought his father to the grave.

Henry was one of the greatest of the English kings. He was richly gifted in person and in mind, and he used his gifts with energy. Though not free from the vices of his race, violence and dissimulation, he governed justly, and carried England a great step onward toward the settlement of her constitution.

He had five sons by his wife Eleanor; *William*, who died in 1156; *Henry*, who died in 1183; RICHARD; *Geoffrey*, who died in 1186; and JOHN. Only Richard and John survived him, and occupied, in succession, the throne of England. He had several natural children; and his intrigue with "the Fair Rosamond" gave rise afterward to the fabulous story of her concealment in the labyrinth of Woodstock, and her discovery and murder by the jealous Eleanor. Of Rosamond's two sons, the elder, William, surnamed Longsword, married the daughter of the Earl of Salisbury; and Geoffrey, the younger, became Bishop of Lincoln and Archbishop of York.

King John. Queen Elinor.

CHAPTER VIII.

THE HOUSE OF PLANTAGENET (*continued*).—RICHARD I., JOHN. A.D. 1189–1216.

RICHARD I. (1189–1199), surnamed CŒUR-DE-LION (the *Lion-hearted*), was born at Oxford, Sept. 13, 1157. He had possessed his mother's duchy of Aquitaine and county of Poitou for several years before the death of Henry II. called him to the throne of England. The sincerity of the grief which he showed at his father's tomb was proved by his retaining his trusted counselors; while he showed his respect for his mother by releasing her from captivity, and his affection for his brother John by the gift, afterward so ill-requited, of honors and estates.

The ten years' reign of Richard was divided into two nearly

equal parts, during the first of which he was absent in the East, and during the second he was chiefly engaged in war on the Continent.

The day of his coronation, Sept. 3, 1189, was marked by a great massacre of the Jews, who had presumed to show themselves in public contrary to the king's orders. There were similar massacres in the following year, especially at York, and the king took severe measures to repress such outrages; but the persecution of the Jews was constantly renewed under the Plantagenet kings. Richard returned to Normandy in December, after filling up some bishoprics and appointing his mother regent.

His whole mind was now given to the Crusade, into which he had been one of the first to enter, and to which Henry had been pledged. Such an enterprise suited him far better than the cares of government. His prodigious strength, his dauntless courage, his military capacity, and his poetic devotion to the honors of chivalry, all combined with the generous enthusiasm of his temper to make him the pattern of a chevalier rather than of a king. From the very first the welfare of his kingdom was sacrificed to this enterprise. Funds were raised by the sale of high offices, as well as of the revenues of the crown; and he even gave up to the king of Scotland, for the small sum of 10,000 marks, the claim of homage which Henry had exacted from him, and the fortresses of Berwick and Roxburgh, the keys of the kingdom.

In April, 1190, he set sail from Dartmouth to meet Philip Augustus at the rendezvous of Vezelay, on the borders of Burgundy, where the united forces amounted to 100,000 men. Rejoining his fleet at Marseilles, he was driven by stress of weather to winter at Messina, where he was joined by Berengaria, the daughter of the king of Navarre, who accompanied him to Palestine, after their marriage on May 12, 1191. On his voyage he took Cyprus, to avenge an insult from its sovereign.

The story of the Third Crusade (1191–1192) belongs rather to the romance of Richard's life than to the history of England. To him was chiefly due the capture of Acre, which had been besieged for two years in vain (July 12, 1191). But in the very hour of victory he gave Duke Leopold of Austria the affront which was afterward so meanly avenged; and Philip Augustus, jealous of being eclipsed by Richard, set sail from Acre homeward on July 31. Amidst tremendous losses Richard marched along the coast to Ascalon, which he took; and he had twice advanced toward Jerusalem, when he found that his unaided efforts were not equal to the enterprise. He made a truce with Saladin, on the terms that Acre, Joppa, and a portion of the sea-coast should belong to the

Christians, and that pilgrims to Jerusalem should be unmolested, Aug., 1192.

Richard's decision had been greatly influenced by the tidings that his brother John was plotting to seize his kingdom, with the support of Philip Augustus. He sailed from Acre on the 9th of October, and, to avoid passing through France, he took his route by the Adriatic, near the head of which sea he was shipwrecked. He set out on his journey through Germany as a pilgrim; but his disguise was discovered at Vienna, and his old enemy, Leopold duke of Austria, arrested him (Dec. 20, 1192), but gave him up on the demand of the Emperor Henry VI., who imprisoned him in a castle in the Tyrol. The beautiful legend of his discovery by the minstrel Blondel belongs to a romance of the 13th century. Richard was brought by the emperor before a diet at Worms (May 20, 1193), where the German princes condemned the conduct of the emperor, whom the pope threatened to excommunicate; and Richard recovered his liberty for a ransom of 150,000 marks.

Meanwhile the news had excited in England an indignation which extended to Richard's enemies at home. Having made a treaty to profit by the king's captivity, Philip Augustus and John began hostilities. The French king was repulsed in Normandy; while John was forced to conclude a truce with the justiciaries who governed England in Richard's absence. He was warned of his brother's return by a letter from Philip in these words: *Take heed to yourself, the devil is broken loose.* All his possessions in England were forfeited by a great council of the barons.

The king sailed from the Scheld, with a fleet sent from England to convoy him, just in time to escape the emissaries of the emperor, who had resolved to recapture him, and landed at Sandwich March 13, 1194. After being crowned a second time at Winchester (April 17), and forgiving his brother John, he passed over into Normandy to avenge himself on the French king. The desultory war which followed was concluded by a truce for five years, Jan. 13, 1199. But three months had not elapsed when Richard ended his brilliant but comparatively useless career by an inglorious death. He was besieging a rebellious vassal in his castle of Chalus, in Poitou, when he was wounded by an arrow in the shoulder, and an unskillful surgeon made the hurt mortal. The castle being taken, the archer, Gourdon, was brought before the king, and defied him to do all that his revenge prompted. Pleased with his boldness, Richard ordered him to be set free, with a sum of money as a present; but the order was disobeyed, and Gourdon was flayed alive and then hanged. The king, who had no children, and who had always treated Arthur, the son of his brother Geoffrey, as his heir, was induced by his mother to acknowledge John as his successor; and he died on the 8th of April, 1199, in the 10th year of his reign and the 42d of his age. He was buried at Fontevraud.

Such a character as Richard's may well be surrendered to the romancer, in whose pages the almost savage grandeur of the warrior is softened by traits of generosity, and adorned by the graces of minstrelsy, in which Richard was a proficient. But history must not fail to record the miseries of the kingdom, abandoned to disorder, and ground down by the expenses of the king's wars and of his ransom. It was reserved for the following reign to reap the memorable fruits of this period of transition.

John (1199–1216), the youngest son of Henry II., was surnamed Lackland (*Sans Terre*) from the circumstance of his having no share in those possessions of the crown with which his brothers were richly endowed; for he had lost the government of Ireland by his own folly. He was crowned at Westminster on the 27th of May, and he set out immediately for France, to resist a movement in favor of his nephew Arthur, duke of Brittany, who claimed the English crown as the son of his elder brother, Geoffrey. This ill-fated young prince was in the hands of Philip Augustus, who wished to use him as the means of weakening John and wresting from him his continental dominions. But Arthur's mother, Constance, being jealous of the designs of the French king, carried off her son from Paris, and caused him to submit to John, who was soon after acknowledged as king by Philip, May 23, 1200.

John now remained in England for more than a year, during which time he divorced his wife, the grand-daughter of the renowned Robert earl of Gloucester, and married Isabella of Angoulême, the betrothed bride of Hugh Lusignan, count of Marche. He also received the homage of the king of Scotland at Lincoln (Nov. 22, 1200).

In the following summer (1201) John visited the king of France, and tried in vain to induce him to give up the cause of Arthur. The English barons also, discontented with John's government, appealed to Philip as his suzerain. A fresh war broke out, in which Arthur openly joined the French, and was taken by John, with many of his principal adherents (July 31, 1202). Arthur was first imprisoned in the castle of Falaise, but afterward removed to Rouen, where John is said to have stabbed him with his own hand, and then to have thrown his body into the Seine (1203).

The murder of Arthur ruined John in France. Neglecting the citation of Philip, as his suzerain, to answer for the crime, he was condemned as a traitor and parricide, and was adjudged to have forfeited all his French possessions. The Bretons took up arms in the name of Eleanor, the sister of Arthur: and, while John first remained inactive at Rouen, and then retired to England (Dec., 1203), Philip easily overran Normandy; and the capture of Rouen (July, 1204) effected the reunion of that province to France, which was followed by the submission of Anjou, Maine, Touraine, and part of Poitou. After some fruitless efforts to recover the lost French provinces, John consented to a truce with Philip, renouncing all the country north of the Loire, 1206.

The loss of Normandy was soon followed by a no less disastrous conflict with the Papal See, which was then occupied by the bold and ambitious Innocent III. On the death of Hubert archbishop of Canterbury, in 1205, the pope set aside two rival candidates for the primacy, and commanded the monks of Christchurch, Canterbury, to elect STEPHEN LANGTON, an Englishman, who had been brought up in France. The king avenged the usurpation by expelling the monks of Christchurch; and the pope replied by laying England under an *interdict* (March 23, 1208). By this act the people were deprived of the offices of religion, except baptism, confession, and the absolution of the dying. Even the dead were not suffered to be interred in consecrated ground, but were thrown into ditches by the way-side. Instead of submitting, John attacked the property and even the persons of the clergy, and this all the more when the pope followed up the interdict by a sentence of excommunication against the king himself (Nov., 1209). The terrified clergy neither dared to obey the interdict, nor to publish the sentence of excommunication. The king showed equal obstinacy in putting down the discontents of his barons, many of whom fled to Ireland and Scotland. John marched northward and received tribute and homage from the Scotch king (Aug., 1209). Next year (1210) he invaded Ireland, and reduced to obedience the English settlers, who had been aiming at independence; and the year after he penetrated into Wales as far as Snowdon, and received the submission of the principal chiefs (1211). These successes were attended with great cruelties, according to the chroniclers, who were John's bitter enemies. Their picture of the king's hateful character is probably faithful; but the events of these three years prove that he was not destitute of energy and courage.

At length the pope produced the last weapon of his spiritual armory. In 1212 he absolved the English from their allegiance to John, and called on the king of France to execute the sentence of deposition. Philip collected a force for the invasion of England, and John saw that the time was come when he must yield. His submission was carried to the length of resigning his kingdom to the Holy See, from which, in the person of the legate Pandolf, he received back his crown anew, to hold it, with all the rites of homage paid to a feudal lord, as a vassal, by the payment of an annual tribute of 1000 marks (1213).

John now turned boldly upon the king of France. The Earl of Salisbury attacked in the French harbors the ships collected for the invasion, and burned Dieppe. John carried the war into the French territories which Philip had wrested from him (1214); but Philip's victory over the Emperor Otho at Bouvines, in Flanders, induced John to conclude a peace at Chinon, Sept. 18, 1214.

Thus ended the second act in the drama of John's reign. The third was as humiliating to himself as the loss of his French provinces or the surrender of his crown to the pope; but it is forever glorious and memorable in English history; for now was laid, by the hands of this unworthy and unwilling sovereign, the foundation-stone of the whole fabric of English liberty.

His rule had by this time become intolerable to every class of his subjects. The Church had found in him a determined enemy. The barons saw their privileges invaded by his tyranny, and the honor of their families outraged by his vices. The commons were treated like serfs, and driven to become outlaws. The property of all classes was subjected to endless exactions. The case of the Jews, who were beyond the protection of the law, served to show the lengths to which he could proceed in extorting money by cruel tortures: for example, a Jew of Bristol, refusing to give up his treasures, was thrown by the king's orders into a dungeon, and one of his teeth was wrenched out daily, until he had lost seven, when he gave in.

The barons of England, who had long cherished the desire to curb the king's tyranny, saw the necessity of redressing the wrongs of the people as well as their own. They found a head in Stephen Langton, archbishop of Canterbury, and a leader in William earl of Pembroke. Their first demand was for the observance of Henry I.'s Charter, a copy of which had been discovered by Langton; and next, at an assembly convened by the primate at St. Edmondsbury, in Suffolk, they framed their requirements for a redress of grievances (Nov. 20, 1214). The king tried in vain to buy over the clergy by a charter, in which he yielded up to them the election of church dignitaries. The barons presented their demands to John at London (Jan. 6, 1215); and, as he deferred his answer, and meanwhile obtained a papal censure against them, they assembled in open war at Stamford, and marched on London, entering the city on the 24th of May, 1215. The king, deserted by all but a few knights, consented to an interview with the insurgents at *Runnymede*—a meadow on the banks of the Thames, near Windsor; and on this ever-memorable spot he signed, on the fifteenth of June, the MAGNA CHARTA or GREAT CHARTER, an instrument which has never ceased to deserve that name, as the chief foundation of the constitutional liberties of the people of England.

The clauses of the Charter in which the barons stipulated for their privileges have now lost their importance, in comparison with those which secured the persons and property of all freemen from the arbitrary power of the crown. The following are the words of the Charter, as confirmed by Henry III.:—NO FREEMAN SHALL BE TAKEN OR IMPRISONED, OR BE DISSEISED OF HIS FREEHOLD OR LIBERTIES OR FREE CUSTOMS, OR BE OUTLAWED, OR EXILED, OR ANY OTHERWISE DESTROYED; NOR WILL WE PASS UPON HIM, NOR SEND UPON HIM, BUT BY LAWFUL JUDGMENT OF HIS PEERS, OR BY THE LAW OF THE LAND. WE WILL SELL TO NO MAN, WE WILL NOT DENY OR DELAY TO ANY MAN, JUSTICE OR RIGHT. In these words were established the great *principles* of *the security of personal liberty* by the process which was afterward more definitely embodied in the writ of *Habeas Corpus*, and that of the right of every accused person to be tried by a *jury of his peers*. The third great principle, of *no taxation without representation*, was embodied in the provision that no "scutage" or "aid" should be imposed without the consent of the great council of the kingdom (except in certain matters personal to the crown); while the mode of constituting this council was laid down, namely, that the superior clergy and nobles should be summoned by the king's writ, and all other tenants in chief by the sheriff. The Charter also secured the *liberties of London and the other great cities*, and protected the people, of every class, from excessive fines; nor did it overlook the meanest of the people, for it provided that even villeins were not to be deprived of their implements of husbandry.

The GREAT CHARTER has always remained the fundamental law of the constitutional monarchy of England. It was confirmed, in succeeding reigns, by no less than 38 solemn ratifications. The most important of these were in the 1st, 2d, and 9th years of Henry III., the last being the form in which it stands to this day unaltered in the statute-book. There were three other ratifications by Henry III., three by Edward I., fifteen by Edward III., six by Richard II., six by Henry IV., one by Henry V., and one by Henry VI. The provision against taxation without the consent of parliament, though removed by Henry III. from the Charter, was confirmed by a special statute in the 25th year of Edward I.

But, besides the special provisions of the Charter, the very fact of its exaction from the king was a consecration of the still deeper fundamental principle, on which the English monarchy itself has always been based, that the crown is held only by the consent of the people, and on the condition that the sovereign shall respect their rights and liberties, and keep his own prerogative within the limits of the law.

To secure the observance of the Charter the king was obliged to give the barons possession of London, and the custody of the Tower to the Archbishop of Canterbury; and twenty-five of the barons were appointed as conservators of the public liberties, with full power over all classes of the people. The king's first act was, in violation of an express oath, to obtain a papal bull annulling the Charter (Sept. 13), while he secretly enlisted a band of foreign mercenaries. With these he overran the kingdom, laying it waste like an enemy's country. The barons, whom his perfidy had taken by surprise, cast off their allegiance, and offered the crown to Louis, the son of Philip king of France. Louis landed at Sandwich, May 21, 1216, took Rochester, and advanced to London, where he received the homage of the barons, June 2. A war ensued, with successes and reverses on both sides. John drew his forces to a head in Lincolnshire, while Louis was detained before Dover, which he had vowed to take; but an accident changed the whole state of affairs. After staying at Lynn, which derived from his favor its appellation of King's Lynn, John was marching into Lincolnshire round the Wash, when, keeping too near its treacherous shores, he lost his carriages, treasure, baggage, and regalia. His health, already much impaired by anxiety, yielded to this final blow; and he reached the castle of Newark, only to expire there, on the 17th of October, 1216, in the 49th year of his age, and the 18th of his reign.

He bequeathed his body to St. Wulstan, the patron saint of the cathedral of Worcester, where he lies beneath a splendid tomb; and to his country the memory of one of the worst men and most tyrannical kings that ever filled her throne, but whose very vices and weakness gave the opportunity for merging the sovereignty of the Norman dynasty in a new constitutional kingdom. This great change was attended by one of no less consequence in the social condition of the people; for it was in the reign of John that the amalgamation of the Normans and Saxons into one people was almost completed. From John also the city of London obtained the right of electing its mayor annually, and the "Old London Bridge" was finished, in place of the former wooden bridge over the Thames.

Convocation of Clergy.

CHAPTER IX.

THE HOUSE OF PLANTAGENET (*continued*).—HENRY III. 1216–1272.

HENRY III., of WINCHESTER, the elder of John's two sons, occupied the throne for a longer period than any English king, except George III., but there are few reigns so barren of events. A boy of nine years old at his father's death, he was in the hands of the wise and brave Earl of Pembroke, who had him crowned at Gloucester (Oct. 28, 1216), when the young king did homage to the pope for his dominions.

Pembroke, appointed protector by a council of the barons at Bristol (Nov. 12), confirmed the Great Charter, thereby conciliating the people and gaining over many of the insurgent barons. Louis and his adherents were excommunicated by the papal legate for continuing the war (April 18, 1217); his army was defeated at Lincoln (May 20); a fleet sent from France with reinforcements suffered the same fate off Dover (Aug. 21); and he himself was besieged in London by Pembroke, with whom he concluded a truce and quitted England (Sept. 11, 1217).

But the barons kept the royal castles that they had seized; and Louis, becoming King Louis VIII. on his father's death (1223), not only broke his promise to restore Normandy, but invaded Poitou, and took Rochelle (1224). Henry crossed over to France, but gained no reputation in the field; while, in every part of his government, he began to show the weakness of his character. He had lost the aid of Pembroke by death (1218), and he quarreled with his faithful counselor, the justiciary Hubert de Burgh (1231), and placed himself in the hands of Peter des Roches, bishop of Winchester, who had formerly gained discredit as a counselor of John, and had been already once dismissed by Henry. This prelate, a Poitevin by birth, filled all offices with his countrymen; and a further irruption of foreigners was caused by the king's marriage with Eleanor, daughter of the Count of Provence (1236). The kingdom was threatened with another civil war, and hostilities actually occurred on the Welsh border and in Ireland with the party hostile to Des Roches; but peace was soon restored, and the insurgents pardoned. During all his reign, however, the king was engaged in conflicts with his nobles.

But before these intestine commotions reached their height Henry engaged in several foreign wars. In 1242 he made war upon Louis IX. of France, and lost his possessions in Poitou. In 1253 he repelled an invasion of Guienne by the king of Castile, but incurred an enormous debt. In 1255 he was tempted by the pope, whom he supported against the Emperor Frederick II., to engage in an enterprise for the conquest of Naples, which only plunged him deeper into debt, and more embroiled him with his barons. Indeed, his subserviency to the pope was one of the chief disgraces of his reign. The best of the ecclesiastical benefices were given to Italians; and the pecuniary exactions of the see of Rome, in various forms, became intolerable.

Meanwhile Henry's favorites were continually leading him to violate the Great Charter, though he had solemnly confirmed it several times. At length the prevailing discontent found an open utterance under the guidance of SIMON DE MONTFORT, earl of Leicester. This celebrated man was the younger son of Simon de Montfort, who had conducted a crusade against the Albigenses, and the brother-in-law of the king. He secretly convened the chief barons, and united them in a confederacy, not only to redress the grievances of the kingdom, but to take its government into their own hands. At a parliament held by the king, to ask supplies for his enterprise against Naples (May 2, 1258), the barons appeared fully armed, and exacted from Henry a promise to assemble another parliament to settle the affairs of the realm.

This "Mad Parliament," as it came afterward to be called, met at Oxford on the 11th of June, and the king was really a prisoner to the armed barons, who appointed fifteen of their own number, with De Montfort at their head, to draw up a scheme of reform, to which they bound the king beforehand by an oath. Their measures, known as the *Provisions of Oxford*, were these — that four knights should be chosen by each county to state their grievances, and that three sessions of parliament should be held every year. There were also provisions for the elections of sheriffs, for guarding estates from foreigners, and for other purposes.

The barons followed up these enactments by taking all power into their own hands, changing all the great officers of state, and even appointing a committee of twelve to wield the whole power of the parliament in the intervals of its session. By enacting that the circuits of the itinerant justices should be held only every seven years they removed a legal check on their power. These excesses led to a reaction in the public mind; and the barons became divided among themselves by the rivalry of the earls of Leicester and Gloucester. At this crisis the king visited France, then under the government of Louis IX., who has gained the name of ST. LOUIS from his personal piety and his crusade against the Moors of Tunis. With him Henry arranged the pending questions concerning his French dominions, by finally surrendering Normandy, which he had no hope of recovering, while he was confirmed in the possession of Guienne, and was to receive Poitou back after the death of Louis (Nov., 1259). These causes of difference being removed, Louis was prepared to mediate between Henry and his rebellious subjects.

During the king's absence in France the dissensions between the barons had threatened a new civil war, in which Prince Edward (afterward so celebrated as Edward I.) prepared to take a part by levying troops. The king mistrusted his son's intentions, but Edward cleared himself of the suspicion of treason by a solemn oath. The Earl of Gloucester went over to the king's party, and Henry was thus encouraged, his conscience being fortified by a papal absolution, to revoke all his concessions; while Edward, pleading the obligation of his oath, sided with the barons. The king fortified himself in London, and De Montfort fled to France; but the death of Gloucester deprived Henry of his main stay, and he was again compelled to surrender to the barons, and to promise to abide by the Provisions of Oxford, which were promulgated in a Great Council held at London, Sept. 8, 1263.

About the same time (Oct. 3) an event occurred in Scotland momentous enough to interrupt the course of our narrative—the defeat of an invading Norwegian host by King Alexander III. at Largs, on the coast of Ayrshire.

The king and the barons at length appealed to Louis, who, in a council at Amiens (Jan. 23, 1264), annulled the Provisions of Oxford, and recommended a general amnesty, declaring also that the people should preserve their ancient liberties. But these terms were distasteful to the barons, and the civil war became fiercer than ever. Henry and Prince Edward returned from France and united their forces; while De Montfort made the castle of Kenilworth his head-quarters; and the country was wasted on every side. At last a pitched battle was fought at Lewes (May 13, 1264), when the king and his brother Richard, earl of Cornwall, were taken prisoners. A truce, called the *Mise* of Lewes, was imposed by De Montfort upon Prince Edward, who surrendered himself a prisoner in his father's place, with his cousin Prince Henry, the son of the Duke of Cornwall. The triumph of the barons was complete. An attempt made by Mortimer, earl of March, to renew the war in Wales was crushed by De Montfort, with the aid of the Welsh chieftain Llewellyn. A fleet collected by the queen to invade England was blockaded in the Flemish ports, till the soldiers dispersed. The Papal bull, excommunicating the barons, was torn in pieces at Dover, and De Montfort kept his Christmas like a king at Kenilworth.

The new year forms an epoch for ever memorable in English constitutional history. On the 20th of January, 1265, there assembled at London, on the summons of De Montfort, a parliament composed on a different model from any previous great council of the kingdom. Besides the chief nobles and prelates, who were summoned by writ, De Montfort directed the return of 100 of the dignified clergy and *of two knights from each shire*, and *two representatives of every city and borough*. These two classes, though for the present sitting in one chamber with the nobles, formed the germ of the House of Commons.

This great service to his country was De Montfort's last act of power. He was deserted by the Earl of Gloucester, the son of his old rival; and Prince Edward escaped ftom his guards (May 28), and joined the army of Mortimer in Wales. De Montfort marched to meet him, under the banner of the king, whose person he carried with him. A battle was fought at Evesham, in Worcestershire (Aug. 4, 1265), in which Prince Edward was victorious, and De Montfort himself was among the slain. His fate was all but shared by Henry, whom he had placed in the front of the battle, and who only saved his life by exclaiming to a knight who had wounded him, "*I am Henry of Winchester, your king.*" The corpse of De Montfort was mangled by the victors; but the people long cherished his memory, as the champion of their liberties; and the impulse which he gave to our constitutional freedom may be allowed to excuse great faults of personal ambition. The remaining partisans of De Montfort, whose chief strong-holds were at Kenilworth Castle and in the Isle of Ely, were gradually brought to submission by Prince Edward, who granted to them terms which are known as "*the Award of Kenilworth.*" A parliament held at that place (Nov., 1266) re-established the king's authority, on the condition of his observing the Great Charter.

The short remainder of Henry's reign was passed in peace. So far, indeed, was tranquillity restored that Prince Edward ventured to follow the impulse of his chivalrous spirit and the example of the French king by embarking in a new crusade (1269); and he was still absent when Henry III. expired at Bury St. Edmunds, on the 16th of November, 1272, in the 66th year of his age and the 57th of his reign. He was buried at Westminster on the 20th, and fealty was at once sworn to his son Edward, "though men were ignorant whether he was alive, for he had gone to distant countries beyond the sea, warring against the enemies of Christ."

The period of nearly a century, from the death of Henry II. to that of Henry III., completed the transition from the Norman sovereignty to English constitutional monarchy. The people had become one; and all between the greater barons and the villeins were equal in the eye of the law. Hence the readiness with which all classes united against the encroachments of the crown; and hence also the necessity, which the barons felt, of acting with the commons. Their close confederacy with the great boroughs is proved by the fact that London was always on their side, except when the king seized the Tower by force. The absence of Richard, the tyranny of John, and the weakness of Henry, forced their subjects to take into their own hands the settlement of that constitution which was founded by the Great Charter and finally established by the parliament of De Montfort.

During this period also was effected the fusion of the *Anglo-Saxon* and the *Norman French* into the ENGLISH LANGUAGE; and the germs of the noble Literature of the next age began to show themselves.

The 13th century was a great period too in the history of English Art; for in it was completed the transition from the heavy Saxon and the massive Norman architecture to that genuine and exquisitely beautiful ENGLISH style which is still unhappily called *Gothic.* Westminster Abbey, which Henry III. nearly lived to complete, may be taken as a type of the many glorious monuments of the art that the present generation is only now recovering.

English Carriages of the time.

CHAPTER X.

THE HOUSE OF PLANTAGENET (*continued*).—EDWARD I., EDWARD II. A.D. 1272–1327.

EDWARD I. (1272–1307), surnamed LONGSHANKS, from his stature, was born at Westminster, June 18, 1239, and married Eleanor of Castile in 1254. He departed, as we have seen, for the Holy Land a few years after his father's recovery of his throne (1270). He first went to join St. Louis before Tunis; but finding that he was already dead, Edward sailed on to Acre, gained several battles against the Saracens, and took Nazareth (1271). One of the fanatic sect called *Assassins* penetrated to his camp and inflicted on him a wound, from which his wife Eleanor is said to have sucked the poison, and so to have saved his life (Ju. 12, 1272). He soon after made a truce with the infidels, and sailed from Acre on the 15th of August.

It was in Sicily that he received the news of his father's death, and of the quiet state of the kingdom under the regency of his cousin the Earl of Cornwall, the Archbishop of York, and the Earl of Gloucester. He spent a whole year in Italy and France, settled the affairs of Guienne, and arranged some commercial disputes with the Countess of Flanders. At length he landed at Dover on the 2d of August, 1274, and was crowned at Westminster, with his queen Eleanor, on the 19th.

Edward's attention was first given to the internal affairs of the kingdom. In a parliament held at Westminster (1275) he took measures for the due administration of justice, and for the suppression of robbery and peculation. In 1278 was enacted the *Statute of Gloucester*, under which commissions were issued to protect and improve the royal demesne and revenue, and to inquire into the encroachments made thereon by the nobles. Turning next to the Church, which had been enriched by large grants from Henry III., the king and parliament enacted the celebrated *Statute of Mortmain*, forbidding lands and tenements to be made over to ecclesiastical corporations without the king's permission. This statute was so called because the members of such bodies, being devoted to the Divine service, were *dead* in the eye of the law, and property held by them was therefore said to be *in mortua manu* (*in a dead holding*). In the same year Edward went over to France, and was confirmed in the possession of Guienne, at the same time renouncing all claim to Normandy.

He now turned his whole attention to the CONQUEST OF WALES. The mountains of that country had afforded a refuge to a large part of the Britons at the Saxon conquest. From that time downward an almost constant state of hostility had been maintained by the incursions of the Welsh princes on the one hand, and the efforts of the English kings to subdue them on the other. The chief leaders of the Welsh had at length come to acknowledge the king of England as their feudal lord; and on such terms LLEWELLYN, the prince of Wales, had received pardon for his adherence to De Montfort. But he disobeyed the repeated summons of Edward to attend the parliament; and in 1276, when his betrothed bride, the daughter of De Montfort, was seized on her voyage to Wales, he broke out into open insurrection. Edward marched at once into the heart of North Wales, secured the passes, and advanced to Snowdon, Llewellyn's last refuge. The prince surrendered at discretion, returned with Edward, and did homage to him at Westminster for the territories which he was permitted to retain round Snowdon and in the Isle of Anglesey, and received back his bride. But his submission served only to rouse the national spirit of the people to a final struggle for their independence. Their bards fanned the flame of patriotism with prophecies, ascribed to Merlin, which marked the present time as the epoch of their liberation. Llewellyn was reconciled to his brother David—who had in the former war placed himself under Edward's protection—and, in 1282, they stormed the castles of Flint and Rhuddlan, which Edward had built as the keys of North Wales. But, while Edward advanced with an overwhelming force, Llewellyn fell in a battle with the marchers, Dec. 11; and his brother David, hunted from hill to hill, was at length betrayed and taken prisoner. He was carried to Shrewsbury, where the king had established the courts of justice, was found guilty by the peers of high treason—that is, the crime of compassing the king's death—and suffered the full extremity of the horrible penalty of treason, which was invented for this occasion, and which has only very recently (1814) ceased to disgrace the statute-book. He was drawn to the gibbet on a hurdle, hanged and cut down before life was extinct, his bowels cut out and burned before his face, and his head struck from his body, which was then divided into four quarters, and these were sent to different parts of the kingdom to be exposed for the terror of traitors (1283). The tradition—so familiar to us by Gray's splendid ode—that Edward's revenge was extended to a general massacre of the bards, does not rest on any sufficient authority.

Wales was now not only subdued but incorporated with England, and brought under the same forms of judicial administration by the "Statute of Wales," which was enacted at Rhuddlan, March 19, 1284. In the following month (April 25) the birth of his fourth son in the castle of Caernarvon gave Edward the opportunity, in a spirit of somewhat ironical conciliation, to restore to his new subjects a native "Prince of Wales." This title was conferred upon the young prince, afterward Edward II., when, by the death of his eldest surviving brother, Alphonso, in the following August, he became heir to the throne; and it has ever since been borne by the heir of the reigning sovereign.

Soon after these events Edward went over to Gascony (1286) and arbitrated a dispute concerning Sicily between the kings of France and Aragon. On his return, after three years' absence, he held a parliament to repress disorders, especially corruption in the administration of justice, for which all the judges, except two, were deposed and fined.

In the following year (1290) the Jews, who had suffered as much since Edward's accession in the name of justice as they had endured from lawless violence in former reigns, were finally banished from the kingdom. Their exclusion remained in force till the time of the Commonwealth.

Meanwhile the troubles of the KINGDOM OF SCOTLAND seemed to offer to Edward the prospect of uniting the whole island under one sovereign—a prospect, however, not destined to be realized for still three centuries. We have already seen the kings of Scotland doing homage to the kings of England for their possessions in the ancient Northumbria; and Alexander III. had rendered that homage to Edward in the parliament at Westminster in 1278. In 1287 Alexander died, leaving only one direct descendant, his granddaughter Margaret, called the Maid of Norway, of which country her father, Eric, was the king. On the birth of Prince Edward his father betrothed him to the Maid of Norway with the consent of the estates of Scotland. But the hope of the peaceful union of the two kingdoms was frustrated by the death of the young Queen Margaret on her voyage to Scotland, Oct. 7, 1290. The crown of Scotland was now claimed by thirteen competitors; but the real question lay between the representatives of the three daughters of David earl of Huntingdon, brother of Malcolm IV. and William the Lion. These were JOHN BALIOL, grandson of Margaret the eldest daughter; ROBERT BRUCE, son of Isabel the second daughter; and Hastings lord of Abergavenny, son of Ada the third daughter. Baliol claimed as the lineal descendant of the eldest daughter; Bruce as being one degree nearer to the common ancestor; while Hastings claimed only a third of the kingdom, which was held by the estates to be indivisible. The parliament of Scotland referred the decision to Edward, who advanced to the frontier with a great army and summoned the competitors and the parliament to meet him at Norham Castle on the south bank of the Tweed. Here he announced his claim to make the decision as suzerain of the whole kingdom of Scotland, and sent back the astonished parliament to deliberate within their own border. Unable to resist, but unwilling to yield, the parliament kept silence. Edward then demanded homage from the candidates; and among those who submitted were Baliol and Bruce. Edward easily obtained the impartial judgments of the highest authorities in Europe in favor of the claim of Baliol, for whom, therefore, he decided, after receiving the renewal of his homage both on Scotch and English ground (Nov. 30 and Dec. 26, 1292). He now began to show his ultimate designs by summoning Baliol to London on trivial complaints, and treating him with marked indignity, evidently to drive him into rebellion, and Baliol returned with the resolution to shake off the English yoke.

An opportunity was soon offered by a war with France, in which Edward became involved by a collision between some Norman and English sailors, when the mariners of the Cinque Ports gained a decisive victory over a Norman fleet (1293). Philip IV. of France cited Edward, as his vassal for the duchy of Guienne, to answer for the alleged outrage; and, by the help of a stratagem not unlike that which Edward himself had practiced on the Scots, he obtained possession of Guienne and declared it forfeit to the French crown (1294). While Edward prepared for war, Philip formed a secret alliance with John Baliol, which proved the beginning of a long and close union between France and Scotland.

As soon as Edward gained a knowledge of this treaty he marched against Scotland and took Berwick, March 30, 1296. Baliol, on his part, openly renounced his allegiance; and a great battle was fought at *Dunbar*, where the Scots were utterly defeated. Baliol surrendered himself and resigned the crown to Edward, who marched unopposed as far as Aberdeen and Elgin, and then returned to London, carrying with him the regalia of Scotland and the venerated stone on which the Scottish kings had been crowned at Scone from time immemorial. This stone may still be seen in the chair of Edward the Confessor, in which the sovereigns of England are still crowned, at Westminster Abbey. Baliol was imprisoned in the Tower for two years and then suffered to retire to France, where he died. The government of Scotland was intrusted to John de Warenne earl of Surrey, with Hugh Cressingham as treasurer, both of whom soon became odious for their tyranny.

The war with France was meanwhile continued with little success, and Edward raised money by the most arbitrary exactions. The clergy submitted, but the nobles and commons made a firm resistance, under the guidance of the constable and the marshal of England—Humphrey Bohun, earl of Hereford, and Roger Bigod, earl of Norfolk. When Edward had crossed over into Flanders, to carry on the war, they obtained from the Prince of Wales that confirmation of the Great Charter which the king had steadily refused. The Charter was sent over to the king at Ghent with an act renouncing his claim to tax the people at his own will. Edward ratified both instruments in the twenty-fifth year of his reign (1297)—a memorable epoch for English liberty.

Edward was released from his French war by the mediation of pope Boniface in 1298; not before all his energies were required to deal with Scotland. The Scots, ground down by their English governors, and distrusting their nobles as either timid or treacherous, had at length found a leader whose name occupies one of the highest places in the Scottish legends of heroism, but many of whose acts are utterly unworthy of such fame. WILLIAM WALLACE was a simple knight of Ellerslie in Renfrewshire. His courage and prodigious personal strength were early proved in encounters with small parties of the English; and he soon had a private cause of vengeance. His house had been sacked and his young wife brutally killed by the governor of Lanark. With an unlimited power of enduring hardship and fatigue, he held out in hiding-places, and gathered about him a hardy band of followers. These he trained in a succession of bold enterprises till he was strong enough to withstand the English in the open field; and he defeated a large army under De Warenne at Stirling, where Cressingham was killed and his dead body flayed in sign of hatred for his cruelty. De Warenne retreated from Scotland, while Wallace ravaged the north of England as far as Durham with the same relentless cruelty that the Scots had suffered. But his forces were no match for the mighty army of 100,000 men which Edward now led into Scotland; and the Scots were utterly crushed in the battle of Falkirk (1298).

But the spirit of the nation was not crushed. While Edward retired for want of supplies, the Scots appointed a regency under Robert Bruce and Comyn, and took Stirling. Pope Boniface VIII. espoused their cause, but his claims were rejected by a parliament held at Lincoln in 1301. Edward, after invading the country several times with partial success, made a grand expedition, supported by a fleet on the eastern coast, and marched through from south to north (1303). Bruce and Comyn, with other nobles, submitted to him, and Stirling surrendered, July 20, 1304. To crown these successes Wallace was captured through the treachery of Sir John Menteith. He was carried to London, tried as a rebel and traitor, and suffered in Smithfield the same cruel death which had been inflicted on David prince of Wales (Aug. 24, 1305).

The conquest of Scotland seemed now complete; and a council was held at London, in September, to regulate its affairs. But even while it was sitting, ROBERT BRUCE, the son of the competitor for the crown, who had died in 1304, left London to claim the crown, to which the death of Baliol had given him an undoubted right. He assembled the Scottish nobles at Dumfries (Feb. 1306), where he found nearly all ready for a new effort, except *John Comyn*, whose name is branded in Scottish history as a traitor. A quarrel ensued, and Bruce stabbed Comyn in the cloister of the Grey Friars. Alarmed at the sacrilege, he exclaimed to Sir Thomas Kirkpatrick, "I doubt I have slain the red Comyn!" "Do you *doubt?*" said Kirkpatrick, "*ich mak sicher*" (*I make sure*); and returning to the cloisters, he dispatched the wounded man. This deed united the nobles by the tie of a common danger, and Bruce was crowned at Scone by the Bishop of St. Andrews as Robert I. (March 25, 1306). The English were driven out of Scotland; but

Edward sent a great army, under Aymer de Valence earl of Pembroke, who defeated Bruce and drove him to take shelter in the Western Isles. The king himself followed and put many of Bruce's chief adherents to death as traitors.

Thus began that series of efforts and reverses which have rendered the name of Bruce so memorable an example of persevering courage. Unable to face the English in the field, he attacked them when and where he could, retreating to his hiding-places in Carrick or the Isles. At length Edward resolved to finish the war by a mighty effort. He advanced at the head of a great army, vowing vengeance against the whole Scottish nation, as far as Carlisle (July 3, 1307), where he was seized with a mortal illness; but, pressing onward, he arrived at Burgh-on-the-Sands, five miles distant (July 5), and died there (July 7), bequeathing to his son his last injunction to complete the enterprise. Such was his devotion to this one desire, that he commanded his corpse to be carried about with the army, and not to be interred till the conquest of Scotland was complete. This injunction, like the rest, was disobeyed, and he was buried at Westminster on the 27th of October. He died in the 69th year of his age and the 35th of his reign.

Edward I. has been called "the greatest of the Plantagenets," and in most respects he well deserved the title. His character was manly and truly royal. He was of a majestic figure and an affable presence, and had great skill in military exercises. He was energetic, industrious, and far-sighted; and his enterprises were planned with great sagacity. He was firm, though severe, in an age when severity was needed, in administering the laws, and in checking the misdeeds of the highest offenders, as well as the lowest criminals. Though of an arbitrary temper, he submitted to the necessity of confirming the privileges of his people by successive renewals of the Great Charter; and in his reign the Commons of England secured the full share of parliamentary power to which they had been first admitted under Henry III. But the chief praise of his government is for those great amendments in the law which have gained for him the title of the English Justinian. But the ambition, the injustice, the treachery, and the cruelty of his dealings with Wales and Scotland are incapable of defense, and betray the entire want of a generous heart.

Of Edward I.'s numerous family seven died before him; and he left three sons and five daughters. The sons were EDWARD II., of Caernarvon; *Thomas*, of Brotherton, afterward Earl of Norfolk and Marshal of England; and *Edmund*, of Woodstock, afterward Earl of Kent: the two latter were quite young at their father's death.

EDWARD II., of CAERNARVON (1307–1327), succeeded his father at the age of 23; and his reign was one of the saddest in English history. He was proclaimed at Carlisle, July 8, 1307, and, after affecting to advance a little way into Scotland, he abandoned the expedition and returned to England. In the following year (1308) he went over to France, and did homage at Guienne to Philip IV., whose daughter Isabella he married. On his return he was crowned at Westminster, Feb. 25.

During his absence in France Edward had intrusted the regency to his worthless favorite *Piers Gaveston*, the son of a Gascon knight who had served the king's father. The young Gaveston had been attached to the household of Edward when Prince of Wales, and his evil influence over the prince was so evident that Edward I. banished him. Edward II. recalled him and loaded him with honors. This conduct roused the jealousy of the nobles; complaints were made against Gaveston at a parliament held in April, and he was banished, but only to be placed by the king in the lieutenancy of Ireland. In 1309 he was recalled, and behaved more insolently than ever. In 1311 the king was compelled by the parliament to agree to certain "ordinances" of reform, including the observance of the charters and the "banishment of evil counselors." On this occasion the principle of parliamentary government was further secured by the provision that the parliament should be summoned once or even twice in each year. But when the king again recalled Gaveston next year (1312) the barons took up arms, under Thomas earl of Lancaster, the king's first-cousin. Edward fled before them, and Gaveston, whom he had placed in Scarborough Castle, was forced to surrender to the barons, who carried him to Warwick Castle, and beheaded him on Blacklow Hill, June 19, 1312. They then exacted a peace, and their own pardon, from the king.

The same year witnessed a most memorable event, in the suppression of the military religious order of the *Knights of the Holy Temple*, or *Templars*, by the pope's bull. This powerful body, which originated in the zeal of the Crusaders, and had rendered splendid services to the Christian cause in the East, had long incurred the suspicion of aiming at supreme power in Europe. They were charged moreover with the practice of unlawful arts, as well as with gross immorality, and their suppression was carried out with great severity. Their estates in England were granted in 1324 to the rival order of the Hospitalers, or Knights of St. John of Jerusalem.

The king now prepared for a final effort to conquer Scotland, where Robert Bruce, after years of wandering, had recovered nearly all the country, and was in the field with a formidable army. Edward marched against him at the head of 100,000 men, and suffered at *Bannockburn*, near Stirling, the most signal overthrow ever inflicted upon the English in their long wars with Scotland, June 24, 1314.

The Earl of Lancaster now openly assumed the government of the kingdom; but Edward did not yield without an effort either to his foreign or his domestic foes. He quelled an insurrection in Wales (1315), and proposed a new invasion of Scotland, in which the party of Lancaster refused to join (1316). In 1319 he concluded a two years' truce with King Robert, Dec. 21. Meanwhile the great barons were in open opposition to his government. In 1318 the parliament appointed a council of sixteen "to assist the king." In 1320 Edward chose a new favorite, *Hugh le Despenser* or *Spenser*, a youth of noble birth and great personal accomplishments, whose father was well fitted to be a counselor to the king. But Lancaster and the barons seized London, and held a parliament, which banished both the Spensers, 1321. Roused by this insult, the king gathered an army, recalled the Spensers, and marched against Lancaster, who drew his forces to a head in the north, and made an alliance with Scotland. The king gained a decisive victory at Boroughbridge (March 16, 1322), when Lancaster was taken prisoner, tried by a military council, and beheaded with every mark of indignity in sight of his own castle of Pontefract. The following year witnessed the close of the long war with Scotland by a truce for thirteen years (1323).

And now a new and final danger was preparing for the unfortunate king in an opposite quarter. Summoned to France to do homage to the new king, Charles IV., surnamed the Fair, and threatened with an attack upon Guienne, Edward sent over in his place his Queen Isabella, who persuaded him to resign Guienne to his son, afterward Edward III. (1325). The queen remained at Paris, and, through an infatuated love for the young Roger Mortimer, who had fled thither when the party of Lancaster was overthrown, she betrayed her faith both to her husband and her king. When recalled to England, she refused to return, unless the Spensers were dismissed; and, raising an army by the help of the Count of Holland and Hainault, to whose daughter, Philippa, she had betrothed her son, she invaded England, and was joined by the earls of Kent and Norfolk, the king's own brothers.

Edward, deserted on every hand, fled to Wales, while his son was appointed guardian of the realm. Both the Spensers were taken and executed. The unhappy king tried to escape to Ireland, but was driven back by adverse winds to South Wales, taken at Neath, and conveyed to Kenilworth. A parliament, summoned by the queen, decreed his deposition, which he was compelled to sign (Jan. 20, 1327). He was carried to Berkeley Castle, and Mortimer sent secret orders to dispatch him. His jailers threw him on a bed and burnt out his intestines with a hot iron, while his screams of agony revealed the murder, of which they had sought to avoid all external marks, by their horrid means of perpetrating it. He perished on the 21st of September, 1327, in the 44th year of his age and the 21st of his reign. His unhappy reign and miserable death bear witness to the fact so often noticed, that in this world the penalty of weakness is worse than that of wickedness. He paid dearly for the negligence and favoritism, which were the only charges that even his betrayers and murderers brought against him. He was never accused of cruelty or exaction. His weakness was not without flashes of a noble spirit; and his memory seems to deserve compassion rather than contempt.

"Oh! give the hapless king his due."

Lollard's Prison.

English Ships of War of the time.

CHAPTER XI.

THE HOUSE OF PLANTAGENET (*continued*).—EDWARD III., RICHARD II. A.D. 1327–1399.

EDWARD III., of WINDSOR, where he was born on Nov. 13, 1312, was in his fifteenth year when he was placed on the throne by his father's deposition, Jan. 20, 1327. He was crowned at Westminster on Jan. 29, when the Great Charter and the Charter of the Forests were confirmed. The parliament nominated a council of regency, with Lancaster at its head; but the real power was in the hands of Queen Isabella and her minion Mortimer. The young king, however, soon found an opportunity to display the warlike spirit for which he was afterward renowned. He took the field in person against the Scots, who invaded England in August, and narrowly escaped falling into the hands of the formidable Douglas. This campaign was closed by an inglorious treaty, by which the king resigned the claim to homage set up by Edward I., acknowledged the independence of Scotland, and restored the regalia (1328). A marriage was agreed upon between Jane, the sister of Edward III., and David, the heir of Robert Bruce, who became King David II. of Scotland by his father's death in the same year, June 7, 1328. This eventful year witnessed also the death of Charles IV. of France, with mighty consequences to England, as will presently be seen.

Edward had already shown a spirit unlikely to submit to the tutelage of his mother and her paramour; and Mortimer soon gave him cause to assert his free-will. Having treacherously got rid of his associates by obtaining the execution of Kent and the imprisonment of Lancaster on a charge of treason (1330), and having enriched himself by many forfeitures, he assumed the title of Earl of March and all the state of a king. Edward took counsel with several of his nobles, and surprised the queen and Mortimer in the castle of Nottingham, to which his party gained entrance by an old subterranean passage. Mortimer was condemned, without trial, by the parliament, and hanged at Tyburn, Nov. 29, 1330. The queen remained in captivity at her own house of Risings for the rest of her life.

The first few years of the reign which Edward now really commenced were occupied in the restoration of internal order and in a war with Scotland. Several of the English nobility, complaining that they had not been restored to their estates in Scotland in accordance with the late treaty, set up Edward Baliol, son of the late John Baliol, as a claimant of the crown, and Edward III. espoused his cause (1332). David fled to France, and the regent Douglas was defeated and slain at Halidon Hill near Berwick, July 19, 1333. Baliol was acknowledged as king by a parliament at Perth; but on the discovery that he had ceded the south of Scotland to Edward, he was obliged to flee to Berwick (1334). In the war which followed the Scots received large succors from the king of France, who thus furnished Edward with a provocation to urge the claim which he had already made to the crown of France.

Thus began those WARS WITH FRANCE which exhausted both countries for a century, and bequeathed to after generations the foolish and fatal legacy of a supposed "natural enmity."

The claim of Edward to the French crown was utterly untenable. It was founded on his descent from Philip III., from whom also the right of the reigning king, Philip VI., was derived. The relation of both to their common ancestor is seen in the following table:

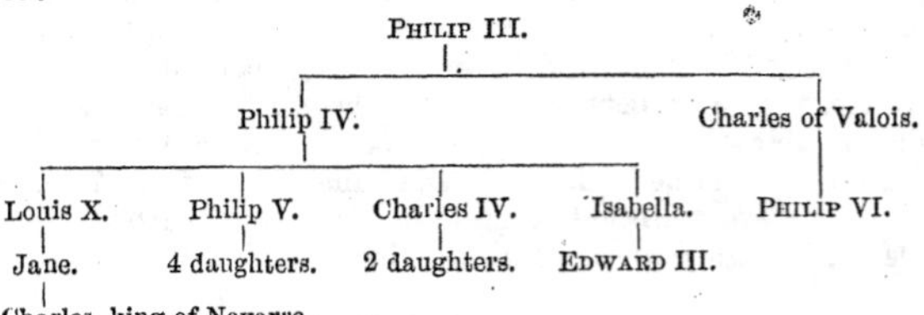

Thus it appears that, if the succession was to be traced through males alone, PHILIP VI. could have no rival. The exclusion of females had been clearly established by the celebrated "Salic Law," which confirmed the right of Philip V. But this law was recent, and the question had been raised whether a female, though herself incapable of reigning, might not transmit her right to a male heir. Even according to this view, the right would have been with the King of Navarre rather than with Edward. His only remaining plea was that, though the son of the younger daughter, he was a step nearer to the common ancestor; but, by a curious fatality, this very point had been decided the other way in the case of Baliol and Bruce. The accession of Philip VI. did not take place without a protest made by Isabella in Edward's favor; but Edward himself had done homage to Philip VI. for Guienne, 1329. In reviving the claim thus virtually abandoned, his first motive seems to have been resentment against Philip for offenses given in Guienne as well as in Scotland; and when once the idea had been really entertained, it ripened in the bold and ambitious mind of Edward into a scheme of conquest. Let it, then, be distinctly recorded, as a turning-point in English history, that the claims of the Plantagenets to the crown of France were only a scheme of downright conquest. No true Englishman regrets their ultimate failure, however proud he may be of the glories of Crecy, Poitiers, and Agincourt. Their success would only have reduced England to a French province and destroyed the independence from which has sprung all her prosperity. The pride of her kings, however, did not suffer the last vestige of the claim to be obliterated till the reign of George III., when the French lilies, first quartered by Edward III., were finally removed from her royal coat of arms.

At first the enterprise seemed only to involve Edward in embarrassments, which led to new measures of constitutional improvement at home. He crossed over into Flanders in 1338, and invaded

France in the following year, but only to retreat. In 1340 he sailed across, gained a great victory over the French fleet off Sluys, and, in the spirit of chivalry, challenged Philip to decide the dispute by single combat. This the French king declined, and a truce was made which lasted for two years. Returning to England, Edward found great disaffection, especially among the clergy and nobles, arising from his arbitrary measures in obtaining supplies for his French and Scottish wars. In the parliament which met in 1341 advantage was taken of his necessities to establish the great principle of *the responsibility of the great officers of state to the parliament.* The nobles also obtained the privilege of exemption from punishment except by the sentence of their peers assembled in parliament. Though the king procured the repeal of the statute soon after, its provisions were destined to endure.

In the same year a war of succession broke out in Brittany. Edward sent succors, under Sir Walter Manny, to the heroic Countess of Montfort, who was defending, in the castle of Hennebonne, the cause of her husband, then a prisoner at Paris (1342). In the autumn—the truce with France having expired—Edward took the field in person, and the war went on in Brittany with no decisive issue.

At length, in 1346, Edward prepared for a campaign in Guienne, but he was compelled by adverse winds to land at Cape la Hogue in Normandy. His army consisted only of 4000 men-at-arms, 10,000 archers, 10,000 Welsh infantry, and 6000 Irish; but, besides the king, it had a chief who proved in himself a host, though then only 16 years of age, EDWARD prince of Wales, called, from the favorite color of his armor, the BLACK PRINCE. The English ravaged the country on the left bank of the Seine almost up to the gates of Paris, and then retreated toward Flanders, pursued by the French king with an immense army. The delay caused in crossing the Somme enabled the French to come up with Edward, who turned to meet them at the village of CRECY, about fifteen miles to the east of Abbeville. His position was a gentle slope, on which he formed his army in three lines, with trenches to protect their flanks, and the baggage in the rear. He gave the post of honor at the head of the first line to his son, who had been knighted only a month before, and himself took the command of the reserve. In his front he placed some cannons, the first that had been used in any great battle; but so little value was yet attached to the invention that the French king had not waited to bring up his artillery. The host of France reached the field after a long day's march from Abbeville, already fatigued, and with their ranks disordered. They also were disposed in three lines. The first consisted of Genoese cross-bowmen, under Doria and Grimaldi; the second was intrusted to the king's brother, the Count of Alençon; and Philip himself was with the third. Around him were all his nobility and great vassals, with the king of Bohemia and his son the king of the Romans. The total force of his army was 120,000 men, while that of Edward was only 30,000; but the French were over-confident and undisciplined, under leaders jealous of each other and blindly contemptuous of the little English army which discipline and a wise general made irresistible.

It was about four o'clock in the afternoon, on Saturday the 26th of August (1346), when the Genoese advanced to attack the English army, who remained firm in their ranks. A thunder-shower had relaxed their bow-strings, and their arrows fell short of the mark, while the English archers, taking their bows out of their cases, poured in their cloth-yard shafts with unerring aim, and put the Genoese to flight. They were cut down by the men-at-arms of their own side; but these also were thrown into confusion by the steady fire of the archers. Then d'Alençon, leading a body of knights past the flank of the archers, closed with the main body of the English. The Prince of Wales was hard beset; and a knight rode out of the battle to Edward, who watched the battle from a wind-mill hill, and asked for help. "Is my son dead, or hurt, or felled to the ground?" said the king; and when the knight answered, "No," he bade him return and tell those who sent him to let the prince win his spurs that day, and to send for no help while he was alive. The like chivalrous devotion was shown by the aged king of Bohemia, who, being almost blind, caused his knights to tie their bridles together, placing him in the midst, and they all fell slain together. Their fate was shared by Alençon and the flower of the French nobility. In vain did Philip try to bring up the reserve; he was forced back by the tide of battle, and his routed army was pursued and slaughtered—for on that day no quarter was given—till the night fell. Then the field of victory was lighted up by torches; and Edward came down from the little hill to reward the prince, who knelt before him, with such words of praise as these: "Fair son, God give you good perseverance. You are my good son, that have acquitted yourself so nobly. You are worthy to keep a realm." This great battle, in which the French left between 30,000 and 40,000 dead upon the field, cost the English only three knights, one esquire, and a very few of inferior rank. In those days of complete armor the loss of life was not so much in the battle as in the pursuit.

In the following week Edward invested Calais, the siege of which lasted just a year. In this interval a great victory was gained over the Scots at Neville's Cross, in Durham, and King David was taken prisoner, Oct. 12, 1346. He was released next year on the payment of 100,000 marks.

The king of France made a vain attempt to relieve Calais at the Whitsuntide of 1347, and the governor, John de Vienne, was reduced to an unconditional surrender, Aug. 4. The beautiful story of the self-devotion of the six burgesses of Calais, who presented themselves before Edward, with halters round their necks, as victims in place of their fellow-citizens, and of their pardon on the intercession of Queen Philippa, can hardly be surrendered to romance without regret. The acquisition of Calais secured an entrance for an army into France; and Edward hastened to people it with English and to make it an English town in all respects. In the following year Edward made a truce with the king of France, during which a treacherous attempt was made to take Calais; but Edward flew to its defense in person, and performed acts of chivalrous valor, followed by equally chivalrous courtesy to his captives. In the same year (1349) he founded the chief of the English orders of knighthood—that of the Garter.

This year was also marked by the first great visitation of that terrible disease the *Plague*, which was said to have originated in the north of Asia. Its victims in London alone were more than 50,000.

The truce with France expired in 1355. Meanwhile John had succeeded his father, Philip VI. (1350); but the kingdom was distracted by the rival pretensions of Charles king of Navarre. Edward invaded it from Calais, and, having gained great booty, returned to repel an invasion of the Scots, whom he drove back, and ravaged the country as far as Edinburgh. The Black Prince had at the same time invaded France from the south, and was returning to Guienne, laden with booty, when he was met at Maupertuis, near Poitiers, by King John, with 60,000 men. By prudence, as consummate as his valor, he gained a decisive victory, and John yielded himself a prisoner. The prince made a banquet for him, and himself waited upon the king at table (Sept. 19, 1356). Having made a truce with France for two years, he conducted his royal prisoner to London, which he entered in procession, riding on a little palfrey by the side of the king, who was mounted on a splendid white steed, and attired in royal apparel. Edward came to meet them, and vied with his son in courtesy to the prisoner. John signed an ignominious treaty, which the French estates refused to ratify; and the country was terribly wasted by a new invasion (1359). Peace was at last concluded at *Bretigni*, near Chartres (May 8, 1360). John regained his liberty for a great ransom.

Edward renounced his claim to the crown of France, as well as to Normandy, Maine, Touraine, and Anjou, and was invested with Poitou and other provinces in the south, besides Guienne, which had not been lost, free from all homage to the king of France. John was released and conducted with honor to France; but, being unable to fulfill all the conditions of the treaty, he surrendered himself again in 1363, and soon after died in the Savoy, the palace where he had resided during his captivity.

In 1367 the Black Prince took part in the war of succession in Castile, between Pedro the Cruel and his brother Henry, on the side of the former. He gained much glory in a bad cause, but incurred debts which led him to impose new taxes on his French subjects, who carried their complaints to Charles, the new king of France. In violation of the treaty of Bretigni, Charles tried to play the suzerain; upon which Edward resumed the title of King of France, and the war was renewed (1369). The Black Prince, disabled by sickness, returned to England, where he died in the 46th year of his age, on the 8th of June, 1376, leaving behind the reputation of all the virtues of perfect chivalry, though stained with some acts of cruelty. His departure from France was the ruin of the English cause; and before his death his father had lost nearly all his old possessions, as well as his new conquests, retaining little besides the cities of Calais, Bordeaux, and Bayonne. Edward concluded a truce with France in 1374.

During the short remnant of his reign he sought relief from the disappointments that thickened round him in the pleasures which he had formerly despised. He had outlived his popularity; and he died, almost deserted, at Shene (Richmond), in the 65th year of his age and the 51st of his reign, on the 21st of June, 1377, and was buried at Westminster.

England has scarcely had a king of more consummate ability and personal virtue than Edward III. He tempered a firm and just administration of the law with a munificent generosity and a noble courtesy. The glory of his foreign wars was tarnished by the badness of his cause and overshadowed by the loss of his conquests; but they contributed most to the welfare of England by the opportunities which they offered for obtaining new grants of liberty in return for the means of prosecuting them.

One of the most important reforms in the criminal law was effected in the 25th year of Edward III. by the "Statute of Treasons," which strictly defined the limits of high treason, to the crimes of compassing the death of the king, levying war against him, and abetting his foreign enemies. The courts of justice rose into higher reputation than ever for the learning both of judges and pleaders.

"At the latter part of this king's reign," says Sir Matthew Hale, "the law seemed to be near its meridian." A new era was opened for commerce by statutes allowing foreign traders within the realm, and by the king's encouragement of Flemish weavers who wished to settle in the kingdom. The progress of literature and art will be noticed at the end of the chapter.

The family of Edward III. is given in the genealogical table at the end of the volume. An accurate knowledge of it is necessary for the understanding of the subsequent history. The dignity of *Duke*, borne by the royal princes, had been introduced by Edward III.

RICHARD II., of BORDEAUX (1377-1399), was the grandson of Edward III., and the son of Edward the Black Prince. He ascended the throne at the age of 11, having been born at Bordeaux in 1366. His fair aspect, and the memory of his father, excited a general feeling in his favor, which was doomed to utter disappointment. His minority was passed nominally under a council named by parliament, but really under the tutelage of his ambitious uncles, the dukes of Lancaster and Gloucester.

The wars with France and Scotland were carried on without any events of importance, but the taxes required to support them led to the celebrated insurrection of the common people under Wat Tyler. In 1380 a poll-tax of three groats (twelve-pence) imposed on every person above fifteen led to an almost universal discontent among the lower orders, on whom it of course pressed most severely. The flame was kindled by an outrage committed at Dartford by one of the collectors upon a peasant girl, under the pretense of assuring himself of her age. Her father, one Walter, a tiler, struck him dead upon the spot with a blow of his hammer. The men of Kent flew to arms, and the insurrection spread to all the eastern and southeastern counties. Besides Wat Tyler, the insurgents had leaders, whose names, partly real and partly affected, proclaimed their mean origin, as Hob Carter, Tom Miller, and Jack Straw, whose name survives on Hampstead Heath. They assembled, to the number of 100,000, on Blackheath, June 12, 1381, where an itinerant preacher, named John Ball, addressed them on the natural equality of all men, asking—

> "When Adam delved, and Eve span,
> Where was then the gentleman?"

Their demands were in accordance with this text: the abolition of villenage, fixed rents in lieu of compulsory service, and freedom in exercising their trades. The king, meeting them in person, promised compliance; but at another meeting in Smithfield, Walworth, the mayor of London, stabbed Wat Tyler, who was dispatched by the king's attendants. His fall was about to be terribly avenged, when Richard rode forward alone, telling them that he himself would be their leader. He succeeded in leading them out of the city and dispersing them; and soon after he took the field with a large army, and executed many of the insurgents, while parliament sanctioned the revocation of his promises.

The spirit shown by Richard on this occasion bore no lasting fruits. He surrendered himself to favorites—Robert de Vere, earl of Oxford, and Michael de la Pole, a foreigner, whom he created Earl of Suffolk and chancellor. But his uncle Gloucester overthrew them both by open force, and obtained his own appointment by parliament as the head of a council of regency (1387). In the following year, however, the king publicly proclaimed his own intention of governing, and procured an opinion from the judges that the council of regency was illegal. Gloucester again took up arms and seized the judges, who were condemned to death, and one of them, Tresilian, was actually executed (1388).

These troubles were somewhat composed by the return to England of the king's elder uncle—

"Old John of Gaunt, time-honored Lancaster,"

who had been engaged in a fruitless contest for the crown of Castile (1389). A truce was concluded with France, while the war with Scotland had become a mere border fray. One of its incidents, however, the battle of Otterbourne, between Douglas and Percy (Aug. 10, 1388), gave occasion to one of the finest ballads in the English language, that of "Chevy Chase." The truce with France, after being more than once renewed, became at length virtually a peace, by an extension for twenty-five years; and thus ended the first series of the great wars between England and France (1396). At the same time Richard married Isabella, the daughter of the French king. He had lost his first wife, Anne of Bohemia, two years before.

He now resolved to make a bold stroke for his personal independence by seizing the Duke of Gloucester, with several of his adherents. His uncles, the dukes of Lancaster and York, supported him. A subservient parliament annulled the commission of regency. Several great nobles were executed or banished, and Gloucester himself was privately murdered in his prison at Calais (1397).

In 1398 a new parliament ratified the acts of the king, and granted him ample supplies. His power seemed firmly established, when he was ruined by his own want of prudence and temper. HENRY duke of Hereford, the son of John of Gaunt, had accused the Duke of Norfolk of slandering the king, and a judicial combat had been arranged, when, in the very lists, the king forbade the fight, and banished Hereford for ten years and Norfolk for life. On succeeding to the dukedom of Lancaster, by his father's death, in the following year, Henry prepared, not only to avenge his banishment and the forfeiture of his estates, but also to frustrate the king's design of settling the crown on Roger Mortimer, earl of March, grandson of Lionel duke of Clarence, the third son of Edward III. (Edward's second son, William, had died without issue). John of Gaunt was Edward III.'s fourth son, but he had married Blanche, the heiress of Henry duke of Lancaster, who was the grandson of Edmund earl of Lancaster, the brother of Edward I. A story had been invented that this Edmund was really the elder brother, but had been set aside for his personal deformity; and thus Henry claimed to be doubly the representative of Henry III.

Taking advantage of Richard's absence in Ireland, Henry sailed from Nantes, attended by several of the banished nobles of Gloucester's party. He had only sixty persons with him when he landed in Yorkshire, but he was soon at the head of 60,000 men; and the adhesion of his uncle, the Duke of York, with the royal army, made him master of the kingdom. Richard hastened back from Ireland, but only to be taken prisoner and forced into an abdication. The parliament, summoned in the king's name at Westminster (Sept. 30, 1399), declared him to have forfeited the crown for his tyranny and incapacity. Lancaster then came forward, and in a set speech claimed the crown by right of blood. His claim was unanimously admitted, and he was placed in the vacant throne by the archbishops of Canterbury and York. The same parliament assembled six days afterward, reversed most of Richard's acts, and consigned him to an imprisonment, from which he was soon released, probably by a violent death, in the 34th year of his age and the 23d of his reign, March, 1400.

He was not destitute of ability; but a weak judgment and a violent temper rendered him unfit to govern. When he at length succeeded in asserting his own will, he became a tyrant; and the unanimous consent of the parliament to his deposition, manifestly expressing the desire of the people, gave a solid title to the house of Lancaster. He left no issue.

With his death closed the fourteenth century, a period during which England made a progress in civilization as great as her advance in military fame, and far more lasting in its results. We have seen the growth of constitutional liberty, and of freedom in the administration of justice, under the Edwards. Though villenage was not yet finally abolished, it had been mitigated by degrees, and the doctrine of man's right to personal freedom was all but established. In ecclesiastical matters, the ground surrendered by preceding kings to the see of Rome was in a great measure recovered. The parliament, in the 20th year of Edward III., declared the homage to the pope, which had been imposed on John, to be null and void (1367); and in the 16th of Richard II. was passed the celebrated statute of *Præmunire*, outlawing all persons who should introduce into the realm any papal bull or other instrument affecting the king (1393). But, more than this, the new doctrine of liberty of conscience had been openly proclaimed, and that even more clearly than it was asserted by the reformers in the next century. JOHN DE WICKLIFFE, a clergyman of Oxford, announced, in the latter part of Edward III.'s reign, the great principle of the reformation—that the doctrines and practices of religion should be conformed to the Holy Scriptures, which he himself translated for the first time into English. Protected by John of Gaunt, he survived the attempts of the church to crush him, and closed his life peacefully at his rectory of Lutterworth, in Leicestershire, in 1385. The royal descendants of his patron cruelly persecuted his followers, who were known by the nickname of *Lollards*.

The latter part of this century was a bright epoch in English literature. GEOFFREY CHAUCER, the friend of Wickliffe, uniting to a poetic genius, which only a very few of his successors have surpassed, a culture derived from the Italian models, and especially from Dante, produced, in his *Canterbury Tales*, a work immeasurably superior to all the efforts of earlier English writers. In this work, and Wickliffe's translation of the Bible, the *English Language* is at length seen perfected in all essential points; and in the reign of Edward III. the English tongue took the place of French in public documents. Latin was, however, still much used, and the earliest state paper that exists in English belongs to the year 1386. Natural science began to shake off the trammels of superstition, and ROGER BACON announced, from his retreat at Oxford, some great discoveries in mechanics and chemistry, including a hint of the discovery of gunpowder.

The glorious art of English architecture advanced to perfection: many cathedrals and churches were built or enlarged; and Edward III. erected the truly regal monument of Windsor Castle; and Westminster Hall, the grandest single chamber in the Pointed style of architecture, was built by Richard II. The splendid works of William of Wykeham at Winchester and Oxford exhibit the noblest use of art in the service of learning and religion. In one word, England had achieved that greatness in arms and law, in arts and letters, which has never since been forfeited.

King, with his Privy Council. (Harleian MS.).

CHAPTER XII.

THE HOUSE OF LANCASTER. HENRY IV. AND HENRY V. A.D. 1399–1422.

HENRY IV. (1399–1413), surnamed BOLINGBROKE, from the town in Lincolnshire at which he was born, in 1366, was the only son of John of Gaunt. He was distinguished for warlike skill and personal courage, which he had proved in wars against the Moors of Barbary. His accession was hailed with joy by the common people, but his title was not recognized by foreign states, and he had to defend it at home against formidable rebellions. The first conspiracy, formed by several of the nobles, was betrayed by the Earl of Rutland and easily crushed (Jan., 1400); but it was followed by an insurrection in Wales, under *Owen Glendower*, who claimed descent from the ancient princes. Glendower captured Lord Grey and Sir Edmund Mortimer, uncle of the Earl of March. Henry, who had the Earl of March in his own hands, was not sorry to be rid of Mortimer, and even refused permission to his kinsman Percy, earl of Northumberland to ransom him. He offended Percy still further by forbidding him to receive ransom for Earl Douglas and other Scotch nobles whom he had taken prisoners (1402). Urged on by his brother the Earl of Worcester, and his fiery son *Hotspur*, Northumberland made a league with Douglas and Glendower, and raised the standard of rebellion. Hotspur, marching at the head of 12,000 men to effect a junction with Owen Glendower, had advanced as far as Shrewsbury when he was encountered by the king (July 23, 1403). A most obstinate and bloody battle followed, in which the Prince of Wales, afterward Henry V., proved himself the heir to the fame of Edward the Black Prince. The fortune of the day was decided by the death of Hotspur, whose fate was shared by many nobles on both sides. Worcester and Douglas were among the prisoners; and the former was beheaded at Shrewsbury.

Northumberland himself, who had been prevented by illness from taking the field, was only sentenced by his peers to pay a fine, and even this the king remitted. Conscious, perhaps, that this clemency showed a fear of his vast power, he renewed his rebellion two years later. But, before he could draw his forces to a head, his confederates, Thomas Mowbray, earl of Nottingham, and Richard Scrope, archbishop of York, were seized by Ralph Neville, earl of Westmoreland, and executed (1405). Northumberland, who escaped to Scotland, was slain in a third attempt at Bramham in Yorkshire (1407). Meanwhile the Prince of Wales carried on the war against Owen Glendower; but that chieftain held his ground till Henry's death.

Scotland might have played an important part in the troubles of Henry's reign; but the dissensions in her own royal family not only crippled her, but resulted in an accident which placed her in Henry's power. The Duke of Albany, not content with ruling his weak brother Robert III., contrived the murder of his eldest son David duke of Rothesay, as a step toward the throne. To save his younger son James, Robert caused him to sail for France; but the ship was taken by the English (1405), and Henry detained the young prince long after his father's death had made him King James I. of Scotland. But, like Henry's other royal captive, the Earl of March, James received an education suited to his rank, and he beguiled his imprisonment at Windsor with some of those poems which have secured for him an honorable place in Anglo-Scottish literature. He was only released under Henry VI., in 1424.

On the whole, the reign of Henry IV., though illustrated by no great achievements, bears witness to the ability of a sovereign who could maintain his questionable title and reduce the disturbed state to order. This was done, however, by a system of terror which caused the king to outlive his popularity, early as was the age at which he died. One great blot upon his administration was his persecution of the Lollards to secure the favor of the church. The year 1401 was the first in which the statute-book was sullied by an act for the burning of heretics; and several executions took place in this and the following reign. The Commons gained an increase of power, both in freedom of debate and in the granting of supplies, and they began to use the right of punishing public officers for offenses against their privileges. It also deserves notice that twice during this reign the Commons proposed to confiscate the temporalities of the church, which were only preserved by the king's refusal to sanction the spoliation.

Henry died at Westminster on the 20th of March, 1413, in the 46th year of his age and the 14th of his reign.

HENRY V. (1413–1422), of MONMOUTH, was born on the 9th of August, 1388. His early exploits in the wars against the Percys and Glendower had been succeeded by an inactivity forced upon him by the jealous state of mind into which his father fell toward the end of his reign. How the prince's restless spirit is said to have found vent in disorders with debauched companions; how he atoned for these excesses by his graceful submission to the judge whom he had insulted on the bench; and how he was at last reconciled to his father; all these are traditions better known through the fancy of Shakspeare than in the actual facts of history. But these faults were all thrown aside when he mounted the throne, and he retained about him his father's wisest counselors.

The beginning of his reign was disgraced by a new persecution of the Lollards. The diffusion of doctrines such as Wickliffe's through Europe alarmed the church, and led to the assembling of the council of Constance, where John Huss was burned (1414). In England Henry may have been the more ready to gratify the zeal of the clergy through being persuaded that the Lollards were disloyal subjects. He suffered the bishops to condemn to the flames the leader of the Lollards, Sir John Oldcastle, Lord Cobham, who had acquired distinction in his father's service and his own. Cobham escaped from the Tower, gathered his followers, and tried to seize the king's person (1414); but, being taken four years later, he was hanged as a traitor and burned as a heretic.

But Henry's whole energies were soon thrown into a new effort to subdue France. During the last reign the war had languished, but the French had more than once attacked the southern coasts of England. Now, however, the internal state of France offered an opportunity which Henry was not the man to lose. King Charles

VI., the grandson of John II., had lost his reason; and the regency was disputed between his brother the Duke of Orleans, and his cousin the Duke of Burgundy, son of the younger son of John. The dispute had broken out into open war, and Burgundy had secretly solicited aid from the king of England. Having strengthened himself by alliances with the Emperor Sigismund and with Ferdinand king of Aragon, Henry openly laid claim to the crown of France, and assembled his forces at Portsmouth in the spring of 1415. He was detained a short time by a conspiracy formed in favor of the Earl of March by the Earl of Cambridge, younger son of Edmund duke of York, Lord Scrope, and Sir Thomas Grey, who were hastily tried and executed.

On the 11th of August, 1415, Henry sailed from Southampton, with 1500 ships, conveying 6000 men-at-arms and 24,000 infantry, chiefly archers. Landing on the 13th, he formed the siege of Harfleur, which capitulated on the 22d of September. But the delay and the heat of the season had been so fatal to Henry's little army that he could proceed no further. Resisting, however, all entreaties to return to England, he resolved to retreat to Calais. By slow stages he reached the Somme, on the banks of which the French army, four times as numerous as his own, were now assembled under the dukes of Orleans and Bourbon. Both armies crossed the river; Henry by an adroit surprise, and the French with a view of barring his progress. Their manœuvre succeeded, though to their ultimate ruin, and Henry found them posted in front of him on the plains of AZINCOUR or AGINCOURT (Oct. 24, 1415). On the following day the scenes of Crecy and Poitiers were repeated, but with a result even more decisive. Standing on the defensive, with their front secured by palisades against the enemy's cavalry, the English archers poured their deadly volleys upon the dense masses of the French, and then charged their disordered ranks. Ten thousand of the French were slain, and 14,000 were made prisoners, among whom were the dukes of Orleans and Bourbon, and many of the highest of the French nobility. The loss of the English was so small that it is stated at only *forty!*

The Duke of Burgundy now openly declared for Henry, who resumed the campaign in 1417 by landing again in Normandy and marching almost unopposed to Rouen, which yielded after a resolute defense (1418). The sense of common danger now led the dauphin to form a secret treaty with the Duke of Burgundy, whose treacherous assassination, however, in a conference with the dauphin at Montereau, broke up the compact again. His son Philip, bent on avenging his father's death, at once made a league with Henry, on terms which placed France at his feet. The treaty was ratified at

Troyes, May 21, 1420. The nominal sovereignty of France was left to Charles VI., but the whole government was committed to Henry, who was to succeed to the crown on the death of Charles. The treaty was cemented by the marriage of Henry to Catherine, the daughter of the French king. Henry at once assumed the government at Paris, where the parliament and the estates of the realm confirmed the treaty of Troyes.

After keeping his Christmas in great state at Paris, and receiving at Rouen the homage of his nobles as regent of France, Henry visited England, where his queen was crowned (Feb. 24, 1421). An incident occurred during this visit which illustrates his want of generosity and conscience where his ambition was concerned. The intimate relations long since established between France and Scotland had led a large body of the flower of the Scottish nation to enter the service of the French king. These Scots, to the number of 7000, had adhered to the dauphin, and had defeated Henry's brother, the Duke of Clarence, at Baugé. Henry now obtained from the captive king of Scotland his consent to the engagement of the Earl of Douglas and other Scottish nobles in the English army. James himself even served as a volunteer, and, under the color of his support, Henry treated the Scots whom he took prisoners as rebels and traitors. No wonder that the feud between Scotland and England grew bitterer in each age!

Returning to France in June, Henry drove the dauphin behind the Loire, and formed the siege of Orleans; but scarcity of provisions compelled him to return to Paris, where his Christmas festivities were gladdened by the news of the birth of a son and heir, at Windsor, on the 6th of December, 1421. He took the field again next year; but an illness, which was beyond the medical skill of the age, brought his career to an untimely end, on the 31st of August, 1422, in the 35th year of his age and the 10th of his reign. He was buried in the chapel of St. Edward the Confessor, in Westminster Abbey, where his effigy is still shown, robbed of the *silver head* with which it was adorned—a stroke of irony emblematic of the fate which awaited not only his conquests, but even his character; for, after conceding to him every quality, whether personal or intellectual, which can win the admiration of the world for a career of martial glory and successful ambition, it remains to be recorded that he was unscrupulous and cruel to all who crossed his path.

The privileges of parliament were further advanced in the reign of Henry V. by the king's consent to abstain from altering the terms of laws which he had consented to enact upon their petition. On the other hand, the king received enlarged powers of taxation, amidst the popular gratitude for the victory of Agincourt, by the grant of the dues of *tonnage* and *poundage* (a certain sum on every tun of wine, and on every pound of some other articles, when imported from abroad), as well as duties on wool and leather, *for his life* (1415).

Henry left but the one infant son with whose unhappy reign the dynasty of Lancaster ended. His widow, Catherine, by her second marriage with a Welsh gentleman, Sir *Owen Tudor*, became the ancestress of a new dynasty, in the person of her grandson, HENRY VII. (*See the Genealogical Table.*)

Henry V.

Marriage of Henry VI. and Margaret of Anjou.

CHAPTER XIII.

THE HOUSE OF LANCASTER (*continued*).—HENRY VI.
A.D. 1422–1461.

HENRY V. left his splendid and hard-won inheritance to his only son, HENRY VI., of WINDSOR, an infant of nine months old, who continued to display childish want of energy during his reign of nearly forty years. This long period of confusion and disaster divides itself into two parts, marked by the loss of the English dominions in France and by the terrible civil conflict known as the "Wars of the Roses."

The king's infancy gave a new opportunity for the parliament to exercise the large powers which it had for some time been steadily acquiring. The administration was intrusted to the elder of the king's two uncles, John duke of Bedford, with the title, not of *regent*, but *Protector of the Realm and Church of England*; and during Bedford's absence as Regent of France, this authority was vested in his younger brother, Humphrey, "the good" Duke of Gloucester. But the protector could do nothing of importance without the consent of a council appointed by parliament. The care of the king's person was committed to Henry Beaufort, bishop of Winchester, the legitimated son of John of Gaunt, in conjunction with Richard de Beauchamp, earl of Warwick.

This arrangement led to the most fatal results. Beaufort was an astute and prudent statesman; while his nephew Gloucester was as headstrong and imprudent as he was generous and popular. Both were unscrupulous in their ambition; and their quarrels not only kept England in confusion, but went far to neutralize all the energy with which Bedford was maintaining the English cause in France.

In that country the power of the late king had been firmly established over the northern provinces; but the dauphin's title was recognized south of the Loire, and the country between that river and the Seine was the seat of active war. New life was thrown into the French party by the death of the poor old imbecile king, Charles VI. (Oct. 21, 1422), when the dauphin claimed the throne, in opposition to Henry, and was crowned at Poitiers as Charles VII. But neither his youthful energy nor the enthusiasm of his adherents could prevail at first against the skill and policy of Bedford. This prince made an alliance with John duke of Brittany; and, in order to secure England from the hostility of the Scots, he persuaded the council to liberate King James I. (A.D. 1424). Bedford was equally successful in his military operations during the first seven years of the new reign. Among other battles, the French suffered at VERNEUIL (Aug. 17, 1424) a defeat almost equal to Crecy or Poitiers, and their Scottish auxiliaries were cut to pieces.

But this was Bedford's last great success; and meanwhile his brother Gloucester had nearly alienated the Duke of Burgundy from the English alliance. Having married Jacqueline of Hainault, who had left her former husband, John duke of Brabant, the nephew of Burgundy, Gloucester attempted to seize on Hainault. On his return to England, his quarrel with Beaufort rose to such a height that Bedford was obliged to go over to effect a reconciliation.

The Duke of Brittany meanwhile declared for Charles, but was reduced to obedience on Bedford's return; and all the advantages which the French might have derived from the disorders of England were neutralized by worse intrigues at the court of Charles.

The year 1429, however, introduced a new scene, marked by one of the most romantic episodes in all history. Bedford had resolved to carry the war to the south of the Loire, and had laid siege to Orleans, the fall of which threatened to be fatal to Charles VII. Now there was a country girl, 27 years old, at the village of Domremi, named JOAN OF ARC.* She had shown hitherto no marks of genius, nor eccentricities of character, but, as the sole servant at a small inn, she had been inured to masculine occupations, such as tending the horses of the guests; and she thus acquired great skill in horsemanship. At length the secret springs of enthusiasm, which so easily vibrate in a woman's heart, were touched by the news of the king's extremity, and Joan believed herself to be the heaven-sent saviour of her country. Presenting herself to Baudricourt, the governor of Vaucouleurs, she related to him her visions, and persuaded him to send her to Charles VII. at Chinon. There, as the story goes, she at once recognized the king, though disguised among his courtiers; she mentioned a secret known only to himself; and she gave a minute description of a sword which was kept in the church of St. Catherine of Fierbois, and which she claimed as the sign and instrument of her mission. That mission she declared to be to raise the siege of Orleans and to crown the king at Rheims.

These and other miracles were eagerly spread abroad by the court and accepted by the people, before whom Joan was exhibited in full panoply on a splendid charger. In this array, unfurling a consecrated banner, she marched to the relief of Orleans. The besiegers, who shared in the first impression of superstitious awe, permitted her to enter the city with a convoy of provisions (April 20, 1429). She forthwith assumed the offensive; attacked and carried the works of the enemy, and compelled the Earl of Suffolk to raise the siege on the 8th of May. This exploit obtained for her the well-known title of LA PUCELLE or the MAID OF ORLEANS.

Charles now consented to accompany her to Rheims at the head of only 12,000 men; and he was crowned in that city, like his predecessors since Clovis, on the 12th of July. Meanwhile his bands gained various minor victories; Suffolk was taken prisoner, and several English and Burgundian garrisons were expelled.

The path of Charles to Paris now seemed open, and even Bedford's tenacity must have yielded, but for a reinforcement of 5000 men, which his uncle, Cardinal Beaufort, was leading through France against the Hussites in Bohemia. Charles was content to avoid a decisive battle, and the war languished for a year, till fortune brought to Bedford a momentary success at the cost of lasting

* Her real name was Jeanne Darc, not d'Arc.

infamy. In a sally from Compiègne (May 26, 1430), the Maid of Orleans was taken prisoner by the Burgundians under John of Luxemburg, from whom Bedford purchased the captive. Whether from revenge, or only from policy, in the hope of depressing the spirits of the French by her fate and exposure, as much as they had been exalted by faith in her divine mission, he had her brought to trial for sorcery and heresy. Her courage at length gave way, when that sentence was pronounced by which the mock mercy of the ecclesiastical courts used to hand over their victims to the secular power; and she confessed that her revelations were illusions or impostures. But the respite thus obtained was soon forfeited by a stratagem of her persecutors, who placed a suit of male attire in her cell, and treated her assumption of that dress as a relapse, excluding her from pardon. Her career was closed, and her fame sealed, by her committal to the flames in the market-place of Rouen, June 14, 1431.

But her work survived her, and her death brought no revival to the English cause. The display of power made by the coronation of Henry at Paris (Dec. 17, 1431) was more than neutralized by the loss of his father's first conquest, namely, Harfleur; and the Duke of Burgundy, who had long been a lukewarm ally, was finally alienated by the death of his sister, the Duchess of Bedford (Nov. 14, 1432), followed by Bedford's marriage with Jaquetta of Luxemburg. After many fruitless attempts at negotiation a congress was held at Arras (Aug. 20, 1435) from which the English envoys retired in disgust (Sept. 6), and the Duke of Burgundy then made a separate treaty with Charles (Sept. 21); while, to complete the blow to Henry, the Duke of Bedford died at Rouen on Sept. 14.

The Duke of York was appointed as Bedford's successor in France; but the needful reinforcements were delayed; and meanwhile Paris opened her gates to Charles, and the citadel was taken, April 13, 1436. The restoration of Charles VII. was now virtually complete; but the war was continued feebly till May 28, 1444, when a truce was made till May 1, 1446, and afterward prolonged to April 1, 1450. By a secret article in this treaty the Earl of Suffolk gave up Anjou and Maine as the price of Henry's marriage with Margaret of Anjou, the niece of the French king; and in 1449 Charles took advantage of the internal troubles of England to break the truce and overrun Normandy and Guienne.

Rouen, the capital of Normandy, fell on the 4th of November, 1449, and on the 12th of August, 1450, the English surrendered Cherbourg, the last remnant of the duchy of the Conqueror. The conquest of Gascony was completed by the fall of Bayonne, August 25, 1451. A revolt of Bordeaux, the ancient capital of the Black

Prince, only led to a last feeble effort, in 1453, for the recovery of Guienne, in which the veteran Talbot and his son were killed at Châtillon, in July, and Bordeaux was taken in October, 1453. Thus were finally lost, together with the conquest of Edward III. and Henry V., all that remained of the hereditary French possessions of the Normans and Plantagenets. CALAIS alone was left, for another century, as a gate through which English armies more than once re-entered France, but never to effect a conquest. But yet these humiliating losses were the beginning of all sound relations between the two countries; though the jealousies kindled by past wars and usurpations postponed for 400 years the career of mutual benefit on which they have at length entered.

The disasters of these thirty years in France were the true index of the weakness and disorder which prevailed in England. The first years of Henry's reign were occupied, as above related, with the contest for power between his uncle, Humphrey duke of Gloucester, and his great-uncle, Henry Beaufort bishop of Winchester, and afterward cardinal. The death of Bedford, in 1435, removed the only check upon their rivalries, which were the immediate cause of the disasters of the following year in France.

In 1441 the party of Beaufort struck a cruel blow at Gloucester by the condemnation of his duchess, Eleanor, for witchcraft; and in 1443 Gloucester brought a charge of treason against Beaufort, who replied by producing a general pardon from the king.

In the two following years Beaufort carried, against the opposition of Gloucester, both the treaty with France and the marriage of Henry to Margaret of Anjou, daughter of Regnier (or René), the titular king of Sicily, Naples, and Jerusalem (1445). The young queen, at once assuming the ascendency over her feeble husband which she ever afterward preserved, threw all her influence into the scale of Beaufort. In a parliament summoned at Bury St. Edmund's, Feb. 10. 1447, Gloucester was accused of treason and cast into prison, where he was found a few days afterward dead in his bed. Just two months later (April 11) Cardinal Beaufort also died, expressing, it is said, great remorse for his nephew's murder. He was succeeded as minister by the Duke of Suffolk, who had negotiated the queen's marriage, and was now her chief favorite. The king himself, though 26 years of age, had shown no capacity for active government; and, besides the other disorders arising out of his long minority, he was burdened with a debt of £372,000.

The fruits of all these evils were now to be reaped by Suffolk. The people, exasperated by the loss of the French provinces, and jealous of the queen as a French princess, hated Suffolk as the negotiator of the treaty with France; but they hated him still more as one of the murderers of the good Duke of Gloucester. That unhappy prince had also friends among the highest nobility who desired to avenge his death, and among these was Richard duke of York, whose claim to the crown began to be put forward. On the 28th of January, 1450, Suffolk was impeached by the Commons, and sentenced to banishment for five years; but his enemies had him seized between Dover and Calais, and he was beheaded on the side of a boat (May 2, 1450), while no inquiry was made after the murderers.

Connected with the movement against Suffolk was the formidable popular insurrection headed by JOHN CADE, a native of Ireland, who had been exiled to France for his crimes. Assuming the popular name of Mortimer, he gathered a force of 20,000 men in Kent (May, 1450), defeated and killed Sir Humphrey Stafford at Sevenoaks, and encamped at Blackheath, whence he sent in to the court a list of grievances. On July 1 he entered London, and beheaded Lord Say and Sele, treasurer of England, and a friend of Suffolk. Four days later the citizens, aided by the governor of the Tower, repulsed him with great slaughter; and his adherents retired and dispersed on receiving a pardon, which was afterward withdrawn. Cade himself was killed in Sussex. There was another insurrection at the same time in Wiltshire, in which William Ascough, bishop of Salisbury, was murdered. Meanwhile the people were again incensed at seeing the government intrusted to the Duke of Somerset, who had just lost Normandy.

This state of utter confusion now seemed to demand that change of dynasty which had been long preparing. To understand the events which followed we must cast back a glance on the family of Edward III. That king had seven sons (*see Genealogical Tables*). When his grandson and legitimate heir, Richard II., was dethroned, the crown went to the family of his *fourth* son, JOHN of Gaunt, passing over that of his *third* son, LIONEL duke of Clarence. (The *second* son, William of Hatfield, died young.) Lionel's only child was *Philippa*, the wife of Edmund Mortimer earl of March. Their son, Roger Mortimer earl of March, died in 1398, leaving a son, EDMUND MORTIMER earl of March, who was the legitimate heir when Richard II. was deposed (1399), though he was set aside by Henry of Bolingbroke. Edmund had also a sister, ANN MORTIMER, through whom the house of York claimed the crown, thus: The *fifth* son of Edward III., EDMUND of Langley, duke of York, left two sons, Edward duke of York, and RICHARD earl of Cambridge, of whom the former died without issue in 1415. The latter, who was executed in the same year for his conspiracy against Henry V., had married Ann Mortimer; and thus their son, RICHARD duke of

York, united in his person the lines of the *third* and *fifth* sons of Edward III. While Richard claimed the throne in right of his mother, he had inherited vast wealth as the heir of the three houses of Clarence, March, and York, and nature had endowed him with ability and valor, but also with gentleness and prudence. Besides all this, he was married to the daughter of Ralph Neville, earl of Westmoreland, who, with his son and grandson, the earls of Salisbury and Warwick, were the most powerful of the nobility. Indeed, the latter, afterward called "The King-Maker," was almost a king himself. Richard duke of York succeeded Bedford in the government of France, whence he was recalled in 1447 by the intrigues of Suffolk and the queen. He was afterward lieutenant of Ireland (1449), where his conciliatory government aided the claims which the Nevilles began to put forward on his behalf. He returned from Ireland in 1451, and in the following year he took up arms, demanding the dismissal of Somerset; but this movement ended by his retirement to his estates.

But on the 14th of October, 1453, the birth of an heir to Henry VI. (Edward prince of Wales) decided the Duke of York to a final assertion of his claim. In the same year the king was seized with an illness which incapacitated him from even the appearance of government. The queen was obliged to admit York and the Nevilles to the council; the parliament appointed York protector during the king's illness, and Somerset was sent to the Tower, under a charge of treason. But next year the king recovered, released and reinstated Somerset, and dismissed the Duke of York, who took up arms, only demanding a reformed government. His army met that of Somerset at *the first battle of St. Albans* (May 23, 1455), where the first blood was shed in that frightful civil contest between the houses of York and Lancaster which exhausted England for 30 years, and in which 12 pitched battles were fought, 80 princes of the blood were killed, and the nobility of England almost destroyed. It may be well here to recall to mind the scene in which Shakspeare describes the choice by the two parties of those symbols which gave to the conflict the name of the "WARS OF THE ROSES:"

PLANT. Since you are tongue-tied, and so loth to speak,
In *dumb significants* proclaim your thoughts:
Let him that is a true-born gentleman,
And stands upon the honor of his birth,
If he suppose that I have pleaded truth,
From this brier pluck a *white rose* with me.
SOM. Let him that is no coward nor no flatterer,
But dare maintain the party of the truth,
Pluck a *red rose* from off this thorn with me.
K. Henry VI., Part I. Act ii. Sc. 4.

The prophecy which the poet puts into the mouth of Somerset was fulfilled in another sense at St. Albans, where his own fall dyed the white rose of York "in a bloody red," and the red rose of Lancaster "looked pale with fear." The king himself was taken prisoner, and treated with great respect. The parliament, which met in July, did justice to the memory of Gloucester, and proclaimed a general pardon. On the return of the king's illness, in November, the Duke of York was again made protector; and Henry, on his recovery, again revoked his appointment (Feb., 1456), when he retired from court; and, after a quiet interval of two years, a formal reconciliation was effected between him and the queen on the 25th of March, 1458.

But this was only a hollow truce; and in the autumn of the same year the slumbering embers of civil war were rekindled by a quarrel between the retainers of the king and those of the Earl of Warwick. Both parties again took up arms, but the Lancastrians proved the stronger; the earls of Salisbury and Warwick retired to Calais (the government of the latter), while the Duke of York himself fled to Ireland; and the chiefs of his party were attainted by a parliament at Coventry (Nov. 20, 1459). In the following year Salisbury and Warwick landed at Sandwich, entered London on the 2d of July, and defeated the queen in battle at Northampton on the 10th, when the king was taken prisoner, and Margaret fled to Scotland with her son.

The Duke of York returned from Ireland in October, and now for the first time made a formal claim to the crown before parliament, who pronounced in favor of his title. They decided, however, that Henry should retain the crown during his life, and be succeeded by the Duke of York, to whose hands the administration should meanwhile be committed; but this compromise was rejected by Queen Margaret, who assembled an army of 20,000 men in the north. The Duke of York, marching to meet her with only 5000 men, was defeated and killed near Wakefield (Dec. 31, 1460). His son, the Duke of Rutland, a fair youth of sixteen, was butchered in cold blood by the Lord Clifford; and the Earl of Salisbury and other noble prisoners were beheaded without trial at Pontefract. Thus began the brutal murders and executions which envenomed the Wars of the Roses.

Richard duke of York, who thus perished in the fiftieth year of his age, left three sons: EDWARD, soon to be King Edward IV.; GEORGE duke of Clarence; and RICHARD, afterward King Richard III. The former, now Duke of York, was still in the field; and against him Margaret sent a part of her army under Jasper Tudor, earl of Pembroke, the second son of Sir Owen Tudor and of Queen Catherine, widow of Henry V. Pembroke was defeated by Prince Edward at Mortimer's Cross in Herefordshire, where his father was taken prisoner and beheaded (Feb. 2, 1461). Margaret herself defeated Warwick, and regained the person of the king, in *the second battle of St. Albans* (Feb. 17, 1461); but she was overmatched by the advancing forces of the Duke of York, reinforced by the remains of Warwick's army; and after ravaging the country round London, the citizens of which shut their gates against her, she retired to the north. On the 28th of February the Duke of York entered London, and on the 3d of March the citizens proclaimed him king by the title of EDWARD IV.

Thus ended the dynasty of Lancaster and the reign of its third king, the former having lasted sixty-two years, and the latter thirty-eight. It is needless to sketch the character of Henry VI. The events of his reign bear their witness to the fatal incapacity which dissipated the fruits of his grandfather's usurpation and his father's victories. But yet, amidst all these public disasters, the gentler virtues of Henry bore other fruits, of more lasting benefit than the crown of Bolingbroke and the laurels of Agincourt. The magnificent schools of ETON and KING'S COLLEGE, CAMBRIDGE, were his foundations—the former in 1440, the latter three years later. *Queen's College, Cambridge*, was founded by Queen Margaret in 1449. The *Public Schools* at Oxford were also founded in this reign (1439), as well as Lincoln and Magdalen Colleges, Oxford (1428 and 1458).

These educational establishments, together with churches, cathedrals, and castles, still afforded ample scope for the art of English architecture, which passed, at the beginning of the 15th century, from the perfect grace of the flowing lines of the "Decorated" style into the somewhat stiffer but even more elaborate forms of the "Perpendicular" or "Florid"—a style which soon afterward culminated in the gorgeous magnificence of St. George's Chapel, Windsor; King's College Chapel, Cambridge; and Henry VII.'s Chapel, Westminster. Literature, however, remained almost stationary after the vast onward stride made by Wickliffe and Chaucer.

The development of the English constitution made steady progress under the house of Lancaster. The doubtful title of Henry IV., the necessities created by the wars of Henry V., and the long minority and weakness of Henry VI., all tended to confirm the privileges of parliament at the expense of the royal prerogative. Parliaments met almost every year; and under Henry VI. the old form of a *petition*—in answer to which the king promulgated a statute, varying the petition as he pleased—was superseded by the *bill*, enacted by the three estates of the realm conjointly, and to which the consent or dissent of the crown must be given without modification. The increased power of the Commons over taxation has been already noticed.

Henry VI. survived his deposition for ten years, the events of which belong to the reign of his successor.

Edward IV. and his Court.

CHAPTER XIV.

THE HOUSE OF YORK.—EDWARD IV., EDWARD V., RICHARD III. A.D. 1461–1485.

EDWARD IV. (1461-1483) was born at Rouen, April 29, 1441, when his father, Richard duke of York, was regent of France. His title to the crown having been accepted by the acclamations of the people assembled in St. John's Fields on Sunday, March 2, 1461, he was proclaimed next day, and installed as king at Westminster on March 4, being not quite 20 years old.

He at once marched northward against Queen Margaret, who had collected a force of 60,000 men in Yorkshire. Edward and Warwick, at the head of 40,000 men, encountered her at Towton, near

Tadcaster, and defeated her in a bloody battle on March 29. Edward gave no quarter, and 28,000 Lancastrians were left on the field, his own loss being 8000. Margaret, with Henry and their son, fled to Scotland, while Edward returned to London and was crowned on the 29th of June. On Nov. 4 parliament recognized his title; and, while confirming the acts of the Henrys, described them as "late in fact, but not of right, kings of England." Numerous executions at once struck terror into the Lancastrians and displayed the innate cruelty of the youthful king.

Meanwhile Queen Margaret sought the aid of the crafty king of France, Louis XI., promising Calais as a bribe. After some futile efforts, made from her retreat in Scotland, she at length marched into England in 1464, and was joined by several of the nobles of the north, where the strength of the Lancastrians always lay; but her army was routed and dispersed by Lord Montacute, the brother of Warwick, in the battles of Hedgley Moor and *Hexham*, April 15 and May 15.

The deposed king and queen escaped in different directions from the battle-field. It is said that Margaret, concealing herself in a forest with her son, fell into the hands of robbers, who took her jewels and treated her with insult. As they were quarreling over their booty, she made her escape into the thickest of the forest; and there, exhausted with fatigue and sorrow, she saw a robber approach with his sword drawn. Forming a resolution worthy of her fortitude, she advanced toward him with the young prince, and said, "Here, my friend, I commit to your care the safety of your king's son." Touched by the confidence reposed in him, the robber devoted himself to their service, and aided their escape to Flanders. Henry was less fortunate. After hiding for some time at the houses of his friends in Lancashire, he was at length betrayed, carried into London by Warwick with his feet tied under his horse's belly, and thrown into the Tower (July, 1466).

Edward was meanwhile indulging in every licentious pleasure, though not to the neglect of public business. Various proposals were made for his marriage, and Warwick was in negotiation with Louis XI. for an alliance with his sister-in-law, a princess of Savoy, when Edward became enamored of the lady Elizabeth Woodville, the young widow of Sir John Grey and daughter of Jaquetta duchess of Bedford, by her second husband, Sir Richard Woodville. The king married her privately on the 1st of May, 1464, and avowed the marriage on the 29th of September; while he created her father Earl of Rivers, and heaped other honors on her relatives. The immediate result was the disgust of the Earl of Warwick, not only at seeing his plans for a more suitable alliance set aside, but because the queen's relatives were all of the Lancastrian party. A prolonged contest for influence at the court ensued between the Nevilles and the Woodvilles. The nobility were naturally disposed to take part with the great Nevilles rather than with the obscure Woodvilles; and even the king's brothers sided with Warwick, especially George duke of Clarence, who married Isabel, daughter of the earl, July 11, 1469.

Meanwhile an insurrection of the peasantry broke out in Yorkshire, and a strange scene of confusion followed. The insurgents were defeated by Neville earl of Northumberland, the brother of Warwick; but they rallied under new leaders who were Warwick's relatives, and raised quite a new cry for the removal of the Woodvilles. Warwick and Clarence, though summoned by Edward to his aid, formed a separate camp in Kent, while a part of the king's army was defeated by the rebels at Edgecote, near Banbury, and the queen's father and brother were taken prisoners and beheaded. The subsequent relations between the king and the Nevilles are involved in great obscurity. At length Edward proclaimed Clarence and Warwick traitors, March 31, 1470. They fled to France; and, under the auspices of Louis XI., formed an alliance with Queen Margaret, who had been residing quietly at her father's court of Anjou. Henry VI. was to be restored to his throne; his son and successor, Prince Edward, was to marry Anne, the second daughter of Warwick; and, in case of failure of male issue, the crown was to descend to the Duke of Clarence, to whom, in conjunction with Warwick, the administration was meanwhile to be intrusted. With a fleet, men, and money, supplied by Louis, Warwick and Clarence landed at Dartmouth, Sept. 13, 1470. Men flocked to them from all sides. Even the king's soldiers could not be trusted: Edward fled to Lynn, and thence embarked for Flanders (Oct. 3). Warwick entered London (Oct. 5), released Henry from the Tower, and again proclaimed him king. A parliament assembled at Westminster (1471) settled the government and succession in accordance with the treaty made with Margaret.

The exiled king had fled to his brother-in-law Charles the Bold, duke of Burgundy, who gave him a small force with which to attempt his restoration. Landing at the mouth of the Humber (March 14), he was admitted into York, joined at Coventry by his brother Clarence, who was discontented with the part allotted to him in the treaty with Margaret (March 30), and received into London (April 11), where he sent poor Henry back to the Tower. He now turned to meet Warwick, who was defeated at Barnet, and left dead upon the battle-field (April 14), the site of which is still marked by an obelisk at the parting of the two great north roads.

But his empty title of "King-Maker" forms in the page of history a more enduring monument of the worthlessness of power, wealth, talent, and favor, when not steadily applied to the one object of the public good.

On the same day Queen Margaret and her son landed at Weymouth with a small French force, and soon gathered an army in the west. Edward hastened to meet her on the fatal field of Tewkesbury (May 4), where the Lancastrians lost their last battle and the life of their young prince, who was foully murdered after the fight. He was taken prisoner in the battle and brought before the king, who, with an insulting manner, asked him how he dared invade his dominions. Prince Edward, a noble youth of eighteen, replied, "To recover my father's kingdom and heritage." The savage victor, stung by his boldness, struck him on the face with his gauntlet, and the dukes of Clarence and Gloucester dispatched him with their daggers. Queen Margaret was also taken prisoner in a convent near the battle-field, and was conveyed to the Tower of London. In the same fortress Henry VI. was shortly afterward found dead; and his body was exposed in St. Paul's on the day after Edward's entry into London, May 22, 1471. It is probable that he was murdered, but there is no reason for fixing the guilt on Gloucester rather than on the king. He was venerated by the Lancastrians as a martyr, and it was even proposed to canonize him; but the pope, as Lord Bacon suggests, thought that "a distance should be kept between innocents and saints."

The direct line of Lancaster in the male branch was now extinct, and its adherents were dispersed and attainted. Some few were pardoned: among them Dr. Morton, afterward the powerful bishop of Ely, and the great lawyer Sir John Fortescue. Edward seemed free to indulge his tastes for voluptuous pleasure and splendid pageantry. But his court was disturbed by quarrels between his brothers Clarence and Gloucester for the inheritance of the Earl of Warwick, which they at length divided; Gloucester marrying Anne, the younger daughter of Warwick.

In 1475 Edward invaded France, relying on the aid of his brother-in-law Charles of Burgundy; but the duke kept aloof, and Louis XI., in a personal interview at Pecquigni, near Amiens, bought over Edward with 75,000 crowns and a promise of 50,000 annually, besides paying 50,000 more for the ransom of Queen Margaret. That noble-spirited but unhappy princess died in 1482.

The rest of Edward's reign was spent in the indolence of a worn-out voluptuary, relieved only by the cruelty which is so often combined with selfish pleasure. The most conspicuous, among many victims, was the king's own brother, the Duke of Clarence.

Edward had never quite forgiven his alliance with Margaret and the Nevilles. He had quarreled with Gloucester, and he had offended the queen. They resolved on his destruction. First, two of his friends were executed on absurd charges of witchcraft and treason; and Clarence's open indignation at their death was construed into a threat against the king. Edward appeared in person against him before the peers, who readily condemned him; and, ten days later, he was *found dead*, like Richard II. and Henry VI., in the Tower, Feb. 18, 1478. The popular rumor that he was drowned in a butt of malmsey, is a significant satire on the horrid mixture of pleasure and cruelty which characterized the reign of Edward.

In 1480 a war broke out with Scotland. That kingdom had been a prey to disorder ever since the captivity of James I. Restored by the policy of the Duke of Bedford in 1424, James had been killed by a conspiracy of his nobles in 1436. His successor, James II., had ended a reign which was almost a constant civil war, by the bursting of a gun at the siege of Roxburgh, then held by the English, 1460. His son, James III., having abandoned himself to low-born favorites, on attaining his majority (1478) had imprisoned his brothers, the Duke of Albany and the Earl of Mar. Mar was put to death, 1479, while Albany escaped and found an ally in England. Edward IV. had, in 1474, betrothed his infant daughter Cecilia to the infant son of James; and the stipulated installments of the dowry had been paid in advance till 1478, when Edward broke off the treaty, preferring a more splendid alliance with the dauphin of France. He now renewed his claim of suzerainty over Scotland, which Albany admitted. The war resulted in Albany's submission to his brother, and in the permanent gain to England of Berwick-upon-Tweed (1482).

Edward's treachery toward James was retorted upon himself by Louis XI., who, in 1483, broke off the marriage contract between the dauphin and the Princess Cecilia. While preparing to avenge the insult Edward was seized with an illness, the fruit of his excesses, and died on the 9th of April, 1483, in the 42d year of his age. He was buried beneath the newly-erected chapel of St. George, at Windsor, in which royal sepulchre the remains of Henry VI. were afterward interred:

> "And blended lie the oppressor and th' opprest."

His vices have been already noticed. They were associated with a freedom of manner which gained him popularity, and they did not destroy, at least till late in his reign, the energy and courage by which he won and kept his crown.

EDWARD V. (April 9 to June 22, 1483), the fourth child, but eldest son, of Edward IV., was born in the sanctuary at Westminster, during his father's brief exile, Nov. 4, 1470. He was, therefore, in his 13th year when he succeeded to the crown. He kept a court, as Prince of Wales, at Ludlow, under the care of his uncle the Earl of Rivers. Richard duke of Gloucester, whom the late king had named regent, was at York, whence he marched to oppose the pretensions of the queen-mother to the regency. At Stony Stratford (April 30) he fell in with the king, who was on his way to London, attended by Lord Rivers and other relatives and partisans of the Woodvilles, whom he seized and sent prisoners to the north, while he conducted Edward to London and lodged him in the Tower, May 4. There the king was soon joined by his brother the Duke of York, whom the queen-mother reluctantly gave up from her sanctuary at Westminster. Richard was appointed protector by a great council of prelates, nobles, and citizens; and he at once began to prepare for his own usurpation. Of his former friends Lord Hastings alone refused to lend himself to the plot. Shakspeare has immortalized the strange scene, first related by Sir Thomas More, who received it from Bishop Morton, an eye-witness, how Richard, with affected rage, at the council-board charged Lord Hastings with plotting against his life by sorcery, in conjunction with Jane Shore, the mistress of the late king; and how Hastings was dragged out into the court-yard of the Tower, where his head was struck off upon a log of wood, June 13. A few days afterward Lord Rivers and his fellow-prisoners were executed at Pontefract.

On Sunday, June 22, Dr. Ralph Shaw, brother of the lord mayor, proclaimed, in a sermon at Paul's Cross, the protector's title to the crown, on the ground that Edward IV. was already married when he espoused Elizabeth Woodville, whose children were therefore illegitimate; and this very day, which had been fixed for the king's coronation, is named in the records as that of his deposition. On the 26th the citizens, headed by the lord mayor and the Duke of Buckingham, waited on Gloucester at his house of Baynard's Castle, with a formal offer of the crown.

RICHARD III. (1483–1485) began his reign with a deed of blood which has thrown all his other atrocities into the shade—the murder of Edward V., and his brother the Duke of York, in the Tower. The story related in the next reign by some of the actors in the deed has been doubted because the Lancastrian authorities always blacken the memory of their opponents, and of Richard in particular, and also because it was the interest of Henry VII. to make out a tale which should disprove the pretensions of Perkin

Warbeck. But these objections are too vague; and the common story was confirmed, in 1674, by the discovery of the bones of two youths under a staircase in the White or "Bloody" Tower. These were interred in Westminster Abbey, by order of Charles II., as the remains of the murdered princes.

The whole character of Richard and his government has likewise been the subject of warm controversy. Those who exalt him into a wise and beneficent ruler are probably influenced chiefly by a natural reaction against the popular picture of the cruel monster "Crookback," deformed alike in body, mind, and soul. The fact seems to be that his person was somewhat insignificant, and one shoulder was slightly raised above the other. He shared the impetuous courage of his brother, as well as his cruel temper and unscrupulous ambition, unrelieved, however, by his gayety. He adhered steadily to Edward, and served with distinction in the civil wars and in the war with Scotland as Warden of the Marches. He shared with the nobility and the people in general in jealousy of the Woodvilles, who are known to have planned his exclusion from all power.

Ascending the throne in the 33d year of his age, he enacted in his only parliament, 1484, various laws for the better administration of justice and the protection of commerce, laws among the best of those made by the Plantagenets. But his energies were demanded by the schemes of the Lancastrians, who had remained safe abroad during the reign of Edward. They had now found a leader in Henry earl of Richmond, the son of Edmund Tudor (son of Catherine, the queen of Henry V., by her second husband Sir Owen Tudor) and of Margaret, the great-grand-daughter of John of Gaunt, by his irregular, but afterward legitimatized, marriage with Catherine Swynford.

Genealogy of Henry of Richmond and of the Duke of Buckingham.

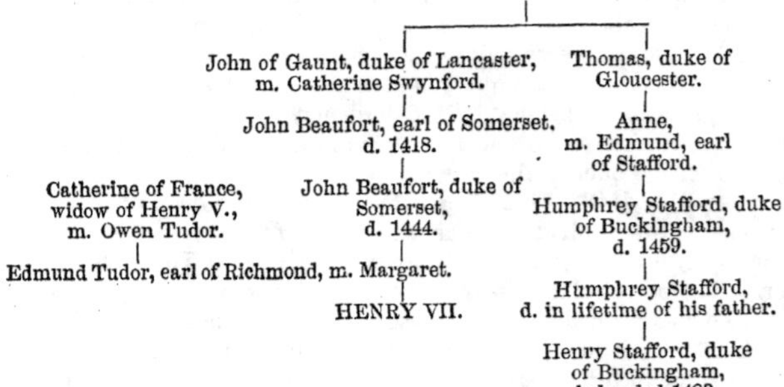

Richmond was also supported by the party of Queen Elizabeth, who had the death of her sons and brother to avenge; and the policy of Morton bishop of Ely devised a happy plan for reconciling the houses of York and Lancaster by proposing a marriage between Richmond and the Princess Elizabeth of York, eldest daughter of Edward IV. Morton also won over the Duke of Buckingham, who had mainly contributed to place Richard on the throne, while the queen-dowager secretly obtained money in the city and sent it over to Richmond in Brittany.

In 1483 Buckingham raised the standard of revolt in Wales; but a flood of the Severn checked his progress, his troops deserted him, and he was taken prisoner and executed at Salisbury, Nov. 1, while Richmond was driven back by a storm from the coast of Dorset. After the death of Richard's queen and his only son, in the following year, he is said to have proposed to marry the Princess Elizabeth himself, and to have obtained the consent of the queen-dowager; but he publicly denied having formed the scheme. Richmond, upon hearing the report, resolved on a new attempt. He sailed from Harfleur on the 1st of August, landed at Milford Haven on the 7th, and advanced through Wales into Staffordshire, gaining partisans; while Richard drew to a head at Nottingham. At length the two armies met at MARKET-BOSWORTH, near Leicester, Aug. 22, 1485. Richmond had 6000 men, and Richard twice as many; but the balance was restored by a force of 7000 under the constable, Lord Stanley, who held aloof till the crisis of the battle, and then decided the victory by taking part with Richmond. Richard was slain fighting with the courage of despair, and seeking to encounter Richmond hand to hand. His body, thrown like a pack across a horse, was carried into Leicester amidst the insults of the populace, and buried in the church of the Grey Friars (Aug. 25). His successor honored him with a mean tomb, which was rifled at the suppression of the monastery, and his stone coffin is said to have been long used as the horse-trough of an inn.

Thus ended the house of York, and with it the dynasty of the Plantagenets, during whose rule of 330 years England had become, in all essential points, the land of constitutional liberty and one of the first powers of the world in arms and commerce, arts and literature. No small advance was made even under the house of York. One most interesting feature of the legislation of these 24 years is seen in the careful enactments for regulating commerce, though on false principles which have only been abandoned in the present generation. In finance Edward IV. introduced the forced gifts strangely called *benevolences*, which a parliament of Richard declared illegal. The short and troubled reign of Richard III. was marked by many important enactments and administrative improvements; and his are the first statutes couched in the English language and embodied in a *printed* form.

Indeed, the great glory of the age was the *introduction of printing into England by* William Caxton, under the patronage of the Lord Rivers who was executed by Richard III. Born at London, about 1412, Caxton learned the art of printing in his intercourse as a merchant with the Continent, and adopted it as his calling. He set up his press in the Almonry at Westminster, in 1477, and died probably in 1492. He issued about sixty-four works, nearly all in English, the last of which bears date in 1490.

Earl Rivers presenting Caxton to Edward IV.

Henry VII.'s Trial of Weights and Measures.

CHAPTER XV.

THE HOUSE OF TUDOR—HENRY VII. A.D. 1485-1509.

We have now reached one of the great *epochs* or turning-points in the history, not only of England, but of Europe and the world. The most natural division between the Middle Ages and Modern History is at this point. The taking of Constantinople by the Turks, in 1453, had destroyed the last remnant of the Roman empire in the East, at the very time when the feudal institutions which had succeeded it in the West were themselves giving way before the growth of commerce and knowledge, and the gigantic power of the press. The supremacy of the great nobles, impaired by their own quarrels, had begun to yield, on the one side, to the authority of the crown, and on the other to the increasing wealth and independence of the people, especially as banded together in the towns. This change led to the substitution of great military sovereignties for the limited monarchies of the Middle Ages in most of the states of Europe, and indeed to some degree in England. The havoc made among the nobility by the Wars of the Roses had left a void in the plan of the state, of which the high-spirited and crafty Tudors were only too ready to step in and take possession; and much of the peculiar character of the history of England, during the next two centuries (1485-1688), results from the efforts of the haughty princes and their feeble imitators, the Stuarts, to assert a prerogative which the Plantagenets never claimed. But these efforts were counterbalanced, and in the end overmastered, by the popular element, which was less powerful on the Continent, and which had gained full expression in the privileges of parliament. The final triumph of the people was even advanced by the very cause which at first threw power into the hands of the crown, the weakening of the nobility, who found themselves driven to seek a solid basis for the dignity of their order in the favor of the people.

A change of vast importance also was effected in the relations of the European states to one another, by those wars and treaties which gradually laid the foundation of the system of international law and "balance of power," which strikingly distinguishes modern Europe from the states of the Middle Ages.

The reign of Henry VII. was a period of transition, during which these great changes began to have full play; otherwise its events are of little interest.

Henry Tudor, earl of Richmond, was in his thirtieth year when Sir William Stanley placed on his head the crown which Richard had worn on the field of Bosworth, and the army saluted him as King Henry VII. So weak was his title that he hesitated whether to base it on his descent from John of Gaunt, or on his proposed marriage with Elizabeth of York, or simply on the right of conquest. At a later period he brought all these shreds of a title to eke out each other, but for the present he was content to be king *de facto*. Parliament settled the crown on his heirs "and none other" (Nov. 7, 1485), *before* his marriage with Elizabeth, which took place on Jan. 18, 1486. In consenting to this union Henry took pains to have it known that he in no degree recognized the title of the house of York. In heart and conduct he was a fierce

Lancastrian; and throughout his reign he made the Yorkists suffer from the bitter hatred with which his heart had been hardened in a long youth of adversity and exile.

He began by removing to the Tower Edward Plantagenet, earl of Warwick, the son of George duke of Clarence, and the heir to the pretensions of Richard duke of York; and he confiscated a large portion of the property of the Yorkists by revoking all grants made from the crown since 1454-5, and by the attainder of the richest of the party. Insurrections soon began. The first, in the north, under Lord Lovel, was easily suppressed (1486); but there were two quarters from which more serious dangers threatened. The English settlers, or *English Pale*, who still held their ground against the Celts in IRELAND, remembered the favor which Richard of York had won from them in his lieutenancy; and in Burgundy the Duchess-Dowager Margaret, sister of Edward IV., made it her chief object to disturb what she regarded as Henry's usurpation.

Pretenders were set up to personate princes of the house of York. The first of these was *Lambert Simnel*, a clever boy of about fifteen, son of a baker (or joiner) at Oxford, who was tutored for his part by an Oxford priest named Richard Simon. Giving himself out to be Edward earl of Warwick, who was then a prisoner in the Tower, he was readily received in Ireland by the deputy, Fitzgerald earl of Kildare, and proclaimed, with the common consent of the people, as King Edward VI. In England, Henry exposed the imposture by the public exhibition of the true Earl of Warwick; while he imprisoned the queen-dowager in a nunnery, and forfeited her lands and revenues.

Meanwhile Simnel landed in Lancashire with a force of 2000 Germans, supplied by the Duchess of Burgundy, under the Earl of Lincoln, son of John de la Pole, duke of Suffolk, and of Elizabeth, eldest sister of Edward IV., whom Richard III. had named his heir, and in whose favor the whole plot seems to have been made. They were utterly defeated by Henry at Stoke-upon-Trent, near Newark, Lincoln falling in the battle, and Simnel and his tutor Simon being taken prisoners (June 16, 1487). These mere tools were treated by Henry with contemptuous clemency. Simon was imprisoned; and Simnel was made a scullion in the king's kitchen, and afterward a falconer. The insurrection formed the pretext for vast exactions of money from the Yorkists; while the king permitted the long-delayed coronation of Queen Elizabeth, whom he habitually treated with cold neglect (Nov. 25, 1487).

Though his policy was averse to foreign war, Henry became entangled in an alliance for the defense of the duchy of Brittany against Charles VIII. (1488), who, by marriage with the Duchess

Anne, finally annexed Brittany to France (1491). Affecting great indignation, Henry levied a "benevolence," and obtained a subsidy from parliament for the ever-popular object of a French war. He crossed over to Calais (Oct. 2, 1492), and, by a show of investing Boulogne, he induced Charles to pay him £149,000, and to promise him a yearly pension; thus, as Lord Bacon says, "making profit upon his subjects for the war, and upon his enemies for the peace."

By this treaty Henry also obtained the removal from France of a second pretender more formidable than Simnel—one, respecting whose claims doubts are entertained even to the present day. While the king was preparing for the war with France, a report was spread that Richard duke of York, the younger of the two sons of Edward IV., whose fate was then a mystery, had escaped from the Tower, and had been concealed for some years in France and Portugal. A youth pretending to be this personage had landed in Ireland, where he was received by the late mayor of Cork and other gentlemen (1492); thence he was invited to France by Charles VIII., who now dismissed him, but refused to give him up to Henry. Retiring to Flanders, he was received by the Duchess of Burgundy, with transports of recognition, as her nephew and the true "White Rose of York" (1493). A letter is still extant, written from Dendermonde to Isabella queen of Spain (Aug. 25, 1493), in which "Richard Plantagenet," as he signs himself, relates his own story of his early life. He professes to have been placed in safety by a lord who had been commissioned to destroy him, but he makes no allusion to the fate of Edward V.; nor have the believers in him ever explained how the one brother's death could be reconciled with the other's preservation. If the story of the murder of the young princes in the Tower was true, the pretender could not be Richard duke of York; if false, there was no room for his claim till his brother was accounted for.

The Yorkists, who were in constant communication with Flanders, gave out in England that their envoys had examined, and were satisfied with, the claims of the young man; and the people in general were in suspense. Henry met the danger both with counsel and energy. The murder of the young princes in the Tower was proved by the evidence of two actors in the deed, named Dighton and Forrest, who were, however, let go unpunished; and the envoys of Henry declared at foreign courts the universal belief that the claim of Richard was an imposture, and that he was ascertained to be a native of Tournay named *Pierce Osbeck*, or, by a corrupted pronunciation, *Perkin Warbeck*. At the same time he bribed Sir Thomas Clifford, one of the Yorkist envoys to Flanders, on whose evidence several gentlemen were executed in 1494. On the 7th of January, 1495, Clifford impeached Sir William Stanley, who had saved Henry's life and crowned him on the field of Bosworth, but whose head was now struck off on Tower Hill, and his enormous wealth swept into the king's coffers (Feb. 16). Henry soon afterward paid Stanley's widow (who was his own mother, the Countess of Richmond) the consolation of a visit.

The treachery of Clifford and the fate of Stanley filled the Yorkists with distrust and dismay. In Ireland, too, their influence was destroyed by the new deputy, Sir Edward Poynings, whose laws, embodied in the *Statute of Drogheda* (1495), formed the basis of the whole Irish government till the Union. Its most important provision was, that no bill could be introduced into the Irish parliament till it had first received the approval of the English council. When, therefore, the pretender was expelled from Burgundy, in consequence of a treaty in 1496, he met with no success in Ireland, and took refuge in Scotland with James IV., who gave him the lady Catherine Gordon in marriage; but when James made an incursion with him into England, the people rose against the invader. Henry's levy of a subsidy to repress such invasions led to an insurrection in Cornwall; and an armed force marched toward London, but were defeated on Blackheath (June 22, 1497). In the autumn the pretender appeared in Cornwall, having lost his asylum in Scotland in consequence of a truce between James and Henry. Landing at Whitsand, near Penzance (Sept. 7), he unfurled his banner as King Richard IV., seized on St. Michael's Mount, where he left his wife, and marched against Exeter. Failing to take that city, and losing courage at the approach of the king's army, he took sanctuary at Beaulieu, in the New Forest (Sept. 21). Thence he came forth, under a promise of his life; was brought to the king at Taunton, and sent to London, where he lived in a sort of honorable captivity. He escaped in June, 1498; and, being pursued, took sanctuary at Shene (Richmond), but at last made a public confession of his imposture, and was committed to the Tower. There he formed a mysterious intrigue with his fellow-prisoner, Edward earl of Warwick, to effect their escape, for which both prisoners were condemned to death. Perkin Warbeck was hanged at Tyburn, Nov. 23, and Warwick was beheaded in the Tower, Nov. 28.

This judicial murder of a helpless prince, whose imprisonment of fourteen years from his earliest childhood, had made him a mere idiot, becomes doubly odious when its true motive is understood. Henry had long been negotiating the marriage of his eldest son, Prince Arthur, to Catherine, the daughter of Ferdinand and Isabella of Spain; and Ferdinand, a prince as astute as himself, had written to the king that "he saw no assurance of his succession as long as the Earl of Warwick lived." The marriage was at length completed (Nov. 14, 1501); but Prince Arthur died in the following April; and Henry, unwilling to repay the dowry, or to weaken his alliance with Spain, obtained a dispensation from Pope Julius II. to contract the young widow to his second son, afterward Henry VIII. When, at a later period, Catherine heard of Henry VIII.'s resolution to divorce her, she said that "it was the judgment of God, for her first marriage was made in blood," meaning that of Warwick.

At the same time (1502) the king contracted his daughter Margaret to James IV. of Scotland; and from this marriage, which was celebrated Aug. 8, 1503, sprung the royal houses of Stuart and Brunswick (see the Genealogical Tables). The queen, Elizabeth, died in 1503.

The long struggle of Henry to maintain his title was at length concluded by his disposal of Edmund de la Pole (the surviving grandson of George duke of Clarence), whom he had created Earl of Suffolk, and who fled to Flanders in 1502. In 1506 Henry extorted from the Archduke Philip the Fair, whom a storm had compelled to put in at Weymouth, the surrender of Suffolk, on the promise of his life. Henry kept the promise while he lived, but made the breach of it one of his dying injunctions to his successor. Suffolk's fate was kept in suspense for four years; but at length he was executed in 1513, without the shadow of any other reason, except to cut off the last male of the line of the Plantagenets.

The last years of Henry's life were devoted to his ruling passion of avarice. His former ministers, Cardinal Morton and Sir Reginald Bray, had kept his extortions within some limits; but they were succeeded by two lawyers, Sir Richard Empson and Edmund Dudley, whose names have been immortalized by their rapacity. Their chief exactions were made by straining the penal statutes to the utmost; but even the parliament was subservient enough to choose Dudley for its speaker (1504). Henry is said to have amassed in the vaults of his palace at Shene the sum of £1,800,000.

At that favorite palace, which he had built at the beautiful spot on the Thames since called Richmond, Henry died of consumption (April 25, 1509), in the 52d year of his age and the 24th of his reign; solacing, or alarming, his last hours by a superstitious devotion to that religion "which never calmed in him an angry passion, nor withheld him from a profitable wrong," and by "a feeble attempt to make amends for irreparable rapine by restoring what he could no longer enjoy." He was buried in the splendid chapel which he had added to Westminster Abbey; and which exhibits, with many other edifices of his time, the last stage of the perfection of the Perpendicular style of English architecture.

So long as ability and success form the chief test of merit, Henry

VII. will be admired as a perfect master of the art of "kingcraft." In this light he is viewed by his great historian, Lord Bacon, who, even while laying bare his avarice and cunning, describes Henry VII., Louis XI., and Ferdinand of Aragon as "the *tres magi* of kings of those ages." But he was destitute of every amiable quality, and even the services which he rendered to his country may be traced to a motive of advantage to himself; but still these services were great, and his profound sagacity and constant vigilance brought England safe out of the confusion and almost ruin of the civil wars.

In this reign constitutional liberty was rather restricted than enlarged; and, amidst an increased severity in administering the law, and sometimes straining it to suit the purposes of the court, we light upon an institution, the very name of which has since become justly hateful—the *Star Chamber*, so called from the decorations of the room in the palace of Westminster in which it met. This court is mentioned under Edward III., but it was revived and reorganized by Henry, for the punishment of offenses against the state, more speedily and secretly than by the usual process of law. The regulation of *weights and measures* was an object of Henry's personal attention. The parliament was still occupied with the supposed interests of commerce; and the treaty with Burgundy, called the *Great Intercourse*, greatly facilitated the commercial relations of England with the chief seats of continental trade.

This reign shares the glory of the discovery of the New World. Deprived by a mere accident of the honor of being the patron of Columbus, Henry favored, though on the limited scale dictated by his avarice, the enterprise of Sebastian Cabot, a Venetian settled at Bristol, who, in 1498, discovered Newfoundland, and coasted along the main land of America as far as Florida. In England, as on the Continent, the 15th century closed with the promise of the mighty events which signalized the following age.

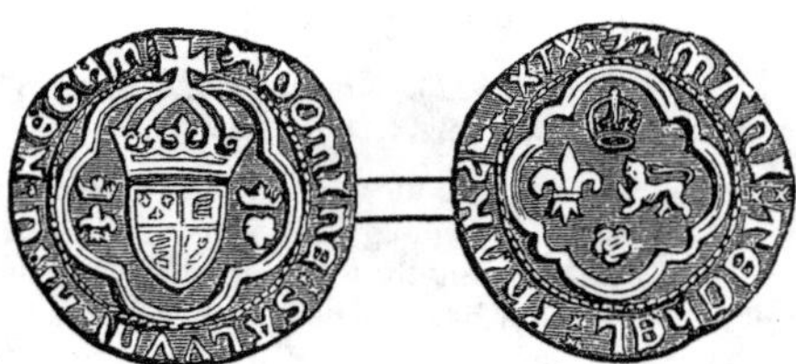

Perkin Warbeck's Groat. A silver coin supposed to have been struck by the Duchess of Burgundy. Preserved in the British Museum.

Henry VIII.

CHAPTER XVI.

THE HOUSE OF TUDOR (*continued*).—HENRY VIII. PERIOD I., TO THE FALL OF WOLSEY. A.D. 1509–1530.

THE new age referred to at the close of the last chapter seemed to be almost personified in the young king who now succeeded to an inheritance which was at length undisputed. The death of Henry VII. was felt as a relief by all his subjects, and the accession of his son was hailed with universal joy. Reuniting in his person the lines of Lancaster and York, he was believed capable of adorning his title with every princely virtue.

HENRY, the second son of Henry VII. and Elizabeth of York, was born at Greenwich on the 29th of June, 1491. On the death of his elder brother Arthur, in 1502, he was created Prince of Wales and betrothed to his brother's widow, Catherine of Aragon, whom he married June 7, 1509, having succeeded to the throne on April 22. The king and queen were crowned at Westminster on June 24, five days before the completion of Henry's 18th year.

His fine person, frank and open countenance, youthful spirit, and proficiency both in martial exercises and in music and other elegant accomplishments, at once commanded the affection of his people, who could not yet see the dangers which lurked beneath his hasty and impetuous temper. In addition to his outward accomplishments, he had received an education far above that of princes in much later times. Having been at first destined by his father to aspire to the papal tiara, he was well versed, not only in polite learning, but in the abstruser studies of theology, and he was diligent in the exercises of devotion.

His first act was to proclaim redress to all who had been injured by the enforcement of obsolete statutes in the late reign, and he gave proof of his sincerity by the imprisonment of Empson and Dudley, who were afterward found guilty of high treason, and executed on Tower Hill, Aug. 18, 1518. The treasures which his father had amassed were employed in maintaining a splendid court, with a succession of pageants and banquets, and of tournaments in which the king was conspicuous among the best lances. His first parliament granted him also a subsidy of "tonnage and poundage" on certain exports and imports.

His chief ministers were *Thomas Howard*, earl of Surrey (afterward duke of Norfolk), the treasurer, and Fox, bishop of Winchester, secretary and privy seal. While the former planned and shared the pleasures of his royal master the latter bore the labor of administration, in which also the king took part with his characteristic energy.

But among the subordinate officers of the court was one destined soon to eclipse all the rest. THOMAS WOLSEY was born in 1471 at Ipswich, where his father, "an honest poor man," acquired a competence in trade; but his having been a butcher is doubtful. The son was educated at Magdalen College, Oxford, where he took his degree of Bachelor of Arts as early as his fifteenth year, and hence was called the "Boy Bachelor." By the interest of powerful patrons he became parson of Lymington in 1500, and one of the royal chaplains in 1505. Henry VII. sent him as a confidential messenger to the Emperor Maximilian, whose daughter the king proposed to marry after the death of Queen Elizabeth, 1507; and Wolsey's speed and address in this mission procured him the deanery of Lincoln (Feb. 2, 1508). At the accession of Henry VIII. we find him royal almoner, a post which gave him free access to the king, whose pleasures he shared with a complaisance scarcely clerical. By his own skill as a courtier, and the influence of his patron, Bishop Fox, who saw in him an invaluable supporter, he obtained a seat at the council, and was made canon of Windsor and registrar of the order of the Garter (1510), prebendary of York (1511), and dean of York and abbot of St. Albans (1512); and he now became the most confidential adviser of the king.

After two years of peace and pleasure the young king found a wider field for his activity and ambition. Europe was convulsed by the conflicts of the powerful and able sovereigns, the Emperor Maximilian, Louis XII. of France, and Ferdinand of Aragon, who, by his union with Isabella of Castile, and by the conquest of Granada from the Moors, had founded the Spanish monarchy; while the sagacious and warlike pontiff, Julius II., threw his weight into which scale he pleased. Louis XII., succeeding Charles VIII. in 1498, had carried on his schemes in Italy, and conquered the duchy of Milan; while his attempt on Naples had resulted in adding that kingdom to the dominions of Ferdinand. In 1508 Louis formed, with Maximilian, Ferdinand, and the pope, the League of Cambrai against Venice, and stripped her of her possessions in Lombardy. But now Pope Julius changed sides, and formed "the Holy League" against France, with Ferdinand, Maximilian, the Venetians, and the Swiss (Oct. 9, 1511); and into this league Henry VIII. was drawn by the pope, who held out to him the hope of obtaining the title of *Most Christian King*, which had hitherto belonged to the crown of France. The decision was not taken without a grave debate in the council, where sage advisers already indicated the true policy of England, to abstain from continental wars and to seek for power on the sea. Henry obtained from parliament a subsidy of two-tenths and two-fifteenths, and declared war against France (June 3, 1512). No honor was gained in this campaign. A small force which Henry sent to Spain, by the advice of Ferdinand, in the hope of recovering Guienne, was kept inactive while Ferdinand overran Navarre, and the army returned greatly weakened by disease (Dec.). Meanwhile the admiral, Sir Edward Howard, wasted the French coasts, and fought an action off Brest, which was claimed as a victory, though the *Regent*, the largest ship in the English navy, was burnt (Aug. 12, 1512). To replace her, the king built the largest ship yet known, the *Henri Grace Dieu;* but he lost the gallant admiral, Sir Edward Howard, in a new attack on Brest, April 25, 1513. The two nations continued to make incursions on each other's shores;

and the importance which naval warfare now began to acquire is attested by an act of parliament, ordering fortifications to be built along the coast between Plymouth and Land's End (1512).

The death of Pope Julius II., who was succeeded by the renowned LEO X. (Feb., 1513), broke up the league against France; but Henry, burning to avenge his disgraces, made a new treaty with the Emperor Maximilian, and, crossing to Calais in person (July 30, 1513), he joined his ally at Terouanne (Aug. 12). Henry's gorgeous display of cloth of gold and trappings contrasted strikingly with the plain simplicity of the veteran Maximilian, who humored the young king by serving under the cross of St. George, while he really directed the campaign. The English and French cavalry encountered on the Lis, near Guinegate, where the latter were seized with a panic, which gave the victory the name of the *Battle of the Spurs* (Aug. 16). Satisfied, for the present, with this first taste of martial glory, Henry only used his army of 50,000 men in taking Terouanne (Aug. 22) and Tournay (Sept. 29), the latter of which towns gave a new bishopric to Wolsey; and he returned to England, Nov. 24, 1513.

In the north a far fiercer contest had been ended by a very different battle. James IV. of Scotland, Henry's brother-in-law, and of a spirit as ardent as his own, had many causes of quarrel inflaming his desire to strike a blow against an hereditary enemy. He made a league with the king of France (May 22, 1512), sent a defiance by his herald to Henry before Terouanne; and, against the advice of his best counselors, and even though he received, as was reported, a supernatural warning, he crossed the Tweed with an army of 50,000 men, Aug. 22, 1513. He was encountered by the Earl of Surrey with 26,000 men, and was slain, with the noblest of his chivalry, on the fatal field of FLODDEN at the foot of the Cheviots, Sept. 9. This was the greatest defeat of Scotland in the long wars between the two countries; and, in our own age, the victory of England has been celebrated by the highest poetical genius of Scotland.

In the following year peace was made both with Scotland and with France; and Henry's youngest sister, Mary, was married to Louis XII., Oct. 9, 1514. Left a widow within three months, by the death of Louis (Jan. 1, 1515), she secretly espoused Charles Brandon, duke of Suffolk, a favorite of Henry, who was reconciled to the match by Wolsey. From this union descended the gifted and unfortunate claimant of the crown, Lady JANE GREY. (See genealogical table.)

During these transactions the internal government had been administered with great ability, and several important enactments were made. The old sumptuary laws were modified (1510); "benefit of clergy" was taken from murderers and felons (1512); the Trinity House was established for the encouragement of navigation (1514); and the great controversy was renewed respecting the exemption of the clergy from the jurisdiction of the royal courts (1515).

The year 1515 forms an epoch in the reign of Henry VIII., both at home and abroad, and several new actors appear upon the stage. First, at home, WOLSEY had now reached the plenitude of his power. Created Bishop of Lincoln, Feb. 6, 1514, and Archbishop of York, Aug. 5, 1514, he now received from Pope Leo X., in compliment to Henry, a cardinal's hat, Sept. 11, 1515, which was soon followed by his appointment as papal legate, 1516. He afterward received also the bishopric of Winchester. He was made chancellor of England on the resignation of Warham, archbishop of Canterbury (Dec., 1515); and he now entered with the king upon the path of arbitrary government, *no parliament being summoned from* 1515 *to* 1523. It must be remembered, too, that he was the representative of the principle of *papal supremacy* in the realm of England. In France Louis XII. was succeeded by FRANCIS I., a young prince in his 21st year, resembling Henry in his gay and ardent spirit and in many points of character. The death of Ferdinand, in 1516, placed the crowns of Spain, Naples, and the Netherlands, and of the Spanish discoveries in the New World, on the head of his grandson, Charles I., who soon became the Emperor CHARLES V. So that, instead of the trio of astute old politicians, Henry VII., Louis XI., and Ferdinand—the "*tres magi*" of Lord Bacon—the fate of Europe rested on the friendships and enmities of three young and gifted competitors in a new and open conflict of ambition. Charles was the youngest of the three, having been born in the year 1500; but nature had endowed him with the subtilty and self-command which Henry and Francis wanted. The keys of St. Peter were held by Leo X., a pontiff as magnificent and able as these kings. Above all, MARTIN LUTHER, now in his thirty-third year, was already prepared—unknown to himself and the world—to maintain the principles before which emperor, kings, and pope must bow. His final breach with the papacy occurred in 1520.

Francis I., having inaugurated his reign by the victory of Marignano, in which he recovered the Milanese (Sept. 13, 1515), sought the friendship of England through the medium of Wolsey. Leo X. exhorted the princes of Christendom to a general agreement, as the basis of which a solemn league was made between Francis and Henry, who restored Tournay and betrothed his infant daughter Mary to the infant dauphin (1518).

On the death of the Emperor Maximilian, Jan. 12, 1519, the kings of France and Spain became candidates for the empire; while Henry sent an envoy, Pace, to the Continent, less with the view of urging his own claim, which was scarcely consistent with the laws of the empire, than in the hope of excluding both the others. The election fell on the king of Spain, who, as the Emperor CHARLES V., added to a power little less than that of Charlemagne in the old world the vast resources of the new, with a mind trained by the precepts of Machiavelli. To recover the dominions of Charlemagne was a natural object of his ambition; and Francis, therefore, had reason to fear as well as hate his successful rival. Henry seemed in a position to hold the balance between them. Both courted his alliance; and, while Francis prepared for a set interview, Charles landed at Hythe, on his voyage from Spain to Flanders, kept Whitsuntide with Henry at Canterbury, and gained over Wolsey by the promise of his influence toward securing him the papacy—a promise which he twice broke.

Charles sailed from Sandwich, May 31, 1520, and on the same day Henry crossed from Dover to Calais. On the 7th of June Francis met him in a field within the English territory, which, from the gorgeous array of the two courts, has obtained the name of the *Field of the Cloth of Gold.* An original picture of the scene is preserved at Hampton Court. The kings, who were the goodliest persons in either host, met on horseback, and embraced with the warmest professions of regard; and the festivities were continued till Midsummer-day. Henry then returned the visit of the emperor at Gravelines, and entertained him at Calais. The result of these interviews was seen in the following year, when Wolsey, while presiding over a pretended mediation at Calais between the emperor and the king of France, secretly visited Charles at Bruges, and concluded an alliance against Francis (Aug., 1521).

The same year witnessed two events of deep significance in connection with Henry's future life. The first was the execution of Stafford duke of Buckingham, a descendant of Edward III., for some unguarded expressions, alleged to have been uttered by him, about his title to the crown. The other was the publication of the king's book, "On the Seven Sacraments," in opposition to Luther, which gained for him and his successors, by a bull of Leo X., the title of "Defender of the Faith" (*Fidei Defensor*)—a title still so prized by a Protestant people that the florin of 1849 had to be recoined because the letters F. D. were omitted in the legend. Shortly afterward Leo X. died, and was succeeded by Adrian VI., a Fleming, who had been tutor to the emperor.

In 1522 Charles again visited England, consoled Wolsey for his disappointment, and persuaded Henry to declare war against France (June). While an invading army, under the Earl of Surrey, did little but return to Calais with great booty, Francis intrigued for diversions in Ireland and Scotland. In the former country the Earl of Desmond, who was to raise the standard of York in favor of Richard de la Pole, was left by Francis without the promised succors; and in Scotland, Albany, regent for the infant JAMES V., was compelled by Lord Dacre to make a disgraceful peace. Meanwhile the war languished for want of money; and, after obtaining a large sum by "benevolence," Henry convened a parliament, after an interval of seven years since the last (April 15, 1523).

Before this parliament, of which the great Sir THOMAS MORE was speaker, Wolsey appeared in person, demanding the enormous sum of £800,000; but they would only grant half, and, when Wolsey attempted to argue with the House, they maintained the privilege of confining all discussion to their own members—a memorable protest and precedent against every attempt of the crown to take part in the debates, in person or by deputy. Henry dissolved the parliament, and governed without one for another seven years; and he levied in one year the subsidy which the parliament had made payable in four. Another fruitless invasion of France was made by Charles Brandon, duke of Suffolk, while Surrey advanced into Scotland and took Jedburgh, Sept. 24, 1523.

On the same day Pope Adrian VI. died, and Wolsey suffered another disappointment in the election of Giuglio de' Medici, CLEMENT VII., a devoted partisan of Charles V. Wolsey now inclined to peace with France; but the defeat and captivity of Francis at the fatal battle of Pavia (Feb. 24, 1525) so revived Henry's ambition to reconquer France that he proposed to the emperor a plan for a joint invasion. The sounder policy of Charles led him to restore Francis to his throne, exacting the cession of Burgundy, the very bait which had been offered by Henry, with other hard conditions (March 17, 1526). Meanwhile, on the emperor's refusal to invade France, Henry had made a treaty with the queen-mother as regent, who engaged to pay him 2,000,000 crowns in installments, besides an annual pension of 100,000 more (Aug. 30, 1525). Another treaty was negotiated by Wolsey, in 1527, by which Henry, in consideration of a payment of 50,000 crowns, engaged to renounce forever all pretensions to the crown of France.

Events of vast moment were meanwhile ripening at home. The illegal attempts to raise money for the invasion of France (1525) had led to open rebellion, which was pacified by the withdrawal of the proposed taxes. The blame was thrown on Wolsey, whose vast wealth and unbounded ostentation at length excited the jealousy of the king, as they had long made him odious to the people. The costly peace-offering which the cardinal made, by presenting his master with the princely residence of *Hampton Court*, only whetted the king's appetite for what was left; and the desire once felt, to shake off the influence of his too powerful minister, was soon ripened by circumstances which called all the passions of the king's nature to the aid of a new policy.

Henry had become weary of his wife as well as of his minister. Catherine of Spain had the grave temper of her nation, was six years older than the king, and all their children, except the Princess Mary, had died young. The king professed to regard their deaths as a divine judgment on him for the offense of marrying his brother's widow; but even he himself would have failed to distinguish the voice of conscience from the sense of disgust, had not his scruples been quickened by his new passion for the Lady Anne Boleyn, a young and beautiful gentlewoman of the queen's suite. It was in the summer of 1527 that Henry first avowed the design of divorcing Catherine and marrying Anne Boleyn. He submitted his scruples to the pope, through his secretary, Knight. Clement, who had been made prisoner to the emperor at the taking of Rome by his ally the constable Bourbon (June 7, 1527), and looked to Henry for his deliverance, gave a favorable reply; but his tone was less decided when he recovered his liberty. In 1528 he granted a commission to the cardinals Wolsey and Campeggio, who cited the king and queen before their court, May 31, 1529. Both appeared; but the queen protested against her judges, and appealed to the pope (June 18). At the next sitting (June 21), instead of answering to her name, she threw herself at Henry's feet and made a pathetic appeal to him, after which she left the court and refused to appear again. The trial was protracted to June 30, when Campeggio suddenly adjourned it to October 1; and in a few days both parties were cited to appear, in person or by proxy, before the pope at Rome. This step was taken through the influence of Charles V., Catherine's nephew and protector; but Henry threw the blame on Wolsey, who had been a warm supporter of the divorce, in the hope of marrying the king to a French princess. But other causes were already working his fall. Henry's was just the temper to take up the old quarrel of Henry II. against the supremacy of Rome, which had been ostentatiously represented in the person of Wolsey. On the very day when the cardinal opened the court of chancery for a new term (Oct. 29, 1529), an indictment of *præmunire* was laid against him in the court of King's Bench by the king's attorney, charging him with receiving papal bulls. On Oct. 17 the great seal was taken from him and given to Sir Thomas More, and he was ordered to retire to Esher from his archiepiscopal palace of York House, which was seized by Henry, and became afterward the palace of Whitehall. On the 18th of October the court of King's Bench sentenced him to imprisonment and the forfeiture of his goods. Henry now sent him a ring, with a consoling message (Nov. 2). Next day parliament met, and agreed to an address, charging Wolsey with many grave offenses, which the king refused to receive; and he afterward showed special favor to Wolsey's old servant, Thomas Cromwell, who defended him in the House of Commons.

Wolsey was left in possession of the archbishopric of York and of part of the revenues of the see of Winchester, and received a full pardon (Feb., 1530). He was soon ordered to reside within his archbishopric, where he spent his time in the observances of religion and hospitality. But suddenly he was arrested at Cawood on a new charge of treason, founded on his correspondence with the pope and the king of France (Nov. 2). His health broke down upon the journey; and as he entered the abbey of Leicester (Nov. 26), he said, "Father abbot, I am come hither to leave my bones among you." On the second day he addressed to Sir William Kingston, lieutenant of the Tower, the memorable words, "If I had served God as diligently as I have done the king, He would not have given me over in my gray hairs"—a self-condemning apology; for that only is true service to man which is based on the service due to God. He added words of deep and prophetic interest, from his knowledge of the king: "He is a prince of royal courage, and hath a princely heart; and rather than he will miss or want any part of his will or pleasure, he will endanger the loss of the one-half of his realm. I warn you; be well assured and advised what ye put into his head, for ye shall never put it out again." That he served a prince of such a temper, and kept him from becoming what he afterward became, has been urged as his best eulogy. His character has been painted by Shakspeare in lines which no feebler hand should try to copy. The most sober reflections on his fate are those of his faithful servant and biographer George Cavendish: "Here is the end and fall of pride and arrogancy of men exalted by fortune to dignities; for I assure you, in his time, he was the haughtiest man in all his proceedings alive; having more respect to the honor of his person than he had to his spiritual profession, wherein should be showed all meekness, humility, and charity, the discussing whereof any further I leave to divines." He died the day after the scene just related, on the 29th of November, 1530, in the 60th year of his age.

Henry VIII. delivering the Bible to Cranmer and Cromwell. (Being a portion of the engraved title-page of Cranmer's or the Great Bible.)

CHAPTER XVII.

THE HOUSE OF TUDOR (*continued*).—HENRY VIII. PERIOD II. A.D. 1529–1536. THE FIRST ENGLISH REFORMATION.

WOLSEY'S dying speech to Sir William Kingston concluded with a long and earnest injunction to the king "that he have a vigilant eye to depress *this new sort of Lutherans*." These words showed a prescience of the great religious change which was already in progress, and of which Wolsey himself was in part the victim. The very year of his fall (1529) was that in which the German princes and deputies of cities who favored the Reformation laid before the diet at Speyer the *Protestation*, which has conferred on them and their followers to this day the name of "PROTESTANTS."

In England the abuses of the church were as gross as on the Continent, and the doctrines of Wickliffe had never been entirely forgotten. One of the earliest English reformers of this age was

WILLIAM TYNDALE, who left England in 1524, repaired to Luther at Wittemberg, and there translated the Gospels and Epistles into English. Thence he removed to Antwerp, and, in conjunction with other English refugees, set up a printing-press for the supply of copies of his Testament and of the tracts of Wickliffe and other early reformers. The king was warned of danger from this quarter in 1525. In 1526 a few thorough adherents of the principles of the Reformation had formed themselves into a society called "the Christian Brotherhood," chiefly with the object of disseminating these tracts and copies of the New Testament.

The new ideas had found their way into the University of Cambridge, whence they were imported into Oxford by some scholars whom Wolsey himself had invited to professorships in his magnificent foundation of "Cardinal's College," afterward called Christchurch (1527). Wolsey applied himself to the rooting out of these heresies; and among those cited before him appears the name of HUGH LATIMER, who was, however, dismissed with a show of favor. Others made a public recantation, and many copies of the obnoxious books were committed to the flames; but as yet the persons of the heretics were spared, and Wolsey's mild measures were attended with no small appearance of success.

Besides these genuine Protestants, who gave a hearty assent to the doctrines of the Reformation, there was a large party that felt disgust at the abuses of the church, the wealth and pomp which overloaded it, and the profligacy of many among the clergy. To this was added so strong a jealousy of the supremacy of the pope within the realm that even Wolsey declared, when Henry was cited to Rome in the matter of his divorce, that a king of England could only appear there at the head of his army.

The king's own mind had been turned, as we have seen, to the disputed questions; and, though he strongly maintained to the last the chief points of Roman Catholic doctrine, he had every temptation to side with the Protestants in the political part of the controversy. The question was at length brought to an issue by his love for Anne Boleyn, who had a strong leaning to the reformed faith, and by the obstacles raised to his divorce through the machinations of the emperor and the pope. Still he abstained from precipitate measures; and, though the new council for the most part represented the views of the queen's friends, the highest officer of state, the chancellor Sir Thomas More, was a stanch adherent to the old opinions, and a much more active persecutor of the Protestants than Wolsey. "With Wolsey heresy was an error; with More it was crime: and no sooner had the seals changed hands than the Smithfield fires recommenced."

Amidst such a state of feeling the parliament assembled which first established the Protestant Church of England under the supremacy of the king (Nov. 3, 1529). Their first act was to draw up a petition, complaining of the growth of heresy, and ascribing it to abuses in the government of the church, which they laid before the king at great length, for "redress, reformation, and remedy." In spite of the opposition of the prelates, headed by FISHER bishop of Rochester, the great leader, with More, of the old high Catholic party, the chief points of the petition were embodied in enactments restraining the arbitrary powers of the bishops' courts, and checking the pluralities and non-residence of the clergy. The session ended on Dec. 17, 1529.

Meanwhile the temporizing policy of Pope Clement was urging Henry on to the extreme course of withdrawing the question of the divorce from his jurisdiction. At length a Cambridge Doctor, THOMAS CRANMER, who now appears in our history at the age of forty, suggested an appeal to the universities of Europe on the legality of a marriage with a deceased brother's wife. The replies were unfavorable to Henry from those universities of Germany and Italy which were under the influence of the Protestants and imperialists, but favorable from the rest. His ally, Francis, overawed the university of Paris into giving the desired answer; and he himself used direct intimidation to the reluctant theologians of Oxford and Cambridge, telling them, under his own hand, that "they had better not stir up a hornet's nest" (1530).

The replies of the universities were laid before parliament, March 30, 1531. They had already, in this new session, taken bolder measures against the clergy and the pope. An act was passed, including the whole body of the clergy under the penalties of *præmunire* for their submission to Wolsey's authority as legate; and they were only pardoned on payment of £180,000. At the same time they were made to confess, by an act of convocation, that THE KING WAS THE PROTECTOR AND SUPREME HEAD OF THE CHURCH AND CLERGY OF ENGLAND, *in so far as is permitted by the law of Christ*—a saving clause carried by Fisher. In the next session, 1532, the power of levying *annates*, or first-fruits on bishops' sees, in favor of the pope, was transferred to the king, and the clergy were commanded to disregard all spiritual censures from Rome for obedience to these enactments. The ecclesiastical revolution was completed by the consent of the convocation of the clergy to surrender their legislative powers. Sir Thomas More's resignation of the great seal (May 16, 1532) proved his own honesty and the discouragement of the Catholic party.

Much of this year (1532) was spent in fruitless negotiations with the pope and emperor concerning the divorce. At length, having renewed his alliance with Francis I. by a personal interview at Calais, Henry celebrated a private marriage with Anne Boleyn (Jan. 25, 1533), who had long resided in his palace with all the state of a queen, and had been created Marchioness of Pembroke in the preceding autumn.

The parliament which met in February passed the "Act of Appeals," forbidding appeals to Rome from the ecclesiastical courts. In cases touching the king and royal family the final appeal was to the prelates in the upper house of convocation. Accordingly, the convocation which met in April decided the questions submitted to them in Henry's favor; and Cranmer, who had just succeeded Warham as Archbishop of Canterbury (March 30, 1533), held a court at Dunstable, and pronounced the king's marriage with Catherine null and void from the beginning, and that with Anne Boleyn good and lawful (May 25–28). On Saturday, the 31st of May, the new queen entered London in procession, and on the next day she was crowned at Westminster with a splendor that seemed designed to gild over all that was dark and doubtful in the manner of her elevation.

Amidst the acclamations of London there was yet so strong a sympathy with Catherine that Charles V., whom Henry vainly attempted to conciliate, cherished hopes of an insurrection. Catherine herself indignantly refused the title of "Princess Dowager," and made her appeal to the pope, who reversed Cranmer's decision. Henry went through the form of appealing to a general council, but his real confidence was in his own power to defy the pope. On the 7th of September his satisfaction was crowned by the birth of a daughter, who, under the name of ELIZABETH, was destined to wield, with glory and success, the power which she derived from the strong will of Henry. The divorced Queen Catherine died at Kimbolton, Jan. 29, 1536.

The parliament, which met on Jan. 15, 1534, confirmed the divorce of Catherine and the marriage with Anne, settled the succession on her children to the exclusion of the Princess Mary, and made any opposition to this settlement by overt act high treason, and any words spoken against it *misprision of treason*.*

The year 1534 is memorable for the final severance of the Church of England from that of Rome, and the entire emancipation of the English state from all control by the pope; for the two changes, though inseparably connected in fact, must not be confounded. The price paid for the church's liberation from Rome was the

* This term, derived from the old French *mespris* (contempt), was applied to crimes which seemed to partake, by necessary inference, of the character of treason.

transference of her legitimate powers to the state, and her subjection to the authority of the king as her supreme head upon earth. This change must be carefully distinguished from the adoption of the broader principle of liberty of conscience—a principle implied in the claims of the Reformers, but unknown to those who framed the reformed establishment. Wickliffe, it is true, had long since asserted that principle, and it was still cherished by a few obscure Protestants, of whom more will soon be heard. But to Henry and his advisers it was as monstrous as democracy could have been; and we must not be surprised, therefore, at seeing religious persecution not only continued, but urged alike against the heartier supporters of the new faith and the obstinate adherents of the old church polity. These persecutions varied with the king's caprice and the changes of his advisers; but, in the main, they were the natural consequence of Henry's continuing to hold Roman Catholic *doctrine* while he cast off the dominion of Rome. It was the glory of a far later age to give up persecution altogether.

The revolution now described was effected by a series of acts of parliament (25 Hen. VIII. cc. 19–21), depriving the clergy of the power—which they themselves renounced in convocation—to legislate even for internal and spiritual affairs, except in convocation with the king's consent, and annulling all canons which were contrary to the king's prerogative—forbidding all payments to the papal see (all appeals had already been forbidden)—transferring the dispensing power from the pope to the archbishops, and confining it to things not contrary to the law of God—doing away with the confirmation by the pope of the election of bishops, and appointing their election to be made by a *congé d'élire* from the crown—exempting monasteries from episcopal visitation, and placing them under the visitation of the crown—and subjecting all who had recourse to Rome for bulls or other instruments to the penalties of *præmunire.* These measures were accompanied by a solemn declaration, that it was not intended to decline or vary from the congregation of Christ's Church in any things concerning the very articles of the Catholic faith of Christendom, but to preserve the peace and unity of the realm by seeking relief within the realm at the hand of the sovereign, to whom there was no superior. The future relation of England to the see of Rome was thus defined by the convocation of York—"that the bishop of Rome had no more power in England than any other bishop;" and he is described in one of the acts as "the bishop of Rome, otherwise called the pope."

These acts make repeated allusions to the king's supremacy, and one of them thus asserts the independence of the realm, as "recognizing no superior under God, but only your Grace," and as free from all laws but "such as have been ordained within it, or *by sufferance of the king to the people taken by their free liberty*, at their own consent to be used among them, not as the laws of any foreign prince, potentate, or prelate." In the following session (Nov., 1534) these principles were made the law of the land by the celebrated Act of Supremacy (26 Hen. VIII. c. 1), enacting that "the king our sovereign lord, his heirs and successors, kings of this realm, shall be taken, accepted, and reputed THE ONLY SUPREME HEAD IN EARTH OF THE CHURCH OF ENGLAND CALLED ECCLESIA ANGLICANA," which title and style is to be annexed to the imperial crown of this realm, with power to correct all heresies and offenses which may be lawfully reformed by any spiritual authority or jurisdiction. This was followed by an act prescribing anew the form of oath to be taken by all the king's subjects, to observe the act of succession already passed, and making the offense of opposition to the settlement, though only in *words, or withholding any of the king's titles*, no longer misprision of treason only, but *high treason*.

Before the passing of these final acts a violent persecution of the Catholic party had commenced. It was not without the provocation of impending danger. Already, in 1533, the king had been threatened with divine judgment by an enthusiast named Elizabeth Barton, "the Nun of Kent," whose pretended revelations were accepted by certain priests and others, and made the foundation of a plot in favor of the Lady Mary, in which Fisher bishop of Rochester was implicated. In March, 1534, parliament, by an act of attainder, condemned the maid and her chief adherents to death for treason, and Fisher and others to imprisonment for misprision of treason. Next month the news arrived that Pope Clement had given judgment against the king's divorce and his new marriage, and had required his submission, under a penalty of excommunication and deposition, to which the imperialists were preparing to give effect by an invasion of England. A commission was issued to administer the oath to the succession. Fisher and Sir Thomas More refused to take that oath, and were committed to the Tower. On the passing of the enactments above mentioned fresh measures of severity were adopted, and Fisher and More were attainted of high treason.

Toward the end of 1534 Clement VII. was succeeded by PAUL III., a pontiff in the interest of France and disposed to an accommodation with England. But Henry distrusted the sincerity of his overtures, and he was further irritated by a rebellion which had broken out in Ireland. He now gave way more and more to the fierce passions of his nature. The penal laws were enforced alike against heretics and Catholics; and while Tyndale's Bible was burnt at Smithfield, and fourteen Anabaptists suffered by fire (May, 1535), the prior and six monks of the Charterhouse were hanged at Tyburn for the treason of denying the king's supremacy (May and June, 1535). Fisher and More were again summoned to submit, and again refused (May 7); and the pope chose this very juncture for making Fisher a cardinal. Stung by this defiance, the king vowed that he might have the hat, but he should have no head to wear it on. And that head, whitened by the cares of eighty years, was meekly laid on the block at Tower Hill on June 22, 1535.

A more illustrious and blameless victim was next brought before the special commission which had condemned Fisher. On July 1 Sir THOMAS MORE appeared before them at Westminster, tottering on a stick from weakness through his long imprisonment. He exposed, with calm contempt, the false evidence of Richard Rich, charging him with treasonable expressions; but as to the king's supremacy, he simply declared that he had never practiced against it, but he could not consent to it. "I will not meddle," he said, "with any such matters, for I am fully determined to serve God, and to think upon His passion and my passage out of this world." When the horrible doom of treason was passed upon him, but commuted to beheading "by the king's *special mercy*"—"God forbid," said he, "that the king should show any more such mercy to any of my friends." Such flashes of his native wit continued to light up the Christian dignity of his few remaining days. The details of the closing scenes are preserved in the exquisite narrative of his daughter, Margaret Roper, who, on his return to the Tower, rushed through the guards and fell upon his neck. On the 6th of July he was brought out to execution on Tower Hill. The weak scaffold shook as he mounted it. "See me safe up," he said to Sir William Kingston, "for my coming down I can shift for myself." Not being suffered to address the people, he asked their prayers and their witness that he died in the faith of the holy Catholic Church, and a faithful servant of God and the king. When he had prayed, the executioner begged his forgiveness. "Friend," said More, kissing him, "thou art to do me the greatest benefit that I can receive. Pluck up thy spirit, man, and be not afraid to do thine office. My neck is very short; take heed, therefore, that thou strike not awry for saving of thine honesty." After laying his head on the block, he moved aside his beard, remarking, "Pity that should be cut, it has not committed treason." And so he died.

If the cause for which he suffered will not justify More's being called a martyr, his death was none the less a judicial murder; and perhaps we may view it as the "baptism of blood" by which Henry committed himself to the crimes and cruelties of his later years. Its immediate effect, following upon the executions of Fisher and the

Carthusians, was a storm of indignation throughout Europe, which Henry attempted in vain to meet with an elaborate apology. The pope drew up the long-threatened bull of interdict and deposition; but its issue was suspended through the interference of Francis I., who warned his holiness against attempting to deal with the crowns of kings. One result of this fresh quarrel with Rome was to draw Henry into a closer union with the German Protestants.

Sir Thomas Cromwell, secretary of state, who had risen to power soon after the fall of his master Wolsey, and had been the chief agent in all the measures of reformation, was now appointed vicar-general or vicegerent of the king in ecclesiastical matters. He at once issued a commission for a general visitation of the religious houses, universities, and other spiritual corporations of the kingdom. Upon their report, exposing scenes of misrule and immorality, over which the veil of decency must be drawn, parliament suppressed (with a few exceptions) all the monasteries, to the number of 376, whose income was under £200 a year, and gave their revenues to the king, amounting to £32,000 a year, besides goods, chattels, and plate, computed at £100,000 more. The universities, on the other hand, received fresh encouragement by the remission of the payment of first-fruits (March, 1536).

By these acts the parliament, which had sat since 1529, set the seal to its work of reformation. It was dissolved on the 4th of April, 1536. Its other chief acts were to increase the severity of the criminal law. The new and horrible punishment of *boiling to death* was not only enacted, but actually inflicted on poisoners, and vagabonds were to be driven to work by severe whippings. It also completed the union of Wales with England, extending to the people of the principality the English laws and liberties, including parliamentary representation, and enjoining the use of the English language in the courts of justice. The county palatine of Chester had recently received the like privileges.

This middle period of Henry's reign has demanded an attention proportionate to its importance. The eleven troubled and tragic years which remain may be disposed of more briefly in the next chapter.

Wolsey's Half-Groat.

Family of Sir Thomas More.

CHAPTER XVIII.

THE HOUSE OF TUDOR (*continued*). — HENRY VIII. PERIOD III., FROM THE EXECUTION OF ANNE BOLEYN TO THE DEATH OF THE KING. A.D. 1536–1547.

The third period of Henry's reign begins with a deed of blood which has delivered his memory to execration—the execution of Queen Anne Boleyn. Even if the charge of adultery were proved conclusively against her, which it never has been, we should scarcely the less abhor the heartless cruelty which could consign to the block the wife whom he had fondly loved, and for whose sake he had divorced Catherine. We need not dwell on the details of the trial, to which the last pang was added by the queen's seeing her sister-in-law, Lady Rochfort, as her accuser, and her uncle, the Duke of Norfolk, among her judges. By a strange inconsistency, the marriage, for unfaithfulness to which she was condemned, was adjudged by Cranmer to have been void from the first on the ground of a precontract. Her alleged paramours, Sir Francis Weston, Brereton, Norris, and Smeaton, from the last of whom a confession had been obtained, suffered at Tyburn, May 12, 1536; her brother, Lord Rochfort, was executed on Tower Hill, for the like unnatural and improbable crime, May 17; and Queen Anne was beheaded within the Tower, May 19, meeting her fate with pious resignation, and sending messages of duty and affection to the king.

The very next day the king married Jane, the daughter of Sir Thomas Seymour, who had been a lady in the train of Queen Anne, as Anne herself had been in that of Catherine. To Henry's extreme joy she bore him a son and heir, afterward EDWARD VI., Oct. 12, 1537; but the queen died on Oct. 24.

A new parliament, which met on June 8 and sat to July 18, 1536, ratified the late acts, and made a new settlement of the succession on the king's heirs by Jane Seymour; and, in case of their failure, the king might dispose of the crown by will or letters patent. A new act was passed against the authority of the pope; and *the first authorized translation of the Bible*, based on Tyndale's, by MILES COVERDALE, was adopted by the king, and ordered to be placed in every parish church.

The popular discontent at the suppression of the lesser monasteries led to insurrections in Lincolnshire and Yorkshire. The latter, under *Robert Aske* of Doncaster, was called the *Pilgrimage of Grace.* It was joined by the Archbishop of York, Lord Darcy, and other noblemen, and was only put down in 1537, when Darcy was executed, with the other leaders, among whom were several abbots.

The occasion presented by this rebellion was seized for the *suppression of the greater monasteries.* The monks generally propitiated the king by a voluntary retirement. The relics, and particularly those of St. Thomas (à Becket) of Canterbury, were exposed to public insult. The property of the suppressed houses was transferred to the king, who pensioned the abbots and priors, erected the six new bishoprics of Westminster, Oxford, Peterborough, Chester, Gloucester, and Bristol, and enriched his courtiers by large grants. Some of the noblest English houses owe their fortunes to this source.

The pope now fulminated against Henry the bull, which had lain dormant for three years, by which his soul was delivered to Satan and his kingdom to the first invader (Dec. 17, 1538). The emperor and the king of France, who had lately made a truce for ten years (June 28), were in vain urged to carry out the sentence. Henry made a characteristic reply, at the expense of several of the relatives of his kinsman Cardinal Pole, who had lately written a book against him. The Countess of Salisbury, mother of the Cardinal, was attainted and imprisoned, while his brother and several other Catholic nobles were beheaded, 1539. (For the relation of the Poles to the royal family see the genealogical tables.)

This same year, 1539, witnessed a great check to the Reformation. In *doctrine* Henry had always been a Catholic, though the influence of Cromwell and Cranmer, and the preaching of Latimer and other earnest Protestants, seemed to have had an effect upon him, the chief sign of which was his authorizing the general reading of the English Bible. But he now attempted to establish uniformity of opinion; and he caused the new parliament (which met April 28, 1539) to enact the *Statute of the Six Articles*, or, as the Protestants called it, the Bloody Bill. It adopted the Romish doctrines of the real presence, communion in one kind, private masses, vows of chastity, clerical celibacy, and auricular confession, as a part of the national creed, all dissent from which was to be visited with the extreme punishment of heresy. The great adviser of this act was STEPHEN GARDINER, bishop of Winchester, the chief rival of Cranmer and Cromwell. Cranmer opposed the bill in the house, but regained the king's favor by dismissing his wife. Bishops Latimer and Shaxton resigned their sees and were imprisoned, a fate which was shared by 500 persons accused under the new act. Cromwell, however, obtained their liberation, and the king granted some compensation to the Protestants by permitting every family to possess the new translation of the Bible. The parliament of 1539 struck also a heavy blow at the civil constitution by giving to the king's proclamations the same force as acts of parliament.

Cromwell was meanwhile planning to draw Henry closer to the Protestant princes of the Continent by his union with Anne, daughter of John III., duke of Cleves. The marriage took place Jan. 6, 1540; but Henry conceived, at the first sight, an aversion to his bride, who could not even converse with him, as she only spoke Dutch. The marriage was pronounced invalid by convocation, on the ground of a pre-contract (July 10), and dissolved by parliament (July 24), with the consent of Anne, who accepted a pension of £3000, with rank next to the royal family. She died at Chelsea in 1557, and was buried in Westminster Abbey.

The divorce of Anne was accompanied by the fall of Cromwell, whose enemies, embittered by the suppression of the monasteries, had a powerful leader in the Duke of Norfolk. The duke arrested him at the council-board and carried him to the Tower on the charge of heresy and treason (June 10), and he was attainted by parliament, June 28. In vain did he implore mercy from the king, who was weary of so able and faithful a servant. He was executed on Tower Hill, July 28, 1540.

On the same day Henry married Catherine Howard, the niece of the Duke of Norfolk. This alliance, and the removal of Cromwell, restored the ascendency of the Catholic party, headed by Norfolk and Gardiner, and the *Six Articles* were rigorously enforced. But the king was equally severe against the deniers of his supremacy; Catholic and Protestant "traitors" were dragged to execution on the same hurdles; and, as was wittily said at the time, those who were against the pope were burned, and those who were for him were hanged. A new rebellion in Yorkshire afforded a pretext for the execution of the aged Countess of Salisbury, mother of Cardinal Pole, who had been attainted in 1539. She was beheaded on the green within the Tower, May 27, 1541. The same fate was soon shared by Queen Catherine Howard, who was clearly convicted of unchastity both before and after her marriage. She was attainted for treason, with her accomplice Lady Rochfort, who had contributed to the death of her own sister-in-law, Queen Anne Boleyn, and both were executed on Tower Hill, Feb. 12, 1542.

From these scenes of blood it is some relief to turn even to the disorders of the sister kingdoms. Ireland had been for some years the scene of wars between her own native parties, and of rebellions against Henry fomented by the Romanists. These tumults were only partially appeased, when Henry assumed the title of King of Ireland, instead of "Lord" (Jan. 23, 1541), an act which was sanctioned by parliament in 1544.

On the Scottish frontier there had been for many years a succession of petty wars and of armed truces. In 1542 Henry declared war against the Scots, who suffered a defeat at *Halidon Hill* (Aug. 25), and one still more disastrous in Cumberland, near the *Solway Moss* (Nov. 25). This disaster is said to have broken the heart of JAMES V., who expired (Dec. 14, 1542), leaving an infant daughter MARY, whose fate was afterward so deeply involved in the destinies of England.

Once more, as in the case of the Maid of Norway (see p. 72), there appeared an opportunity of uniting the crowns by a marriage of the young Prince of Wales with the infant Queen of Scots. The alliance was nearly concluded by Henry and the regent Earl of Arran, when it was broken off by the influence of Cardinal Beaton, the head of the Catholics in Scotland, who was already engaged in his conflict with the Scottish Reformers; and an alliance was made between Scotland and France, against which country Henry had lately formed a league with the emperor (Feb. 11, 1543).

On the 10th of July, 1543, Henry made his sixth and last marriage, with Catherine, widow of Lord Latimer, commonly known by her maiden name of Catherine Parr. She was a woman of virtue and good sense. It is said, though on doubtful authority, that her leaning to the reformed doctrine at one time endangered her; but she escaped by her tact in managing the king's temper. At Gardiner's instigation he had given orders for her arrest, when the following scene took place: "Kate," said he, sharply, "you are a doctor." "No, Sir," she replied, "I only wished to divert you from your pain by an argument in which you so much shine." "Is it so, sweet-heart?" exclaimed the king; "then we are friends again." She had the rare fortune to survive her husband. The same year that Henry died (1547) she married Sir Thomas Seymour, admiral of England, and died in 1548.

The wars with Scotland and France were actively prosecuted in 1544 and the following years. In May the English burnt Edinburgh and Leith, and they continued to ravage the south of Scotland. In July Henry himself invaded France and took Boulogne; but the emperor suddenly concluded a separate peace with Francis at Crêpy, and Henry returned to England (Sept. 30). In the next year (1545) the French fleet harassed the English coast, and an indecisive action was fought off the Isle of Wight. At length peace was concluded both with France and Scotland, June 7, 1546. The chief obstacle to an accommodation with the latter country had been removed by the assassination of Cardinal Beaton, at St. Andrews, just when his triumph over the reformers seemed complete (May 28).

At home these last years of Henry's reign are filled with events illustrating the increasing power of the Reformation, the violent resistance of its enemies, and the inconsistencies and cruelty of the king. In 1544 Henry sent to Cranmer a translation of the Litany, for general use in solemn processions; and in the following year he added forms of morning and evening prayer, in English, to be used instead of the Breviary.

Henry's last parliament met Nov. 23, 1545; and, after voting a subsidy for the war, and passing a new law against heretics, it proceeded to settle the question of ecclesiastical property. The property of all hospitals, colleges, and chantries was vested in the crown; and the uneasiness created by the measure was removed by the magnificent foundations of *Trinity College, Cambridge, and The Hospital of St. Bartholomew.*

On Christmas-eve it was prorogued by the king in person. His speech, the last he uttered in parliament, exhibits the state of his mind in a most interesting light. Bursting into tears, he deplored the want of charity between man and man, and the prevalent religious dissensions. He exhorted his hearers to reform these evils in themselves, and the bishops and clergy to agree in teaching truth, which is one. Though the use of the Scriptures had been permitted in the English tongue, they must not be expounded by each man as he pleased, nor "disputed and jangled in every alehouse and tavern." Thus did Henry, while pointing to the true source of knowledge, claim to subject its use to his own will, and teach, as the remedy for all evils, the charity which he never learned. Here, too, is the key to the perplexities of his character—qualities of the highest order, intentions of the best aim, overmastered by self-will. During the remainder of his reign that one "tyrant passion" had full play. Yet we must not ascribe to him all the blame of the measures urged on by bad advisers. Gardiner and Norfolk, seconded by BONNER bishop of London, renewed their persecution of the Protestants. Latimer again escaped, by the favor of the king; but they sent other victims to the flames, and the fate of the young and beautiful Anne Ascue, who suffered, with more than manly firmness, for denying the doctrine of transubstantiation, deserves perpetual pity (July, 1546). At this very time Henry proposed to the reformed princes of Germany a new "League Christian;" and we have the best assurance of his intention to have carried on the work of the reformation.

But his career was run. A wound in his leg grew worse, and confined him to his couch (Nov., 1546). All thoughts were turned toward the succession. By a third and final act of succession (1544) the claims of the princesses Mary and Elizabeth had been admitted, next in order after their brother Edward. The Prince of Wales was a delicate child of nine years old, and there must be a protector during his minority. The most likely candidate was Edward Seymour, lord Hertford, the young prince's uncle, who had distinguished himself in the late wars, but was wanting in sound judgment. As the head of the Protestants he was obnoxious to the Catholics, to whose leaders he had given personal offense. Those leaders were the veteran Duke of Norfolk and his celebrated son, Henry Howard earl of Surrey, who was the most accomplished man of his age, and whose writings have given him a high place in English literature. His splendid virtues have cast into the shade his faults of imprudence, haughtiness, and ambition; and it was in part owing to those faults that he now fell a victim to the jealous fears of Henry. On the charge of his aspiring to marry the Princess Mary and succeed to the crown he was arrested and committed to the Tower, with his father (Dec. 7). They were also charged with intrigues with Gardiner for the restoration of the papacy. Surrey was tried and found guilty by a special commission, Jan. 13, 1547, and executed Jan. 19. The parliament, meeting on Jan. 14, passed an act of attainder against Norfolk, the king urging on the proceedings from the desire, as he told them in his message, to provide a successor to the dignities of Norfolk at the coronation of the

Prince of Wales. But this last victim was snatched from him by a power to which even kings must yield. On Thursday, Jan. 27, the royal assent was given by commission to the bill of attainder, and two hours after midnight Henry was no more. In his last moments he had sent for Cranmer, but when he reached Whitehall the king was speechless. Cranmer, "speaking comfortably to him, desired him to give some token that he put his trust in God through Jesus Christ; therewith the king wrung the archbishop's hand" and expired. He died on Jan. 28, 1547, in the 56th year of his age and the 38th of his reign.

He was buried on Feb. 16, in St. George's chapel, Windsor, in accordance with the directions of his will, which also bade the remains of Queen Jane to be interred beside him. The masses, which he ordered to be said forever, combine with his prayers to the Virgin and other expressions in the will to mark it as that of a doctrinal Catholic. The same instrument arranged the succession in accordance with the last act of parliament, but added that, in case of the failure of his children and their issue, the crown should pass to the issue of his sister the Princess Mary and the Duke of Suffolk, thus excluding the Scottish royal family. A council of fifteen "executors" was named to administer the government during his son's minority.

Henry's reign was one of the most, if not the most, memorable for its acts in English history. Besides all its ecclesiastical reforms, and notwithstanding the increased power of the crown, parliament gained a vast addition to its importance by Henry's constant appeals to it to sanction his acts, and by the use he made of the commons to overcome resistance in the lords. Of Henry himself it has been well said that his history is his best character and description. The popular tradition vacillates between admiration of "bluff King Hal" and execration of a blood-stained tyrant; and, while one historian holds him up as all but "the ideal model of perfect wickedness," another ingeniously hammers out the treasures of our old records into leaves to gild over his idol. In his own time it was said of him that "Harry loved a *man*"—and it was because he was a *man* himself—not a hero, nor a saint, nor a monster, but a man—whose fierce temper exaggerated human faults and vices, but whose reign bears witness to many manly virtues; and after both have been judged with the severest impartiality, it remains to be recorded, even of him, that

"The man's the man, for a' that."

Paul's Cross.

CHAPTER XIX.

THE HOUSE OF TUDOR (*continued*).—EDWARD VI. A.D. 1547–1553.

HENRY VIII. left three children: MARY, the daughter of Catherine of Aragon; ELIZABETH, the daughter of Anne Boleyn; and EDWARD, the son of Jane Seymour. Mary was in her 32d year,

Elizabeth in her 14th, and Edward in his 10th; the first being the hope of the Catholics, and the other two of the Protestants. With Norfolk in the Tower, where he remained during Edward's reign, none were so rash as to move in Mary's favor, and Edward became king by the title of Edward VI.

EDWARD VI. was born at Hampton Court, Oct. 12, 1537. We learn from his own diary of his reign that "he was brought up till he came to six years old among the women." He had then for tutors Dr. Cox, afterward his almoner, and John Cheke, one of the first cultivators of Greek learning in England. He had a competent knowledge of Latin, Greek, French, and Italian, and was able to converse intelligently on questions of philosophy and religion, nor was he deficient in manly exercises. His sincere piety ever showed itself in the desire to do right. After all allowance has been made for the language of flattery and for the promises of hope, we may accept the praises of the great men who knew him as proofs of his rare virtue and attainments.

During most of his reign, however, Edward was in the hands of statesmen who were little fit to be the advisers of such a prince. His uncle, the Earl of Hertford, postponing the announcement of Henry's death till the third day, conducted Edward from Hertford to his sister Elizabeth at Enfield, and brought him to the Tower (Feb. 1, 1547), his proclamation having been made in London the day before. The council of executors appointed by Henry only met to subvert the principles of the late king's will. He had desired that there should be no protector, and that no new measures of importance should be taken during his son's minority. But Hertford obtained his own nomination as protector, and he was at the same time created Duke of Somerset; the chancellor, Wriothesley, being made Earl of Southampton, and John Dudley viscount Lisle, Earl of Warwick. Wriothesley was the head of the Catholic party and the great opponent of Somerset, who very soon obtained his dismissal and imprisonment for an irregularity in his office of chancellor (March 6). Dudley, whose name soon becomes and remains in his descendants so conspicuous, was the son of Edmund Dudley, the creature of Henry VII. For his bravery in the Scotch wars he had been favored by Henry VIII. and created Viscount Lisle. Gardiner bishop of Winchester had been originally nominated among the executors, but Henry had struck out his name for his treasonable practices with Norfolk. Cranmer was there as the moderating spirit between the extreme parties.

Edward was crowned on Feb. 28, and on March 13 he granted a new commission to Somerset with enlarged powers, the body of executors being transformed into a council and placed under Somerset's control. His administration may be regarded as the temporary triumph of the Protestant party, to be followed by the reaction under Mary, before the final settlement of the Reformation by the firmness of Elizabeth.

The state of affairs was such as to demand the utmost prudence, but to tempt a man like Somerset to rashness. On the Continent the Reformation seemed in danger. Luther had died shortly before Henry VIII. (1546). The *Council of Trent* had assembled in 1545 to relay the foundations of the Catholic Church. The Emperor Charles V. had defeated the Protestant princes at Mühlberg (April 22, 1547). Francis I. died March 22, and was succeeded by HENRY II., who began his reign by assisting the Scottish Catholics, and encouraging them to break off the projected marriage of their young queen to Edward VI. He was prompted to this course by the princes of Lorraine, whose sister, Mary of Guise, was the widow of James V. and mother of the Queen of Scots.

The castle of St. Andrews, where the slayers of Cardinal Beaton had taken refuge, surrendered to a French force, Aug., 1547, whereupon Somerset invaded Scotland and gained a great victory at Pinkie, near Musselburgh, Sept. 10. But the humiliation of this defeat, and the cruelty of the English after the battle, only the more alienated the Scotch Catholics, who very soon sent the infant queen to France and betrothed her to the dauphin, afterward Francis II.

Meanwhile the Reformation had been pushed forward at home. The zeal of one London parish had purged its church of images, pictures, and even the crucifix; a general ecclesiastical visitation had been instituted for the removal of images, the assertion of the royal supremacy, and the use of the English tongue in the church services; and Bonner and Gardiner had been imprisoned for protesting against these measures (Sept.), though they were soon released. The parliament, which met Nov. 4, placed all offices, including bishoprics, in the king's hands, and the bishops were reappointed, *during pleasure*, without even the show of a *congé d'élire.* They repealed the statutes of Henry IV. and Henry V. against the Lollards, with the Six Articles, and other penal measures of the last reign. They enjoined communion in both kinds, and imposed severe penalties for speaking irreverently of the Eucharist. They vested all the remaining property of ecclesiastical corporations in the crown, to be employed for uses of learning and religion; but much of it was diverted to the enrichment of the new nobility. They abolished the many treasons created in the last reign, restoring the statute of Edward III., and they increased the severity of the laws against vagrancy. The work thus begun was carried on by the council, who had already regulated preaching by the publication of twelve homilies to be read in all churches, and who now issued proclamations against superstitious popular customs (1548). A committee of bishops and divines was appointed to amend the offices of the church; and the result of their labors was the FIRST BOOK OF COMMON PRAYER, the use of which was enjoined by parliament in the first *Act of Uniformity* (Jan., 1549). A revised edition, called the *Second Book*, was published in 1552. This work was, in all essential points, the basis of the present Prayer-book. The chief subsequent alterations were made in the reigns of Elizabeth and Charles II. Perfect liberty was given for the use of the English Bible, many editions of which were published during Edward's reign. The same parliament permitted the marriage of the clergy; and they continued fasting, not as a religious act, but to encourage the fisheries.

But a change more important than all the rest was the establishment of *the theological doctrines* of the continental reformers. Luther's *articulum stantis aut labentis ecclesiæ*, the doctrine of justification by faith, was fully adopted by the English reformers; while in most points they followed the guidance of JOHN CALVIN.

Meanwhile the course of politics was far from running smooth. The opposition of Gardiner and Bonner was again silenced by imprisonment, soon followed by deprivation of their sees; but a more formidable danger arose from the intrigues of the protector's brother, Lord Seymour of Sudeley, Admiral of England. He had married Queen Catherine Parr, and on her death he had formed a plan to marry the Princess Elizabeth and to obtain possession of the king's person. He was attainted by parliament and executed on Tower Hill (March 20, 1549), his brother, the protector, reluctantly consenting to sign his death-warrant.

The following summer was marked by popular insurrections, partly against the new order of things and partly caused by pressing social disorders which had arisen during the state of transition. While prices were vastly enhanced by the discoveries of gold and silver in the New World, the coin had been repeatedly debased to meet the necessities of the court. While the suppression of monasteries had not only deprived the poor of the alms they gave, but thrown monks and friars upon the world, the means of subsistence were narrowed by the inclosure of vast parks, chiefly by the new nobility, and the poor were crushed by the vagrant laws. Somerset's efforts to give redress by a personal hearing of complaints, and by a proclamation against inclosures, had only sanctioned the popular discontent. An insurrection in the west, demanding the complete restoration of Romanism, was put down by Lord Russell, who was created in the next year Earl of Bedford, and was the ancestor of the ducal house. "Ket's rebellion," in Norfolk, was suppressed still more severely by Warwick.

These disorders were laid at the door of Somerset, who was also accused of desiring to make peace with France and Scotland, without gaining any success in war. Besides, he had made himself unpopular by his arrogance, and especially by his demolition of several churches and bishops' palaces to clear a site for his mansion in the Strand. (That mansion, "old Somerset House," deserves notice as the first specimen of Italian architecture in England. Its site is now occupied by the noble Italian edifice designed by Sir William Chambers for George III.) A party was formed in the council by Warwick and Southampton against Somerset, who was deserted by nearly all his friends save Cranmer and the secretary Cecil, afterward the great Lord Burleigh. He sought safety in submission, and confessed, on his knees, the charges against him. An act of parliament deprived him of all his offices and sentenced him to a fine of £2000 a year in land (Dec., 1549). The king, however, remitted the fine, and Somerset was soon restored to the council and apparently reconciled to Warwick (April, 1550).

Warwick had to cope with the same difficulties as Somerset, and, with more than Somerset's imprudence, he wanted his sincerity. He concluded peace with France and Scotland, giving up Boulogne for 400,000 crowns (March, 1550). While his partisans were enriched by the forfeiture of several Catholic bishops, he obtained for himself the dukedom of Northumberland (1551), and signalized his elevation by the destruction of his old rival. Somerset had formed a conspiracy to recover his power and seize the persons of his enemies at the council. He was arrested at the council-board (Oct.), tried at Westminster Hall, and beheaded on Tower Hill, Jan. 22, 1552.

The Reformation proceeded meanwhile under the auspices of Cranmer and his friends; of whom Ridley had been made bishop of the united sees of London and Westminster, Hooper bishop of Gloucester, and Miles Coverdale bishop of Exeter. Forty-two *Articles of Religion* were drawn up (1551), a second Act of Uniformity was passed, and fasts and holidays were regulated by parliament (1552). Though there were no executions of Catholics to excuse the cruelties of the next reign, yet the pains of heresy were enforced against Protestant schismatics; and, among others, Joan Bocher was burnt as an Anabaptist (1550). Great efforts were made to induce the Lady Mary to conform, but she steadfastly refused; and, out of deference to the power of her cousin Charles V., she was allowed the private exercise of her religion.

Northumberland, though in his last moments he professed to have always been a Catholic, now brought his affected zeal for Protestantism to the aid of his family ambition. The king's health was giving way. An attack of small-pox in April, 1552, had been followed by consumption. Northumberland worked upon his fears of a Catholic revolution to induce him to assume the power, which his father had only exercised by the sanction of parliament, to dispose of the crown by will, in favor of the Lady Jane Grey, of whose parentage and character we shall speak presently. Edward summoned the judges to draw up the necessary deed; and, on their objecting to it as illegal, the dying king showed a flash of his father's temper, and "asked, with sharp words and an angry countenance, where were the letters patent." Northumberland threatened furiously. The deed was drawn and signed by the council, Cranmer hesitating to the last (June 21, 1553).

Meanwhile the king was rapidly sinking; his physicians gave place to an ignorant woman, who promised a certain cure; and, while rumors of poison were spread among the common people, Mary and Northumberland were seeking aid—the one from the emperor, and the other from France—for the impending conflict. The king expired at Greenwich on Thursday the 6th of July, 1553, in the 16th year of his age and the 7th of his reign; and with him ended the male line of the house of Tudor. Besides all the good that was hoped or said of him, he left deeds as his imperishable memorials in the grammar-schools which bear his name throughout the land, and especially in the magnificent hospitals, for the mind and body, of Christ's Church and St. Thomas.

Old Somerset House.

King Philip, husband of Queen Mary.

CHAPTER XX.

THE HOUSE OF TUDOR (*continued*).—LADY JANE GREY AND QUEEN MARY I. A.D. 1553–1558.

History presents no greater contrast than that between the characters, as well as the fate, of the two ladies who became, on the death of Edward VI., competitors for the crown. The last act of parliament and the will of Henry VIII. had settled the succession, after Edward, on the princesses Mary and Elizabeth in order, and after them on the heirs of the two daughters of MARY TUDOR (daughter of Henry VII.) by her second marriage with Charles Brandon duke of Suffolk. The following table shows their genealogies:

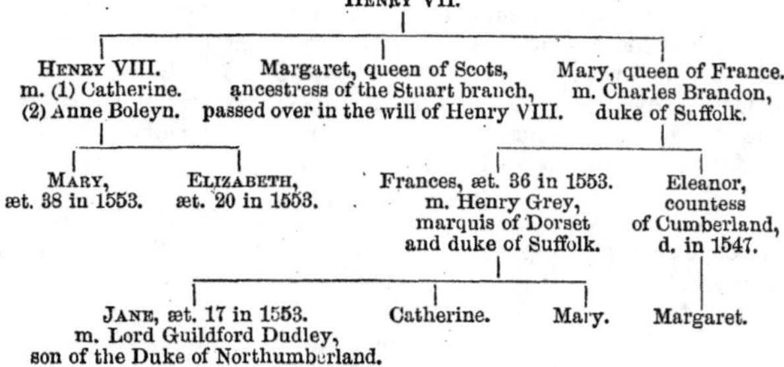

Thus Lady JANE GREY was the eldest of the four representatives of Mary Tudor. She added to the most gentle temper and the rarest piety and virtue accomplishments in learning which distinguished her above all the women even of that learned age, though the princesses Mary and Elizabeth were but little her inferiors. For this she thanked her tutor, whose gentle methods of instruction were the more winning from their contrast to the severity of her parents. She knew Greek, Hebrew, and Arabic, and devoted the hours which her friends spent in hunting to such reading as the "Phædon" of Plato. From these studies she was called, sorely against her will, to the throne, the prison, and the block. She was married to Lord Guildford Dudley, Northumberland's fourth son, May 25, 1553, and was at Sion House when Edward died. When Northumberland came to conduct her to the Tower, which was first her palace and then her prison, she showed the greatest reluctance and alarm, but yielded, praying for strength, and was proclaimed amidst the ominous silence of the people (July 9). To increase her disgust she learned that her husband was to be made king; and she plainly warned him that he, at least, had no title to the crown.

Meanwhile the Lady MARY, summoned by Northumberland to the death-bed of her brother, had stopped at Hunsdon (Hoddesdon) in Hertfordshire, just in time to escape into Norfolk, whence she wrote to the council to claim the crown. Her letter arrived the day after the proclamation of Queen Jane. Friends gathered round her; and, when Northumberland marched to meet them, the members of the council who remained in London escaped from his guards in the Tower and proclaimed Queen Mary, amidst the exultation of the people (July 19). Northumberland, deserted by his army, was arrested at Cambridge (July 20) and committed to the Tower (July 25), with his sons, the Lady Jane, Bishop Ridley, who had preached against Mary at Paul's Cross on Sunday the 16th, and many other leaders.

On Aug. 3 the queen entered the city, attended by the Princess Elizabeth and the ex-queen Anne of Cleves. She went straight to the Tower, and released the Duke of Norfolk, Bishop Gardiner, Lord Courtenay (the young and handsome son of that Marquis of Exeter who had been beheaded in 1539), and other prisoners. She assured the lord mayor and aldermen that, "albeit her own conscience was stayed in matters of religion, yet she meant not to compel or strain men's consciences." But her own convictions were too strong, and party-spirit ran too high, for neutrality or even moderation. A tumult at Paul's Cross the next day, on Bonner's restitution to his see, was made the occasion for forbidding any to preach without a special license, which was only granted to known Romanists.

On the 18th the Duke of Northumberland, and his son the Earl of Warwick, pleaded guilty of treason before their peers; and the next day Sir Andrew Dudley and three other gentlemen were tried before a special commission and also pleaded guilty. Northumberland, after abject entreaties for life, was beheaded, with Sir John Gates and Sir Thomas Palmer (Aug. 22). All died professing themselves Catholics, and exhorting the people to return to the faith. Warwick was respited, and died in the Beauchamp Tower (Oct. 21, 1554), on the wall of which he has left his name, "JOHN DUDLE," with floral emblems of the names of his four brothers. Seldom has the triumph of a sovereign over rival claimants been attended with so little severity.

The remission of the second portion of the last subsidy raised the tide of Mary's popularity to its height, and the religious reaction was scarcely opposed, except by the foreign refugees for conscience' sake; and they were ordered to leave the country. Among them was the illustrious Peter Martyr. Mass was said in St. Paul's in Latin, the crucifix was replaced, and the "real presence" was defended from the pulpit. The marriages of the clergy were no longer recognized. Gardiner was appointed chancellor (Aug. 23), and was associated with the lately restored bishops in a commission to purify the episcopal bench. Hooper, bishop of Gloucester, the most zealous Protestant on the bench, was deprived and imprisoned in the Fleet (Sept. 1); Latimer, who had boldly come to London though warned to escape, was sent to join Ridley and Coverdale in the Tower (Sept. 4). Cranmer was also warned; but, far from flying, he published a protest against the restoration of the mass, and was committed to the Tower (Sept. 14). He was tried for treason before a special commission (Nov. 13), with Lady Jane Grey, her husband, and his brothers Ambrose and Henry Dudley. All pleaded guilty, and were respited for the time. Negotiations were secretly opened with Rome, and Commendone, the envoy of Julius III., came privately to court and carried back a letter from Mary praying for the reconciliation of England to the church; but the time was not yet come to receive Cardinal Pole, whom the pope, on hearing of Mary's accession, had appointed legate to England, and who was impatient to return.

The emperor's envoy, Renard, had been Mary's constant adviser; and, under the guise of a politic moderation, had recommended a thorough suppression of heresy. He now urged the marriage of Mary to his master's eldest son, Don Philip, prince of Castile. The proposed marriage was most unpopular. The council and the people were averse to any foreign marriage; and the queen, in the first days of her accession, had promised compliance with their wishes. But in an alliance with the imperial family they saw too true an earnest that the religious persecution, which had raged for years in the Netherlands and Spain, would be imitated in England; nay, that even the horrors of the Inquisition might be introduced. The popular feeling leaned toward Courtenay, whom the queen had created Earl of Devon; while a party among the Protestants desired his union to the Princess Elizabeth.

Mary was crowned on Oct. 1, and parliament met on Oct. 5. They declared the queen's legitimacy and right to the crown, annulled all the religious laws of the last reign, abolished all the new treasons, restricted the *præmunire*, and restored the form of public worship as it had been in the last year of Henry VIII. They also reversed the attainder of the Duke of Norfolk. But to the Spanish marriage they showed an invincible dislike, and their petition against it was received with a Tudor explosion of anger (Nov. 16). They were equally firm against the queen's desire to exclude Elizabeth from the succession. That princess, who had carried compliance so far as to hear mass, now withdrew from the court; her life was threatened several times, and was only protected by the politic advice of the emperor.

The marriage treaty was concluded before Christmas, the emperor consenting to Philip's exclusion from the crown in case of Mary's death, and to other securities against foreign influence. The discontent of the people broke out into open insurrection, with the new year (1554). Sir Thomas Wyatt rose in Kent, Sir Peter Carew in Devonshire, and the Duke of Suffolk in the midland counties, against the Spanish match and for the Lady Jane. Wyatt alone had some success, and forced his way to London. But here his troops deserted him, and he was taken prisoner (Feb. 7). This movement sealed the fate of Lady Jane Grey, who, after a vain attempt to convert her, suffered, with characteristic meekness, within the Tower (Feb. 12). Her husband, Lord Guildford Dudley, was beheaded just before her on Tower Hill. Her father, the Duke of Suffolk, and Wyatt, were executed soon after, with sixty or seventy others, while 400 more were conducted before the queen with ropes round their necks and pardoned (March and April). The acquittal of Sir Nicholas Throgmorton is a memorable example, thus early in English history, of the firmness of a jury on a state trial. Gardiner was also defeated in his attempt to re-enact the Six Articles and to obtain power to execute the sentence of convocation, condemning Cranmer, Ridley, and Latimer as heretics (April and May). The Princess Elizabeth was at first committed to the Tower, but afterward conveyed to Woodstock (May 19) and placed under the custody of Sir Henry Bedingfield. When queen, she forbade Sir Henry to come to court, adding, "God forgive you, and we do; and if we have any prisoner whom we would have hardly handled and straitly kept, then we will send for you."

Meanwhile the queen was married to Philip by proxy (March 6), and he arrived with a great fleet at Southampton, July 20. Thence he traveled, through a pouring rain, to meet the queen at Winchester, where the marriage was celebrated by Gardiner, July 23; and henceforth all acts of Government were issued in the names of King Philip and Queen Mary. The union proved a wretched one. Mary was now thirty-eight, and Philip eleven years younger. He was cold, haughty, and neglectful; and she had not the art of winning the affection for which she yearned. She already suffered from the hysterical fits which tormented her last days; and before long the mistaken hope of offspring revealed to her the incurable malady by which those days were numbered. Her only consolation was in her religion, which, though unquestionably sincere, assumed the form of cruel bigotry, under the influence of her evil counselors and of her own morose temper.

The parliament, which met on Nov. 12, reversed the attainder of Cardinal Pole, received absolution from him as legate, and completed, under his auspices, the reconciliation of England to the see of Rome. With the new year began the MARIAN PERSECUTION, which has conferred on the queen the title of the *Bloody Mary*. Gardiner was the prime instigator, though he died before the persecution reached its height, and not before he had shown symptoms of relenting. Pole, though naturally humane and gentle, shares the guilt of sanctioning it; but the chief agent was BONNER, bishop of London, in whose diocese the majority of all the executions took place. *Christopherson*, bishop of Chichester, vied with him in cruelty; but nine of the fourteen dioceses were exempt from bloodshed. Even King Philip, deep as is the stain upon his memory from the subsequent cruelties of Alva in the Netherlands, employed his chaplains to preach against these proceedings. The total number of men, women, and children who were burnt—for even *children* were thrown into the flames, and some at the very moment of their birth—is computed as follows:

1555, from February	72
1556	94
1557	79
1558, from February to September	39
Total	284
Annual average	71

The proto-martyrs were JOHN ROGERS, a canon of St. Paul's, and HOOPER, ex-bishop of Gloucester. The former was burnt in Smithfield, the usual site of these executions, February 4; the latter at Gloucester, Feb. 9, 1555. RIDLEY and LATIMER suffered together at Oxford, Oct. 16, when Latimer uttered, with the keen quaintness which adorns his sermons, the prophetic words, "Be of good comfort, Master Ridley; play the man; *we shall this day light such a candle, by God's grace, in England, as I trust shall never be put out.*"

CRANMER had been tried and condemned with Latimer and Ridley, but he was reserved for humiliation before death. Irresolute by natural temper, he yielded to the unwearied artifices of his enemies, and was betrayed by the promise of pardon into signing a recantation; but when he found that he was to die after all, he redeemed his error like a brave Christian man. On the day of his execution (March 21, 1556) he was placed upon a platform in St. Mary's, Oxford; and after a sermon by Cole, the provost of Eton, recounting his crimes, but comforting him as a penitent, it was Cranmer's turn to speak. First uttering a fervent prayer, he exhorted the people against prevailing sins; and then, instead of the expected recantation, "Now I come," said he, "to the great thing that troubleth my conscience more than any other thing that ever I said or did in my life, and that is the setting abroad of writings contrary to the truth, which here I now renounce and refuse, as things written with my hand contrary to the truth which I thought in my heart, and written for fear of death to save my life." And after other such words, he declared that the hand which had offended should be first burnt. As he went on to denounce the pope as antichrist, they pulled him down and hurried him to the stake. There, as he had said, he held his right hand steadily in the flame, crying with a loud voice, "This hand hath offended." When the fire got up he was very soon dead, never stirring or crying all the while. The effect of his martyrdom, as described by a Catholic eye-witness, was probably the greatest check that the persecution had yet received.

On the following day Cardinal Pole was made Archbishop of Canterbury. He was now Mary's chief support. Gardiner had died Nov. 12, 1555; and Philip had returned to the Continent to receive the sovereignty of the Netherlands, which his father abdicated in his favor at Brussels, Oct. 25, 1555. The other dominions of Charles V. were soon added, except the hereditary states of Austria and the elective dignity of the empire, in which he was succeeded by his brother Ferdinand. Charles retired to a Spanish convent, where he relieved his hours of devotion with the construction of mechanism; and it is said that the impossibility of making his clocks keep together taught him at last the folly of his life-long effort to make the minds of men move in uniformity.

Passing over the conspiracies which added to Mary's troubles, we come to the closing scene. In 1557 Philip revisited England, only to induce Mary to join in his war with France, which, after one brilliant success at the battle of *St. Quentin* (Aug. 10.), led to the loss of CALAIS, the last remnant of the conquests of the Plantagenets. Left without succor from England, the city was surprised and taken by the Duke of Guise, Jan. 7, 1558. The people of England resented this loss as the greatest national disgrace, not being yet prepared to welcome it as their final deliverance from an unwise ambition. The queen felt it as the climax to her troubles. In September she was attacked by a prevailing fever, and she died Nov. 17, 1558, in the 5th year of her reign and the 43d of her life. She was buried in Henry VII.'s chapel, Westminster, Dec. 13. Her minister and kinsman, Cardinal Pole, died on the same day with herself.

The reigns of Henry VIII., Edward VI., and Mary, corresponding very nearly to the first half of the 16th century (A.D. 1509-1558), form a distinct period in the history of *English literature*, which has been called the "Age of the Protestant Reformation." Its character was determined by the *revival of classical learning*, and by the great religious movements of the time. Men had little time or inclination for the lighter graces of literature, and even poetry had a serious complexion. JOHN SKELTON (d. 1529), the tutor of Henry

VIII., was the chief of a number of quaint satirists who did not spare the abuses of the church. The ill-fated Henry Howard earl of SURREY (1516–1547) created a new epoch by the twofold service of giving the earliest example of English *blank verse* in his translation of the *Æneid*, and of being the first to imitate the great Italian poets, especially Petrarch, and to introduce the form of poetry called the *sonnet*. His contemporary, the elder Sir THOMAS WYATT, wrote satires, epigrams, and other miscellaneous poetry. Both attempted versions of the Psalms; and these, with other efforts, formed the basis of the complete metrical translation which was published early in the next reign, under the names of *Sternhold and Hopkins*, and which is known as the "Old Version," in contradistinction to the feebler "New Version" of Tate and Brady. The *drama* began to form itself out of the "Mysteries" and "Miracle-plays" of the Middle Ages.

The *prose* of this age is of two kinds: works modeled on the Greek and Roman classics, and theological compositions. The printing-press already multiplied copies of the classics, and *Greek* learning fought its way against the "Trojans," as its opponents were called in the universities. ERASMUS, whose own visit to England had great influence, praises the exactness of English scholarship. ROGER ASCHAM'S *Schoolmaster* is still one of the best works on education in the English language; and Sir THOMAS MORE imitated Plato's vision of an imaginary republic in his celebrated *Utopia*.

In religious literature the period derived its glory from the *English versions* of the Bible, the chief of which were: 1. *Tyndale's New Testament* (1526) and *Pentateuch* (1531); 2. *Coverdale's Bible* (1537), the first complete and authorized translation, and still used in the English Psalter; 3. *Matthew's Bible*, edited on the Continent by *John Rogers*, the proto-martyr; 4. *Cranmer's*, or the *Great Bible* (1540); and 5. The *Geneva New Testament*, a revision of Tyndale's, by *Whittingham*, a refugee in the reign of Mary. The composition of the *English Prayer Book* has been already noticed.

Most of the original works in theology were in Latin—those of the reign of Henry VIII. almost entirely so. The English works are chiefly *Tracts* and *Sermons* by the reformers and martyrs, especially TYNDALE, RIDLEY, CRANMER, and LATIMER. Latimer's Sermons are perhaps the best of all, for their simple energy and quaint wit. The great work of JOHN FOX, commonly known as "The Book of Martyrs," belongs to the latter part of this period.

In *history*, the *Chronicles* of HALL and HOLINSHED, the *Life of Wolsey* by GEORGE CAVENDISH, and the *Journal of King Edward's Reign* by himself, are valuable sources of information.

Kenilworth Gate.

CHAPTER XXI.

THE HOUSE OF TUDOR (*continued*).—ELIZABETH. A.D. 1558-1603.

SECTION I.—PROGRESS OF THE REFORMATION.

THE long reign of ELIZABETH (1558-1603) contains three series of chief events: the history of the Reformation at home and in France and the Netherlands: the affairs of Scotland and the fate of its unhappy queen; and the final period of security which followed the destruction of the Spanish Armada. These will be related separately, as far as possible, though the first two are for the most part contemporaneous.

Elizabeth was proclaimed by the council Nov. 17, 1558, and proceeded from Hatfield to London (Nov. 24) amidst universal rejoicings. All prisoners for religion were at once released, and proclamation was issued forbidding unlicensed preaching, and restoring part of the English service (Dec. 27). The queen was crowned on Jan. 13, 1559, by the Bishop of Carlisle, the only prelate who would officiate, and parliament met on Jan. 21. They declared Elizabeth's legitimacy and title, and restored the supremacy of the crown as settled by Henry VIII., and the laws enacted for religion under Edward VI. The denial of the queen's title was again made treason. The queen was empowered to intrust her spiritual jurisdiction to a commission, and hence arose the too famous *Court of High Commission.* The English Liturgy was restored, and its use prescribed under heavy penalties by a new *Act of Uniformity.* Some resistance was shown in convocation, and a public disputation in Westminster Abbey was cut short by the withdrawal of the Catholics. Nearly all the bishops refused the oath of supremacy, and were deprived; and it was some years before the bench was fully reconstituted under the primacy of Archbishop Parker (consecrated Dec. 17, 1559). The ministers who chiefly directed these changes were the lord keeper, Sir Nicholas Bacon (father of the great Lord Bacon), and the secretary of state, Sir William Cecil, afterward Lord Burleigh.

Before their prorogation (May 8) parliament had addressed the queen very earnestly on the subject of her marriage. Elizabeth, who had already refused the overtures of Philip II., her late sister's husband, now expressed her resolution to have for her epitaph, "Here lies Elizabeth, who lived and died a maiden queen;" and she kept her word, in spite of all that her detractors have said. It is true that, at different periods of her reign, she entertained the advances of several suitors; and in 1579 she went so far as to order the drawing up of her marriage contract with the Duke of Anjou, but the marriage was ultimately broken off. Her relations with the Earl of Leicester need further elucidation, but she probably never contemplated marriage with him.

In foreign politics a new scene was opening. Ever since the accession of Charles V. the constant wars between France and the Empire had left England free to choose her part; but now that Philip saw his hopes of union with Elizabeth gone, and England fully committed to the Reformation, he hastened to conclude peace with France. The general pacification of *Câteau-Cambresis*, between France, England, and Spain, was completed in April, 1559; and the new alliance between Spain and France was cemented by the marriage of Philip II. to Elizabeth, daughter of Henry II. Henry was accidentally killed at the tournament held on the occasion (July 10, 1559), and was succeeded by his son FRANCIS II., whose marriage with Mary queen of Scots had been completed a year before (April 24, 1558). The young king was weak, both in body and mind; and the Guises, who were now all-powerful, commenced the persecution of the *Huguenots*, as the French Protestants were called, by a curious corruption of the name they had borrowed from Germany, *Eidgenossen* (i. e. *confederates*). The death of Francis II. (Dec. 5, 1560), and the accession of his brother CHARLES IX., under the regency of the queen-mother, the infamous CATHERINE DE' MEDICI, led to the great religious wars, in which the cause of the Huguenots was upheld by the two Henrys of Navarre, father and son, the Prince of Condé, and the three brothers Coligny, against Catherine and the Guises; in which they suffered the great defeats of *Jarnac* and *Moncontour* (1569) and the atrocious *Massacre of St. Bartholomew* (Aug. 24, 1572); and which were only ended by the accession of Henry of Navarre as HENRY IV., and his great victory at *Ivry* (1589).

The influence of these events in England, though indirect, was most important. On the queen's accession, Mary of Scotland and her husband the dauphin quartered the arms of England on their shield, and assumed the royal title. No notice was taken of the remonstrances of Elizabeth, who on her part complied with the requests for aid made by the Protestants both in Scotland and in France. A fleet sent to the Firth of Forth (Jan., 1560) compelled a French army to capitulate at Leith; and a treaty was made at Edinburgh, by which the French evacuated Scotland, and Francis and Mary engaged to lay aside the arms and title of the crown of England (July 6). In 1562 Elizabeth sent a force, under Ambrose Dudley earl of Warwick, to the aid of the Protestants in Normandy. They took Havre; but on the pacification which followed between the Catholics and Huguenots both united against the English, who were driven from Havre (July 28, 1563) and other towns which they had garrisoned. On April 1, 1564, peace was concluded with France; and the claim of England to Calais was finally, though tacitly, relinquished.

Meanwhile the final settlement of the reformed Church of England was made by the parliament of 1563, and convocation drew up the 39 Articles, as they now stand. Having reached this point, the queen was resolved, like her father, to bring all her subjects to uniformity in religion; and henceforth she was involved in an incessant conflict with two opposite parties. The Catholics were repressed by the penal laws, and in some cases their share in treasonable plots seemed to justify severe measures. But at the other pole of the ecclesiastical world a party had arisen, including many shades of opinion, which were long confounded by their adversaries under the common name of *Puritanism*. They desired a form of worship more thoroughly purified from the usages of the Church of Rome than that which was now established in England. Their chief objections were against the decorations of the churches, the vestments of the clergy, the use of the ring in marriage, and the sign of the cross in baptism. Such objections had already been made to the settlement arranged by Cranmer, chiefly among the more zealous refugees from the Marian persecution; and there were disputes on these matters at Frankfort in 1554. But the exiles brought back with them further views respecting Calvinistic theology, civil liberty, and other peculiar doctrines, which were most distasteful to Elizabeth, but were secretly favored by some of her council, including Cecil and Walsingham. Many openly refused to conform to the worship of the established church, and were called *Nonconformists*. When they proceeded to form congregations of their own, they became "the Separation," or *Dissenters*. As early as 1564 we find the queen issuing strict orders to the bishops to enforce conformity; while the cause of the Nonconformists was supported, for his own ends, by the queen's favorite, Robert Dudley earl of Leicester, son of the late Duke of Northumberland. Nonconformist divines were deprived of their preferments (1565), their books condemned (1566), their congregations broken up, and the worshipers imprisoned and brought before the bishops, who failed to convince them of their errors (1567). Neither the primate Parker (d. 1575), nor his successor Grindal (d. 1583), was disposed to more severe measures; but Elizabeth at length found a zealous servant in Archbishop Whitgift, who used the Court of High Commission as a sort of inquisition, only stopping short of torture and death. The most eminent of the Nonconformists was *Thomas Cartwright*, Margaret professor of divinity at Cambridge, who had a warm controversy with Whitgift; he fled to the Continent (1573), was imprisoned by the Court of High Commission (1590-1593), and died at Warwick 1603. *Robert Browne* also deserves notice, not so much for his own merits as for the accident which gave his name to the party who were afterward called *Independents*. Their entire denial of the authority of civil magistrates in matters of religion was construed into a treasonable attack on the queen's supremacy, and many of them were hanged at Tyburn. The most celebrated of these "Brownist" martyrs were Barrow, Greenwood, and Penry, who suffered, under circumstances of great cruelty, in 1593. Still the power of the Puritans increased steadily during the reign of Elizabeth, and it was only by her direct authority that some of their proposals failed in parliament. On one of these occasions (1571) the queen stretched her prerogative so far as to imprison the mover of the obnoxious bill.

But there were other sectaries who were regarded as outside of the widest limits of toleration, and for whom the fires of Smithfield were still kindled. In 1575 a congregation of Anabaptists were seized; some recanted; eleven were sentenced to the stake, but banished; and two were burnt. Fox, the martyrologist, prayed the queen to inflict some other death than burning—a decisive proof of the opinions then held about the suppression of heresy by capital punishment. Elizabeth's whole ecclesiastical policy may be explained by her preference of Lutheranism to Calvinism, and her resolve to enforce uniformity and to maintain her own supremacy.

The Bloody Tower.

Wollaton, Nottinghamshire. (Specimen of Architecture of the period.)

CHAPTER XXII.

THE HOUSE OF TUDOR (*continued*).—ELIZABETH. SECTION II.—MARY STUART AND THE CATHOLICS. A.D. 1558–1587.

THE great drawback on Elizabeth's prosperity was MARY STUART queen of Scots, whose superior beauty hurt the vanity of the woman as much as her rival claims troubled the policy of the queen. Mary was a princess of the house of Tudor, through her father James V., son of Margaret Tudor, the second daughter of Henry VII. After Elizabeth, therefore, she was the legitimate heir to the crown of England, though her branch had been passed over, by the will of Henry VIII., in favor of his younger sister's children. Her mother was Mary of Guise, the sister of the Duke of Guise and the Cardinal Lorraine. Her father died a week after her birth, which took place Dec. 7, 1542. Her training devolved upon her mother;

while the government of Scotland fell into the hands of Cardinal Beaton, who defeated the attempt to unite her to Edward prince of Wales, and betrothed her to the Dauphin Francis. In her fifth year she was taken to the court of France, and educated there till her marriage (April 24, 1558). It is no wonder, therefore, though it was the chief source of all her troubles, that she became a bigoted Catholic and a thorough Frenchwoman. Unhappily, too, the court of France, at that time the most dissolute in Europe, gave the worst possible training to a temper too prone to levity.

Thus born and thus brought up, she became, by inevitable necessity, the rival of the Protestant Elizabeth, in the eyes of the Catholics, except that large party in England who held fast to loyalty and to a settled government. We have referred (chap. xxi.) to the assertion of her claims, and the events which led to the peace of Edinburgh (July 6, 1650). That event left Scotland in the hands of the Protestants, whose leaders had formed a confederacy by the name of the *Lords of the Congregation.* The life and soul of their party was the great preacher, JOHN KNOX, who had brought back from his exile at Geneva the most devoted attachment to the doctrines of Calvin, and to the Presbyterian model of church government; and who added to an uncompromising hatred of Popish usages a morose dislike to every form of worldliness. Added to this was the extremest assertion of the principle, not merely of the union of Church and State, but that all civil government must be conformed to those maxims of religion which the Church teaches. Every departure from this principle was stigmatized as *Erastianism*, a name derived from *Erastus*, a Swiss physician, who opposed the views of Beza and Calvin upon ecclesiastical discipline.

Such was the platform upon which the Scottish parliament of 1560 framed their establishment of religion, and of which Francis and Mary did not conceal their dislike. On the death of Francis (Dec. 5, 1560) Mary would fain have staid in France, but the jealousy of the queen-mother, Catherine de Medicis, decided her departure. She took a piteous farewell of the beloved shores, and landed at Leith, Aug. 19, 1561, "a stranger to her subjects, without experience, without allies, and almost without a friend."

The celebration of mass in her chapel, on the first Sunday, was the signal for a riot. Next Sunday John Knox preached against idolatry, and in personal interviews he spared neither the pride of the sovereign nor the feelings of the light-hearted woman of nineteen. Henceforth she looked on him as an enemy, and he regarded her as a Jezebel. But her beauty and her spirit won the chivalrous affection of the youthful portion of her subjects: the few Catholics were still loyal; and the fanaticism of her enemies was kept in check by the ability and moderation of her natural brother, *James Stuart*, prior of St. Andrews, whom she created successively Earl of Mar and *Earl of Murray*.

Elizabeth corresponded with her in a tone of sisterly affection, which became, however, more imperious when she gave advice on Mary's marriage. But the Queen of Scots chose her cousin Henry, lord Darnley, son of the Earl of Lennox, whose countess was the daughter of Margaret Tudor and sister of James V. Darnley therefore stood in the same degree of descent from Henry VII. as Mary, and was, after her, the next heir to the crown of England (see the genealogical table of the House of Tudor). They were married July 29, 1565; and Mary conferred on Darnley the title of King.

Incensed at this union of two rival claimants of her crown, and at Darnley's disobedience (for she claimed his allegiance, as born in England), Elizabeth began to intrigue with the Lords of the Congregation, to whose party the Earl of Murray went over. But the popular feeling was now with Mary; and the lords, who had taken up arms, fled to England. Elizabeth received them angrily, and disavowed their cause; while Mary, intoxicated with success, joined the *League of Bayonne* for the destruction of Protestantism.

Darnley had meanwhile revealed his heartless and profligate character. Wearied of his society, the queen sought the amusements which she had loved at the court of France. A Piedmontese, named *David Rizzio*, son of a teacher of music, pleased her so much that she made him her French secretary, and passed much time in his society. Her jealous husband resolved to strike her through her favorite, and allied himself, for this object, with the party of the Douglases. As Mary was supping in private with Rizzio and her servants, the conspirators burst into the room, guided by Darnley himself; and, in spite of the cries and resistance of the queen, who was in the sixth month of her pregnancy, Ruthven stabbed Rizzio before her face, and the rest dragged him into the next apartment, and dispatched him with fifty-six wounds (March 9, 1566). On learning that he had expired, Mary said, "I will then dry my tears, and study revenge." She dissembled her feelings, pardoned the conspirators, and appeared to be reconciled to her husband, while she restored to her favor Murray and the other banished lords, whom Darnley had called back to Scotland to strengthen his party. On the 19th of June, 1566, she gave birth to a son, who was baptized, according to the rites of the Church of Rome, by the name of JAMES, and became afterward king of Scotland and England.

Darnley, continuing his profligate course of life, had again left the court, when he was taken ill, it was said with the small-pox, near Glasgow. Mary brought him to Edinburgh, where he was lodged in a solitary house called the *Kirk of Field*. Early on the morning of Feb. 10, 1567, the house, with all its inmates, was blown up with gunpowder, and the dead body of the king was found in a neighboring field. Suspicion at once fell upon the queen and James Hepburn *earl of Bothwell*, who had for some time been her chief adviser. The Earl of Lennox openly accused Bothwell, who was acquitted by the use of intimidation (April 12). He formed a league among the nobles, carried off the queen as she was returning from a visit to her son at Stirling (April 24), and married her on the 15th of May, having divorced his wife a little before. The celebrated Sir James Melville, who was in the queen's retinue, bears witness to the absence of any show of reluctance on her part when she was carried off.

At this last outrage on all decency the Protestants took up arms and defeated Mary and Bothwell at *Carberry Hill*, near Edinburgh. Bothwell escaped to end his days in a Norwegian prison, where he was confined for piracy, and Mary was taken prisoner and conveyed to the castle of *Lochleven*. Here she was forced to resign the crown in favor of her infant son, and to commit the government to a council with Murray as regent. The king, who had just completed his first year, was crowned at Stirling, as James VI., July 29, 1567. But a party was formed for the queen, who made her romantic escape from Lochleven Castle, May 2, 1568, only to suffer a final defeat from the regent at *Langside*, near Glasgow (May 13), whence she fled to the Solway Firth, and crossed over into Cumberland (May 16) to throw herself on the protection of Elizabeth.

During these scenes Elizabeth had affected to mediate between Mary and her subjects. She now sent her a message of sympathy, but refused to see her till she had cleared herself of her husband's murder. Mary, taken by surprise, consented to submit her cause to so good a friend, and she was removed to Bolton, while Murray was summoned to send envoys to justify his conduct. A formal inquiry was opened at York before the Duke of Norfolk (son of the Earl of Surrey whom Henry VIII. beheaded), the Earl of Sussex, and Sir Ralph Sadler, when the Scotch lords were startled by the revival of the old claim of English supremacy, and some of them on their part commenced an intrigue for the marriage of Mary to Norfolk, who was the head of a strong party comprising the moderate Catholics and many Protestants. Elizabeth and Cecil disconcerted the plot by transferring the commission to Hampton Court, and adding to it her most trusted counselors, while Mary was removed, from a neighborhood where the Catholics were strong, to Tutbury in Staffordshire. After some reluctance Murray produced love-letters between Mary and Bothwell, and other papers which left no doubt of her guilt. Mary's commissioners then fell back on her claim as a sovereign princess to refuse an answer to any earthly tribunal. Upon this Elizabeth assembled her council, and declared her conviction of Mary's guilt. She offered, however, to forgive the past if Mary would resign the crown or recognize James's joint title, under the regency of Murray, which Mary steadfastly refused.

Plots now began to be formed for her liberation. Norfolk continued his correspondence with a view to a marriage, and Leicester entered into the plan, which the queen cut short by committing Norfolk to the Tower, Oct. 11, 1568. He was afterward liberated, having satisfied Elizabeth of his loyalty. Meanwhile the northern Catholics took up arms under the earls of Northumberland and Westmoreland. They were dispersed by the Duke of Sussex without a blow, and many of their followers were executed (1569).

On Jan. 23, 1570, the regent Murray was assassinated at Linlithgow; and a war ensued on the border between Mary's partisans and the English. Insurrections of Catholics broke out in Ireland; in the Netherlands the Duke of Alva was plotting with English Catholics, and planning an invasion of the realm (see ch. xxiii.); and the Guises were victorious in France (see ch. xxi.). A special provocation was given to Elizabeth by the publication of a bull of excommunication by Pope *Pius V.* (April 25, 1570), which was affixed to the gates of the Bishop of London's palace by one Felton, who was seized and executed as a traitor (Aug. 8). Several other executions took place, and new laws were enacted against the Catholics (1571). Norfolk, having not only renewed his correspondence with Mary, in spite of his solemn promise, but entered into Alva's plans of invasion, was convicted of a treasonable plot to dethrone the queen (Jan. 16); but it was only at the instance of the House of Commons that she at length sent him to the block (June 2). She refused their prayer for the judgment of the Queen of Scots as the mover of all these seditions; and was not hurried into rash measures even by the horrible news of the massacre of St. Bartholomew in France (Aug. 24, 1572).

The seven years from 1572 to 1579 were a period of great tranquillity in England. The important events that occurred meanwhile in the Netherlands and in the Spanish seas are related in the next chapter. But, in 1580, Pope Gregory XIII. sent a mission of Jesuits, the first who had appeared in England, under Robert Parsons and Edmund Campion. A proclamation was issued against them, to which Campion replied by a challenge to a public disputation. The next parliament (1581), among other severe acts, made it treason to reconcile any one to the Church of Rome; and

Campion was seized, tortured, and at length executed for high treason, with two other priests, Dec. 1, 1581. The records of the next few years are full of plots, real or pretended, by Jesuits and others for the liberation of Mary and for a Spanish invasion, which led to new penal laws and executions.

At length, in 1586, some priests of the English seminary at Rheims sent over an assassin, named John Savage, in conjunction with a priest named Anthony Ballard, to kill the queen and raise an insurrection, which the Spaniards were to support by an invasion. Among several Catholic gentlemen who joined the plot, was one from whom it is known as *Babington's Conspiracy*. The design was betrayed to the watchful secretary, Walsingham, by Gifford, a seminary priest, and fourteen of the chief conspirators were executed (Sept. 20, 21).

This plot sealed the fate of Mary, whose detention had long been odious, while her release would only have given a rallying-point for civil and foreign war. A correspondence which Babington had held with the ex-queen was made the ground for a charge of treason against her; and she was removed to Fotheringhay Castle, there to be tried before a board of forty-seven commissioners (Oct. 11). At first she refused to plead; then she acknowledged that she had corresponded with foreign powers to gain her freedom, but indignantly denied all schemes against the life of Elizabeth. When the letters to Babington, in which she approved his design, were produced and supported by the evidence of her two secretaries, she charged the latter with perjury, and Walsingham with forging the letters, which he expressly denied. After the trial the commissioners adjourned to the Star Chamber at Westminster, and, having found her guilty, sentenced her to death for compassing the destruction of the queen, Oct. 25.

But Elizabeth still showed a real or affected hesitation. She called a new parliament, which met on October 28; and which, after attainting Babington and his associates, prayed the queen to consent to Mary's execution. She begged them to consider if there were any other possible expedient; and on their replying that they could find none, she dismissed them with what she herself called "an answer without an answer." Parliament was prorogued, Dec. 2; the council confirmed the sentence against Mary, Dec. 4; and it was published, "to the great and wonderful rejoicing of the people of all sorts," Dec. 6. Mary received the news as a relief from long suspense, and claimed the character of a martyr. She wrote a touching and dignified letter to Elizabeth, asking to be buried in France, and making some requests for her servants. She did not ask for life; but urgent entreaties were made for her by the king of France, while her son, the king of Scotland, added threats. Again

Elizabeth seemed to hesitate; and when at last she signed the warrant, and gave it to Davison the secretary (Feb. 1), she affected to attempt its recall; but the council took the responsibility, which they afterward threw upon Davison, who was fined £10,000 and imprisoned by the Star Chamber.

The warrant was directed to the earls of Shrewsbury and Kent, who proceeded to Fotheringhay, where Mary received them with a cheerful resignation, which she maintained to the last. The next morning (Feb. 8, 1587) she was beheaded in the castle hall, in the 45th year of her age and the 19th of her captivity, amidst a pity for her fate which has too often warmed into the chivalrous but vain desire to reverse the just judgment of her own age upon her crimes.

Elizabeth affected surprise, grief, and indignation at the execution of the sentence. She shut herself up and wept, railed at her ministers, and ruined Davison. James expressed his resentment by recalling his embassador, and the states of Scotland offered to support him in taking vengeance. But the grief of Elizabeth gave James a fair pretext to lay aside his wrath; and both were calmed down into contentment for the security of their crowns by the skill of Walsingham, and by the sense of their common interest in the cause which had now to undergo its last great peril.

The Old Palace at Greenwich.

Military Costume.

CHAPTER XXIII.

THE HOUSE OF TUDOR (*concluded*).—ELIZABETH. SECTION III.—THE SPANISH ARMADA. THE QUEEN'S DEATH. A.D. 1587–1603.

At the time of the execution of Mary Stuart, Philip II. of Spain had been for some time preparing his great scheme for the destruction of Protestantism by at once invading England and subduing the revolted provinces of the Netherlands. A short retrospect is necessary to understand the story of the "Invincible Armada."

The provinces of the *Netherlands*, or the *Low Countries*, now forming the kingdoms of *Holland* and *Belgium*, having passed by marriage from the house of Burgundy to that of Austria, were inherited by Charles V. from his father. They were, even before England, the chief seat of trade and maritime enterprise; and the burghers of their great cities, such as Amsterdam, Leyden, Antwerp, Brussels, Ghent, and Liège, with their increasing wealth, had acquired a spirit of independence which often showed itself in turbulence. The revived learning and the new religious doctrines of the 15th and 16th centuries had found in them a congenial home; and Charles V. had persecuted the Dutch and Flemish Protestants with a cruelty which he was restrained from exercising in Germany. On his abdication at Brussels (Oct. 25, 1555) he transmitted his maxims of government to his son, Philip II.; but neither the father who bestowed, nor the son who received the crown of a bigot and a tyrant, knew that it was destined to be cast down by a young man on whose shoulder the emperor leaned—the Prince of Orange, afterward known as WILLIAM THE SILENT.

Philip resided chiefly in the Netherlands till 1558, occupied with the affairs of England and France; after his refusal by Elizabeth, and his marriage to Isabella of France, he retired to Spain, leaving the regency to his natural sister, Margaret duchess of Parma; but he continued, from his writing cabinet in the Escurial, to direct those persecutions which soon drove the provinces to rebellion. In 1567 the *Duke of Alva* was sent with an army to crush both heresy and disaffection; and the king literally passed *sentence of death on the whole population of the Netherlands* by what has been well called "the most compendious death-warrant ever framed." The following year (1568) was marked by the judicial murders of the *counts Egmont* and *Horn* at Brussels, and by the first campaign of the Prince of Orange, who had previously escaped. It was about this time that England became concerned in the affairs of the Netherlands. Some merchantmen from Spain, laden with specie for the army in the Netherlands, had been chased into English ports by French cruisers; and Elizabeth, always ready to assist the insurgents if she could also benefit herself, had seized the treasure, alleging that it really belonged to certain Genoese merchants, from whom she had simply borrowed it, to keep it safe for her brother of Spain! Alva retaliated, and English commerce was driven from the Netherlands to Hamburg (1569); and at the same time plots against the queen's life were fomented both by Philip and Alva. (See chap. xxii.) Meanwhile the Prince of Orange obtained a footing in the provinces of *Holland* and *Zeeland;* Alva was recalled: Elizabeth coquetted with both parties, but many of her subjects joined the insurgents. In 1575 the Estates offered her the sovereignty of the revolted provinces, while she declined, tendering her good offices to reconcile them with their sovereign. Besides hesitating to come to open war with Philip, she was no doubt influenced by her lofty ideas of kingly right, and by dislike to the extreme Protestanism of the insurgents. In 1578 she entered into a treaty of alliance, and aided them with ships, men, and money; but a coolness arose from their overtures to the Duke of Anjou (formerly Alençon), the brother of Henry III. of France; for though Anjou was now her suitor, and apparently a favored suitor, she was not willing to see French influence paramount in the provinces. Her ministers were opposed to her coquettish policy in both cases; and would have had her reject Anjou and openly espouse the cause of the Netherlands, while the sympathies of the people were entirely with the Hollanders. In 1580 the liberated States made a formal declaration of their independence, and in the following year they placed themselves under the sovereignty of Anjou, who took his final departure from England as a rejected suitor. His unsuccessful government was closed by his death, in the same year in which an assassin, instigated by Philip, murdered the Prince of Orange (July 10, 1584).

Philip's intention to dispose of Elizabeth by the same means was made clear by repeated discoveries of plots, but she still hesitated to declare war. Embassies passed between her and the States, whom private Englishmen were serving as soldiers, while English sailors were harassing Philip's American possessions in a manner which savored somewhat of piracy. The chief of these adventurers was Sir *Francis Drake.* At length, in 1585, when Henry III. of France rejected the overtures of Holland, and the Catholic League of Joinville was formed for the suppression of heresy throughout Europe—when Philip's schemes against England were placed beyond all doubt—and when the loss of Antwerp by the patriots, after a terrible siege, brought danger to her very doors—Elizabeth accepted the protectorate of the Netherlands, and sent over an army under her favorite, *Robert Dudley earl of Leicester.*

The calumnies of his enemies in his own age, and the pens of the poet and novelist in ours, have consigned the name of Leicester to such odium that it becomes difficult to estimate his character truly. The calmest of his contemporaries judged that there was no clear evidence of the great crimes with which he was charged, such as the murder of his first wife, Amy Robsart (his marriage with whom is mentioned in King Edward's diary), and the poisoning of the Earl of Essex as a step to his second marriage. That his leaning to the Puritans was all hypocrisy has been taken for granted, with many other charges, for which we have only the statements of his great enemies, the priests and the emissaries of Philip. All agree that he was a man of unbounded vanity and ambition, but a brave and experienced soldier. In this quality, however, he was far overmatched by the governor of the Netherlands, Philip's nephew, *Alexander Farnese prince of Parma*, who was reputed the most skillful captain of his age.

Leicester landed at Flushing (Dec. 19, 1585), whither his celebrated nephew, Sir PHILIP SIDNEY, had preceded him. He was received enthusiastically, and installed as governor-general at the Hague; but he soon fell into suspicion, through the ambiguous policy of Elizabeth and his own eagerness to place English garrisons in the chief fortresses. Succors from England were delayed, while a party of the ministers, headed by Burleigh and prompted by the queen, carried on secret negotiations with Parma.

But while they wavered Philip well knew that Holland was the true portal of England, and he was now (1586) deep in correspondence with Parma respecting the plan of invasion which was to subdue the latter and regain the former. Parma was to be rewarded with the hand of Mary Stuart, who was to be queen of England under Philip. The English people were stanch; and they saw that the present conflict was a training for the coming death-grapple. "God hath stirred up this action," wrote one in Leicester's army, "to breed up soldiers to defend the freedom of England, which through these long times of peace and quietness is brought into a most dangerous estate, if it should be attempted." And this new martial spirit was inflamed by the return of Drake from the New World, whither he had been sent out with a fleet of twenty sail, and whence he came back laden with spoil, having taken San Domingo, Porto Rico, Santiago, and Carthagena, and ravaged the shores of Florida. These successes made it more difficult for Philip to raise money in Flanders, where the army of Parma lay inactive for want of it. When the campaign of 1586 opened on the Meuse, Leicester's first successes only served to puff up his vanity; the tide soon turned; and his fruitless siege of *Zutphen* led to the loss of Sir Philip Sidney, who was mortally wounded in a skirmish and carried to Arnheim (Sept. 22, 1586). As he left the battle-field, in extreme pain from his shattered thigh, he saw a wounded soldier look wistfully at a bottle of water which his attendants had just brought him. "Thy necessity is greater than mine," said Sidney, handing him the bottle to drink first. He lived long enough to surprise, by the calmness of his last hours, the friends who had delighted in his life as the perfect model of every virtue and accomplishment, and died with these words: "Love my memory. Cherish my friends. Above all, govern your will and affections by the will and word of your Creator; in me beholding the end of this world, with all her vanities."

The events which followed are too complicated to be related here. While the feeling of republican independence grew stronger and stronger in the States, under the guidance of patriots like *Barneveld*, English influence grew weaker and weaker, through the faults of Leicester, the treachery of his lieutenants, and the vacillating policy of Elizabeth, who reopened negotiations with Parma, even after the plot of Babington and the death of Mary Stuart had removed the last semblance of the possibility of peace between her and Philip. Meanwhile Sir Francis Drake attacked Philip on his own coasts, captured and destroyed several ships in the harbors of Cadiz and Lisbon (for Portugal, since 1580, belonged to Spain), and thus inured the English sailors to the encounters of their little vessels with the huge ships of Spain (April, 1587). Leicester was finally recalled from Holland in Dec., 1587; and the following winter was one of expectation on the part of England, and of active preparation in Spain and Flanders.

History presents no more memorable example than that of the attempted invasion of England by Philip II., to show how the grandest schemes of conquest may overreach themselves by their very vastness, and may be baffled by the blessing of God upon means not only simple but even feeble.

Philip had gradually collected, in the ports of the Peninsula, a fleet of 130 ships of war, many of them new vessels of a size hitherto unknown. There were 60 great *galleons*, 4 large *galleys*, and 4 still larger *galeasses;* all of which had huge castles at the stem and stern, while the galeasses were decorated like floating palaces. In vain had Parma urged upon his master the need of handier vessels for throwing an army upon an enemy's coast. Philip relied on vastness, and thought only of sweeping the sea. The fleet carried 20,000 soldiers, among whom were 2000 grandees, and 300 friars and inquisitors. Their instruments of conversion were placed with the arms and stores on board the transports, in the shape of fetters, whips, thumb-screws, and other machines of torture. This "Invincible Armada," as it was fondly called, crowned with the pope's benediction and consecrated banner, was placed under the command of the Duke of Medina Sidonia, a grandee of the purest blood, and utterly ignorant of naval affairs. He was to sail from Lisbon to Calais, and there effect a junction with the force which Parma had collected in the Netherlands, amounting at first to 30,000, but reduced by sickness to 23,000. But how Parma was to put to sea and effect the junction, was a point for which Philip had not provided. After many delays, the Armada sailed from Lisbon on the 18th, 19th, and 20th of May, 1588. A storm off Cape Finisterre drove it back to Corunna, whence it finally sailed on July 12.

The preparations in England to receive it were more satisfactory for their patriotic ardor than for their promptness or sufficiency. It was very late when the danger was fully credited. Levies were hastily made throughout the kingdom, and three armies were collected: one of 30,000 to attend the queen's person, one of 20,000 to guard the south coast, and a third of 23,000 in the camp at Tilbury under Leicester. Through this camp the queen rode on horseback, declaring to the soldiers her resolution to lead them in person to the field, and rather perish there than survive the ruin of her people. But these armies were not collected till the end of July, and then they were undisciplined and even mutinous; and the queen's harangue at Tilbury was only delivered on the 9th of August, *a week after the dispersion of the Armada.*

Well it was for England that she was readier at sea, though even here her force seemed quite disproportioned to the danger. She possessed only 14,000 sailors, and a fleet of 34 sail, none larger than frigates, and most much smaller. There was scarcely a merchant vessel exceeding 400 tons, while the ships of the Armada were from 300 to 1200 tons; but, such as they were, ships were at once furnished by the commercial towns and by the gentry and nobility, and manned by sailors full of enterprise. Above all, there were the veteran adventurers, such as Drake, Hawkins, and Frobisher, with Lord Howard of Effingham as admiral, whose high character moderated the jealousies of his captains, and who possessed the prudence which the service in hand especially required.

Even after the Armada had sailed, the damage it suffered off Finisterre gave rise to the report that the enterprise was abandoned for that year: but Howard kept good watch, and on Friday, July 19, he received intelligence that the gigantic fleet was off the Lizard. Putting out from Plymouth Sound with 67 ships, he first encountered the Armada on Sunday, July 21. It spread over seven miles of sea, in the form of a vast crescent, facing up the Channel. Avoiding all close encounters with the vast ships, the English gained the weather-gage, and used their swifter and handier vessels to harass the unwieldy enemy at their pleasure. In this manner a running fight was maintained all up the Channel. The English were reinforced from every port. The Spaniards suffered many losses, and two of their largest ships were taken by Sir Francis Drake.

At last, however, they cast anchor in Calais Roads (July 27), still strong enough apparently to crush the English fleet; but they waited in vain for the Duke of Parma, whose army, long since ready, was blockaded in the Flemish ports by a swarm of small vessels collected by the Dutch. It was vain to attempt to cross the Channel till it was cleared of the English fleet; and it was equally impossible to sail out and join the Armada, which lay waiting for him off Calais, with the English fleet lying within two miles.

On the night of Sunday, July 27, Howard directed six fire-ships against the Armada. The Spaniards were seized with a sudden panic, and cut their cables. Two large ships caught fire; several fell aboard of each other; and on the Monday morning the whole fleet, except some ships that had run ashore, was seen drifting before a southwest wind past the Flemish coast. *The plan of invasion had failed.* One last battle was fought with the pursuing English fleet off Gravelines, and lost by the Spaniards, who then, with their best ships crippled, were driven before the wind into the German Ocean (July 29). Owing to want of supplies, the English were compelled to relinquish the chase off the coast of Scotland (Aug. 2), while Medina Sidonia attempted to return home round the British Isles. Between the Orkneys and Hebrides he was overtaken by a storm which completed the dispersion of his fleet, of which scarcely more than a third returned to Spain. He himself bore the news of the disaster to Philip, who submitted to it as the will of God, and began to write dispatches ordering Parma to build a new Armada.

The joy in England was unbounded. The queen went in state to St. Paul's to return thanks for deliverance from a danger greater than any to which the country was ever exposed between the times of William the Conqueror and Napoleon. But few knew how narrow the escape had been. "A great kingdom is a grand wager," wrote the admiral. "Security is dangerous; and if God had not been our best friend, we should have found it so." When all fear of the Armada's return had ceased, the war was carried on vigorously against Spain on the high seas and on the coasts of America, under Drake, the two Hawkinses, and Sir Walter Raleigh; and attacks were made upon Spain itself, with partial success, under Drake and Norris (1588), and afterward under the Earl of Essex (1596). The enterprises in the American seas bore lasting fruit, as they led to the foundation of England's colonial empire, a beginning of which had been attempted by Raleigh some years before, in the settlement which he named *Virginia* in honor of the queen. (See p. 186.)

Shortly after the defeat of the Armada the religious wars of France were brought to an end. Henry III. was the last king of the house of Valois. In the early part of his reign he had favored the princes of Lorraine (the Guises), but in 1576 he made a peace with the Huguenots. Upon this the Duke of Guise formed the "*League*," an organization of the extreme Catholics throughout France. After the death of Henry's brother, the Duke of Anjou, the succession was disputed between Henry of Navarre and the princes of Lorraine. The latter formed a secret treaty with Philip of Spain at the château of Joinville (Jan., 1585). The League took up arms, while Henry found unexpected aid from Henry of Navarre. A period of confusion, in which the king sided alternately with each party, ended in placing him more entirely than ever in the hands of Guise (May, 1588). Henry III. only regained his freedom by foully assassinating the Duke of Guise, and his brother the Cardinal of Lorraine, at Blois (Dec., 1588). Paris and the League rose in insurrection. Henry again sought the alliance of Henry of Navarre (April, 1589); and the two kings were besieging Paris when Henry III. was stabbed by a Dominican monk named *Jacques Clement* (July 31), and expired after naming Henry of Navarre as his successor (Aug. 2), who, by the title of HENRY IV., became the first king of the house of Bourbon.

Elizabeth sent the new king £22,000 and 4000 men under Lord Willoughby (1590), and larger forces, under the Earl of Essex, in the two following years. To conciliate the Catholics, Henry IV. abjured the Protestant faith (July 25, 1593); but the war was still maintained in Normandy by the League and the Spaniards; and Elizabeth continued her succors to Henry, though indignant at his apostasy, till he made peace with Spain in 1598. One memorable action of this war was the taking of Brest from the Spaniards (1594), when the gallant Sir Martin Frobisher was killed.

In the year 1598 England was relieved of her great enemy, Philip II., by death (Sept. 13); but Elizabeth also lost her great minister Burleigh. His death gave freer scope to the ambition of the young Robert Devereux earl of Essex, who had been advancing in the queen's favor ever since the death of Leicester. He had shown, in several military enterprises, more gallantry than ability; and his rash temper was not restrained even by the queen's presence. On one occasion he is said, in the heat of a dispute, to have turned his back upon her; she gave him a box on the ear, and he clapped his hand to his sword, swearing that he would not bear such usage, were it from Henry VIII. himself. Still his favor survived these quarrels, and he was now appointed lord-lieutenant of Ireland (March 12, 1599).

That country had never been thoroughly subdued; and under the Tudors it was ever ready to rise, first for the house of York, and then for the Catholic cause and the Spanish schemes. It was now in open rebellion under Hugh O'Neale, earl of Tyrone. Essex landed at Dublin with 18,000 men (April, 1599); but after a fruitless campaign he entered into suspicious conferences with Tyrone. On hearing of the queen's displeasure he hastened back to England against her orders, and rushed, besmeared with dust and sweat, into her bedchamber. Elizabeth received him graciously; but on recovering from her surprise she altered her conduct, and committed him to the custody of the lord keeper Egerton, though still consoling him with marks of her affection.

Essex had powerful enemies at court; Sir Robert Cecil, secretary of state, and younger son of Lord Burleigh; Sir Walter Raleigh, his rival in the personal favor of Elizabeth; and Sir Francis Bacon, whom he himself had greatly befriended. But he might probably have recovered the queen's favor, could he have bowed his spirit to her caprice. Among other indignities, she refused to renew a patent giving him a monopoly of sweet wines, saying that, "in order to manage an ungovernable beast, he must be stinted of his provender." Essex lost his head. He talked of the queen like a madman. He intrigued secretly with the Catholics, and ostentatiously patronized the Puritans. At length he formed a plot to seize the palace and compel the queen to dismiss her ministers, call a new parliament, and acknowledge James of Scotland as her successor.

On Sunday, Feb. 8, 1601, the earls of Southampton and Rutland, the lords Sandys and Monteagle, and about 300 gentlemen of quality, were summoned to Essex House in the Strand; and the earl informed them that his life was threatened by Raleigh and his party. The queen sent the lord keeper, with other counselors, to know the meaning of the assembly. Essex detained them prisoners, and sallied forth with about 200 followers, to raise the citizens; but as no one joined him, he returned home, and surrendered the same evening to the Earl of Nottingham. On Feb. 19 he was arraigned, with Southampton, before a jury of 25 peers, and found guilty. His contrition moved the pity of the queen, who countermanded the death-warrant she had already signed; but at last, offended at his not asking for mercy, she left him to his fate. He was privately beheaded in the Tower at the age of 34, giving every proof of penitence and piety, Feb. 25, 1601.

During the last two years of her life Elizabeth was the victim of a dejection which some ascribed to her remorse for the fate of Essex, but which was probably the result of natural decay and of exhaustion after the cares of her long and vigorous reign. Her greatest anxiety was about the succession to her crown. She had survived all the family of Charles Brandon, whom her father's will had named as her successors; and there remained only the claim of James Stuart king of Scots, who, besides being the legitimate heir, was a Protestant. But James was personally most distasteful to Elizabeth, and her ministers taxed their ingenuity to conceal their correspondence with him. Sir Robert Cecil, the secretary, and the chief manager of this affair, was one day riding with the queen when a courier delivered some dispatches. "Whence are they?" said Elizabeth. "From Scotland, please your grace," replied the courier. She ordered Cecil to open the packet. As he cut the string he affected to smell some offensive odor from the papers. The queen, always most sensitive on such points, bade him take the papers and have them fumigated before she saw them.

Still her sound judgment perceived the true interest of her kingdom and of the Protestant cause; and there is no good reason to doubt that in her last moments she accepted the King of Scots as her successor. After assuring the Archbishop of Canterbury of her trust in God, she fell into a lethargic slumber and quietly expired, in the 70th year of her age and the 45th of her reign, March 24, 1603.

Her personal character is impressed upon the annals of her reign. With the haughty spirit of her father, she carried her prerogative sometimes even further than he ventured; but she possessed a far sounder judgment. Early adversity had taught her to put some restraint upon her temper, and she had the wisdom to follow wise counselors. The feminine fault of coquetry affected the policy of her government as well as her personal relations to her favorites, and she suffered for the fault; but, as the bride of her country only, her vigor and patriotism well deserved that same chivalrous devotion which has been renewed in our day to the best of her successors, excusing the faults of the one, and exalting the almost faultless virtue of the other. In one word, the reign of Elizabeth has no parallel in English history save that of Victoria.

The annals of Elizabeth are adorned with some of the greatest names of English literature. The majesty of English prose was formed by the hand of Hooker; the harmony of English verse flowed from the lips of Spenser. The drama, the surest proof of an advanced civilization, had then its first beginnings, and was perfected by the immortal genius of Shakspeare; while Bacon opened up a new method of philosophy, whose practical fruits we may be said even now to gather.

Gold Angel of Elizabeth.

James I.

CHAPTER XXIV.

THE HOUSE OF STUART.—JAMES I. A.D. 1603–1625.

In the peaceable succession of James VI. of Scotland as James I. of England we see the full establishment of the principle of *legitimacy*, as opposed to election or selection among members of the royal house, but not as overriding the constitutional liberties of the people.

The Scottish family who now wore the crowns of both divisions of Great Britain were descended from the great Anglo-Norman house of the Fitz-Alans. Walter Fitz-Alan was seneschal or *steward* of Scotland under David I., the contemporary of Stephen. The office became hereditary, and the title was used as a surname. Walter, the sixth high steward, one of Robert Bruce's bravest companions in arms, married the king's daughter, Marjory Bruce; and on the death of Bruce's only son, David II., their only child succeeded him as ROBERT II. (1371); and from him the crown had been transmitted in the direct line of descent for eight generations. But the personal history of the Stuarts had been marked by strange misfortunes. Since Robert II. himself, there were only two who had not suffered a violent death; and they died broken-hearted—the one for his family troubles, the other for national disaster. *Robert II.* died naturally (1389); his son, *Robert III.*, died of a broken heart (1406); his son, *James I.*, was murdered (1435); his son, *James II.*, was killed by the bursting of a gun (1460); his son, *James III.*, was assassinated (1488); his son, *James IV.*, fell on Flodden Field (1513); his son, *James V.*, died of a broken heart (1542); his daughter, Mary, was beheaded (1587); and her son, *James VI.*, was born amidst national and domestic tumults (June 19, 1566), and placed on the throne as rival to his mother (July 24, 1567). He was carefully educated by the celebrated George Buchanan; and his real learning might have escaped the contempt of pedantry, had it been associated with manly qualities; but of these he was utterly destitute, and he even disgraced his lineage by personal cowardice. On assuming the government, at the age of fourteen, he gave himself up to worthless favorites; and he opposed to the turbulence of his nobles and the zeal of the reforming clergy a wretched sort of cunning which he was pleased to call *kingcraft*, and which indeed had somehow helped him through formidable dangers, including two conspiracies—the *Raid of Ruthven* (1582) and the *Gowrie Plot* (1600). He was married, in 1590, to Anne of Denmark, daughter of Frederick II., by whom he had two sons and a daughter: *Henry*, born Feb. 19, 1593; CHARLES, born at Dunfermline, Nov. 19, 1600; and *Elizabeth*, born Aug. 19, 1596, and married in 1612 to Frederick the elector palatine. The children of this marriage were the princes Rupert and Maurice, so distinguished in the civil wars, and *Sophia*, who became Electress of Hanover, and mother of GEORGE I.

The proclamation of James was received in England with universal favor; and in Scotland with a feeling which he himself expressed when he called his new kingdom the *Land of Promise.* But his popularity was dissipated by what was seen of him during his journey to London. The subjects of the Tudors looked with contempt upon his ungainly person and clumsy carriage, his awkward manners and disgusting habits, his airs of conceit, and that affectation of wisdom which his courtiers humored by addressing him as Solomon, while the great Duke of Sully more aptly described him as *the most learned fool in Christendom.* To his contempt was added jealousy at the rewards which he showered upon his Scottish followers, and his cheapening of titles of honor. He made no less than 700 knights during the first three years of his reign.

James was crowned at Westminster, July 25, 1603. He retained Elizabeth's ministers, against whom a plot was soon formed by Lord Cobham, the friend of Sir Walter Raleigh. This plot was called the *Main*, to distinguish it from a contemporaneous conspiracy called the *Bye*, or the plot of the priests, and also the *Surprising Treason*, because its purpose was to surprise and imprison the king. The two plots were much mixed up; and Philip of Spain was concerned in one or both. One object was to set aside the king in favor of his cousin, *Arabella Stuart*, daughter of the Duke of Lennox, Darnley's younger brother. Raleigh was charged with accession to the *Main*, on the sole testimony of Lord Cobham. After a trial, memorable for his dignity in bearing the scurrilous abuse of Sir Edward Coke, he was found guilty of high treason (Nov. 17). He was reprieved and confined in the Tower till 1616, where he occupied himself with his noble "History of the World." After the death of Arabella Stuart, Raleigh was released, but without a pardon, March 20, 1616. Having tempted the king with hopes of finding a rich gold-mine, he sailed for Guiana (1617); but, after a fruitless attack on the Spanish settlement of St. Thomas, on the Orinoco, his crews mutinied, and he retorned to certain death, that he might keep his pledged word. The Spanish minister, Gondomar, now demanded his life; and James, who was then in treaty for his son's marriage to a Spanish princess, had the cruel meanness to send him to the block on the sentence passed fifteen years before. Raleigh died with Christian dignity on Oct. 29, 1618.

The Lady Arabella Stuart, whose name had been used in the *Main* and *Bye* plots, continued in favor with James till 1610, when she was privately married to William Seymour, son of that Lord Beauchamp who was the representative of the line of Mary Tudor and Charles Brandon, and the idea of whose succession Elizabeth had rejected with scorn. Seymour was sent to the Tower, and Arabella was placed in custody at Highgate. Both escaped: Seymour fled to Ostend, but Arabella was captured on board a French bark and committed to the Tower, on no charge known to the law. There she died in 1615, after her reason had given way under the severity of her treatment. Her death left James and his children the sole representatives of the house of Stuart.

Early in his reign James undertook the settlement of the questions at issue between the church and the Puritans. A conference was opened at Hampton Court (Jan. 14, 1604), in which "the modern

Solomon" took an active part, making a vast parade of his learning, and soon showing that, now he was free from the galling yoke of his native Presbyterian divines, he had embraced the principles of high episcopacy. *No bishop, no king,* was one of his favorite maxims. The conference broke up, leaving the two parties where they were. The Book of Common Prayer was slightly altered; and a beginning was made of that translation of the Bible which has ever since been used as the *Authorized Version*—a noble work, though in some respects inferior to the earlier translations.

James's first parliament met on March 19, granted the king duties of tonnage and poundage, and confirmed the edicts of Elizabeth against Jesuits and recusants of the king's supremacy. The House of Commons also framed an 'Apology made to the King touching their Privileges,' showing that they held their privileges of *right* and not of *grace*, as James had proclaimed. Thus early began the conflict of the free people and parliament of England against that doctrine of

"The right divine of kings to govern wrong,"

which James left as a fatal legacy to his house. In the same year peace was made with Spain and Austria, the king binding himself not to aid the Hollanders (Aug. 18); and James was proclaimed by the new title of "King of Great Britain, France, and Ireland" (Oct. 24, 1604). On his medals he assumed the title of "Imperator."

The Catholics had watched for the new reign with deep anxiety. Their hopes from the son of Mary Stuart were at first strengthened by James's promises of toleration. But when the first acts of the king and parliament taught them that he had neither the power nor the will to change the temper of the people toward them, certain fanatics planned that strange stroke of revenge known as the "Gunpowder Plot." The parliament of 1605 was about to meet, after several prorogations, on the FIFTH OF NOVEMBER. On the 26th of October, Lord Mounteagle, a Catholic peer, waited upon Cecil, now Earl of Salisbury, with an anonymous letter, which had been sent to warn Mounteagle from attending the parliament, which, the writer said, "shall receive a terrible blow, and yet they shall not see who hurts them." It is now pretty certain that the letter was a pretense, to cover the more direct betrayal of his fellow-conspirators, by Francis Tresham, the brother-in-law of Lord Mounteagle. Cecil proceeded with great coolness, first consulting other members of the council. After six days he waited upon James, who was engaged in his usual occupation of hunting, at Royston. Prompted, doubtless, by a hint not too broad, the sagacious king conjectured that the above words and others in the letter pointed at "a blowing up of powder;" and Cecil was too good a courtier to prevent the discovery being blazoned abroad, as, in the words of Sir Edward Coke, "a divine illumination of the royal mind." No alarm was given, either to the people or the conspirators. On Nov. 4 the lord chamberlain made a cursory examination of the vaults under the House of Lords, and observed a large stock of coals and wood in a cellar, where they found "a very tall and desperate fellow," who called himself the servant of Mr. Percy. A second visit was made soon after midnight, when the same man was seized with slow matches and touchwood and a dark lantern. The coals and wood proved, on a search, to be a covering for thirty-six barrels of gunpowder. The prisoner was taken to Whitehall, and declared before James and the council that, if he had not been apprehended, he would have blown up the parliament-house, with the king and royal family, the peers and bishops; for he was authorized to destroy them as excommunicated heretics. On the following day his real name was extorted from him by the rack, the terrible effect of which is still attested by the signature to his confession. He proved to be one GUIDO or GUY FAWKES, the son of a notary of York; a convert to Catholicism, and for some time a soldier in the Spanish army of Flanders, where he had learned how to treat heretics. He had been brought to London in 1604, by *Thomas Winter*, as a fit instrument for the plot, which had been formed early in that year by *Robert Catesby*, a gentleman of good family, who had been concerned in the insurrection of the Earl of Essex. Catesby had sought the aid of *Thomas Percy*, a relative of the Duke of Northumberland, and of another old friend, named *John Wright;* they were soon joined by *Winter*, then by *Fawkes*, and afterward by *Robert Keyes* and *Christopher Wright*. Binding themselves by an oath of secrecy, which they took at the hands of *Henry Garnett* and other Jesuits, these seven men, with the aid of Catesby's servant, *Thomas Bates*, labored incessantly for eighteen months, collecting gunpowder at a house at Lambeth, which formed their head-quarters, and bringing it over to the cellar under the House of Lords, which was hired in Percy's name, after they had toiled for some time in digging a mine. In the summer of 1605 Fawkes went to Flanders to engage the Spaniards in the conspiracy, and Catesby raised a troop of horse. Meanwhile the plot was communicated to Sir Everard Digby, Ambrose Rookwood, and Francis Tresham, all country gentlemen connected with the Jesuits, and the last a cousin of Catesby, who distrusted him from the beginning.

On the 5th of November there was a general rendezvous of the conspirators at Dunchurch, to follow up the blow which should have been struck in London, by seizing the Princess Elizabeth. Sir

Everard Digby was already there with a large party, when Catesby, Percy, and others arrived from London with the news of Fawkes's arrest. Marching to Holbeach in Staffordshire, they made a brave defense against the forces raised by the sheriff; Percy and Catesby were killed by one shot as they fought back to back. Several others were taken and executed, as was Garnett the Jesuit. The immediate result of the plot was the enactment of severer laws against the Catholics (1606); and the oath of allegiance was devised, abjuring the doctrine "that princes excommunicated or deprived by the pope may be deposed or murdered by their subjects." Arians and other heretics were still sent to the stake (1612).

The reign of James I. witnessed the foundation of our colonial empire. In 1607 a permanent settlement was effected at James Town in Virginia, Raleigh's settlement having been abandoned (see p. 177). In 1610 a charter was granted for the colonization of Newfoundland; and in 1620 a band of Nonconformist exiles, the celebrated "Pilgrim Fathers," sailed from Holland and landed at Massachusetts Bay, and there formed the germ of the New England States. The charter granted by Elizabeth (1600) for fifteen years to the East India Company was renewed in perpetuity (1609; a factory was established at Surat, and their trade was extended to Java and Sumatra (1611). In the same year, an English adventurer, Sir Thomas Sherley, arrived as embassador from the Shah of Persia, and in 1615 an embassy was sent to the Great Mogul at Agra.

Nearer home a great step was taken toward the civilization of Ireland by the formation of a company in London for the colonization of Ulster. To provide funds for its defense the new order of "Baronets" was founded (May 22, 1611); but the fees for their patents were also applied to other uses. The *bloody hand* on a baronet's shield is the cognizance of Ulster.

The year 1612 was marked by the deaths of the minister Robert Cecil earl of Salisbury (May 24), and of HENRY PRINCE OF WALES (Nov. 6), of whose talents, virtues, and manly accomplishments his contemporaries speak in the warmest terms. A mystery hangs over his fate. Three months later (Feb. 14, 1613) the Princess Elizabeth was married to Frederick, the elector palatine. All these three events had, sooner or later, the gravest consequences.

Cecil's successor was a young Scot, named Robert Carr, who had come to court in 1609, been installed as the king's favorite, and created Viscount Rochester (1611). James not only aided him in gratifying his passion for the Countess of Essex by procuring her divorce from the earl, but he gave Rochester, on his marriage, the title of Earl of Somerset. Then followed a terrible tragedy, the poisoning of Sir Thomas Overbury, the friend of Carr, who had opposed his passion for Lady Essex (Sept. 15, 1613). The crime was brought to light by the free talk of the person who had prepared the poison, and the Earl and Countess of Somerset were convicted by their peers (May, 1616). They were pardoned by James, whose whole conduct in the matter is most suspicious.

But meanwhile the king had transferred his affections to a new favorite, GEORGE VILLIERS, who appeared at court in 1615. He was a young man of twenty-one: and with a fine person he had all the arts of pleasing a weak and vain man like James, who created him, in rapid succession, Viscount Villiers, Earl, Marquis, and Duke of Buckingham; loaded him with wealth, and conferred on him some of the highest offices of the realm. These favors engendered in Villiers a capricious insolence, which rendered him hateful to the people, while the king was alternately terrified and coaxed into submission to his temper. Under his guidance the court became more than ever a scene of debauchery, which disgusted all who remembered the stately decorum of Elizabeth. Not even the plays of Shakspeare nor the masques of Ben Jonson could redeem the low coarse sensuality of the king, and the unbridled profligacy of his favorite, which the new nobility, dependent on court favor, made haste to imitate. That the severity of the Puritans was provoked by the dissoluteness of the court is at least as true as that the vices of the Restoration were a reaction from their moroseness.

But public affairs were escaping from the grasp of king and favorite, both abroad and at home, in the church and in the state. "Your queen," wrote a courtier to Harrington, "did talk of her subjects' *love and good affection*, and in good truth she aimed well. Our king talketh of his subjects' *fear and subjection*, and herein I think he doth well too, *as long as it holdeth good.*" But James had neither the power nor the industry to make it hold good; while his frivolous pleasures and the grants to his courtiers constantly drove him to appeal to parliament for money. In 1605 the commons demurred to granting a supply; and in 1610 they voted one amounting only to £100,000, and passed a bill forbidding illegal exactions by the king's sole authority. They offered James a settled revenue of £200,000 in lieu of the feudal prerogatives by which he claimed to raise money. They also remonstrated against the abuse of proclamations, and the proceedings of the court of high commission. This first parliament of James was dissolved (Feb. 9, 1611) after sitting seven years.

James's second parliament met April 5, 1614; and set the great example of *declining to grant supplies till the illegal impositions and other grievances were redressed.* This is the first clear and direct use of the constitutional "power of the purse," by which the commons ultimately secured the whole direction of legislation. The obvious reply was for the king to use his prerogative of dissolving parliament, and he dismissed them angrily without their passing a single act. Hence this was called the "*Addled Parliament.*" But meanwhile money must be had. It was raised by a *benevolence;* and now the conflict passed into its second stage, *individual resistance* to the illegal use of the prerogative. A gentleman, named Oliver St. John, was fined £5000 in the Star Chamber for condemning this method of raising money. But he had on his side the highest legal authority, Chief-Justice Coke, who had already on other occasions given offense by maintaining the laws of the land where they opposed the king's will. On one occasion he had said that "his highness was defended by his laws;" but James told him "he spoke foolishly, for he was not defended by his laws, but by God;" and Coke had to beg pardon on his knees! He was at length dismissed (Nov., 1617), while Sir Francis Bacon, who had maintained the king's prerogative against Coke, was made lord keeper (March 7, 1617), and in the following year lord chancellor. He was also created Viscount St. Albans.

James was equally eager to assert his authority in religious as in civil matters, and he dealt with both in the same petty and ineffectual manner. By issuing a proclamation allowing of public sports on Sundays after divine service, he irritated the Puritans to no purpose, and exposed himself to a rebuff from Archbishop Abbot, who forbade the reading of the proclamation in churches (1618). The year before James had revisited his native country for the first time, only to impose episcopacy upon a people who had cast it off (1617). Scottish preachers soon began to declaim against prelacy, though it was reserved for the next reign to reap the fruits of all these measures.

Another root of discord and a new power of opposition was being rapidly developed from the king's foreign policy. He had made peace with Spain, as we have seen, in 1605, abandoning the Hollanders, and only stipulating for the *moderating* of the powers of the inquisition over English subjects trading in Spain. In 1609 he mediated a twelve years' truce between Spain and Holland, an unforeseen effect of which was to send the English and Dutch privateers, who had preyed upon the Spaniards, to the seas of the West Indies, where they became the terribly renowned *Buccaneers,* while others joined the Barbary corsairs in the Mediterranean.

The murder of Henry IV. of France by the fanatic Ravaillac (1610) made the people more averse than ever to alliances with Catholic powers; and they viewed the death of Raleigh as a sacrifice to propitiate Spain, with which power James was already meditating a closer connection by the marriage of his son Charles, now Prince of Wales, to the infanta Maria, second daughter of Philip III. The Spanish embassador, Gondomar, protracted the negotiations, to prevent James from aiding the Protestants of Germany, whose cause was in the greatest peril.

The Emperor Matthias died in 1619, and was succeeded by Ferdinand II., who also claimed the kingdom of Bohemia by right of inheritance from Matthias. But the Bohemians, who had heartily embraced the Reformation, offered the crown to Frederick, the elector palatine, son-in-law to James I. and nephew of Prince Maurice of the Netherlands, in the hope of forming a great Protestant alliance. James at first held aloof, till the popular indignation forced him to send 4000 volunteers, not to aid Frederick in Bohemia, but only to defend the palatinate. Meanwhile Frederick was defeated by the Austrians at Prague (Nov. 7, 1620), and the father of the future kings of England fled for his life to Holland; while the Spaniards, under Spinola, ravaged the palatinate, meeting with little resistance except from the small English force under Sir Horace Vere. The battle of Prague proved the death-blow to Protestantism in Bohemia and Southern Germany.

To crown all these provocations, James closed the year with a proclamation, "forbidding any of his subjects to discourse of state matters, either foreign or domestic" (Dec. 23, 1620).

The temper of the people was reflected in the new parliament, which the king's wants compelled him to call after an interval of seven years (Jan. 30, 1621), and to whom he afterward said—"I have often piped unto you, but you have not danced." They granted him a small subsidy, and then turned to the redress of grievances, in a spirit of vengeance on their authors. The system of granting monopolies and patents as a source of revenue had grown into an enormous abuse; and the commons impeached Sir Giles Mompesson, who had patents for licensing ale-houses, and for gold and silver thread, which he had made of base metal. He fled beyond seas. A still greater evil was the venality of the judges; and it is mournful to record the name of the great Lord Bacon as one of the chief offenders. He was impeached by the commons before the lords, for corruption in his office of chancellor. He confessed to twenty-eight articles; his only apology being that the presents he had accepted had never influenced his decisions, and that his frailty had lain in partaking of the abuses of the times. But such excuses were unheeded by a parliament which had set about a new work of reform; in which his old enemy, Sir Edward Coke, was a chief leader; and where so many remembered his treatment of Essex as well as his flattery of James. The late chancellor was sentenced to pay a fine of £40,000, to be imprisoned in the Tower during the king's pleasure, to be banished from court, and to be incapable of holding any state office or of sitting in parliament. The king remitted his fine and soon released him, providing for him by a pension of £1800 a year; and Bacon spent the remaining five years of his life in the uninterrupted study of philosophy, by which his name has been immortalized. His own reflection on his fall was this: "I was the justest judge that was in England these fifty years; but it was the justest censure in parliament that was there these 200 years."

This praise could not be awarded to the cruel sentence passed on a Roman Catholic barrister, Edward Floyd, for expressing his joy that "goodman Palsgrave and goodwife Palsgrave (*i. e.* Mr. and Mrs. Elector Palatine) had been driven from Prague." The commons, without hearing him, sentenced him to be whipped, to have his ears nailed to the pillory, and his tongue bored. He denied the charge and appealed to the king, who demanded of the commons how they dared to judge offenses which did not touch their privileges. The case was transferred to the Star Chamber, and Floyd was fined £5000 and imprisoned for life. The whole affair is a memorable example, to show how the country party were driven by passion into the very outrages upon justice and into acts of cruelty from which they themselves were soon to suffer.

The parliament was prorogued on June 4; but before separating they recorded a unanimous resolution to spend their lives and fortunes in defense of their religion and of the palatinate. They met again on Nov. 20, indignant at the imprisonment of one of their members, Sir Edwin Sandys, during the recess, and at the news that the Austrians had overrun the palatinate, inflicting all manner of cruelties on the Protestants. The commons presented to the king a petition, drawn up by Coke, against the growth of Popery in general and the Spanish alliance in particular, praying that the palatinate might be defended, and that Prince Charles might be married only to a Protestant. James, who had already made a treaty with Spain for the marriage, and for the toleration of Popery (April 27, 1620), wrote to the speaker, commanding the house not to meddle with any matter which concerned his government or the mysteries of state, as things far above their reach and capacity! To their renewed claim of liberty of speech, he replied that *their privileges were derived from the grace and permission of his ancestors and himself.* Upon this the commons drew up their celebrated PROTESTATION, asserting that "*the liberties, franchises, privileges, and jurisdictions of parliament are the ancient and undoubted birth-right and inheritance of the subjects of England.*" James sent for their journals, and in full council tore out the record with his own hand, and prorogued the parliament (Dec. 9), which was soon after dissolved (Feb. 8, 1622). The authors of the Protestation, COKE, PYM, and SELDEN, were imprisoned, with other members, as well as the Earl of Oxford; for it deserves especial notice that the peers had acted with the commons. In this parliament the die was cast, and that contest was fairly begun between the crown and the country, in which James had sown the wind; and his son, trained in his principles, was to reap the whirlwind.

Thus left to his own counsel, the king proceeded with the Spanish match, and hoped by its means to obtain the peaceable restoration of the elector palatine. PHILIP IV., who had succeeded to the throne of Spain (1621), promised to obtain the necessary papal dispensation, while James engaged not only to tolerate Catholic worship, but to endeavor to reunite the churches, and gave an earnest of his intentions by releasing persons confined as Popish recusants. Philip promised his good offices toward restoring the elector palatine. Things were in this position when Buckingham proposed to Prince Charles to give the court of Spain the pleasing surprise of a visit, and James somewhat reluctantly consented (Feb. 1623). The prince and Buckingham traveled in disguise, under the names of John and Thomas Smith.* At Paris "John Smith" saw and fell in love with the Princess Henrietta Maria, sister of Louis XIII. This accident, and Buckingham's disorderly conduct at Madrid, ruined the whole scheme. The prince and Buckingham returned to England (Oct. 5); and after some further negotiation the match was broken off in December, James losing the two millions of promised dowry, and all hopes of the recovery of the palatinate.

Parliament met on Feb. 19, 1624. Buckingham satisfied the house with a garbled version of the recent negotiations, the truth of which Prince Charles came forward to attest; and this was the first public exhibition of that vice of insincerity which afterward ruined him. War was declared with Spain for the recovery of the palatinate, and £300,000 were voted. An act was passed, declaring monopolies illegal; and an impeachment was preferred against the Earl of Middlesex, lord treasurer, for corruption in his office. He was found guilty by the peers, and fined £50,000.

Parliament was prorogued May 29, and James found himself crossed in his favorite schemes, committed to war against his will, and treated with contempt by his son, over whom Buckingham had acquired a complete ascendency. He consented to the prince's marriage with Henrietta Maria, and the treaty was concluded Nov. 12.

* This genuine English name was also taken by the late King Louis Philippe, who fled into England as "William Smith" in 1848.

In the following spring the king caught an ague among the damps of his favorite residence at Theobalds, in Hertfordshire, and died (March 27, 1625), in the 23d year of his reign over England, and the 59th of his age. His better qualities were neutralized by his overweening conceit of his own wisdom and his royal authority. Though the conflict which he provoked only came to an issue under his son, there was not a claim of prerogative made by Charles, nor an assertion of privilege by his earlier parliaments, which had not been first put forward under James.

The growing intercourse with Italy gave a new direction to art under the Stuarts; and the style of architecture which *Palladio* had invented from the classical models was cultivated in England by *Inigo Jones*. His great design was the new palace of Whitehall, a vast edifice, of which the Banqueting-house was the only part completed. It now forms the Chapel Royal. The wealthy merchant, Sir *Hugh Myddelton*, led the way in civil engineering, by the construction of the *New River* for supplying London with water. Hudson, Baffin, and other intrepid navigators, opened a new path of maritime enterprise in the Arctic regions.

House of the Conspirators at Lambeth.

Charles I. and Armor-bearer. (Vandyke.)

CHAPTER XXV.

THE HOUSE OF STUART (*continued*).—CHARLES I. FROM HIS ACCESSION TO THE MEETING OF THE LONG PARLIAMENT. A.D. 1625–1640.

CHARLES I. (1625-1649) was born at Dunfermline, Nov. 19, 1600. Soon after his father's accession to the throne of England he was created Duke of York, and, in 1612, the death of his elder brother

Henry made him Prince of Wales. Succeeding his father on March 27, 1625, he was married by proxy (June 13) to the Princess Henrietta Maria of France, whom Buckingham conducted to England (June 25).

The personal character of Charles presented a marked contrast to the undignified conceit, the childish frivolity, and the gross sensuality of his father. He was dignified and devout, and grave even to melancholy. He applied himself steadily to the business of the state, and set about the payment of his father's debts by the sacrifice of the royal forests, in which James had delighted. "The face of the court was much changed in the change of the king." But the hopes of serious men of all parties were destined to disappointment, partly through the pernicious influence of Buckingham, partly through the bad advice of the queen, but chiefly through Charles's high views of prerogative, and the strange mixture of violence, irresolution, and duplicity displayed in his dealings with his subjects.

A new parliament met on June 18; and after voting two small subsidies (about £140,000) for the war with Spain, they required an account of former subsidies, and a redress of grievances. In vain did Charles urge on them his necessities. Their spirit of opposition was inflamed by the discovery that Buckingham, as lord admiral, had lent some ships to the king of France, to be employed against the Huguenots, who were defending themselves in their last stronghold at Rochelle. This parliament, in fact, was entirely guided by the old popular leaders, Coke, Selden, Pym, and others, to whom must now be added the names of Sir John Eliot and Sir Thomas Wentworth. They had removed from Westminster to Oxford on account of the plague; and the appearance of the disease in the latter city gave Charles a pretext for dissolving a parliament from which he could obtain no supplies (Aug. 12, 1625).

After an attempt to raise money by loan, and an abortive attack on Cadiz under Lord Wimbledon, Charles summoned a new parliament (Feb. 6, 1626). The sheriffs had been directed to exclude the chief patriots; and no writ of summons was issued to the Earl of Bristol, the late embassador to Spain. These stretches of prerogative both recoiled on the court. Bristol appealed to the lords, and his writ was then issued; and on a new attempt to intimidate him, he accused Buckingham as the author of the war with Spain. Meanwhile the commons presented to the peers articles of impeachment against Buckingham (May 8). The king sent the managers (Sir Dudley Digges and Sir John Eliot) to the Tower, but released them on the refusal of the House to proceed with business. The same method was tried with a peer, the Earl of Arundel, with the like result; and this *second* parliament was dissolved (June 15, 1626).

Among various attempts now made to raise money without the sanction of parliament was a *general loan*, for refusing to contribute to which several gentlemen were imprisoned; and the judges set at naught the chief provision of the Magna Charta by deciding that a special mandate from the king justified this step. Meanwhile Cardinal Richelieu, the prime minister of Louis XIII., had laid siege to La Rochelle; and England, already at war with the whole Austrian power in Germany and Spain, declared war also against France. Buckingham, who was believed to be the chief adviser of this measure, sailed with a fleet and army to La Rochelle; but the Huguenots distrusted and refused to receive him. He landed at the Isle of Rhé; and after losing two-thirds of his men, and all his hope of military reputation, he returned to England (Oct. 12, 1627).

The want of money compelled the calling of a *third* parliament (March 17, 1628), which was conspicuous for the station, wealth, and learning of its members, among whom were many of the gentlemen who had suffered for resisting the general loan. In his opening speech the king told them that, if they refused to relieve his necessities, he would resort to other means; but yet they set to their work with perfect temper; and after voting five subsidies, but before completing the grant, they embodied their claim for the redress of grievances in the memorable PETITION OF RIGHT, which has been called the *Second Great Charter* of the people of England. The grievances complained of were these: Forced loans and benevolences; taxes imposed without the consent of parliament; arbitrary imprisonments; the billeting of soldiers; and martial law. The remedy asked was not the grant of any new liberties, but the observance of the ancient rights of the people, as embodied in Magna Charta. The king tried all methods of evasion, and asked the commons to trust him for their rights and liberties, "to the preservation of which he held himself in conscience as well obliged as of his prerogative." To show that they were in earnest the commons commenced proceedings against Buckingham. Upon this the king gave way, and the *Petition of Right* passed into the statute which bears the same title (3 Car. I. c. 1; June 7, 1628). The proceedings of this parliament against the prelates of the court party will be noticed presently.

Buckingham was saved from impeachment by the prorogation of parliament (June 26), but in two months he fell a victim to the knife of Felton (Aug. 23). The assassin, a lieutenant in the army, was a man of melancholy temperament, who had served under Buckingham at the Isle of Rhé, and had been disappointed of promotion. He obtained entrance into the house at Portsmouth where the duke, surrounded by his officers, was preparing a new expedition to aid La Rochelle, and stabbed him with a knife. Amidst the confusion that ensued Felton was seen walking composedly in front of the house. He at once avowed the deed, but would confess to no other motive than that he had killed the duke as a public enemy. Charles wished to have him racked, but the judges declared the practice illegal; and thus ended the horrid system of extracting evidence by torture. Felton was executed on Nov. 27. Meanwhile the fleet prepared by Buckingham had sailed under the Earl of Lindsay, but nothing was effected; and the fall of La Rochelle (Oct. 28) left Cardinal Richelieu at liberty to perfect his great scheme of absolute monarchy, which ultimately proved the ruin of the Bourbons.

Charles's feebler attempt at the same policy was hurrying the Stuarts to speedier ruin. The concession of the Petition of Right and the death of Buckingham instead of turning the king into a new path seemed only to irritate his opposition to the popular party, both in Church and State. The former subject now claims our attention. The great body of Protestants throughout Europe had by this time been parted into two chief doctrinal sections, by the same controversy respecting the sovereign grace of God and the free-will of man which had been discussed in the 5th century between Augustin and Pelagius. The leaders of these two parties were Calvin and Arminius. The views of Calvin were adopted, in general, by the English reformers under Edward VI., and still more decidedly by John Knox and the Kirk of Scotland. James I. was long a Calvinist, and took part, by his envoys, in the condemnation of the Arminians at the *Synod of Dort* in Holland (1618); but a party was gaining strength in the Church of England who combined with Arminian views a leaning to the ceremonies of the Church of Rome, and an extreme assertion of the divine rights both of bishops and of kings. James at last joined this party, forbade the clergy to preach predestination, and conferred bishoprics on several leading Arminians. Charles, who had early adopted the same views, encouraged their avowal from the pulpit, especially by Dr. Mainwaring, who, preaching before the king at Whitehall, condemned those who refused the general loan as enemies of God and of the king. The leader of this party was WILLIAM LAUD, who was born at Reading, Oct. 7, 1573. While a student at Oxford his opposition to the Puritans incurred the censure of the vice-chancellor Abbot. He became chaplain to Neile, the Arminian bishop of Rochester, who introduced him to James I. Having accompanied the king to Scotland, and aided him in the restoration of episcopacy, Laud was made Bishop of St. Davids (1621), and translated by Charles I. to the see of Bath and Wells (1626). One passage in Laud's diary speaks volumes. When fined by the Long Parliament (Dec. 21, 1640) for an illegal imprisonment, he writes, "Say the imprisonment were more than the law allow; what may [not] be done for honor and religion sake?"

The king's favor to this party had from the first given dissatisfaction to his parliaments. In 1625 they condemned the "Appello Cæsarem" of Dr. Montagu, a king's chaplain, who had already been censured by the last parliament of James, and silenced by Archbishop Abbot. The parliament of 1628, after the enactment of the Petition of Right, framed a remonstrance accusing Bishops Neile and Laud of favoring Popery. Charles replied by advancing Laud, directly after the prorogation, to the bishopric of London (July 11), with the powers of the primacy, Archbishop Abbot having been suspended for his opposition to the high-church party; and about the same time Montagu was made Bishop of Chichester.

Dangerous as was such a counselor as Laud, whose learning and earnestness of purpose only made his extreme littleness of mind the more mischievous, it was Charles's fate to gain over from the popular ranks a new adviser, whose nobler qualities proved still more fatal. Sir THOMAS WENTWORTH, of a wealthy Yorkshire family, was born in London in 1593. He sat for Yorkshire in several parliaments, where he was one of the most eloquent leaders of the country party; and he was imprisoned for refusing to contribute to a forced loan. In 1628, after the death of Buckingham, he was gained over to the court by the offer of a peerage, and was created Baron Wentworth. His old comrade Pym said to him, "You are going to be undone; but remember that, though you leave us now, I will never leave you while your head is on your shoulders." Wentworth's was a deliberate choice. His clear mind saw that the constitution had lost its balance; that either the king or the parliament must be supreme; and he chose the part most congenial to his pride of birth, his haughty courage, and his boundless ambition.

When the parliament reassembled (Jan. 20, 1629) they refused all supplies till they should have discussed grievances, and resolved that "whoever should bring in innovation of religion, Popery, or Arminianism, and any that should advise the taking of tonnage and poundage not granted by parliament, or that should pay the same, should be accounted enemies to the kingdom." This resolution was passed on March 2, amidst a strange scene of confusion. The speaker, Finch, who was soon afterward made chief justice, refused to put it, and said that he had a command from the king to adjourn and to put no question. He then left the chair, but he was forced back into it, and held there by Hollis and Valentine while the remonstrance was passed by acclamation. During this scene the doors were locked; and the gentleman usher, who had been sent by the king, was kept waiting outside. He now entered, and ended the sitting by removing the mace from the table. Eight days later (March 10) the king dissolved the parliament with a speech which characterized his opponents as "vipers;" and a proclamation was issued, intimating his intention to govern without parliaments (March 22). Sir John Eliot, Hollis, and Valentine were imprisoned for refusing to answer in the court of King's Bench for their conduct in parliament. They disdained to accept of liberty on the condition of finding sureties for their good behavior; and Sir John Eliot died in prison (Nov. 27, 1632).

The great experiment of absolute government, to which Charles had now committed himself, lasted for eleven years (1629–1640). His chief advisers were the queen, Laud, and Wentworth. Royal proclamations were declared to have the force of statutes. The taxes condemned by parliament were levied, and peace was made with France (April 14) and Spain (Nov.). The courts of High Commission and the Star Chamber became more active and arbitrary than ever, imposing heavy fines and inflicting cruel punishments for sedition, libel, and nonconformity. Two examples may suffice. Dr. *Alexander Leighton*, a Scottish divine, was imprisoned and put in the pillory (Nov., 1630) for writing a book entitled "Zion's Plea against Prelates," in which, besides attacking the bishops, he called the queen a "Canaanite and idolatress." He was twice whipped and branded, had his ears cut off and his nose slit, and remained in prison eleven years, till he was released by the Long Parliament. His son became Archbishop of St. Andrews under Charles II. *Prynne*, a barrister of Lincoln's Inn, had written a quarto of 1000 pages, entitled "*Histriomastix*," against stage plays, interludes, music, dancing, and other festivities. As some of these amusements were patronized by the court, the Star Chamber condemned the book as a seditious libel, and sentenced Prynne to be put from the bar, to stand in the pillory at Westminster and Cheapside, and to have one of his ears cut off at each place, to pay a fine of £5000 to the king, and to be imprisoned for life (1633). The "Book of Sports" was again issued; and all the clergy were commanded to read in their churches the proclamation which enjoined the king's subjects to amuse themselves on Sundays, after morning service, according to its directions (1633).

While Laud, now Archbishop of Canterbury, was sitting in the Star Chamber to direct these measures and to punish the Puritans, and was conforming the worship of the Church of England nearer and nearer to the Romish model, Wentworth was maturing his plans for making the king absolute. In 1629 he was created a viscount, and made lord president of the Council of the North, an office of almost despotic authority. In 1633 he was sent to Ireland as lord deputy, and there he put in practice the model of government which he designed to introduce into England. "You may govern as you please," he wrote to Laud. "I know no reason but you may as well rule the common lawyers in England as I, poor beagle, do here, and that upon the peril of my head. I am confident that the king is able to carry any just and honorable action *thorough* all imaginable opposition." *Thorough* is the constant watchword of his correspondence with Laud.

Passing over innumerable details of this despotic government, we come to the great act of opposition which has immortalized the name of JOHN HAMPDEN. Having been rated at 20*s*., as ship-money, for his estate in Buckinghamshire, Hampden refused to pay the tax as illegal. His example was followed by others. The recusants were cited into the Exchequer Chamber, where, after an argument which lasted for six weeks, the twelve judges, with two exceptions, gave their sentence for the crown; "which judgment," says Clarendon, "proved of more advantage and credit to the gentleman condemned than to the king's service" (June 12, 1637). In the same year the press was placed under the most rigorous surveillance by a decree of the Star Chamber (July 1); and a proclamation (April 30) restricting emigration to America seemed to shut out the oppressed from the last sad refuge of voluntary exile.

At length a crisis was brought on by Charles's determination to force the English ecclesiastical system upon Scotland. Though never recognized as the head of the Scottish Church, and without consulting the General Assembly, he issued a set of canons, and a liturgy, slightly varied from that of the Church of England. On Sunday, July 23, 1637, the liturgy was appointed to be read for the first time in the cathedral of St. Giles at Edinburgh; but the dean no sooner appeared in his surplice than his voice was drowned by the cries of, "A pope! a pope! Antichrist! Stone him!" When the bishop mounted the pulpit to appease the tumult a stool was thrown at his head; and the magistrates could scarcely disperse the congregation. The nobility and gentry, for the most part, made common cause with the people; and when they found the king inflexible, they organized a provisional government, consisting of four "*Tables*," the nobility, gentry, ministers, and burgesses. The Tables drew up the celebrated instrument called the COVENANT, which contained a renunciation of popery, and an engagement for mutual defense in resisting religious innovations (March 1, 1638). Almost the whole people flocked to subscribe the Covenant. Charles made great concessions, but it was too late. Without reference to his authority, a general assembly met at Glasgow (Nov. 21, 1638), and abolished episcopacy, the court of High Commission, the canons, and the liturgy; while the nation prepared for war, seizing the fortresses and opening communications both with France and with the English malcontents. Charles levied a large army (Feb., 1639), and joined them in person at York; but when he reached Berwick he suddenly made a pacification with the Scots, conceding all their demands, and engaging that a parliament and a general assembly should be called to compose all differences (June 18, 1639). These bodies met in August, when the parliament made such proposals for limiting the king's authority that they were prorogued by the royal commissioner. They sat on in defiance of his authority, and the war recommenced.

In England preparations for the new campaign involved Charles in the necessity of calling a *fourth* parliament, after an interval of eleven years; but the day of reckoning for the misrule of that period was still postponed for a few months. The parliament, which met April 13, 1640, proving to be resolute in discussing grievances before supply, was dissolved abruptly on the 5th of May. It is sometimes called the *Short Parliament*. On the night of the 11th an attack was made by a mob on Laud's palace at Lambeth. This riot was construed into treason, as being a levying of war, and one of the rioters was executed.

Meanwhile the Scots were preparing to enter England with an army of 25,000 men to back their petition for a redress of grievances. They passed the Tweed on the 20th of August. On the 27th they defeated a detachment of 4500 men under Lord Conway at Newburn-upon-Tyne, and took possession of Newcastle. The king was now at York with Wentworth, who had returned from Ireland, and had been created Earl of Strafford. Charles summoned a great council of the peers to meet him at that city; and by their advice he consented to a treaty, and commissioners were appointed on both sides to meet at Ripon. Here an armistice was agreed on (Oct. 26). The negotiations were transferred to London, and a weekly subsidy of £5600 was granted to the Scots while they remained in England.

The system of governing without a parliament had now finally broken down; and Charles, making a virtue of necessity, announced to the peers at York his intention to call a parliament. This step was virtually a surrender of the government to the popular party, and the commencement of the FIRST ENGLISH REVOLUTION. The returns to the writs included all the surviving popular leaders, who had directed the course of former parliaments and had suffered in the cause of liberty, such as Pym, Hampden, Hollis, Vane, and St. John. The coming change was preceded, as is usual, by popular commotions. A mob broke into St. Paul's, where the court of High Commission was sitting, and tore up the benches, with cries of "No bishop! no High Commission!" And this was the last sitting of that odious court (Oct. 22). Strafford and Laud were especially threatened. Even the former quailed before the coming storm, and wished to return to Ireland; while Laud committed his fears to the pages of his diary, and saw in the fall of his portrait from a wall in his palace too true an omen of his own approaching fate.

Amidst these signs of the times met that memorable assembly, the *Fifth* parliament of Charles I., which has obtained, from its duration, the name of the LONG PARLIAMENT. It sat from Nov. 3, 1640, till it was turned out by Cromwell, April 10, 1653, and was not finally dissolved till 1660. (See p. 227.) It formed for those twelve years and a half the real government of Great Britain, for the power of Charles ceased with its meeting, though his nominal reign was prolonged till his unhappy death on Jan. 30, 1649.

House at Portsmouth in which the Duke of Buckingham was assassinated.

Puritans destroying the Cross in Cheapside.

CHAPTER XXVI.

THE HOUSE OF STUART (*continued*).—CHARLES I. FROM THE MEETING OF THE LONG PARLIAMENT TO THE EXECUTION OF THE KING. A.D. 1640-1649.

CHARLES went down to his new parliament with but little state, and opened it with a speech inviting the laying aside of suspicion on both sides. But confidence was irreparably destroyed. The commons elected Lenthall for their speaker, in opposition to the king's wishes. Petitions for the redress of grievances poured in from all sides; but the first hearing was given to those of the imprisoned and mutilated victims of the Star Chamber, who were released and compensated for their fines and sufferings. On the 9th of November Strafford came to London, in dependence on the king's promise, that "not a hair of his head should be touched by the parliament;" and on the 11th, Pym moved his impeachment for high treason. The debate was conducted with closed doors, lest Strafford should learn what was doing and advise a dissolution. The vote was passed unanimously, with the concurrence even of the moderate royalists, among whom HYDE and FALKLAND now became conspicuous. A crowd of members followed Pym to the House of Lords: the bill of impeachment was presented, and Strafford, coming down to the house in haste, was at once ordered into custody. He was removed to the Tower on Nov. 25. The lord keeper Finch, and Sir Francis Windebank, who were next attacked, fled to Holland and France. Then came the turn of Laud, who was denounced by the Scots as "the great incendiary." The new canons framed by him were declared by the commons illegal (Dec. 16), and he was ordered into custody by the lords (Dec. 18). Commissions were sent out to deface and remove all images and superstitious ornaments of churches (Jan. 23, 1641); but they also destroyed many beautiful monuments, and, among the rest, Cheapside and Charing Crosses. Persons who had exercised illegal powers, including the levy of arbitrary taxes, or who had concurred in the sentences of the courts of the Star Chamber and High Commission, were proceeded against as "*delinquents*" (Jan., 1641).

On the 15th of February the *Triennial Act* was passed to prevent any further attempt to govern without a parliament. It provided that a parliament should meet at least once in every three years; that the lord chancellor and other officers should take an oath to issue the necessary writs; that, if the chancellor failed to issue the writs by the 3d of September in each third year, any twelve peers might do so; that, in default of the peers, the sheriffs, mayors, and other municipal officers should summon the voters; and, as a last resort, that the electors might meet and choose representatives, who should assemble on the third Monday in January. Nor could the parliament be adjourned, prorogued, or dissolved, without their own consent, within fifty days after their meeting. On the 10th of March the commons passed a bill to prevent clergymen from holding any civil office, and the bishops from sitting in the House of Lords; but it was rejected by the peers. This was the first instance of any serious difference between the two houses.

The trial of Strafford was now at hand. The charges against him, in twenty-eight articles, had been laid before the lords on Jan. 30, and his case had been referred to a joint committee of the two houses, who were sworn to secrecy. The trial commenced on March 28, in Westminster Hall, which was fitted up with great state. The peers sat as judges on raised benches, with Lord Arundel as high steward on the woolsack; and on another stage of raised seats were placed the commons as accusers. The throne was vacant, but beside it was a closed gallery for the king and queen, who were present throughout the trial. The accusation set forth all Strafford's illegal and arbitrary measures, his acts of individual oppression, and his supposed plot to subvert the constitution by help of an army raised in Ireland. There was quite enough of proof (and much more has since been brought to light) to bear out the resolution of the commons "that the Earl of Strafford had endeavored to subvert the ancient and fundamental laws of the realm, and to introduce arbitrary and tyrannical government." But it was difficult to bring his conduct under the legal definition of high treason. The essence of that crime was in attacking the king's person, or certain points of his prerogative, all of which were strictly defined by the statute of Edward III. How then could acts done in the king's service, and in extension of his prerogative, be construed into treason against him? or, if they could, under which head of the statute could Strafford's acts be classed? Pym argued, with great power, that, as the king was the head of the state and the central point of the constitution, with the ruin of which he must fall, there could be no higher treason against him than to subvert the constitution. Treason against the people he maintained to be treason against the throne, especially for the consequences it threatened to the king himself. "Arbitrary power," said he, "is dangerous to the king's person, and dangerous to his crown." He proved this from the examples of Eastern despotisms, and from English early history, and he added, in a prophetic spirit, that the sovereign who abetted such treason was not himself safe from "a miserable end." To bring Strafford's acts under the Statute of Treasons, reliance was placed on his scheme for using the Irish army in England, which was construed into a "levying war against the king." To prove the scheme itself, Pym at length produced the notes of a deliberation in the council, taken by the secretary Sir Harry Vane, and found by the younger Sir Harry Vane in his father's cabinet. It was now the 13th of April; and Strafford, who had borne himself most nobly through the trial, spoke for two hours and a half in his defense, though suffering from illness, with an acuteness and eloquence never perhaps surpassed even in Westminster Hall. He protested against the whole doctrine of constructive treason as injustice, and unanswerably exposed its impolicy. "No man," he said, "will know what to do or say for fear of such penalties." His peroration was as touching as his argument was powerful; and, as one of the bitterest of his enemies records, "he moved the hearts of all his auditors, some few excepted, to remorse and pity." Even Pym betrayed some such feeling as, in his concluding speech, he encountered the glance of his ancient friend. But he and his comrades were convinced that either Strafford's head must fall or theirs, and with theirs the liberties of England.

To insure his condemnation they took another course, while the trial was still in progress. On the 10th of April Pym brought in a *Bill of Attainder*, which the commons passed on the 21st, 59 members voting against it in a house of 263. We find Hampden voting with Digby in the minority, while Hyde and Falkland were strong supporters of the bill. In the House of Lords, only 45 peers were present when the question came on, though about 80 had attended the trial; and the bill was only carried by 26 to 19 (April 29). The debate in the lords throws a most interesting light on the opinions of the day concerning constructive treason. The judges, being asked whether the articles on which the lords found Strafford guilty amounted to treason, replied that he "deserved to undergo the pains and forfeitures of high treason by law."

The Bill of Attainder now only awaited the king's assent, which was loudly demanded by the people. Strafford wrote to Charles, offering himself as a sacrifice to the public peace. At this juncture an officer named Goring betrayed to the commons a plot, to which the king had assented, for bringing up the army of the north, nominally to protect parliament, but really to overawe or forcibly dissolve it. The commons drew up a protestation, to defend the Protestant church, his Majesty's person and power, and the lawful rights and liberties of the people; which was signed by every member of both houses, except two of the peers, and by multitudes of the people. They next passed a bill to prevent the dissolution of the present parliament without its own consent, thereby making themselves independent of their constituents as well as of the king. On the 10th of May the royal assent was given by the same commission to this bill and to the attainder of Strafford; and, after a feeble show of pleading for his life on the next day, Charles left him to his fate. Strafford received the intelligence with the exclamation, "Put not your trust in princes, nor in the sons of men; for in them there is no salvation." He preserved his calmness and courage to the last. In passing from his apartment to Tower Hill he stopped under the window of his fellow-prisoner Laud, and asked his blessing. One blow of the axe put an end to his ambitious career, in the forty-ninth year of his age (May 12, 1641). The justice of his death is still a question of dispute; as to its policy, few will now defend such a mode of punishing a minister even for political crimes, so long as a milder sentence will suffice to deter others from plots against the constitution.

"The one supremely able man the king had" being thus removed, the parliament proceeded to abolish the courts of Star Chamber and High Commission; and, with the former, the arbitrary jurisdictions of the king in council, the councils of the North and of the Welsh Marches, and of the counties palatine of Lancaster and Cheshire. They voted £300,000 to the Scots, who had remained in England, and imposed a poll-tax for the payment of both armies, which were disbanded August 6. They granted a subsidy of tonnage and poundage to the king, to last only from May 25 to July 15; and before adjourning (Sept. 8) they appointed a committee of both houses to sit during the recess, with large powers. The commons' committee occupied itself with the affairs of the church. The personal conduct of the clergy was inquired into by what was called the committee of *scandalous ministers*—a name deserved by some of those who were deprived, though there were also many cases of oppression. The deprived ministers were allowed one-fifth of their former incomes.

Early in August the king went to Scotland, where he made large popular concessions, conformed to the Presbyterian worship, and received several Covenanters into the privy council. Meanwhile a terrible rebellion broke out in Ireland. The disbanded soldiers of Strafford's army joined with the discontented Catholics in a rising which began in Ulster (Oct. 23, 1641) and soon spread over the whole country, even the Catholics of the "English pale" joining in it. The other English settlers were almost exterminated, death being the least of the cruelties inflicted on them. The number that perished is estimated at from 40,000 to 200,000; and Dublin was the only spot of Irish soil preserved to England.

Parliament reassembled on Oct. 20, and on the 25th they received the news of the Irish rebellion, which inflamed their animosity toward the Catholics, and their suspicions against the king, who returned to London on Nov. 25. The commons had already drawn up a REMONSTRANCE, in 206 articles, enumerating all the grievances of the last sixteen years, and vehemently ascribing them to a popish faction in the king's councils. It was only carried, after a warm debate of fourteen hours, by the small majority of eleven (Nov. 22). Among its opponents were Falkland and Hyde, the latter of whom had now secretly gone over to the court, as the former did soon after. It was presented to the king (Dec. 1) without being sent to the peers for their concurrence. It was, in fact, an appeal to the people, for whose use it was printed and widely distributed. An answer was also published, drawn up by Hyde on the part of the king.

When Charles returned from Hampton Court to keep Christmas at Whitehall, several reduced officers and gentlemen of the inns of court offered themselves as his body-guard, under Colonel Lunsford, a man of bad character; and daily conflicts ensued between them and rioters of the popular party, especially the London apprentices. The latter, from their close-cut hair, were nicknamed *Roundheads* by their opponents, who called themselves *Cavaliers;* and these terms were soon applied to the two parties in the coming conflict. In these riots the bishops were so repeatedly insulted that they were hindered from attending in parliament; and on Dec. 28, twelve bishops joined in a protest against all acts passed in their absence as illegal. They were at once impeached by the commons and committed to the Tower (Dec. 30). On the next day the king refused the request of the commons for a body-guard under the Earl of Essex, the late commander of the army.

The year 1641 closed with these signs of the contest of open force which began with the new year. On Jan. 3, 1642, the attorney-general, in his Majesty's name, exhibited articles of treason in the House of Lords against Lord Kimbolton and five members of the House of Commons—namely, Hampden, Pym, Sir Arthur Hazelrig, Hollis, and Strode. The next day the king went in person to the house to arrest the five members, who were not present; and his retiring was accompanied with loud cries of "Privilege! Privilege!" The five members took refuge in the city, whither Charles went the following day (Jan. 5) to address the common council and demand their surrender, while parliament met only to adjourn, after appointing a committee to sit at Merchant Taylors' Hall, where defensive measures were organized. Charles now retired to Hampton Court (Jan. 10), while the members were brought back in triumph to the house, escorted by the London trained bands under Skippon (Jan. 11). The next day Lord Digby and Lunsford appeared in arms for Charles at Kingston. They were voted traitors by the commons. Digby escaped to the Continent; but Lunsford was taken and committed to the Tower.

The king now listened to the wiser counsels of Hyde, Colepepper, and Falkland. On Jan. 20 he sent a message to the house, offering to consider their grievances. They returned their thanks, but required that the command of the militia and of the chief fortresses should be placed in their hands. At the same time they directed Goring and Hotham, the governors of Portsmouth and Hull, to hold those fortresses "for king and parliament." They proceeded to raise men and money under the pretext of the Irish rebellion. The king made a last concession by assenting to a bill excluding the bishops from the House of Lords; and then escorted the queen to Dover, whence she passed over to Holland (Feb. 16), carrying with her the crown jewels, which she pawned to buy arms for the king.

From Dover Charles went to Theobalds (Feb. 28); and, refusing the request of the parliament to remain near London, he proceeded slowly northward with the Prince of Wales and the Duke of York. At Newmarket (the race-course of which place was established by him) he held an angry conference with the earls of Pembroke and Holland and the commissioners of the commons, and finally refused to give up the command of the militia (March 9). He reached York on the 19th, and was well received in the county, which levied a guard for his person. On April 23 he presented himself before Hull, but was refused admission by Sir John Hotham.

The parliament meanwhile made active preparations. They issued new commissions of lieutenancy (April 15), and appointed the Earl of Essex to the command of an army hastily raised, to which London furnished 4000 men in one day, besides large contributions of money, plate, and female ornaments. After some fruitless proposals for peace, and denunciations of treason by each party against the adherents of the other, the king marched southward at the head of his army and gave the signal of CIVIL WAR by unfurling his standard at Nottingham, a ceremony which was equivalent to the proclamation of martial law (Aug. 22, 1642).

It is impossible to do more than indicate the leading points of the conflict which ensued; most lamentable in itself, but yet glorified by the chivalrous loyalty of the one party, and the devoted patriotism of the other. On the side of the king were most of the nobility and principal gentry, who viewed his cause and theirs as one, all of the clergy who had adopted high-church principles and feared the growth of Presbyterianism and other forms of dissent, and the fiery youth of the upper classes, together with many adventurers of profligate character and broken fortunes. He had the able counsel of Hyde, Falkland, Colepepper, and other moderate statesmen, who had now finally retired from the parliament and accepted office from the king. His troops were animated by the fiery courage of his nephews Maurice and "Rupert of the Rhine." But he wanted abler generals, and the supplies of arms and money which the queen contrived to send him were quite inadequate to his necessities.

The people in general favored the cause of the parliament, whose strength lay in the great towns, and especially in the sturdy trained bands of London. At a time when standing armies were not yet formed, the militia were a very effective infantry. In cavalry the army of the parliament was much the weaker. Some gentlemen, such as Hampden, raised troops from the young farmers on their estates; others, like OLIVER CROMWELL, who now began his military career as a captain of horse, were careful to "raise such men as had the fear of God before them, as made some conscience of what they did." But for the rest, he thus described them: "Your troops are most of them old decayed serving-men, and tapsters, and such kind of fellows; and their troops are gentlemen's sons, younger sons and persons of quality: do you think that the spirits of such mean and base fellows will ever be able to encounter gentlemen that have honor and courage and resolution in them?" Both parties were scantily provided with artillery and fire-arms, and many a lance and sword, breast-plate and steel cap, were brought out after long disuse. But both sides found another weapon in the now free press, which teemed with pamphlets and ballads, while the newspapers, or *Diurnals*, as they were called, spread intelligence and kept alive party-spirit in every corner of the realm. JOHN MILTON, whose mighty pen labored for the cause of the parliament, and who has left the noblest defense of the freedom of the press, in his "Apology for the Liberty of Unlicensed Printing," thus describes the state of London: "Behold now this vast city; a city of refuge, the mansion-house of liberty, encompassed and surrounded with His protection. The shop of war hath not there more anvils and hammers working, to fashion out the plates and instruments of armed justice in defense of beleaguered truth, than there be pens and heads there, sitting by their studious lamps, musing, searching, revolving new notions and ideas." But there was still another and a mightier force at work. It was a war of religion; and here the advantage was on the side of the parliament. Men of the purest piety, like Bishop Ken, were to be found on the king's side; but the cry of "Church and King" meant, in most mouths, only a venerable institution; while "the Cause" of the other party signified an earnest, though often fanatical belief, sustained by religious habits which gave the camp the aspect of a conventicle. But neither in church nor state was there any great spirit of hostility to the ancient institutions of the kingdom. As, in quieter times, it is the boast that, with few exceptions, the highest Tory and the greatest Liberal are still attached to the constitution, so, even in this war of opinion, the advocates of despotism in the one camp, and the theoretical republicans in the other, formed as yet an insignificant minority. In religion, the great mass of the people were still attached to the Church of England, and it was only the refusal of moderate reforms that led to the triumph first of Presbyterianism and then of Independency.

From Nottingham the king sent proposals to the parliament (Aug. 29), but they would listen to no terms till he should furl his standard and give them the command of the militia. On Sept. 9 they published a declaration of the causes of the war, and on the same day the Earl of Essex marched from London with the trained bands, to take the command of the army at Northampton, which now numbered 15,000 men. The king retreated to Shrewsbury, where his army mustered 10,000 men, under the command of the Earl of Lindsay. The cavalry were under Prince Rupert, who had already opened the campaign by seizing Worcester, and routing a party of the parliamentary horse. Advancing again toward the capital, Charles encountered Essex in a bloody but indecisive battle at EDGEHILL in Warwickshire, where Lord Lindsay was mortally wounded (Sunday, Oct. 23, 1642). Essex retired to Warwick, and the king advanced to Oxford, which was entirely devoted to him, and became his head-quarters for the most part of the war. Marching on toward London, he seized Reading, and defeated a parliamentary detachment at Brentford (Nov. 12); but Essex, who had reached London by hasty marches, met him at Turnham Green with superior forces, and the king retired to Oxford (Nov. 29).

After fruitless negotiations for peace, Essex opened the campaign of 1643 by taking Reading (April 27); but the war languished in the south, the only action worth recording being a mere skirmish at Chalgrove in Oxfordshire (June 18), which is memorable for the fall of JOHN HAMPDEN, who died of his wounds on June 24. In the north the royalist spirit enabled the Earl of Newcastle to keep the upper hand against the parliamentary general, Lord FAIRFAX, who was completely routed at *Atherton Moor*, near Bradford. But the chief scene of action was in the west, where an indecisive battle at *Lansdown*, near Bath (July 5), was followed by a complete victory gained by the royalists, near Devizes, over Sir William Waller (July 13), who surrendered Bristol to Prince Rupert (July 27). The king now formed the siege of Gloucester (Aug. 10), but raised it on the approach of Essex, who on his part retired to avoid an engagement; but at *Newbury* in Berkshire he found the king before him, and a battle, in which both sides displayed desperate valor, was closed by night (Sept. 20). Here died the devoted FALKLAND, who, since the outbreak of the war, had fallen into deep dejection, and kept reiterating the cry of "Peace! peace!" Both armies, exhausted by this battle, retired into winter-quarters.

Falkland's cry for "*Peace*" had been uttered also in London; and a conspiracy to force the parliament to accept terms had been formed by the poet *Edmund Waller*, himself a member. But the leaders were still resolute. They formed with the Scots the "SOLEMN LEAGUE AND COVENANT," which the parliament subscribed themselves, and ordered to be signed by all under their authority. This celebrated instrument bound the subscribers to extirpate popery and prelacy, superstition, heresy, schism, and profaneness; to maintain the rights and privileges of parliaments, together with the king's authority; and it pledged them to mutual defense. The Scots received a subsidy of £100,000, and prepared to enter England, in Jan., 1644, with an army of 40,000 men, under the Earl of Leven. The king, on the other hand, had already sought aid from Ireland, where the Marquis of Ormond was now at the head of 50,000 men. Concluding an armistice with the Irish (Sept. 15, 1643), he sent over a large force, who landed at Mostyn in North Wales, but were routed by Fairfax at Nantwich (Jan. 25, 1644). Fairfax united his victorious army with the Scots, and formed the siege of York, whither Lord Newcastle had retired. Prince Rupert advanced to its relief with 20,000 men. Fairfax and Leven raised the siege, and the armies met at MARSTON MOOR (July 2). Cromwell, at the head of his "Ironsides" (as his troops were called from their armor), broke the right wing of Rupert's army, under the prince himself; while the royalists had the like success on the other wing. The victorious bands, finding themselves face to face as they returned from the pursuit, renewed the combat, which ended in the complete defeat of the king's forces, and established the military reputation of Cromwell. York surrendered to Fairfax, the Scots took Newcastle, and the authority of the parliament was supreme in the north (Oct. 1644).

We must now return to the south and the west. At the beginning of this year Charles called the parliament to Oxford. The summons was obeyed by the majority of the peers, but the commons were only half as numerous as the house at Westminster. The Oxford parliament sat from Jan. 22 till April, and endeavored to raise money by an excise. The king had also a mint at Oxford, while parliament made a new great seal in place of that which was in the king's possession. In April Essex and Waller marched against Oxford. Charles retired to Worcester, but returned suddenly and defeated Waller at *Cropredy Bridge*, near Banbury (June 29), three days before the battle of Marston Moor. He then turned against Essex, who had meanwhile advanced into Cornwall, and who now found himself surrounded. The infantry under Skippon surrendered, with their arms, baggage, and ammunition; while the cavalry passed the king's outposts in a mist, and Essex escaped in a boat to Plymouth. But a new army under the Earl of Manchester (formerly Lord Kimbolton) defeated Charles at Banbury, though not decisively, drove him back to Oxford, and then retired into winter-quarters. This campaign is memorable for the first appearance of ROBERT BLAKE, afterward the celebrated admiral, who was now a colonel in the parliamentary army, and took Taunton. In Scotland the royal standard was raised by James Graham earl of Montrose, who, with the aid of a body of Irish, defeated Lord Elcho at *Tippermuir*, near Perth (Sept. 1), and sacked Aberdeen (Sept. 12). The year closed with the condemnation of Archbishop Laud by bill of attainder (Dec. 17). He was beheaded on Jan. 10, 1645.

Meanwhile a schism, which had long existed among the popular party, had come to a head. As opinions against episcopacy had grown stronger the minds of men were turned toward the *Presbyterian* model of church government; and this movement was aided by the close alliance with Scotland. The celebrated *Assembly of Divines*, which met at Westminster (June, 1643), framed a Calvinistic and Presbyterian model of doctrine and discipline, to which parliament adhered; but some of the ablest leaders, including Cromwell and Sir Harry Vane, had adopted the views of the *Independents*, who maintained that each congregation formed a complete church, and that the civil power had no authority in matters of religion. These doctrines spread rapidly in the army, in close connection with republican theories of government; and the Independents now aimed at supremacy. In November, Cromwell accused Manchester in parliament of backwardness in the field, while Essex and the Scottish commissioners were plotting against Cromwell himself. At length the House of Commons passed the "Self-denying Ordinance," by which the members of both houses were excluded from civil and military offices (Dec. 21). The army was remodeled. Essex and Manchester were excluded. Sir THOMAS FAIRFAX was made general, and, by his special desire, the services of Cromwell were retained as lieutenant-general and commander of the horse, notwithstanding the ordinance. The peers agreed to the ordinance on April 3, 1646.

During these proceedings serious negotiations for peace were carried on at Uxbridge. The conferences were opened on Jan. 30, and a truce was agreed on for twenty days. The demands of the parliament embraced the abolition of episcopacy and the liturgy, the settlement of Ireland by their authority, and the command of the militia. Charles had consented to sign a treaty, when he received a letter from Montrose, announcing a great victory over the Marquis of Argyle at Inverlochy, and praying him not to treat with rebels. The negotiations were broken off on Feb. 22; and it was afterward proved, from the king's private correspondence, that he had never entered on them in good faith.

In May, Charles marched from Oxford, relieved Chester (May 15), and seized Leicester (May 31). On the news of these successes, Fairfax, who had laid siege to Oxford in the king's absence, marched northward, while Charles turned back to relieve Oxford. The armies met at NASEBY, near Market Harborough, in a fiercely-contested battle. Charles displayed great ability and courage; but by the rashness of Rupert, and the skill and courage of Fairfax and Cromwell, this last great battle was lost, and the cause of the king was ruined (June 15, 1645). His private cabinet, which was among the spoils, furnished the parliament with terrible proofs of his bad faith. Charles escaped to Wales, where the Scots advanced on him from the north; and Fairfax overran the west, while Cromwell reduced the midland counties. Rupert surrendered Bristol (Sept. 10); and Charles, after attempting the relief of Chester (Sept. 23), shut himself in Oxford (Nov. 5). His last hopes from Scotland were extinguished by the defeat of Montrose by Lesly, at *Philiphaugh* (Sept. 13). His overtures to the parliament met with no response; and the secret negotiations which he attempted with the Scots and the Independents were fraught with mutual suspicions of insincerity. At last, on the approach of Fairfax to Oxford, he resolved to throw himself into the hands of the Scots, who, besides being his ancient subjects and fellow-countrymen, began to view with alarm the progress of independency. He escaped from Oxford in disguise (April 26), and reached their head-quarters near Newark (May 5). Though treated with all respect, he was required to issue orders for the surrender of all his garrisons in England, and also of Dublin, to the parliament; he was urged to take the Covenant; and was involved in a controversy with Henderson, a Scotch divine, in which Charles showed much learning.

Retreating to Newcastle, for the greater security of their prize, the Scots proceeded to treat with the English parliament, who were at first disposed to resent their reception of the king. At length they agreed to retire from England, receiving £400,000 for pay and expenses, and to surrender the person of the king, who was accordingly given up to the parliamentary commissioners at Newcastle (Jan. 30, 1647). Charles was kept in close custody at his own house of Holmby in Northamptonshire, cut off from his friends, and refused even the ministration of his own chaplains, because they had not taken the Covenant (Feb.). Oxford had surrendered to Fairfax in the preceding summer; the Prince of Wales had escaped to Scilly, and thence to France; and, on March 30, the surrender of Harlech Castle put an end, for the present, to the first civil war.

The parliament now attempted to get rid of the army by sending part of it to Ireland and disbanding the remainder, dismissing all officers above the rank of colonel, except Sir Thomas Fairfax—a direct blow at Cromwell and the other leaders of the Independents. The soldiers persuaded Fairfax to advance toward London; and from their head-quarters at Saffron Walden they addressed an imperious petition to the parliament, who sought to conciliate them by sending Cromwell, Skippon, Ireton, and Fleetwood, to inquire into their distempers. These generals appointed a council of the principal officers, with a representative assembly composed of two privates or inferior officers from each company, who were called *adjutators*, or, by a happy corruption, *agitators*. They at once drew up a statement of their grievances; and they took the best means of enforcing them by seizing the person of the king. This bold measure was effected by an "agitator" named Joyce, on June 4; and on the 7th the king had an interview with Fairfax and Cromwell at Royston, and expressed his wish to remain with the army. On the 5th the army, encamped on Newmarket Heath, took a solemn engagement not to suffer themselves to be disbanded. The Presbyterian leaders now resolved to make a charge of treason against Cromwell, who had returned to London; but he fled back to the army at Triplow Heath, and was received with acclamation. He was followed by the parliamentary commissioners, who rode with Fairfax to the head of each regiment, and read to them the votes of parliament. In each case an officer stepped forward and promised a reply when the votes had been laid before a council of officers and adjutators. The men were asked if this was their answer, and they replied, "All! all!" (June 10.) The same day they moved on toward London, having sent forward a letter to the lord mayor and aldermen, declaring their desire for a settlement of the kingdom on the basis proposed by parliament before they took up arms. A respectful answer was sent to their head-quarters at St. Albans; and on June 16 they demanded the impeachment of eleven leading members, and marched to Uxbridge on the 25th. The next day the eleven members retired from the house, upon which the army fell back to Reading. During all this time the king was with them, treated as if he were on a royal progress, and receiving his friends freely. At length a demonstration of the apprentices against the change in the officering of the militia, which parliament had yielded to the army, provoked a fresh advance to Hounslow Heath, where the speakers of both houses (Manchester and Lenthall) presented themselves, with their maces, attended by eight peers and about sixty commoners. Armed with this show of constitutional authority, the army entered London without opposition, conducted the speakers to Westminster, leveled the lines that had been thrown up round the city, and placed the whole government in the hands of the Independents—the parliament quietly submitting, and rescinding all their votes against the army.

Charles was now brought to Hampton Court, where he lived, in outward appearance, as a king; but his position caused the greatest perplexity to his guardians as well as to himself. While Cromwell and Ireton were holding frequent conferences with him, risking their favor with the army, and incurring the suspicion of the republicans by their efforts to save him, there is every reason to believe that he was conspiring with the Scots for their destruction. At length he solved their perplexity and sealed his own fate by escaping from Hampton Court on the night of Nov. 11, and taking refuge with Colonel Hammond, the governor of the Isle of Wight, who conducted him with much respect, but really as a prisoner, to Carisbrooke Castle (Nov. 14).

Cromwell, now master of the king and parliament, took prompt measures to restore his authority over the army, which had been shaken by the extreme fanatics, who were called *Levelers*. He ordered the meetings of the agitators to cease; and, on being disobeyed, he openly seized the ringleaders at a review, and had one of them shot on the field by sentence of a court-martial. The momentous questions of the settlement of the kingdom and the disposal of the king's person were debated in a secret council of officers which Cromwell held at Windsor; and it was at the sittings of this council that the daring scheme was first opened of bringing the king to justice. Fresh overtures from Charles were met by the parliament with four proposals, which would have left all civil and military affairs in their hands. The king refused, and renewed negotiations with the Scots. He attempted to escape through a window of his apartments in Carisbrooke Castle, but stuck fast between the bars (Dec. 28), and his confinement was made more rigorous. It was now voted that no more addresses should be made to him, or communications received from him (Jan. 13, 1648). This vote was virtually a renunciation of allegiance.

Meanwhile the Scots were preparing to aid the king, and a royalist reaction broke out in England. There were riots in London and insurrections in Wales and Kent, which were put down by the energy of Cromwell, Fairfax, and Skippon. The young Duke of York (afterward James II.) escaped from St. James's (April 22), and the crews of seventeen ships of war lying at the mouth of the river sailed for Holland and put themselves under the command of the Prince of Wales. In accordance with the "*Engagement*" formed at Carisbrooke to restore Charles, the Scots entered England on July 5, with a large army under the Duke of Hamilton, and were joined by the royalists of the north under Sir Marmaduke Langdale. They were met by Cromwell and Lambert, who defeated Langdale at Preston (Aug. 17) and Hamilton at Uttoxeter (Aug. 20). The more ardent Presbyterians, who were opposed to the "Engagement," now rose in the western lowlands and marched on Edinburgh, in conjunction with the highlanders of Argyle. This was called the "Whiggamore Raid," from the cry "*Whig*" (get on) used by the Scottish carters to their horses; and this strange nickname is still the title of the great party of progress. (The opposite name of *Tory*, which came into use later, was the native name for the Irish banditti.) On Sept. 20 Cromwell entered Scotland, joined Argyle at Edinburgh, and arranged the government according to the views of the Whigs. In England this *second civil war* was finished by Fairfax's capture of Colchester (Aug. 28), when Sir George Lisle and Sir Charles Lucas were shot by sentence of a court-martial—an exception to that general abstinence from military executions which forms so favorable a contrast to the Wars of the Roses.

During the absence of Cromwell the moderate party renewed negotiations with Charles by sending commissioners to treat with him at Newport (Sept. 18). The king's appearance—care-worn, but not dejected by his captivity, during which his hair had turned gray—moved compassion, as much as his ability in the discussions commanded admiration. But while he was secretly writing, "My great concession this morning was made only to facilitate my approaching escape," he could not make up his mind to a sufficient show of concession on the question of the Church; and the conferences, after being protracted above two months, were broken off on Nov. 28. The delay had given time for Cromwell to reappear. He had been detained in the north by the resistance of Pontefract; and on the 20th of November he forwarded to Fairfax the petition of his army against the treaty of Newport; while the army of Fairfax, moved by Ireton and Ludlow, presented a remonstrance, demanding the punishment of the king and the dissolution of the parliament, which they charged with perfidy to the cause (Nov. 30). On the same day the king was seized at Newport by order of the council of the army, and imprisoned in Hurst Castle, while the army advanced to London. Even then, Hollis proposed to proclaim the officers traitors; and the parliament, though shrinking from such extremes, had the courage to adopt the concessions of the king, as a sufficient basis for a treaty, by a majority of 129 against 83 (Dec. 5). The next day Ireton prepared for action, and on the 7th Colonel Pride surrounded the house with two regiments, seized 52 members, and shut out 160 others. This process was called "*Colonel Pride's Purge.*" The remnant of 50 or 60 members (nicknamed the "*Rump*"), who were all of the Independent party, reversed the recent vote. Cromwell reached London during the night of the 7th, and declared that "he had not been acquainted with this design, yet since it was done he was glad of it, and would endeavor to maintain it."

All was now prepared for the closing act. While Charles lived he might always be used by the Scots and Presbyterians to destroy the present leaders. To bind his conscience by a treaty with rebels had been found impossible. The leaders of the popular party thought his death necessary for their self-preservation. But few will now defend the policy of the deed. It spread a thrill of horror through Europe, and gave a pretext for the misgovernment of the Restoration.

While the council of the army framed the plan of a republic, under the name of "The Agreement of the People," the House of Commons appointed a committee to prepare a charge against the king (Dec. 23). They declared it treason for a king to levy war against his parliament (Jan. 1, 1649), and, in spite of the refusal of the peers (Jan. 2), of whom only sixteen met, to concur in the bill, they passed an ordinance, appointing a high court of justice for the trial of "Charles Stuart, King of England" (Jan. 6). Charles had been brought from Hurst Castle to St. James's (Dec. 18), and thence to Windsor (Dec. 22). He was now conducted to Whitehall by Major Harrison, a furious republican (Jan. 19). On the next day the high court of justice met in Westminster Hall. Its original plan included 150 members; peers, commoners, and aldermen of London. The refusal of the peers to concur reduced it to 135, of whom only 69 answered to their names. Bradshaw sat as president. The king, when brought in, sat down in the chair prepared for him, still wearing his hat, and none of the members uncovered to him. His demeanor was that of stern contempt. He spoke firmly against the jurisdiction of the court, which adjourned to the 22d. On that and the following day the same scene was repeated. The 24th and 25th were spent in collecting evidence, which was produced in court on the 26th, and on the 27th the court assembled to pronounce sentence. The king asked for a conference with the parliament in the Painted Chamber, which was refused. After a speech from Bradshaw to the king, enumerating all his offenses, the clerk read the sentence, that his head should be severed from his body.

The Scots protested against the proceedings; the Dutch interceded in the king's behalf; the Prince of Wales sent a blank sheet of paper, subscribed with his name and sealed with his arms, on which his father's judges might write what conditions they pleased as the price of his life. Solicitations were found fruitless with men whose resolutions were fixed and irrevocable.

There were only two clear days between the sentence and its execution. They were spent by Charles in devotion, and in taking leave of his third son, Prince Henry, and his daughter, the Princess Elizabeth. The death-warrant was signed on Jan. 29, and the open street before Whitehall was named as the place of execution. At ten o'clock on the morning of the 30th Charles walked across the park from St. James's to Whitehall, where he spent about three hours in prayer, and then received the sacrament. Between two and three o'clock he was led out on to the scaffold, which was erected in front of the central window of the banqueting-hall. When Charles stepped out of the window upon the scaffold he found it so surrounded with soldiers that he could not expect to be heard by any of the people. He addressed his discourse to the few persons who were about him; justified his own innocence in the late fatal wars, though he acknowledged the equity of his execution in the eyes of his Maker; and observed that an unjust sentence, which he had suffered to take effect, was now punished by an unjust sentence upon himself. When he was preparing himself for the block, Bishop Juxon, who had been allowed to attend him, called to him, "There is, Sir, but one stage more, which, though turbulent and troublesome, is yet a very short one. Consider, it will soon carry you a great way; it will carry you from earth to heaven; and there you shall find, to your great joy, the prize to which you hasten, a crown of glory." "I go," replied the king, "from a corruptible to an incorruptible crown, where no disturbance can have place." At one blow his head was severed from his body. A man in a vizor performed the office of executioner; another, in a like disguise, held up to the spectators the head streaming with blood, and cried aloud, "This is the head of a traitor!" (Jan. 30, 1649.)

Charles died in the 49th year of his age and the 24th of his reign; and was buried at Windsor, Feb. 8. Nearly two centuries later his coffin was opened in presence of George IV., and the features still showed that melancholy which is seen in the portraits by Vandyke, and especially in that triple likeness which struck an Italian artist as stamped with the presage of misfortune.

Medal struck in honor of the Earl of Essex, bearing on one side a portrait of the Earl, and on the other the two Houses of Parliament; the King presiding in the Lords, and the Speaker in the Commons. Engraved from the Parliamentary series executed by Simon, the celebrated Medalist of the period.

Great Seal of the Commonwealth: obverse.

CHAPTER XXVII.

THE COMMONWEALTH. A.D. 1649–1660.

About an hour after the death of Charles I. (Jan. 30, 1649) proclamation was made in London that whoever should proclaim a new king without the authority of parliament should be deemed a traitor. On Feb. 6 the commons voted the House of Lords "useless and dangerous," and it sat no more till the Restoration. On the 7th they declared the office of king "unnecessary, burdensome, and dangerous, and therefore to be abolished." They adopted a new great seal (Feb. 8), reopened the courts of law (Feb. 9), and committed the executive government to a council of state consisting of thirty-eight persons (Feb. 14), of which Bradshaw was made president, and Milton Latin secretary. The appointment of Colonels Blake, Dean, and Popham as admirals (Feb. 24) soon led to great results abroad; but it was first necessary to restore order at home, and in Ireland and Scotland. The Duke of Hamilton, the Earl of Holland, and Lord Capel were tried and executed for a royalist con-

Great Seal of the Commonwealth: reverse.

spiracy (March 10). A mutiny of the "Levelers" in the army was suppressed by the energy of Fairfax and Cromwell; and Lilburne, their leader, was imprisoned (March 27).

The government of Ireland had been delivered up by the Marquis of Ormond to the parliament in 1646. After the king's death Ormond was recalled by the Irish Catholics, and took nearly all the fortresses, except Dublin, Belfast, and Londonderry. Cromwell was now appointed general-in-chief and lord-lieutenant of Ireland (June 22). He left London on July 10, and sent on to Dublin a reinforcement, which enabled Colonel Jones, the governor, to inflict on Ormond a disastrous defeat (Aug. 2). Cromwell himself reached Dublin on Aug. 18, stormed Drogheda (Sept. 12) and Wexford (Oct. 9), and by putting their garrisons to the sword, intimidated the other fortresses into surrender, and struck terror alike into the native Irish and the royalist English. "Truly I believe," he wrote, "this bitterness will save much effusion of blood;" and whatever judgment may be passed upon the means, this end was secured *for the time.* The conquest was finished by a short campaign in the following spring; more than 40,000 Irish were permitted to take service in the armies of France and Spain; and Cromwell, leaving Ireton as his deputy, returned to London (May 31, 1650) to meet new dangers from the side of Scotland.

The triumph of the Independents and the execution of the king had entirely alienated the Scots, who hastened to proclaim CHARLES II. at Edinburgh (Feb. 5, 1649). But the rigid Presbyterians, who then ruled the kingdom, had no intention of receiving him, except upon their own conditions; and when Montrose raised the royal standard in the north he was treated as a public enemy. This gallant nobleman was taken prisoner, and, under an old act of attainder, passed in 1644, he was hanged at Edinburgh with the most cruel insults (May 31, 1650). Charles, who had inherited the fatal duplicity of his family, disavowed the commission which he had given to Montrose, accepted the Covenant, and arrived in Scotland on June 16. Meanwhile both sides had prepared for war; but Fairfax was unwilling to lead against the Scots, and resigned his commission. Cromwell was appointed his successor as "captain-general and commander-in-chief of all the forces raised and to be raised within the commonwealth of England" (June 26), and he left London on June 29. The veteran Lesly prepared to receive him by wasting all the country south of Edinburgh, so that, when Cromwell crossed the Tweed (July 16), he was dependent on his fleet for supplies. Marching along the coast to Musselburgh, he found Lesly posted between Edinburgh and Leith in a position too strong to be attacked (July 29). Failing to tempt the wary Scot to a battle, Oliver retired to Dunbar (July 31). Lesly followed him, and blockaded the passes toward England; and Cromwell's army daily wasted away by sickness. At length the imprudent zeal of the preachers drove Lesly to try a battle, and he led down his right from the hill of Doon to the level ground (Sept. 2). Cromwell saw the blunder, and exclaiming, "The Lord hath delivered them into our hands!" gave orders for attacking the exposed wing at dawn. The result was the famous victory of DUNBAR, in which 4000 Scots were killed, and above 10,000 taken prisoners (Sept. 3, 1650). Edinburgh submitted at once; its castle surrendered on Dec. 18, and Cromwell became master of all the country south of the Forth.

Meanwhile Charles endeavored to escape from the Covenanters to the highlands; but he was brought back to Perth, almost as a prisoner (Oct. 25), and crowned at Scone (Jan. 1, 1651). Cromwell, who had fallen ill through exposure to the weather in a march to Stirling (Feb.), took the field again in June, and secured Perth, while the Scots army lay at Stirling. At this juncture, Charles, with the vigor which he could occasionally assume, resolved on a rapid march into England. Starting from Stirling on July 31, he advanced through Cumberland, Lancashire, Cheshire, and Shropshire, and stopped to rest his army at Worcester (Aug. 22). But few joined his standard. The parliament proclaimed him and his adherents traitors, and sent new forces to join Cromwell, who had followed in rapid pursuit, leaving Monk to guard Scotland with 6000 men. He reached WORCESTER on Aug. 28, and, after storming the forts, he fell upon Charles's army in the city, on the anniversary of the battle of Dunbar (Sept. 3). The Scots were slain or taken prisoners almost to a man. Charles escaped, and found shelter in a lone house, called *Boscobel*, through the noble loyalty of the farmer, Penderell, and his four brothers. On the approach of a party of soldiers Charles took refuge with a companion in a large oak-tree, standing in an open space on the edge of the wood; and, to use his own words, "while we were in this tree we see soldiers going up and down in the thickest of the wood, searching for persons escaped; we seeing them now and then peeping out of the wood." This "*Royal Oak*" was long an object of veneration, and the descendants of the Penderells still receive a pension for their loyalty. Other hair-breadth escapes followed; and, after trying successively at Bristol, Bridport, and Southampton, Charles at length embarked at Shoreham (Oct. 15), and landed at Fécamp in Normandy (Oct. 17). Cromwell returned to London (Oct. 12), and took up his residence in great state at Hampton Court.

While Cromwell conquered Ireland and the Scots, Blake and other admirals had established the power of the Commonwealth on the seas. The fleet which had deserted to Charles (p. 215) had infested the Channel and threatened Dublin under the command of Prince Rupert, who eluded the blockade of Blake at Kinsale and got safe to Lisbon. Blake, having been refused admission into the Tagus, captured a richly laden fleet of Portuguese ships (March, 1650), and brought the king of Portugal to sue for a new alliance with England (Jan., 1651). Blake next subdued the Scilly Isles (May), which had given refuge to royalist privateers, and then detached a part of his fleet under Ayscue, who reduced the American plantations, all of which, except New England, had adhered to the royalist party. Guernsey was reduced in October, Man in November, and Jersey in December, while Monk completed the subjection of Scotland; and Ireton had nearly subjugated the Irish rebels, when he died of the plague at Limerick (Nov. 1650), and left the command to Ludlow. Galway, the last strong-hold of the Catholics, was surrendered July 10, 1651. The final settlement of both kingdoms was intrusted to parliamentary commissioners.

The relations of England with Holland become now most interesting. The death of the Prince of Orange, the son-in-law of Charles I. (1650), seemed to open the way for an alliance between the two republics; but the royalist refugees at the Hague insulted the English commissioners; the envoys of the Provinces, who came over to renew the negotiations after the battle of Worcester, met with a cold reception; and the parliament aimed a heavy blow at Dutch commerce by the celebrated *Navigation Act*, forbidding the importation of goods in foreign vessels, except those of the country that produced them (Oct. 9, 1651). At the same time, among other demands, a claim was made for the salute of the English flag. Mutual animosity led to open hostilities. A battle took place in the Downs between Blake and a large fleet under the Dutch admiral Van Tromp (May 19, 1652), and the English parliament declared war (July 8). Ayscue fought an indecisive action with De Ruyter off Plymouth (Aug. 16). Blake and Penn defeated Van Tromp and De Ruyter in the Downs (Sept. 28). In a subsequent action (Nov. 28) Van Tromp's superior numbers forced Blake to retreat to the Thames, while the Dutch admiral carried a broom at his mast-head as a sign that he had swept the seas of the English; but the insult was avenged by a new fleet which parliament fitted out, and Van Tromp was entirely defeated by Blake off Portland (Feb. 18). The action continued across the Channel for three days, till the Dutch escaped into the Scheldt. Another victory was gained off the North Foreland (June 2 and 3); and the Dutch were blockaded in the Texel by Monk and Penn, Blake being ill on shore. In attempting to escape thence their fleet was almost entirely destroyed, and Van Tromp himself was killed (July 31).

Meanwhile a new revolution had been effected in England. From the conclusion of the Irish and Scotch wars a permanent government had become necessary. The general feeling was in favor of some form of mixed monarchy—a view supported by Cromwell, though without a hint of who should be the sovereign. On his return from the battle of Worcester he had urged an amnesty and a law for the election of future parliaments. The parliament, by a small majority, fixed Nov. 3, 1654, for its own dissolution (Oct., 1651), and they passed an act of amnesty (Feb. 24, 1652). On the other hand, they reduced the army to 25,000, and were meditating a further reduction (Aug., 1652), when Cromwell resolved to wrest the government from them. After the army had sent up an imperious petition Cromwell led 300 soldiers down to the house, ordered them "to take away that bauble" (the mace), drove out the members with objurgations, and locked the doors (April 20, 1653). This proceeding was sanctioned by addresses from the army, the fleet, and many of the chief corporations of England.

Cromwell formed a council of state, consisting of himself and 8 other officers, with 4 civilians (April 30), and summoned a small parliament of his own nominees (128 from England and Wales, 5 from Scotland, and 6 from Ireland), to whom he nominally committed the supreme power till Nov. 3, 1654. This assembly was called the "Little Parliament," and sometimes "Barebone's Parliament," from the ludicrous name of one of its members—*Praise God Barebone.* It met on July 4, 1653, and showed itself more disposed to settle the government on extreme republican principles than to submit to Cromwell. At length, on Dec. 13, Sydenham, an Independent, suddenly proposed that the parliament should resign its power into Cromwell's hands. The speaker, who was a party to the scheme, adopted the proposal by leaving the chair, the members disposed to remain were dispersed by soldiers, and a majority afterward signed the deed of resignation. An "*Instrument of Government*" conferred on Cromwell the title of "His Highness the Lord Protector." He was to have a council of 21 members, and a standing army of 20,000 foot and 10,000 horse; and he was bound to summon, every three years, a parliament of 460 members, who were to sit for five months without prorogation or dissolution, and whose acts would become law even if he withheld his assent. The office of protector was for life, and on his death his successor was to be appointed by the council (Dec. 16, 1653).

The short period of the PROTECTORATE is marked by the establishment of the power of England abroad, but by dissension and suspicion at home. On the 5th of April, 1655, Cromwell signed a treaty of peace with Holland, and a close alliance was formed between the two republics, comprehending also Denmark, the Hanseatic towns, and the Protestant cantons of Switzerland. In the same month a treaty was concluded with Sweden, and, soon after, one with Portugal. Overtures were made by France, where the wily Cardinal Mazarin governed with the queen-mother Anne of Austria during the minority of Louis XIV.; and Cromwell consented to join in hostilities against Spain. He sent a fleet into the Mediterranean under Blake, who forced the Dey of Algiers to promise the repression of piracy, and destroyed the forts and fleet of Tunis. Another squadron sailed for the West Indies under Penn and Venables, who were repulsed from St. Domingo, but made the important conquest of JAMAICA. The admirals, however, were sent to the Tower for not effecting more.

War was now declared by Spain, and vigorously prosecuted by the English fleet under Blake; but his health had long been failing, and after a glorious victory at Santa Cruz in the Canaries (April 20, 1657) he died within sight of his native shores. BLAKE was the first of that noble race of sailors of whom Nelson is the type, whose one watchword is Duty, and whose aim is not so much to bring their ships safe home as to inflict all possible damage on the enemy.

England was now restored to more than the foreign power of Elizabeth, for Cromwell knew nothing of Elizabeth's vacillation between parties. "The cause of God and his country" was his single motto; and even the persecuted Vaudois of the Piedmontese valleys found protection in his remonstrances with the Duke of Savoy and the king of France. James I. had stipulated for "moderation" in the treatment of English subjects by the inquisition; but under Cromwell they might repeat the calm boast, "Civis Romanus sum," and find the name of their country a safeguard from insult. He proved his desire for universal toleration by attempting to readmit the Jews into England. The last act of his foreign policy was the campaign of 1658, in combination with the French under Turenne, against the Spanish Netherlands, which gave England a compensation for Calais in Dunkirk (June 25, 1658), till it was *sold* to France by Charles II. (See p. 231.)

The protector's domestic government was equally energetic, but on this field his foes were his own countrymen. His first parliament met (Sept. 4, 1654) only to question the very foundation of his power, and he dismissed them in anger (Jan. 31, 1655). Plots were formed both by the royalists and the republicans, and most inflammatory pamphlets appeared against the protector. There were royalist risings in several counties, and an open insurrection in Scotland under Middleton. The latter was kept in check by Monk, while Cromwell put down the former, dealing severely with the royalists, but trying to gain over the republicans. England was divided into eleven military districts, under as many major-generals, with parliamentary commissioners who levied taxes and imprisoned suspected persons. The government of Ireland was intrusted to Henry Cromwell, the protector's second son, whose amiable character was allied with vigor and ability.

A second parliament met on Sept. 17, 1656, about 100 members being excluded by warrants of the council. The majority thus secured offered Cromwell the title of King (March 25, 1657), which the opposition of his generals induced him to decline, after long hesitation (May 8). The house then presented to him a second "humble petition and advice," renewing the title of Lord Protector, and authorizing him to name his successor and to create a House of Peers (May 26). He was inaugurated anew with great pomp in Westminster Hall (June 26), and he appointed 60 peers. The parliament reassembled Jan. 20, 1658, but was dissolved in consequence of the opposition of the commons to the new peers (Feb. 4).

Meanwhile Spain was busy, as in the time of Elizabeth, with her old arts of assassination. In 1656 she employed Colonel Sexby, a Leveler, to get up an insurrection. Syndercombe, an agent of Sexby, made an attempt on Cromwell's life (Jan. 19, 1657); and similar acts were invited by a pamphlet with the title of "Killing no Murder," which was written by Colonel Titus, a royalist, and widely disseminated by Sexby. At last Sexby was seized (Dec., 1657), and, like Syndercombe, escaped execution only by dying in the Tower. A more formidable royalist plot was organized by the Marquis of Ormond, in conjunction with a projected invasion by Spain from Flanders; and the plan was favored by Lord Fairfax and other leading Presbyterians (Jan. and Feb., 1658). The conspiracy was detected, and two leading royalists were executed. But these repeated dangers destroyed Cromwell's peace, and at last broke down his health. He was seized with a slow fever, which settled into a tertian ague, and he died on the anniversary of his victories at Dunbar and Worcester (Sept. 3, 1658), in the 60th year of his age and the 4th of his protectorate. We have attempted to record his acts without discussing those features of his character which have long been treated with passion and prejudice. It only remains to add that he was a liberal patron of art and literature, and a great lover of music. He saved from destruction the cartoons of Raffaelle, and other noble works of art; he fostered the genius of Milton; he projected a revised translation of the Bible; and the magnificent "Polyglot Bible" of Brian Walton was published under his auspices.

Cromwell's private life was safe from the reproach of his bitterest enemies. His wife, Elizabeth Bourchier, bore him three sons—*Oliver* (who fell in battle in 1648), *Richard*, and *Henry*—and four daughters: *Elizabeth*, Mrs. Claypole (d. 1658); *Bridget*, married successively to Ireton and Fleetwood (d. 1681); *Mary*, viscountess Fauconbridge (d. 1712); and *Frances*, lady Russell (d. 1721). His descendants are still numerous, especially in Cambridgeshire and Herts. He was always conspicuous for duty and affection to his mother, a most pious and virtuous lady named Stuart,* who died at an advanced age during his protectorate.

On the death of Cromwell his son RICHARD was named protector by the council, and universally acknowledged. A new parliament (Jan. 29, 1659) confirmed the basis of government as settled in the "humble petition and advice." But Richard's temper was too mild for the times. The army became threatening, and he was forced by his uncle Desborough and his brother-in-law Fleetwood to dissolve the parliament (April 22, 1659), leaving the government to the

* Her alleged relationship to the royal family rests on no good evidence.

council of officers, who recalled the remnant of the Long Parliament (May 7), and appointed a committee of safety (May 9) and a new council of 31 members of the old Presbyterian party (May 13). The army and fleet adhered to this revolution, and Fleetwood was appointed lieutenant-general. Richard Cromwell made a formal demission of his office (May 25) and retired to the Continent. Some years after he returned to England, and lived quietly at Cheshunt till 1712. Henry Cromwell resigned his command in Ireland (June 15) and retired to Cambridgeshire, where he died in 1674.

Dissensions soon arose between the army and the parliament, who were expelled by Lambert (Oct. 13, 1659), and a military "Committee of Safety" administered the government. Lambert had meanwhile suppressed an insurrection of the royalists and Presbyterians (Aug. 19). But the balance of England's destinies was held by Monk and his army. Monk commenced his march from Scotland, nominally to restore the parliament. Lambert advanced to meet him as far as Newcastle, but found his soldiers falling away. The garrison of Portsmouth and the army round London declared for the parliament, which reassembled on Dec. 26; and on the 3d of February, 1660, Monk, who had been joined at York by Lord Fairfax, entered London without opposition. On the 13th the "Engagement" to the Commonwealth was again agreed to, and on the 25th Monk was appointed captain-general. Monk now entered into secret negotiations with Charles, and persuaded him to escape from Brussels to Breda, lest the Spaniards should detain him as a pledge for Dunkirk; and the advice came only just in time. Meanwhile the reinstatement of the excluded members by Monk (Feb. 21) had given the moderate party a majority in the parliament, which repudiated the Engagement (March 13), and dissolved itself (March 16), after appointing a new parliament to meet on April 25. Thus at last the "Long Parliament" came to an end.

The Presbyterians united with the old royalists in the elections for the "Convention Parliament," in which the ancient peers returned to their house. On the 1st of May Sir John Grenville appeared with a letter from the king to both houses, accompanied by a declaration promising liberty of conscience and a general amnesty, with no exceptions but such as parliament should itself make. The soldiers were assured of the continuance of their present pay, with all arrears. An answer was at once prepared, and both houses attended the proclamation of King Charles II. (May 8), who landed at Dover (May 25), and entered London on his 30th birthday, May 29, 1660. So enthusiastic was his welcome that he pleasantly said it must have been his fault only which had kept him so long from a people so devoted to him.

Medal exhibiting a first-rate Ship of War: struck to commemorate the appointment of James Duke of York, Lord High Admiral.

CHAPTER XXVIII.

THE HOUSE OF STUART (*continued*).—CHARLES II. A.D. 1660-1685.

CHARLES II., the first Englishman of the Stuart dynasty, was born at St. James's, May 30, 1630. He became "king *de jure*," by his father's death, on Jan. 30, 1649, from which day the years of his reign are legally computed, so that the *first* year of his actual reign (1660-1661) is numbered in the statutes as his *twelfth*. During the Commonwealth he was for a short period "king *de facto*" in Scotland (1650-1651); but the battle of Worcester made him an exile in France, Germany, and Holland, till his restoration, May 29, 1660.

He was possessed of many external advantages—a fine person, a ready wit, graceful manners, and the greatest affability—but his face, the complexion of which was extremely dark, was cast in a harsh and forbidding mould. He was faithless, selfish, and utterly unprincipled; indolent in business, and given up to sensual pleasures. Even adversity seemed to have taught him no lesson, except meanness in revenging and unscrupulousness in enjoying himself; together with a selfish prudence which kept his arbitrary ideas in check, and which he once expressed to the Duke of York by saying, "Brother, I have no wish to go on my travels again." His character was summed up in a mock epitaph by his boon companion Rochester:

"Here lies our sovereign lord the king,
Whose word no man relies on;
Who never said a foolish thing,
And never did a wise one."

"Quite true!" rejoined the king, "for my words are my own, and my acts are my ministers'."

The convention parliament, which continued to sit after the Restoration, settled on the king an income of £1,200,000; abolished the feudal revenues of the crown, granting hereditary excise duties in lieu of them; and voted duties of tonnage and poundage for the king's life. They passed an act of pardon and indemnity, from which the regicides and some others, including Vane and Lambert, were excepted by name. The regicides, both living and dead, were attainted. Twenty-nine of them were tried before a special commission (Oct. 9–13), and ten were executed, the others having surrendered on the promise of their lives by a royal proclamation. The remains of Cromwell, Ireton, and Bradshaw were disinterred by order of parliament, and on the anniversary of the late king's death they were hanged on the gibbet at Tyburn, under which the bodies were buried, the heads being struck off and exposed on Westminster Hall (Jan. 30, 1661). Vane and Lambert were brought to trial later. The former sealed his fate by his bold defense, and was executed June 14, 1662; the latter saved his life by his submissive demeanor, and lived thirty years as an exile in Guernsey, where he died a Roman Catholic.

The king dissolved the convention parliament Dec. 29, 1660. The army was next disbanded, except a force of 1000 horse and 4000 foot, which formed the first nucleus of the *standing army*. In Scotland the royal authority was entirely restored by a parliament which met Jan. 1, 1661. The Marquis of Argyle and a preacher named Guthrie were brought to trial, convicted on the feeblest evidence, and executed—the former on May 27, the latter on June 1.

The restoration of the church kept pace with that of the crown. Favor was at first shown to the Presbyterians, some of whom were appointed to high office; and the eminent clergymen, Baxter and Calamy, were made royal chaplains. While restoring the bishops to their sees, and filling up the vacant bishoprics, the king issued a declaration promising to the Presbyterians and Independents a consideration of their objections to the liturgy (Oct. 25). For this purpose a conference was held at the Savoy between twelve bishops and twelve leading Presbyterian ministers, but the result was only to widen their differences (April 15 to July 25, 1661).

The king was crowned April 25, 1661; and on May 8 he met his new parliament, which proved at first devoted to the church and subservient to the court. It lasted, though with some long prorogations, till Jan. 24, 1679; and earned the title of the "Pension Parliament" by the bribes which its members received from the kings both of England and of France. Its first act was one "for the security of the king's person and government," by which the Covenant was pronounced unlawful, and parliament was declared to have no legislative power without the king. By the *Corporation Act* all corporate officers were required to receive the sacrament in the Church of England, to abjure the Covenant, and to take an oath of *non-resistance*, renouncing the lawfulness of bearing arms against the king or his officers, even in self-defense. In the next session was passed the celebrated ACT OF UNIFORMITY (May 29, 1662), which required all clergymen to express their "unfeigned assent and consent to all and every thing in the Book of Common Prayer," as recently revised and settled by convocation; to receive episcopal ordination; to abjure the Covenant, and take the oath of non-resistance. All who refused to submit to these conditions were to be *ipso facto* deprived of their preferments on the ensuing St. Bartholomew's day (Aug. 24), and on that day nearly 2000 clergymen left their livings. They were acknowledged to be among the most learned and pious, as their very sacrifice itself proved them to be among the most conscientious, of the clergy. The government tempted many of them with offers of high preferment, which were refused, with scarcely an exception. Even bishoprics were offered to Baxter, Calamy, and Reynolds, but accepted only by the last. Severer measures followed. The deprived ministers were forbidden by the Act of Uniformity to exercise their ministry, under the penalties of fine and imprisonment; and the like penalties, up to transportation for seven years, were imposed on their hearers by the *Conventicle Act*, if as many as five persons, besides the members of the same household, should assemble for worship (1664). The very means of subsistence left to the deprived clergy were struck at by the *Five Mile Act*, which prohibited those who had refused to take the oath of non-resistance from coming within five miles of any corporate town, except in traveling, and also disabled them from keeping schools (1665). The Nonconformists were also included in the disabilities of the *Test Act*, which was passed against the Catholics in 1673 (see p. 235). These persecuting acts were only repealed in the reign of George IV.

In foreign politics a new era was opened in 1661 by the rise of Louis XIV., who was born Sept. 5, 1638, and succeeded to the throne of France, by his father's death, May 14, 1643. His minority was passed under the tutelage of Cardinal Mazarin; but on that minister's death (March 8, 1661) the young king announced to his council his intention of directing his own government, and at once gave proofs of the vast powers and vaster ambition which held France in awe and Europe in alarm for more than half a century (Louis XIV. died Sept. 1, 1715, after a reign of 72 years). A close alliance was now formed between the courts of France and England, and both united to support Portugal against Spain. Henrietta, the sister of Charles II., was married to Philip duke of Orleans, the brother of Louis XIV., and Charles himself espoused Catherine of Braganza, daughter of John IV. of Portugal (May 21, 1662), a woman of sense, spirit, and virtue, whom he treated with heartless neglect, while he lived openly in the society of his mistresses. Her chief value in the king's eyes was her dowry of £500,000, with the fortresses of Tangiers in Africa and Bombay in India. The money was squandered on his pleasures; but his returning necessities led him to sell Dunkirk and Mardyke (Cromwell's conquests) to the king of France for £400,000 (Nov. and Dec.).

The Dutch and English meantime continued their rivalry for commercial supremacy at sea. A new "African Company," formed under the auspices of the Duke of York, came into collision with the Dutch settlements on the Guinea coast;* and their fleet, under Sir Robert Holmes, captured the Dutch settlement of New Amsterdam (since the great city of *New York*) on the coast of America (Aug. 27, 1664). Parliament voted £2,500,000 for the war; and the clergy were for the first time included in the tax, instead of voting separate supplies in convocation. War was declared against Holland, Feb. 22, 1665; and a great naval victory was gained off Lowestoft by the English fleet under the Duke of York, Prince Rupert, and Lord Sandwich (June 3). Louis XIV. now came to the help of the United Provinces, with whom he had previously made an alliance against Spain, and declared war against England, Jan. 16,

* *Guineas* were first coined in the year 1663 from gold imported by this company.

1666. The French fleet of 40 ships sailed from Toulon, and Albemarle detached Prince Rupert with 20 of his 74 ships to keep them in check. During his absence, the Dutch fleet of 80 sail, under De Ruyter and the younger Van Tromp, appeared off the North Foreland, and were engaged by Albemarle. The battle lasted *four days* (June 1–4). On the second the Dutch were reinforced by 16 ships, but the arrival of Prince Rupert on the third saved Albemarle from destruction; and after a violent combat on the fourth, both fleets returned to their harbors. A more decisive battle on the 25th of July gave the English the mastery of the sea.

These two years, however, are still more memorable for *pestilence* and *fire* than for war. The mysterious epidemic, called distinctively THE *Plague*, which has been known on the shores of the Levant from the earliest ages, had long since appeared in Europe (imported, as some said, by the Crusaders), and the close streets of old London were seldom free from its ravages; but in 1665 it broke out with a violence unexampled except by the great plagues of Athens (B.C. 430) and Florence (A.D. 1348). In July the weekly deaths were 1100, in September they increased to 10,000, and in the course of the year 100,000 perished. The parliament removed to Oxford; the court and nobility fled from London; the houses were shut up, and whole streets deserted, except by the solitary passenger staggering home to die, and the heavy sound of the death-cart, with the voice of the bellman crying, "Bring forth your dead! Bring forth your dead!" The rites of burial were soon neglected, and the corpses were flung into great pits. As in all such seasons, the presence of death gave new license to wanton pleasure; and the sounds of revelry were mingled with the cries of fanatics who stalked about denouncing "Woe unto the city!" The pestilence declined when winter had fairly set in (1665).

The new year (1666) earned from the pen of Dryden the celebrated title of "Annus Mirabilis" (the Year of Wonders), partly by the great sea-fights related above, but chiefly by the "*Great Fire*," which almost totally destroyed the city of London. It broke out before daybreak on Sunday, Sept. 2, in a baker's house near London Bridge, at the spot marked by the column of Sir Christopher Wren called "the Monument;" and, aided by an east wind and a dry season, it devoured the close wooden houses from the Tower to the Temple, and as far north as Holborn Bridge and Cripplegate. It raged for three days and nights, defying the efforts to arrest it, which were directed by the king and his brother in person. It was only on Sept. 5 that its progress was stayed at great gaps made by blowing up houses with gunpowder. It destroyed about 400 streets and 13,000 houses, though only 8 lives were lost; but the remnants of the plague were burnt out as by a refiner's fire, and the city rose from its ashes, with the magnificent dome of new St. Paul's on its central hill, under the master hand of Sir CHRISTOPHER WREN. His plans, if fully carried out, would have made of London the noblest and most convenient city ever built, and of its cathedral the grandest basilica devoted to Christian worship; but the city was cramped by haste and economy, and the church was altered by the desire of the court to prepare it for Catholic worship. In the mean time the origin of the fire was falsely ascribed to the Papists; and the popular prejudice was commemorated on the Monument by an inscription which has been only recently removed.

These calamities favored the desire for peace, and negotiations were opened at *Breda* (May 14, 1667). During their progress the fleet was neglected, and the Dutch seized the opportunity for striking a terrible blow at English naval power. De Ruyter suddenly appeared at the Nore, took Sheerness (June 9), burnt some ships at Chatham (June 12), and ascended the Thames as far as Tilbury, where he was repulsed by Sir Edward Sprague (June 29). But Louis held aloof, not wishing that any one power should be supreme at sea, and peace was concluded at Breda, July 21, 1667.

To appease the national indignation at this disgrace, and at the growing profligacy of the court, a victim was found in the EARL OF CLARENDON, the only great statesman Charles had. We have seen him, as Sir Edward Hyde, among the popular leaders in parliament, and then passing over with Falkland to Charles I. He shared the exile of Charles II., and kept him back from much folly. After the Restoration he remained Charles's chief adviser, was made Earl of Clarendon and lord chancellor, and had all the power of a modern prime minister. By the marriage of his daughter Anne to the Duke of York he became the grandfather of two queens of England—Mary and Anne. But he was disliked by the queen-mother, detested by Charles's licentious courtiers, and hated by the people for his haughtiness and avarice. To retain Charles's favor he had sanctioned his most arbitrary acts, and had even advised the sale of Dunkirk; and now he fell unpitied before the anger of parliament and the intrigues of George Villiers duke of Buckingham, the worthy son of his father. He was insultingly deprived of the seals (Aug. 30), impeached by the commons (Nov. 12), and banished to the Continent by Charles (Nov. 29). He spent his exile in writing the "History of the Great Rebellion"—a work of great eloquence and power, but in many parts willfully inaccurate, and therefore untrustworthy. He died at Rouen in 1674.

In the government which succeeded Clarendon we have the first resemblance to the more modern "Cabinet;" for it bore the equivalent name of "Cabal"—that is, a secret committee. Its chief members were the Duke of Buckingham, Lord Arlington, and Sir William Coventry, with whom were associated Lord Ashley and Sir Thomas Clifford. Scotland was still governed by the Earl of Lauderdale, who was chiefly engaged in a cruel persecution of the Covenanters. The derivation of "cabal" from the initials of these statesmen is merely founded on a curious coincidence, but it may help the memory to perpetuate the infamy of the ministers who sold their country to the king of France.

Louis XIV. had married Maria Theresa, the daughter of Philip IV. of Spain; and on the death of that king (1665) he laid claim to the Spanish Netherlands in right of his wife, and an army under Turenne overran Flanders in the summer of 1667. Upon this, the first of the many leagues formed to check the ambition of the "Grand Monarch" was devised by Sir WILLIAM TEMPLE, our embassador at Brussels. The *Triple Alliance*, between England, Holland, and Sweden, was signed on Jan. 13, 1668; and it led to the treaty of Aix-la-Chapelle, by which Spain gave up the towns conquered by Louis, who renounced all claim to the rest of Flanders (April 25). Meanwhile Charles was secretly selling the common cause to Louis for the promise of a revenue which might enable him to govern without a parliament; and at length a secret treaty was signed at Dover (May 22, 1670), by which Charles engaged to make an open profession of the Catholic religion, and to assist Louis in his schemes on Spain and Holland, and Louis promised Charles a pension of 3,000,000 livres (£120,000) while the war lasted, and the aid of 6000 men in case of an insurrection in England. Clifford and Arlington were parties to the treaty. The Duke of York had already avowed his conversion to Romanism (1669); and his wife died, confessing herself a Catholic, March 31, 1671. About the same time great scandal arose out of the attempt to seize the regalia in the Tower by Colonel Blood, a notorious ruffian (May 9, 1671), who was not only pardoned by the king, but presented with an estate of £500 a year in Ireland. But even if Charles had been an accomplice in the robbery it would not have been more shameful than his seizure of £1,300,000 which had been deposited by the bankers in the exchequer, in order to prepare for a Dutch war (Jan. 2, 1672).

War was declared against Holland, March 17, 1672, and a desperate naval action was fought in Southwold Bay between De Ruyter and the Duke of York, the French fleet standing aloof. The Dutch retired, and on the side of the English Lord Sandwich was killed (May 28). On land, a small English force under the Duke of Monmouth and JOHN CHURCHILL (afterward Duke of Marlborough) followed Louis, who overran the United Provinces. The Dutch army was commanded by WILLIAM PRINCE OF ORANGE, then in his 22d year. He retired into Amsterdam, and laid the surrounding country under water. The government, headed by the pensionary JOHN DE WITT, a great and virtuous statesman, but the firm opponent of the house of Nassau, shrunk from such extremities, and inclined to peace. This excited the fury of the populace; the great towns rose in tumult; the brothers De Witt were barbarously massacred; the Prince of Orange was elected to the office of stadtholder, which had been vacant since his father's death in 1650; and under his guidance the people were again united in defense of their independence. "There is one certain means," said the prince, "by which I can be sure never to see my country's ruin—I will die in the last ditch." In the following campaign a coalition between the empire, Spain, and Holland, forced Louis to act on the defensive; while Charles, though he continued the war at sea with doubtful success, had new difficulties to occupy him at home, in the increasing indignation of the people and the altered temper of the parliament.

The people were thoroughly alarmed at the influence of France and the growth of Catholicism. Parliament, meeting on Feb. 4, 1673, complained of a *Declaration of Indulgence* by which the king had suspended the penal laws. Charles gave way, and the TEST ACT was passed, binding all persons holding any public office to receive the sacrament in the established church, and to take the oaths of allegiance and supremacy, with another, abjuring belief in transubstantiation. In consequence of this, Lord Clifford and other Catholic noblemen resigned their offices; and the Duke of York gave up the command of the fleet to Prince Rupert. New offense was given by the Duke of York's marriage to Mary of Modena, against which the commons in vain protested. The opposition now found an able leader in the versatile and unprincipled Anthony Ashley Cooper, already mentioned as Lord Ashley, and now Earl of Shaftesbury. He had been made lord chancellor Nov. 17, 1672, but was deprived of the seals Nov. 9, 1673. The Duke of Buckingham also joined the opposition, and the Cabal ministry was broken up. The office of lord treasurer was conferred on Thomas Osborne viscount Latimer, who was soon created Earl of DANBY. After the Revolution he was made Marquis of Carmarthen and Duke of Leeds. He was an honest statesman, and opposed to the French policy, but of high monarchical principles.

Finding that he could obtain no supplies, Charles made a separate peace with Holland (Feb. 9, 1674), receiving £300,000 from the States. He even affected to yield to the desire of the commons, that he would support the Dutch against France, at the very time when he secured the renewal of his pension from Louis as a bribe for his neutrality (Feb., 1676). By the advice of Danby and Sir William Temple he arranged a marriage between the Prince of Orange and the Princess Mary, daughter of the Duke of York, who afterward reigned as WILLIAM AND MARY (Nov. 4, 1677). Peace was concluded between France and Holland at *Nimeguen* (Aug. 10, 1678).

During the last three years the opposition in parliament had constantly gained strength, and an event now occurred which made the "No Popery" party for a time triumphant. This was the discovery of the pretended "POPISH PLOT" by TITUS OATES, a man of infamous character, who was first an Anabaptist, then a clergyman, next a convert to Romanism and a member of the English college of St. Omer, from which he had been expelled, but where he had obtained much information useful for his present purpose. He caused the king to be informed of a plot against his life, and himself laid an information before Sir Edmondsbury Godfrey, an active justice of the peace, to the following effect: The pope had delegated the sovereignty of Great Britain to the Jesuits; the king was to be assassinated as a heretic; London was to be fired, and the Protestants every where massacred; the crown was to be offered to James as a gift from the pope, on condition of the extirpation of Protestantism; and, in case of his refusal, he also was doomed to death. The chief agent in the plot was said to be Père la Chaise, the confessor of Louis XIV., but the Duke of York's confessor was also implicated (Aug., 1678). When examined before the council, Oates contradicted both himself and well-known facts in the grossest manner. Nevertheless he obtained credence from the people, and even from the ministers, while the opposition took up the "plot" as a party weapon. Coleman, the late queen's confessor, was arrested; and his papers furnished evidence, not indeed of *the* plot, but of *a* plot with France for converting the nation and bribing the king to popery. At this juncture the magistrate, Sir Edmondsbury Godfrey, was found murdered in a ditch at Primrose Hill; and his death, the real manner of which is still a mystery, was universally ascribed to the Papists (Oct. 15). Charles treated the whole matter with characteristic levity, saying that "he was accused of being in a plot against his own life;" but the Duke of York insisted on inquiry; while Danby, in a strong anti-Catholic spirit, laid the case before parliament at its meeting (Oct. 21). A solemn fast was appointed; addresses were voted; several Catholic peers were committed to the Tower; both houses declared their belief in the plot; and, amidst this excitement, an act was passed to exclude Catholics from either house of parliament. The commons proceeded to impeach Danby of high treason, on the evidence of a letter produced by Montagu, the embassador at Paris, demanding money from Louis for the king

(Dec. 21); but the lords refused to commit him, and Charles prorogued the parliament (Dec. 30), which was soon afterward dissolved, having sat for eighteen years (Jan. 24, 1679).

Meanwhile the "plot" went on bravely. When Oates was rewarded with a lodging at Whitehall, and a pension of £1200 a year, he naturally found imitators. A wretch, named *William Bedloe*, came forward with new evidence; and both the informers began to attack the queen. Executions became frequent. The first victim was Coleman (Dec. 3). He was followed to the scaffold by three priests (Jan. 24); and three of the queen's servants suffered for the murder of Godfrey on the sole evidence of Bedloe (Feb.). The new elections were decidedly in favor of the opposition, and it was thought prudent for the Duke of York to retire to Brussels.

Parliament met on March 6, 1679, in a temper most hostile to the court. The impeachment of Danby was revived, and he was committed to the Tower, though he had received a pardon from the king (April 16; the privilege thus asserted was confirmed by the Act of Settlement in 1701). Charles consented to govern by the advice of a council of 30 persons, of which Shaftesbury was president; the Earl of SUNDERLAND (Robert Spenser) being secretary of state. A sort of inner council, or *cabinet*, was formed by Sir William Temple, Shaftesbury, Sunderland, and Lord HALIFAX (George Savile). By the influence of Shaftesbury a bill was brought into the commons to exclude the Duke of York from the succession to the throne, and was carried by a majority of 79; but its progress was stopped by the dissolution of parliament (May, 1679).

To this parliament we owe the celebrated HABEAS CORPUS ACT, "for the better securing the liberty of the subject, and for prevention of imprisonments beyond the seas" (31 Car. II. c. 2). It forbids the judges, under severe penalties, to refuse to any prisoner a *writ of habeas corpus*, directing the jailer to produce the body of the prisoner in court, and to certify the cause of his imprisonment. It requires that every prisoner shall be indicted the first term after his commitment, and tried in the subsequent term. It secures a person, once set free by order of the court, from being again committed for the same offense. This statute forms a safeguard of English liberties only second to Magna Charta, of which it is the necessary complement.

Scotland had now been driven into open rebellion by the tyranny of Lauderdale and Sharp, Archbishop of St. Andrews and a recreant Presbyterian. As early as 1666 an insurrection broke out in the west, where the strength of the Covenanters lay; but the insurgents were defeated at the Pentland Hills (Nov. 28), and many of them were executed. From this time the penal laws were enforced most cruelly by the council of Scotland, their chief agent being Colonel JOHN GRAHAM OF CLAVERHOUSE, afterward VISCOUNT DUNDEE. Sharp was the chief object of popular hatred. One James Mitchell tried to assassinate him in 1668; and he was at length cruelly murdered by a party of Covenanters at Magus Muir in Fifeshire (May 3, 1679). The assassins retired toward Glasgow, gathered an armed force, and defeated a small body of cavalry under Claverhouse at Drumclog (June 1). They made themselves masters of Glasgow, and raised an army of 8000 men; but were totally defeated and dispersed at Bothwell Bridge, on the Clyde, by the Duke of Monmouth, whom the king had sent on a special commission into Scotland (June 22, 1679).

That unfortunate nobleman now begins to play an important part in state affairs. He was Charles's favorite illegitimate son, by Lucy Waters, whom it was afterward pretended that the king had married. He was of a mild and generous disposition, but utterly wanting in judgment and firmness: hence he easily became the tool of the opposition; and in the celebrated poem of Dryden he is *Absalom*, and Shaftesbury *Ahithophel.* He was especially odious to the Duke of York as a possible rival for the crown.

The first success of the anti-Catholic party was followed by some reaction. The accusations of Oates and Bedloe had hitherto insured conviction; but they now received a check in the acquittal of Sir George Wakeman, the queen's physician, and three others (July 18). The Duke of York returned from the Continent, and superseded Monmouth as lord high commissioner in Scotland, where he renewed the cruelties of Lauderdale. Shaftesbury was dismissed (Nov. 17), and the council modified. But the flagging credit of the plot was revived by a fresh informer named *Dangerfield*, who accused the Presbyterians as well as the Papists. This new invention was called the "*Meal-tub* Plot," from the place where the papers were alleged to have been discovered. Meanwhile Shaftesbury was bent on revenging his disgrace. He procured many addresses praying for the speedy meeting of parliament; while the court party got up counter addresses, expressing abhorrence of such an interference with the king's prerogative. Hence the two great parties of *country* and *court* obtained the appellations of *Addressers* and *Abhorrers*, which were soon superseded by the nicknames of WHIG and TORY. To keep up the excitement Shaftesbury made a formal presentment to the grand jury of Middlesex, with a view to indicting the Duke of York as a Popish recusant (June 26, 1680); but the jury were dismissed by the chief justice Scroggs. This summer Monmouth made a progress through the west of England, and was received almost as a king (Aug. 1680).

At length the new parliament assembled (Oct. 21, 1680), and proved more violent than the last in their hostility. They renewed the vote of faith in the plot, and rewarded the principal informers. The *Exclusion Bill* passed the commons by a large majority (Nov. 15). In the lords it was supported by Shaftesbury, Sunderland, and Essex, but opposed by Halifax in a speech of surpassing ability, and thrown out by 63 to 33, after a debate of unprecedented length, during the whole of which the king was present. The commons gave vent to their disappointment by the impeachment of the Catholic lords who were prisoners in the Tower. The aged Earl of Stafford was found guilty, after a trial of six days, and Charles had the weakness to consent to his death; but the shamelessness of the witnesses on his trial, and the sympathy which he excited on the scaffold, sealed the fate of the "plot," and his was the last blood shed for it (Dec. 29, 1680). An end was put to the violence of parliament by a dissolution (Jan. 10, 1681).

A new parliament, the last in Charles's reign, was convened at Oxford (March 21, 1681). The Earl of Shaftesbury, the city members, and other leading exclusionists, came with numerous followers, many of them armed; and the king's guards were mustered. The parliament consisted nearly of the same members as the last; they showed the same spirit, and took up the same measures—the impeachment of Danby, the Popish plot, and the Exclusion Bill. But they had overestimated their strength; and when the king, who had just concluded another pension-treaty with France, ventured on the decisive step of a dissolution in a week after their meeting (March 28), it became evident that he was backed by a strong national party. In fact, the counsels of "Ahithophel" had been "turned into folly," or rather Shaftesbury's advice had been foolish from the first. No confidence could be reposed in his character; the exposure of the "plot" had recoiled on those who adopted it as a party weapon; and the native loyalty of the English revolted from the exclusion of the rightful heir, and still more from the mad scheme of setting a bastard on the throne. A reaction had set in, which the court followed up without even a pretense of mercy or moderation. While the clergy preached "passive obedience" and "non-resistance," servile judges and packed juries began those judicial murders which have handed down the names of Scroggs and Jeffreys to perpetual infamy. The first victim was Stephen College, a London joiner, who had been in arms at Oxford. He was condemned for conspiracy on the testimony of the very same wretches who had lately given evidence against the Catholics, and who were now taken into the pay of the court. Shaftesbury himself was next committed on a charge of high treason; but the grand jury ignored the bill, amidst the plaudits of the city (Nov. 24, 1681). To prevent a similar miscarriage of "justice" for the future, it was necessary to have such sheriffs as would return juries whose verdicts might be relied on; and, after a long contest, Dudley North and another nominee of the court were elected sheriffs of London and Middlesex (1682). Upon this Shaftesbury fled to Holland, with his friend the celebrated JOHN LOCKE, and there his troubled career was closed by death (Jan., 1683).

The Duke of York had meanwhile been showing in Scotland what might be expected of him when he should mount the throne. To the sternest bigotry he added the most cold-blooded cruelty. He seemed to gloat over the sufferings of his victims, and a savage taunt was his usual answer to an appeal for mercy. Of his perversion of justice the case of Argyle is a memorable example. For a simple and honest explanation of the sense in which he took a new test imposed by the Scottish parliament he was found guilty of treason and "leasing-making;" but his escape to Holland postponed his fate to the following reign. Well might Charles predict *to the Prince of Orange*, in 1681, that, "whenever the duke should come to reign he would be so restless and violent that *he could not hold it four years to an end*."

London now paid the penalty of her long-tried devotion to the popular cause by the prosecution of her leading citizens. But this was not enough. An inquiry was directed into the validity of the city's charter, and on the flimsiest pretexts it was pronounced by the judges to have been forfeited. Charles only restored it on condition of his having the disposal of the chief municipal offices (June, 1683). Most of the other corporations in England surrendered their charters, and received them back on the like terms, paying heavy sums for the favor.

By such proceedings the gauntlet was fairly thrown down to those who held the lawfulness of resistance to illegal government. Lord WILLIAM RUSSELL and ALGERNON SIDNEY were now the most conspicuous leaders of the country party. Russell, a younger son of the Earl of Bedford, held the principles of the "constitutional Whigs" of the present age; and his character was adorned with virtues which were fostered by the matchless piety and intelligence of his wife, Lady Rachel Russell. Sidney, a son of the Earl of Leicester, was a republican of the Spartan and Roman school, and no stranger to the darker paths of state intrigue. As early as 1681, when the king was ill, a scheme had been formed, with Monmouth and Shaftesbury, for an armed resistance to the Duke of York's succession; and now a more definite conspiracy was organized. A council of six—namely, Monmouth, Russell, Sidney, the Earl of Essex, Lord Howard of Eskrick, and John Hampden, grandson of the great patriot—concerted measures with Argyle and other Scottish malcontents for risings in the city, in Cheshire, and in the west. At the same time another plot was formed, without their knowledge, to assassinate the king on his return from Newmarket, by stopping his coach and shooting him, at a farm called the *Rye House*, on the Lea in Hertfordshire, which belonged to Rumbold, an old republican officer. Charles escaped the snare by leaving Newmarket eight days earlier than he had proposed, and the discovery of the "Rye-House Plot" was followed by the betrayal of the Whig conspiracy. Monmouth escaped; but the other leaders were taken, and Lord Howard made a confession of the whole scheme. It was well known that the two conspiracies were unconnected, but the court made every effort to fasten on the Whig leaders the guilt of the Rye-House plot. Lord William Russell was the first tried. He acknowledged the plan of insurrection, but denied all thoughts of attempting the king's life; and the evidence for the crown confirmed his statement. Though no overt act of treason was proved, he was found guilty; and neither the prayers of his wife, nor the stronger motive of £100,000 offered by his father to the king's mistress, could obtain his pardon. "If I do not take his life," said Charles, "he will soon have mine." "Arbitrary government," said Russell, "can not be set up in England without wading through my blood." His noble wife, who had acted as his secretary at the trial, fortified his resolution by her Christian courage; and after a calm but affecting parting with her, he was beheaded in Lincoln's Inn Fields, July 21, 1683.

Against Sidney Lord Howard was the only witness; and as the law of treason requires two, the defect was supplied by a manuscript found among his papers, advocating republican government, and approving of conspiracies against such tyrants as Caligula and Nero. Under the direction of Jeffreys, who had lately been made chief justice, these abstract theories were taken as evidence of compassing the death of the reigning king; and Sidney was found guilty (Nov. 21) and beheaded (Dec. 7), glorying that he suffered for "the good old cause." Hampden, against whom no second witness could be invented, was convicted of misdemeanor only, and fined £40,000 (Feb. 6). Essex was found in the Tower with his throat cut, probably by his own hand, on the morning of Lord William Russell's trial. Monmouth was pardoned, bnt soon afterward banished from court, and he fled to Holland early in 1684.

The ascendency of the Duke of York at court was now established. He obtained the liberation of Danby and other political prisoners on bail (Feb., 1684), and was reinstated in the office of lord high admiral, the king assuming the power to dispense with the test.

Titus Oates was convicted of libeling the duke, sentenced to £100,000 damages, and imprisoned in default of payment. Charles, freed by his French pension from the want of supplies, continued to govern without parliaments; if the entire neglect of business, and the passing all his time in indolence and profligacy, can be called government. At length, on Feb. 2, 1685, he was seized with an apoplectic fit; and in spite of the most violent remedies, he expired on Feb. 6, in the 55th year of his age and the 25th of his reign, after being reconciled to the Church of Rome, of which he professed to have been long secretly a member. He was buried at Westminster, Feb. 14.

Light-house erected at Plymouth, 1665.

Medal of Archbishop Sancroft and the Seven Bishops: obverse.

CHAPTER XXIX.

THE HOUSE OF STUART (*continued*).—JAMES II. A.D. 1685–1688.

THE brief reign of James II. of England and VII. of Scotland contains the history of that catastrophe which Charles II. had predicted and prepared, but which he had had the tact and good fortune to postpone till after his own death. James was alike destitute of the good-humor which made Charles popular, and of the skill to turn aside opposition. He professed indeed to his council his resolution to maintain the established government in church and state, and he retained his brother's ministers; but he went openly to mass, and ordered by a proclamation the payment of taxes as before. At the same time he secretly formed a council of Catholics, and opened a negotiation with Pope Innocent XI.

He was crowned, with his queen, on April 23, 1685, the communion being omitted; and parliament assembled May 19. They proved devoted to the court; granted the king tonnage and poundage, with other duties, for his life; and discharged Danby and the Catholic lords accused by Oates. The punishment inflicted on that miscreant excited almost as much abhorrence as his crime itself. Being convicted of perjury, he was sentenced to be degraded, heavily fined, whipped at the cart's tail from Aldgate to Newgate on one day, and

Medal of Archbishop Sancroft and the Seven Bishops: reverse.

from Newgate to Tyburn on the next, imprisoned for life, and pilloried five times every year. Contrary to the manifest intention of his judges, he survived the infliction of 1700 lashes, and lived till after the Revolution, when he received a pardon and a pension of £500 a year. His accomplice Dangerfield died from the severity of a like punishment; but his death was laid to the door of a person named Francis, who struck him in the eye with a cane on his way back to Newgate, and was hanged for the murder. On the same day (May 30) the venerable RICHARD BAXTER, to whom Charles had even offered a bishopric, was tried for a seditious libel against the church, in his *Paraphrase of the New Testament*, and sentenced to fine and imprisonment, amidst ribald insults which surprise us even from the lips of Jeffreys, who is said to have wished to have him whipped, like Oates and Dangerfield. At a later period (Nov., 1686) the Rev. Samuel Johnson, who had been the chaplain of Lord William Russell, was found guilty of a seditious address to the army, and sentenced to a severe whipping; the king's only reply to all intercessions being, that, "*since Mr. Johnson had the spirit of martyrdom, 'tis fit he should suffer.*"

The accession of James was a signal for insurrection, but the first attempts had a disastrous issue. Monmouth, whom the Prince of Orange prudently dismissed from his court, retired to Brussels, and joined Argyle in a rash plan of invasion. Early in May Argyle landed in Cantyre and raised about 2500 of his own clan, but his force was dispersed by the militia; he himself was captured in the disguise of a peasant (June 17, 1685), and beheaded at Edinburgh on his former sentence (June 30). His calm sleep on the night before his execution is portrayed on the walls of the new legislative palace at Westminster, in contrast with the indignities inflicted on the last moments of Montrose. The Scottish parliament, meeting on April 23, had already passed new laws against the Covenanters, who were delivered over to the cruelties of Claverhouse.

On June 11 Monmouth landed at Lyme Regis in Dorsetshire with scarcely 100 followers, but with equipments for an army. His popularity in the west soon placed him at the head of more than 2000 men, almost entirely of the lower orders. Advancing to Taunton, he assumed the title of "King James II.," having already issued a declaration stigmatizing "James duke of York" as "a traitor, a tyrant, an assassin, and a popish usurper." He marched on slowly, gathering more adherents than he could arm, and neglecting to take any decisive measures. The news of Argyle's fate had already led him to despair, when he met the royal army under Feversham and Churchill. Seizing a favorable opportunity, he attacked them at Sedgmoor, near Bridgewater (July 6); but his peasants were dispersed after a brave resistance, and Monmouth himself fled. He was found concealed in a ditch, in the disguise of a peasant (July 8), and carried to London. On the journey he wrote the most submissive letters to the king, who admitted him to an interview, but only to endeavor to extort from him the names of his accomplices (July 13). At this insult Monmouth's courage revived; and he met his fate calmly, the last scene being painfully protracted by the irresolution of the executioner (July 15, 1685). His followers were devoted to destruction. Many suffered military execution from the ferocious Colonel Kirke, who had long served at Tangiers, and who inflicted on the towns that had favored Monmouth the barbarities learned in his intercourse with the Moors. Others were reserved for the more systematic cruelty of Jeffreys, who was sent down on a special commission, long remembered in the west as the "*Bloody Circuit.*" Besides those already butchered by Kirke and his "lambs," as he called his soldiers, 330 are computed to have fallen by the hand of justice. The whole country was strewed with the heads and limbs of traitors. The convictions of Mrs. Gaunt, Lady Lisle, and Alderman Cornish, were particularly cruel and unjust. The last two were reversed after the Revolution. Even those who received pardon were obliged to atone for their guilt by fines which reduced them to beggary; or where their former poverty made them incapable of paying, they were condemned to cruel whippings or severe imprisonments. Some bought a pardon by bribing the judge, who made a large sum of money by selling his protection. Jeffreys, for these eminent services, was soon after invested by the king with the dignity of chancellor (Sept. 28). Courtiers, and even the ladies of the court, nay, the queen herself, made large gains by a traffic in pardons, and by the sale of prisoners for field labor in the West Indies. The maids of honor received more than £2000 as the price of a pardon to the young girls of Taunton, who had presented Monmouth with an embroidered banner and a Bible. While these scenes were passing in England Louis XIV. revoked the *Edict of Nantes*, by which Henry IV. (1598) had established liberty of worship in France (Oct. 12, 1683). Above half a million of Protestants, many of them the most industrious subjects of the crown, left France: nearly 50,000 settled in England, destined to plant the silk manufacture, with other arts, there, and meanwhile exciting new fears of papal persecution. About the same time James dismissed the Marquis of Halifax, who, as the head of the party called "Trimmers," had kept the court within some show of moderation (Oct. 21).

The king now commenced that contest for the power of "*dispensing*" with the provisions of the Test Act, which ended in the loss of his crown. He first proposed to keep Catholic officers in the army; and being unable to obtain the assent of parliament, which met on Nov. 9, he dismissed them on Nov. 20. He was equally unsuccessful with the parliament of Scotland. The question was next brought before the judges by a feigned action against Sir Edward Hale, a new convert to Romanism, who had accepted a commission of colonel. The bench having been purged by the dismissal of four judges, the twelve judges, with one exception, declared that there was nothing with which the king could not dispense (June 21). The clerical converts to Romanism received dispensations from the Act of Uniformity, and preachers were ordered to abstain from controversy. To enforce this order a new ecclesiastical commission was issued (July 14, 1686), which suspended Compton bishop of London for not silencing a clergyman who had preached against popery. Catholic worship was celebrated in public; schools were opened by the Jesuits; several monastic orders settled in London; and Catholics were appointed as heads of houses in both universities. The king even went so far as to send an embassador to Rome, and to give a public reception to a papal nuncio (July 3, 1687).

James attempted to recommend these measures by the false pretense of universal toleration. He published declarations for liberty of conscience, first in Scotland (Feb. 12, 1687), and then in England (April 4 and 27); and in a progress through the country (Sept.) he paid court to the Dissenters, few of whom, however, were deceived. The best commentary on these professions was furnished by his conduct in Ireland. Tyrconnel, a most bigoted Catholic, was appointed lord-lieutenant (1687); and he proceeded to expel the Protestants from all civil and military offices, to annul the charters of Dublin and other corporations, and to increase the army. In England, also, James endeavored to gain over the army to Romanism, and formed a camp at Hounslow Heath.

A crisis was brought on by the publication of a second *Declaration of Indulgence* (April 25, 1688), with a command that it should be read in all churches on the two Sundays, May 20 and 27. Upon this the primate, Sancroft, united with six other bishops in a private petition to the king, praying him not to insist on their reading the Indulgence from the pulpit, which their consciences forbade them to do (May 18). James resolved to deal with the petition as a seditious libel. The seven bishops were brought before the Council, and committed to the Tower; the people lining the banks of the river, and entreating their blessing as they passed along (June 8). The scene was repeated when they were called into court to plead (June 15), and again when they were brought to trial (June 29). A conclusive defense was made by their counsel, and especially by SOMERS; and after several hours of deliberation, or rather of a contest of endurance between the court and country parties on the jury, the verdict of "*Not guilty*" was pronounced (June 30). Westminster Hall rang with bursts of cheering, which were re-echoed through the country, and even in the camp at Hounslow, where James was present. "So much the worse for them," he exclaimed, on learning the cause of the uproar.

In the very midst of these proceedings the queen gave birth to a son, who was baptized by the names of JAMES FRANCIS EDWARD (June 10, 1688). This event hastened on a scheme already in progress for the liberation of the country. WILLIAM prince of Orange, the son-in-law of James, had sent over an emissary, Dykvelt, to sound the feelings of the English Protestants. His mission had been successful, and now another envoy, Zuylestein, who was sent to congratulate James on the birth of an heir, brought back to William an invitation from several nobles and other leading statesmen to appear in arms as their defender. The prince's preparations were made known to James by Louis XIV.; but he slighted the information, till he received a letter from his minister at the Hague, warning him of an immediate invasion. The king was thunderstruck; the letter dropped from his hands, and he began to retrace his steps with a precipitation which only proved his fear, and brought him into contempt (Oct.). The Prince of Orange was now on his way to England. He published a declaration of his intention in coming, to protect the rights and liberties of the people, to procure a free parliament, and to examine the suspicions that were current respecting the birth of the Prince of Wales (Oct. 10). Great hopes were excited by the declaration. On Oct. 19 he set sail from Helvoetsluys, with 500 ships and 14,000 men, for Yorkshire; but he was driven down the Channel by a gale of wind, during which he passed the king's fleet in the Downs, and, after spending his birthday in devotion, within sight of the shores of England (Sunday, Nov. 4), he landed at Torbay, Nov. 5, 1688, and advanced to Exeter. His unexpected arrival in this quarter, and the terror struck by the suppression of the late rising, made his first reception somewhat cool. But Sir Edward Seymour and other gentlemen soon joined him. Symptoms of disaffection appeared in the king's army at Salisbury; Lord Cornbury, the eldest son of James's nephew the Earl of Clarendon, went over to William (Nov. 12); there were riots in London, and risings all over the country. James declared his intention of calling a parliament (Nov. 16), and hastened to Salisbury. His officers promised to stand by him; but one of the most conspicuous and favored of them, Lord Churchill, deserted to the opposite camp a few days after, with the Duke of Grafton, a natural son of Charles II. (Nov. 22). The king now retreated. At Andover he was abandoned by Prince George of Denmark, the husband of his daughter Anne (Nov. 24); and, on reaching London, he found that Anne herself had fled to Nottingham with Lady Churchill and the Bishop of London (Nov. 26). "God help me!" he exclaimed; "my own children have forsaken me!" He now seemed passive in the hands of his council, composed of the peers who were in London. By their advice he proclaimed an amnesty, summoned a parliament to meet on Jan. 15, and sent Halifax, Nottingham, and Godolphin as commissioners to treat with William (Nov. 30). Meanwhile he was planning his escape, without waiting for the result of the negotiations, which went on at Hungerford (Dec. 8 and 9). The queen and her infant son left Whitehall, Dec. 10, and sailed for France; and at three o'clock the next morning the king stole away in disguise from Whitehall, carrying with him the Great Seal, which he threw into the river, as he hastened to Sheerness, where a vessel waited for him. By these acts he left the country without a government; and his reign is held to have terminated on this day, Dec. 11, 1688.

THE INTERREGNUM: Dec. 11, 1688, to Feb. 13, 1689.

The populace of London were in riot; Catholic chapels were sacked; the detested Jeffreys had been seized at Wapping, and conveyed to the Tower; the disbanded troops of Feversham were let loose upon the country; when the peers and bishops who were in London formed a provisional government, under the presidency of Halifax (Dec. 11 and 12), and invited the Prince of Orange to advance on London. Meanwhile James had been recognized at Sheerness and detained by the populace (Dec. 12). His friends escorted him back to Whitehall (Dec. 16); where, misled by the compassion shown him by the people, he resumed the airs of a monarch. Next day the council advised him to retire to Ham; but he preferred Rochester. There he waited for a few days, hoping to be recalled; and at last he sailed for France (Dec. 23). He was kindly received by Louis, and took up his abode at St. Germain's, which henceforth became the court of the exiled Stuarts.

The Prince of Orange arrived at Whitehall the same day that James departed (Dec. 19), and assembled a body of about seventy peers, with the lord mayor and aldermen and about fifty citizens, and several members of former parliaments. Rejecting a premature offer of the crown, William, by their advice, summoned a "Convention of the Estates," consisting of the peers, and commoners elected just as for a parliament. The wants of the Exchequer were supplied meanwhile by a free loan from the merchants of London.

In SCOTLAND, the royal troops having been withdrawn, the Covenanters proclaimed William king, at Glasgow, and a deputation waited on him at London (Jan. 10, 1689), requesting him to summon the Estates for March 18.

The CONVENTION met on Jan. 22, 1689. After much discussion, and with no little opposition in the peers, they resolved that James, by violating the constitution, breaking the original contract between king and people, and withdrawing from the kingdom, had *abdicated* the throne; and, further, that the rule of a Romish prince had been proved inconsistent with the safety of the Protestant religion. Still more discussion arose respecting a successor. The Prince of Orange refused the proposal of a regency; and, before filling the vacant throne, the commons drew up, and the lords accepted, the memorable "DECLARATION OF RIGHTS," which might be called the *Magna Charta of the Revolution*, only that its origin was above that of any royal charter, in the will of a united people. It recapitulated the offenses of the late king; reasserted the ancient rights of the people; settled the crown, first on William and Mary, as king and queen; next on the survivor of them; then on the queen's issue; failing them, on the Princess Anne and her issue; and lastly, failing them, on the issue of the Prince of Orange. It concluded by prescribing new oaths of allegiance and supremacy. On the 13th of February, 1689, the Convention met at Whitehall; the declaration was read; the crown was offered to the Prince and Princess of Orange, and accepted by William in a few quiet words; and, amidst the shouts of the people, WILLIAM and MARY were proclaimed king and queen of England, France, and Ireland.

Medal of William and Mary.

CHAPTER XXX.

THE REVOLUTION DYNASTY.—WILLIAM AND MARY, A.D. 1689–1694. WILLIAM III. ALONE, A.D. 1694–1702.

William Henry of Nassau, prince of Orange, was born at the Hague, Nov. 4, 1650, eight days after the death of his father, William II., stadtholder of the United Provinces. His mother was the Princess Mary, daughter of Charles I.; and thus he was the nephew, as well as the son-in-law, of James II. He had trained his slender body and weak constitution to endure fatigue. His pale and impassive countenance was lighted up by piercing eyes and dignified by an ample forehead. His demeanor was grave and reserved almost to moroseness; and his taciturnity might have earned the epithet of his great ancestor (see p. 172). When he spoke, it was little and very slowly, with what Bishop Burnet calls "a disgusting dryness," but "well and to the point," and his words could always be implicitly relied on. His excellence lay in action. He freed England from tyranny, placed her civil and religious liberties on a firm basis, and raised her to the foremost rank among the states of Europe. And all this he did amidst danger, ingratitude, and opposition, even from those who had invited him to the work. His letters to his friend

Heinsius show how keenly he felt these obstacles; for "few men had stronger passions, and few had the art of concealing and governing passion more than he had" (Burnet).

Though the crown was shared alike by William and Mary, the government was entirely committed to the king. He chose his ministers from both political parties, of course excluding declared *Jacobites*, as the partisans of the Stuarts are henceforth called (from *Jacobus*, the Latin form of *James*). Danby and Nottingham were associated in the same council with Halifax and Shrewsbury; and high offices were conferred upon some of his Dutch followers, as Bentinck, Schomberg, Zuylestein, and Auverquerque. Bentinck was made Earl of Portland, and was the ancestor of the present duke. William was his own foreign minister, and the one object of his European policy was to check the aggrandizement of Louis XIV. The king and queen were crowned on April 13, 1689.

The Convention, having declared itself a parliament (Feb. 13), proceeded to settle the revenue of the crown on a scale of frugality bordering on distrust; and they assumed, for the first time, the power of *appropriating* the supplies; half of the whole income of £1,200,000 being devoted to the public expenses, and half to the civil list. William resented their parsimony, but we can hardly blame their fear lest, having the resources of Holland at his disposal, he should be too little dependent upon parliament. Indeed it was only by the aid of Dutch troops that he was able to surmount his first difficulties, and to persevere in his foreign policy. He used them to suppress the mutiny of a Scotch regiment, soon after his accession. This led to the first *Mutiny Act*, which has since been renewed annually, for placing the troops under martial law. The army was remodeled under the care of Lord Churchill, who was soon made Earl of Marlborough, and who led several regiments to serve against Louis in Flanders, Dutch troops replacing them at home.

Freedom of worship was secured to Protestant Dissenters by the Toleration Act (May 24); but Unitarians were excluded from its benefits, and there was no relaxation of the penal laws against Roman Catholics. In the Church of England, the primate Sancroft and seven other bishops refused to take the new oath of allegiance, and were suspended. Their example was followed by 400 of the clergy, who suffered deprivation, and, under the name of *Nonjurors*, formed a class devoted to the exiled house of Stuart.

In Scotland a convention of the estates declared James to have *forefaulted* the crown, which was conferred on William and Mary. Episcopacy again gave place to Presbyterianism as the established religion, but the covenant was tacitly abandoned, to the great scandal of the extreme party. Still the Stuarts had a large body of adherents, especially in the highlands. The Duke of Gordon held the castle of Edinburgh for King James; and Claverhouse, now Viscount Dundee, raised his standard at Stirling and assembled an army of 2000 or 3000 highlanders. He gained a complete victory over General Mackay in the pass of *Killiecrankie*, south of Blair Athol; but he himself fell in the battle (July 13, 1689). Gordon had already surrendered the castle of Edinburgh (June 13), and all resistance ceased with the death of Dundee.

A far more formidable civil war had broken out in IRELAND, where James himself landed on March 12, having been furnished by Louis XIV. with a fleet, but he had only 1200 of his own soldiers and 100 French officers. Tyrconnel met him at Cork, with a horde of wild Irish, far more than he could arm. With this force, and with only twelve field-pieces and four mortars, he laid siege to Londonderry, which raised the long-celebrated cry of "No surrender." The city was blockaded for 105 days by Marshal Rosen, and both inhabitants and garrison suffered the last extremities of famine; but their heroic resistance, under Major Baker and a clergyman named Walker, was at last successful. They were relieved by Kirke, July 30, and on August 1 the besieging army broke up, after burning their huts. On the same day Lord Mountcashel was defeated at Newton Butler by the Protestants of Enniskillen. On Aug. 12 Marshal Schomberg landed at Donaghadee, with 10,000 men, and took and sacked Carrickfergus. James, after in vain offering him battle, retired into winter-quarters. During the summer he had held a parliament at Dublin, which voted some violent reactionary measures.

The English parliament reassembled Oct. 25, and converted the *Declaration of Right*, with some enlargements, into a statute, which, under the name of the BILL OF RIGHTS, forms, after Magna Charta and the Petition of Right, the third great charter of English liberties. They also reversed the attainders of Lord William Russell, Algernon Sidney, Cornish, and Mrs. Lisle, and gave compensation out of the estate of Jeffreys for the illegal fines inflicted by him. The unjust judge himself had died in the Tower, April 18, 1689.

The convention parliament was dissolved Feb. 6, 1690, and succeeded by one in which the Tories had a majority. They sat from March 20 to May 23; passed an Act of pardon and indemnity; settled a pension of £20,000 a year on the Princess Anne; presented Marshal Schomberg with £100,000; and voted William £1,200,000 for the war in Ireland. The king landed at Carrickfergus, June 14; and, having joined Schomberg, advanced against James, who retreated to a strong position on the steep banks of the river *Boyne*. On July 1, 1690, William crossed the river, and utterly defeated

James, whose army at once dispersed, while he himself fled to France, and landed at Brest, July 9. The BATTLE OF THE BOYNE has perhaps cost more lives by its factious celebration in after-years than fell in the action itself. The vanquished lost only 1500, and the victors 500; but among the latter were Marshal SCHOMBERG, and Walker, the defender of Londonderry. William followed up his victory by taking Waterford and other towns; but Limerick made good its resistance (Aug. 8-30), and he returned to England, Sept. 6. Marlborough then made a short campaign of only a month, and returned home after capturing Cork and Kinsale (Sept. and Oct.). Tyrconnel, James's deputy, also left Ireland for France; and the Jacobite cause was intrusted to James Fitz-James, *duke of Berwick*, an able general, the natural son of James, and the nephew of Marlborough, and to *Patrick Sarsfield*, the popular leader of the Irish, who had distinguished himself in the defense of Limerick. Ginkell commanded for William, and, in the following year, he brought the campaign to a successful close by the masterly capture of Athlone (June 30), the defeat of the French general St. Ruth at Aghrim (July 12), and the surrender of Limerick after a siege of six weeks. The war was concluded by the *Pacification of Limerick*, which secured to the Irish Catholics the exercise of their religion, and permitted those who wished to retire to the Continent at the expense of government (Oct. 3, 1691). Sarsfield and about 12,000 men entered into the service of Louis XIV.; and the Irish "brigade" will be seen playing a distinguished part in subsequent wars.

The support given to James by Louis led to hostilities in the Channel. War was declared against France, May 7, 1689. On June 30, 1690, the English and Dutch fleets, under the Earl of Torrington, were defeated off Beachy Head by Admiral Tourville, and driven to take shelter in the Thames; while the French remained masters of the Channel, but they attempted nothing further, except burning Teignmouth. In 1691 William went to Holland to arrange for a grand European coalition against Louis XIV. (Jan. 16—April 13), and he spent all the summer there, with Marlborough, in an indecisive campaign (May—October).

At the close of 1691 the new government was established in the three kingdoms. A pacification of the Scotch highlands had been made in August, granting pardon and indemnity to all who should lay down their arms and take the oath of allegiance before Dec. 31; but subjecting defaulters to military execution. These terms were complied with by all the Jacobite heads of clans, except M'Ian, the chief of the M'Donalds of *Glencoe*, a wild valley of the western highlands, opening upon Loch Levin, and accessible on the land side only by a few difficult passes. M'Ian repaired to Fort Augustus on Dec.

31, but found no one authorized to administer the oath. He was directed to Inverary; but owing to the difficulty of the passes, which were blocked with snow, he arrived there only on Jan. 6. Sir Colin Campbell, the sheriff of Argyle, yielding to M'Ian's earnest entreaties, received his oath, and he returned home in security. But he had a deadly enemy in the Scottish Secretary, Sir John Dalrymple (afterward Earl of Stair), who availed himself of M'Ian's legal default to plan the massacre of his whole tribe. The horrid deed was carried into execution, with as much treachery as cruelty, on the night of Feb. 13, 1692; and it was only the late arrival of one party of soldiers that enabled a portion of the clan to escape through some unguarded passes. The *Massacre of Glencoe* set the stamp of execration on William's name in the highlands; and, though he was doubtless imposed on by Dalrymple, it is impossible to acquit him of culpable negligence, if he was not guilty of direct connivance. No measure could have been more favorable to the cause of James in Scotland.

In this year (1692) a formidable attempt was made for the restoration of the Stuarts. The schemes of the Jacobites were favored by some of the leading Whigs, especially Marlborough, who induced the Princess Anne to write a penitent letter to her father. The conspirators called in the aid of Louis. The Irish brigade, now numbering 20,000 men, with 10,000 French troops, formed a camp at Cotentin, near La Hogue, and a fleet of eighty sail was fitted out to convoy them to the coast of England. The impolitic manifesto issued by James contrasted strongly with the wise and resolute conduct of Queen Mary, who had the charge of the government during William's absence in the Netherlands. Having reason to believe that Russell, the English admiral, was in the Jacobite conspiracy, she addressed a letter to him, expressing confidence in the fleet, and ordered him to read it to all his officers on his quarter-deck. When the French fleet under Tourville put out from Brest for the camp, it was encountered by the English and Dutch off Cape la Hogue, and utterly defeated (May 19, 1692). In commemoration of the BATTLE OF LA HOGUE, Queen Mary gave up the palace of Greenwich as a hospital for disabled seamen, and the erection of the present *Greenwich Hospital* was begun by William in 1696.

Louis had some compensation for his loss at La Hogue, in the defeats of William by Marshal Luxemburg, near Namur (Aug. 3, 1693), and at Landen (July 19, 1694), and in the naval victory of Tourville over Sir George Rooke and a valuable convoy, near Lagos (June 17, 1694). These reverses were the more serious for the encouragement they gave to the Jacobites. Bristol, Exeter, and Boston declared for James, and Marlborough's intrigues frustrated an expedition against Brest. The pressure of war taxes became severe; and the parliament, which met Nov. 12, 1694, seized the opportunity to carry the bill for *Triennial Parliaments*, to which William had refused his assent in a former session. (This statute, which provided for a *new* parliament every three years, was repealed under George I., in 1716.) During the same session the *Freedom of the Press* was established by the non-renewal, on its expiration, of the act to restrain unlicensed printing. Severe steps were taken to punish the prevalent corruption of public officers: among whom, Sir John Trevor, the speaker, had to suffer the ignominy of putting the question for his own expulsion from the House of Commons.

The loss of Queen Mary, who died of small-pox on Dec. 28, 1694, deprived the throne of William of the appearance of legitimacy given by her sharing it, and plots began to be formed by the Jacobites against the king's life, with the sanction of James. William spent the summer in the Netherlands, and achieved one of his greatest successes, the taking of Namur and its citadel (Aug. 4 and Sept. 1, 1795). The new parliament, which met on Nov. 22, passed a most important Act for regulating *Trials for Treason*, giving the accused a right to a copy of the indictment, the aid of counsel, and other advantages. A list of the witnesses to be called was granted by a later statute of Anne (1709). Meanwhile the plots mentioned above went on, and a scheme was laid by Sir George Barclay, a Scotch officer, and others, to assassinate William on his way to hunt at Richmond, as was his custom every Saturday (Feb. 15). The conspiracy was betrayed, and a "loyal association" was formed by both houses of parliament to protect the king's life. Five of the conspirators were condemned and executed (March 18 and April 3), having been publicly absolved on the scaffold by Jeremy Collier, a nonjuring divine. Sir John Fenwick, against whom only one witness could be produced, was at length attainted by act of parliament, and executed on Tower Hill, Jan. 28, 1697. While in prison he offered to give evidence against Marlborough, Godolphin, Admiral Russell, and other leading men, who are now known to have been in treasonable correspondence with James; but he gained no credit, and only sealed his fate by rousing their enmity. The Whigs had now regained their ascendency, and several of their leaders received new titles. The great lawyer, SIR JOHN SOMERS, was made lord chancellor and a peer (April 22, 1697).

Another indecisive campaign in the Netherlands had made Louis desirous of closing the war; and, after protracted negotiations, the general PEACE OF RYSWICK was signed, Sept. 10, 1697. Louis relinquished most of his conquests, and acknowledged William as king of Great Britain and Ireland.

About the same time England was visited by another potentate, destined to raise his barbarous and little-known dominions to the rank of a first-rate power, and to prepare his successors for leading on a European coalition to the overthrow of Louis XIV.'s most powerful successor. This was PETER THE GREAT, czar of Russia. He lived at Mr. Evelyn's house at Deptford, while he spent his days in the dock-yard, and worked with his own hand, to acquire the knowledge of ship-building. Another great event of this year was the opening of *St. Paul's Cathedral* for public worship, on the thanksgiving day for the peace of Ryswick (Dec. 2, 1697).

The peace was of short duration. While parliament was pressing on William the reduction of the army, Louis was planning no less a scheme than the addition of Spain to his dominions, on the approaching death of Charles II. The table on the opposite page shows the state of the royal family of Spain.

The rights of the several claimants are too complicated to be discussed here; nor had they much to do with the issue. William favored the expedient of a partition of the vast Spanish empire, by incorporating with France the provinces north of the Pyrenees; giving to the dauphin Naples and Sicily, with the other Italian possessions, except Milan, which was assigned to the Archduke Charles; while the electoral prince of Bavaria, Joseph Ferdinand, whom Philip IV. had named as his heir, was to inherit Spain, the Netherlands, and the Indies. A secret treaty to this effect was signed by William and Louis at Loo (Oct. 1, 1698), but frustrated by the death of Joseph Ferdinand (Feb. 8, 1699). They made a second treaty of partition in the spring of 1700, giving Spain, the Netherlands, and the Indies to the Archduke Charles, and Milan to the dauphin, in addition to the share already allotted to him. But, in the autumn, the emperor rejected all plans of partition, and Louis induced the king of Spain to make a will in favor of his grandson, Philip duke of Anjou, who became King PHILIP V. of Spain on the death of Charles II, (Oct. 21, 1700). The emperor took up arms against the French in Italy, in favor of his son, who assumed the title of CHARLES III.; and thus began the great *War of the Spanish Succession* (1701). William at first acquiesced in the accession of Philip V.; but a sense of common danger soon led him to form the *Grand Alliance* of England, Holland, and the empire, for depriving Philip, or rather Louis, of Flanders and the Milanese (Sept. 7, 1701).

At this very moment an event occurred which caused the people to unite heartily in the policy of the king. His course at home had not been smooth. The parliament of 1688 had deprived him of his Dutch guards, and revoked enormous grants of forfeited lands in Ireland which he had made to his Dutch favorites, be-

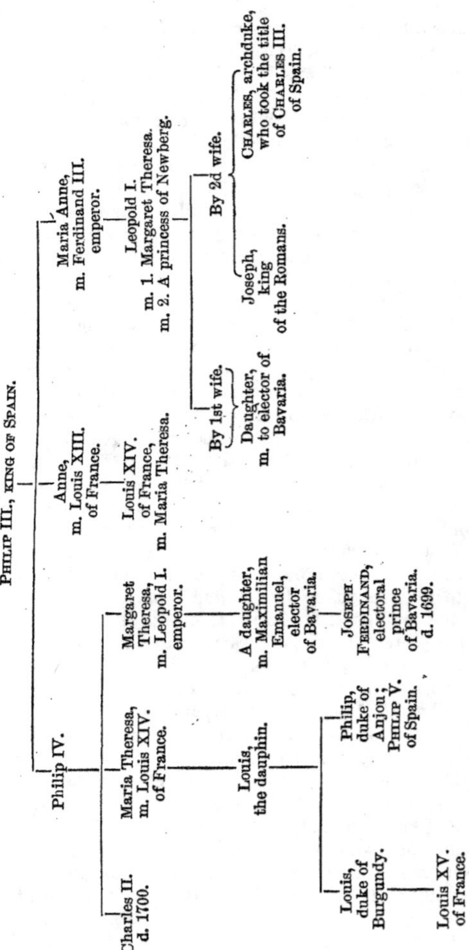
PHILIP III., KING OF SPAIN.
Philip IV.
Anne, m. Louis XIII. of France.
Maria Anne, m. Ferdinand III. emperor.
Charles II. d. 1700.
Maria Theresa, m. Louis XIV. of France.
Margaret Theresa, m. Leopold I. emperor.
Louis XIV. of France, m. Maria Theresa.
Leopold I. m. 1. Margaret Theresa. m. 2. A princess of Newberg.
Louis, the dauphin.
A daughter, m. Maximilian Emanuel, elector of Bavaria.
By 1st wife.
Daughter, m. to elector of Bavaria.
By 2d wife.
Joseph, king of the Romans.
CHARLES, archduke, who took the title of CHARLES III. of Spain.
Louis, duke of Burgundy.
Philip, duke of Anjou; PHILIP V. of Spain.
JOSEPH FERDINAND, electoral prince of Bavaria. d. 1699.
Louis XV. of France.

sides excluding them from the council. In the next parliament, which met Feb. 6, 1701, with the celebrated Robert Harley for speaker, the Tories had a majority. The partition treaties were censured as prejudicial to the Protestant religion; and the earls of Portland, Halifax, and Orford (Admiral Russell), with Lord Somers, were impeached for their share in them. But now arose that new form of making public opinion felt by a hostile parliament, which has often since proved its power. A *Petition* was presented by the gentlemen and freeholders of Kent, praying the house to abandon factious disputes, and to grant the king supplies for the aid of his allies (May, 1701). Though the house committed the leading petitioners, they suffered the impeachment to fall to the ground, and parliament was prorogued on June 24. Their one great measure was the Act of Settlement, for securing a Protestant succession to the crown. William was childless; and the death of the young Duke of Gloucester, the only son of the Princess Anne (July 30, 1700), had left her also without heirs. A successor was found in Sophia, the daughter of the unfortunate Frederick elector palatine and Elizabeth daughter of James I. She was married to the elector of Hanover, and was the only descendant of James I. who adhered to the reformed faith. On her and her heirs, therefore, being *Protestants*, the crown was settled in case of the deaths of both William and Anne without issue. New securities for the liberties of the people were incorporated in this act.

The Act of Settlement had been passed only a few months, and the Grand Alliance had been signed only a week, when James II. died at St. Germain's, Sept. 16, 1701. Louis XIV. at once acknowledged his son, James Francis Edward, as king of Great Britain and Ireland, in defiance of the treaty of Ryswick. This outrage roused all England. The voice of the people found utterance in the new parliament (Dec. 30), which responded loyally to a noble speech from William; voted £600,000 and large land and sea forces for the war; resolved that no peace should be made till France had given reparation for the insult; and attainted the "pretended Prince of Wales" and his adherents of high treason. William, care-worn and enfeebled by disease, found himself once more the trusted leader of his people, united with him in the cause of freedom and religion, which was dearer to him than his crown.

But the triumph was his last, and others were to reap its fruits. He was riding from Kensington to Hampton Court when his horse fell with him, and he broke his collar-bone (Feb. 21, 1702). There seemed at first no danger. He transacted business; sent a message to parliament on the 23d; gave his assent to several bills; and on the 28th was pronounced convalescent. But the shock had been fatal, and he died on the 8th of March, 1702, in the 52d year of his age, and just after completing the thirteenth year of his reign. His memory has only received full, though perhaps partial, justice from the most eloquent writer of our own day.

REVIEW OF THE SEVENTEENTH CENTURY.

The age from the death of Elizabeth to that of William (1603-1702) coincides almost exactly with the duration of the 17th century, and forms a period of mortal conflict between the principles of liberty and despotism. That conflict had been carried on, in practice, ever since the reign of John. Constitutional liberty had been obtained under the Plantagenets; but the strong will of the Tudors seemed to have left the victory with the crown, though all the forms of a free constitution were preserved, ready to start into activity under a less vigorous hand. The Stuarts, too weak to continue this system in its power, yet committed themselves more openly to the assertion of its *principles*. James I. summed up the theory of divine right in the simple maxim, "*a Deo rex, a Rege lex*" (the king is from God, the law from the king); and Charles I. and James II. staked life and crown on its maintenance in practice. The parliamentary leaders opposed force to force; while the theory of popular rights was argued out by Milton, Sidney, and Locke; and the revolution of 1688 was avowedly based on the union of right and might. The abstract theories involved in the dispute have ever since been open to debate; but the practical result, as embodied in the *Bill of Rights* and the *Act of Settlement*, is accepted, alike by Whigs and Tories, as equally binding on the sovereign and the people. In religion, also, the conflict between the Catholic and Protestant churches, after being more and more complicated by the innumerable forms into which the latter branched out, was tending to the wider question of liberty of conscience, which was for the first time publicly, though very partially, recognized under William. In the foreign relations during this period there were strange vicissitudes. Elizabeth had established the power of England abroad and on the seas, as the guardian of her own independence and the champion of the oppressed. This proud position was regained by Cromwell, after it had been abandoned by James I. and Charles I.: it was recklessly sacrificed by Charles II., the pensioner of Louis; and was revived by William in the new form of wars for the maintenance of the "balance of power" in Europe. The supposed connection between peace and liberal principles is not borne out by the experience of this century; nor does that experience justify the assumption that the honor of the crown in the eyes of Europe is best maintained by the extreme advocates of its prerogatives at home. One result of foreign and domestic war was the establishment of a permanent military force. We have noticed the commencement of a standing army under Charles II. It increased under James II. to 20,000 men; and under William it became an institution. The navy was a favorite object with the Stuarts; and James II. especially, both as Duke of York and king, deserves lasting praise for his efforts to maintain an efficient fleet, seconded by the celebrated Pepys, as secretary to the Admiralty.

Amidst all its troubles the country made steady progress in population, civilization, and wealth. The great colonies of North America—Virginia, New England, Maryland, New York, New Jersey, Carolina, and Pennsylvania—were established by religious refugees and speculative settlers, or gained as the prizes of war; and many of their names still bear witness to their origin. The fruits of war were also reaped both in the West and East Indies; and in the latter the East India Company, besides gaining enormous profits, began to obtain a permanent footing in the country. A rival association sprang up about the time of the Revolution, and the two were finally incorporated together in 1702. Commerce was extended by other companies of merchant adventurers, and it received a vast impulse from the naval successes against the Dutch. Enormous fortunes were realized in trade; and Sir Josiah Child may be mentioned as the representative of English "merchant princes." The association of such men supplied funds to the parliament and to Cromwell; and such an association, which came forward under William with a loan of £1,200,000, was incorporated as the *Bank of England.* Taxation gradually took more of its modern form, in the imposition of numerous duties of customs and excise; and the *National Debt* may be said to have originated in the wars against Louis XIV., for at the Revolution it was little above a million, and at the death of Anne (1714) it had reached 50 millions. It must not be concealed that with the increase of wealth there was a frightful increase of corruption. Kings and statesmen bribed each other, and the merchants bribed them all.

Art received some encouragement during this age, chiefly by the employment of foreign artists, among whom the greatest was Vandyke. English architecture ceased to live; but the new semi-classic style of Palladio was introduced by Italian architects, and developed with great magnificence by *Inigo Jones* and Sir *Christopher Wren.*

Literature, which had culminated under Elizabeth, maintained an elevation in which only a severe taste could detect incipient decline. *Shakspeare* belongs to James as well as Elizabeth. He found a worthy successor in *Ben Jonson;* but when the drama rose again from its suppression under the Commonwealth, it was debased by the prevailing immorality, which infected the whole literature of the Restoration. *Milton* belongs, by his sympathies and earlier writings, to the Commonwealth; but his great poem was the solace of his blind old age, when he had "fallen on evil days and evil tongues." His sublime blank verse remains without a rival; but the stately and nervous couplets of *Dryden* gave birth to a new school, while his death (in 1700) closes the poetical literature of the century.

Bacon stands at the head of the prose writers of the century, which ends with his worthy disciple in philosophy, *John Locke;* the intervening period being marked by the great names, but opposite principles, of *Cudworth* and *Hobbes.* Science was pursued on the principles of Bacon by *Boyle*, *Wren*, *Hooke*, *Harvey* (the discoverer of the circulation of the blood), and other worthy associates, who formed the *Royal Society* under Charles II., and its achievements were crowned by SIR ISAAC NEWTON. In the vast field of religious literature BUNYAN is unrivaled. *De Foe* devoted his almost equal genius to political conflict as well as to popular fiction. The Diaries of Pepys and Evelyn give us striking pictures of the manners of the Restoration and Revolution, and Bishop Burnet's Memoirs are a valuable authority. *Newspapers* began to acquire their modern influence upon the abolition of the censorship under William.

Reverse of Medal struck to commemorate the Battle of the Boyne.

Great Seal of Queen Anne, after the Union with Scotland (reverse).

CHAPTER XXXI.

THE REVOLUTION DYNASTY (*continued*).—ANNE. A.D. 1702–1714.

ANNE, the second daughter of James II., was born at St. James's, Feb. 6, 1665. She was educated by Dr. Compton, afterward Bishop of London, who made her a firm Protestant. Her hand was sought by the electoral prince of Hanover, George Louis, who ultimately became her successor; but she married Prince George of Denmark, a weak, coarse, indolent man, who never had any influence in England, though he held the office of lord high admiral from Anne's accession. Their children all died in infancy. The last survivor of them was William duke of Gloucester, a boy of much promise, who was born July 24, 1689, and died July 30, 1700. Prince George himself died Oct. 28, 1708. A much more important person than Anne's husband was her chosen friend *Sarah Jennings*, to whom she became attached when a young girl. In 1681 this lady married

Colonel Churchill, bringing to the aid of his advancement an ambition as eager and unscrupulous as his own. At the Revolution Lord and Lady Churchill induced Anne to desert her father; and all the favors with which William rewarded Marlborough's military genius did not prevent him and his countess from forming a "princess's party," and intriguing with the court of St. Germain's. When Anne ascended the throne she was still entirely subject to Lady Marlborough, with whom she affected to lay aside the queen, calling her friend *Mrs. Freeman*, and being called by her *Mrs. Morley*. She made Marlborough a knight of the Garter and captain-general of all her forces; and gratified his military ambition by continuing the warlike policy of William III. Her ministers were chosen from the Tories, Godolphin being lord high treasurer. Their contest with the Whigs, which nearly ended in bringing back the "Pretender," and the victories of Marlborough, are the two great subjects of interest in Anne's reign.

Its chief domestic event is the Union of England and Scotland into the one kingdom of Great Britain. This great measure was recommended by the queen in her first speech to parliament (March 11, 1702), and she was empowered to appoint commissioners to treat for the union; but the negotiations were not fairly commenced till April, 1706. There was violent opposition to the union in Scotland: and the Scottish parliament passed an act, at the beginning of the queen's reign, refusing to settle the crown of Scotland on the heir to that of England. The more moderate party proposed a federation; but eventually, by the help of unsparing bribery, the Act of Union passed the Scottish parliament on Jan. 16, 1707, and the English parliament on March 6, and came into operation on May 1. The two countries were united into one kingdom; but they preserved their respective religious establishments — the Episcopal Church of England, with the queen at its head, and the Presbyterian Kirk of Scotland, acknowledging no head on earth. The laws and customs of each of the ancient kingdoms were to be preserved unaltered, except as the united parliament might from time to time determine; and hence the Scotch system of law, founded on the Roman code, is very different from that of England. Scotland was to send 45 members to the House of Commons, and 16 peers, elected for life, to the House of Lords. The crown abandoned the power of creating new Scotch peers; and it was provided that, if their number should be reduced to a limit which is now nearly reached, the remnant should become peers of the United Kingdom. The "Union jack," bearing the red cross of St. George and the diagonal white cross of St. Andrew (though as yet wanting the cross of St. Patrick), was appointed by proclamation to be the national flag (July 28).

The popular feeling of hatred to the union lasted in Scotland for many years, and all manner of evils were most absurdly ascribed to it; but statesmen had long seen its necessity on political grounds; and its advantages to the commerce and civilization of both countries, adding wealth to Scotland and energy to England, have been proved by the experience of 155 years.

We now turn to foreign politics. Early in 1702 Marlborough went as embassador to Holland, to concert measures against Louis XIV., and on his return war was declared against France and Spain (May 4). In July he took the command of the allies in Flanders, and reduced Venloo, Ruremonde, and Liège. He returned to England in November to receive the thanks of parliament and the patent of a duke, with a pension of £5000 a year, which was afterward made perpetual. The fleet, under Sir George Rooke, failed in an attack on Cadiz, but captured and destroyed several French men-of-war in the bay of Vigo. Admiral Benbow pursued the French West Indian fleet, and engaged them for five days, though they had fifteen ships, and his seven were reduced to two by the desertion of his captains, whom he lived long enough to punish before dying of his wounds at Kingston in Jamaica (Aug., 1702).

The campaign of 1703 was indecisive. In Southern Germany the French and Bavarians were successful against the Austrians; but Marlborough took Bonn on the Rhine, and the fall of the fortresses of Huy, Limburg, and Gueldres made him master of the line of the Meuse as a base for his operations in the following year. The Duke of Savoy and the king of Portugal joined the alliance this year, and the nominal king of Spain, Charles III., paid a visit to England. The beginning of winter was marked by a tempest of unparalleled fierceness called the "Great Storm" (Nov. 26—Dec. 1). The royal navy lost 12 ships and 1500 men; the damage in London was computed at £1,000,000; and, among much other loss of life, Bishop Kidder and his wife were killed by the fall of part of the Episcopal palace at Wells.

In 1704 Marlborough concerted with Prince EUGENE of Savoy a masterly scheme for the relief of the emperor. Carrying his army across the Rhine, Main, and Neckar, to the Danube, while Eugene secured the line of the Upper Rhine, he took Donauwerth, cutting in two the enemy's forces on the line of the Danube, and securing a bridge over the river. The armies of the Upper Rhine now came through the Black Forest to the aid of the main bodies; the French, under Marshal Tallard, joining the elector of Bavaria, and Eugene uniting his forces to Marlborough. The French and Bavarians took up a strong position on the heights of *Hochstadt*, behind the village of BLENHEIM, which lies on the south bank of the Danube, in

Bavaria. To secure the village Marshal Tallard weakened his centre, and upon that point Marlborough flung all his force, cut the line, pushed the right wing of the enemy into the Danube, or forced them to surrender, Tallard himself being among the prisoners. On the left the Bavarians held their ground against Eugene till the right was defeated, and then retreated to Ulm. The Battle of Blenheim is one of the most complete victories in history. It enabled the imperial forces to overrun Bavaria and to pursue the French into Alsace, where they took Landau and Traerbach; while Marlborough went to Berlin to secure the aid of the king of Prussia, and returned to London in December. His reception was most magnificent, and his rewards substantial. The manor of Woodstock was adorned, at the public cost, with the splendid mansion of *Blenheim House*, and granted to him and his heirs forever. They hold it by the tenure of presenting to the sovereign annually, on the anniversary of the battle, a small flag embroidered with the *fleur-de-lys* of the Bourbons, which hangs in the armory of Windsor opposite to the tricolor, which is also annually presented for the manor of Strathfieldsaye in memory of Waterloo.

In the same summer the English fleet, under Sir George Rooke, made the important conquest of Gibraltar, through the negligence of its garrison (July 23); and it was held against a combined attack by the French and Spanish fleets (Oct.). Another French squadron, sent to reinforce the besiegers, was totally defeated by Sir John Leake (March 10, 1705), with the result of raising the siege of Gibraltar, and destroying the naval power of France in the Mediterranean. The shores of Spain now witnessed the daring exploits of Charles Mordaunt, earl of Peterborough, who, in conjunction with a fleet under Sir Cloudesley Shovel, took Barcelona, and reduced all Catalonia and Valencia under the authority of Charles III. (May—Oct., 1705). Marlborough was occupied this summer in defending the Dutch frontier. He was made a prince of the empire by Joseph I., the successor of Leopold.

The timid policy of the Dutch again kept Marlborough in the Netherlands in 1706, but gave him thus the opportunity of winning the brilliant victory of Ramillies (near Tirlemont), over Marshal Villeroi (May 23). The French were expelled from Italy by Prince Eugene and the Duke of Savoy; and an Anglo-Portuguese army advanced to Madrid, but were driven out again by the Duke of Berwick. The British fleet, under Sir John Leake, took Majorca and Iviza. These victories gave a prestige to the government which aided them in carrying the Union; and they postponed the fall of Marlborough, whose influence at court was now giving way before an intrigue to be related presently. Their effect abroad was to make Louis desirous of peace, but his overtures were distrusted by the allies.

In 1707 Majorca was retaken by Marshal Villars; but Eugene invaded France from Italy, and laid siege to Toulon (July 26). The town made good its defense against both the prince and a blockading fleet under Sir Cloudesley Shovel. That brave admiral, who had risen from before the mast, perished with four of his ships on some rocks off the Scilly Isles, on his voyage home (Oct. 22). There were no decisive actions this year in Germany or Flanders.

The season of 1708 opened with an attempt of the Pretender to invade Scotland from Dunkirk (March 6); but his fleet was dispersed by Sir George Byng, after a panic had been created in London, and the Habeas Corpus Act suspended. In the Netherlands Marlborough conducted one of his most brilliant and decisive campaigns, and won the great victory of OUDENARDE over Marshal Vendôme (July 11), which made him master of all Flanders. Next year, with Prince Eugene, he followed up his success on the French frontier by the victory of MALPLAQUET over Villars (Sept. 11), and the capture of Mons (Oct. 20, 1709); and in the year after they made further progress in Artois and Picardy (March to June, 1710). The fleet had its full share in the honors of war. *Sardinia* and *Minorca* surrendered to Sir John Leake in 1708, and the French settlement of Port Royal in *Acadia* (now *Nova Scotia*) was taken in 1710, and named Annapolis in honor of the queen. In Spain there were great vicissitudes during these three years. The victories of Count Stahremberg, aided by General Stanhope, at *Almenara* (July 27, 1710) and *Saragossa* (Aug. 20) put Charles III. in possession of Madrid; but he was soon driven out by Marshal Vendôme, who forced Stanhope to surrender (Dec. 10) and defeated Stahremberg (Dec. 20). In the summer of 1711 Charles III. had scarcely a footing left him in Spain. He returned to Germany (Sept. 27), and was elected emperor by the title of CHARLES VI. Within a month afterward (Oct., 1711) Marlborough, after obtaining some successes against Villars, took his final departure from Flanders, his enemies having obtained complete ascendency at court. This change demands a review of domestic politics.

In Anne's first new parliament, which met Oct. 20, 1702, the commons chose ROBERT HARLEY as speaker, and showed a violent Tory spirit, which was only kept in check by the lords. Their great party measure was a bill against "*occasional conformity*" (that is, the practice adopted by some of the less scrupulous Dissenters of taking the sacramental test merely to qualify for office), which the peers threw out. The convocation of the clergy was strongly divided this session by the parties of *High Church* and *Low Church*, the latter supporting and the former opposing a revision of the Liturgy, with a view to the comprehension of Dissenters, and *Dr. Atterbury* made his appearance as a leader of the high-church party. In 1703–4 disputes arose between the two houses from the violent measures of the commons to coerce the Scots into making a settlement of the crown as in England, and from the attempts of the commons to "tack" the bill against occasional conformity to a money bill. Marlborough was disgusted at these party conflicts, and Godolphin was anxious to keep terms with the Whigs, who formed a powerful opposition party called the "*Junto*," under Lords Somers, Halifax, Wharton, Orford, and Sunderland. The ministry was strengthened by the introduction of Robert Harley and HENRY ST. JOHN, whom the two great leaders hoped to find devoted to them; but Harley undermined the influence of the Marlboroughs with the queen, who began to weary of Sarah's temper, by the introduction of a new favorite, *Abigail Hill*, who soon became Mrs. Masham. They revenged themselves on Harley by driving him from office, on a false charge of being implicated in a treasonable correspondence which one of his clerks, named Gregg, had carried on with France. Harley and St. John, who resigned with him, were replaced by two Whigs—ROBERT WALPOLE and Cardonnel (Feb., 1708). In the autumn of the same year the cabinet became still more Whiggish by the appointment of Somers as lord president; and the parliament, which met Nov. 16, chose Sir Richard Onslow, a Whig, for speaker.

The tables were, however, soon turned again by the popular outburst in favor of *Dr. Sacheverel*, who, preaching before the lord mayor at St. Paul's (Nov. 5, 1709), advocated passive obedience, virulently abused Dissenters and Low Churchmen, inveighed against the Whig ministers, and made a personal attack upon Godolphin. The commons voted the sermon scandalous and seditious, and resolved to impeach Sacheverel. He was brought to trial before the lords at Westminster Hall (Feb. 27, 1710), and condemned to silence for three years, and his sermon to be burnt by the common hangman. But the temper of the people, who escorted the high-church champion to and fro with loud cheering, encouraged Anne to make a gradual alteration in the ministry. The change was completed by the dismissal of Godolphin (Aug. 8); and a Tory administration was formed under the Duke of Shrewsbury, with Harley as chancellor of the exchequer, and St. John, who was now a decided Jacobite, as a secretary of state, specially charged with the foreign correspondence. They were supported by a new Tory parliament, which met Nov. 25, 1710, and passed the act against occasional conformity, and the *Schism Act*, requiring all teachers to conform to the established church. Both were repealed under George I. in 1719.

Thus far Marlborough's military ascendency was respected. The queen's speech had expressed a desire for peace, but urged the vigorous prosecution of the war, for which the commons voted £14,000,000. But no mention was made of Marlborough's services, a motion in the lords for a vote of thanks to him was defeated, and the duchess was dismissed with insult from her offices about the queen's person. The advancement of Harley was aided by a strange accident. Guiscard, a French adventurer, whom St. John had employed, being brought before the council on the charge of a treasonable correspondence with France, stabbed Harley with a penknife, the blade of which fortunately broke against his breast-bone. St. John and others dispatched Guiscard with their swords (Mar. 18, 1711). Harley's slight wound earned for him the sympathy of the people, the parliament, and the queen. He was made EARL OF OXFORD (May 24) and lord high treasurer (May 29). But his good fortune brought upon him the envy of St. John, for whom Guiscard's blow seems to have been meant, and who now began to intrigue against his former comrade. Their rivalry became more marked when St. John obtained his peerage as VISCOUNT BOLINGBROKE (July 7, 1712).

Meanwhile the ministry had begun to treat secretly for peace. After the campaign of 1711 the elevation of Charles to the imperial crown, the repeated overtures of Louis, and the exhaustion of all parties, furnished solid grounds for proposing peace; negotiations were opened (Oct. 20), and *Utrecht* was named as the place where the conferences were to be held.

At this juncture Marlborough returned to London (Oct. 18). He defended his character and conduct in parliament, which met on December 7, repelling the insinuation, which had been made even in the queen's speech, against "the arts of those that delight in war," and protesting that "he was ever desirous of a safe, honorable, and lasting peace." That no peace could be so which left Spain and the West Indies to the house of Bourbon, was resolved by 62 against 44; but the same amendment was rejected in the commons by 232 against 106. The ministry then proceeded with their personal attack on Marlborough. A report was laid before the commons, charging Marlborough, Walpole, and Cardonnel with peculation (Dec. 21). The two commoners were expelled from parliament, and the great duke was dismissed from all his offices. He was succeeded as commander-in-chief by the Duke of Ormond (Jan. 1, 1712), with instructions not to press the war during the negotiations, which were opened at Utrecht, in spite of the opposition of the allies (Jan. 29, 1712). Twelve new peers were created to secure the consent of the lords to the proposed terms, against which there was still a strong party headed by Marlborough. But his opposition in the senate was neutralized by his absence from the field. Ormond, after taking Quesnoy (July 17), made a separate armistice; Eugene was defeated; several fortresses in Flanders were retaken; and France was enabled to insist on moderate terms. Marlborough retired from England in November. He returned on the very day of the queen's death (Aug. 1, 1714), but was received coldly by George I. He was, however, restored to his old office of captain-general, and aided, by his advice, in suppressing the rebellion of 1715. He died June 16, 1722, and was buried in Westminster Abbey. His duchess, who survived till 1744, published a *Vindication* of his conduct and her own, against the charges of treason, avarice, falsehood, and unscrupulous ambition, on which the verdict of posterity has generally been passed against them, perhaps too severely. It was on hearing the memory of Marlborough thus assailed, that Bolingbroke, his constant enemy, replied, "*He was a great man, and I have forgotten all his faults.*"

The conferences for peace at Utrecht lasted for more than a year. The English plenipotentiaries were the Earl of Strafford, John Robinson bishop of Bristol, and subsequently Matthew Prior the poet. The throne of Spain proper and its colonies was abandoned to the house of Bourbon, on the promise of Louis that the crowns of France and Spain should never be united; but Naples, Milan, and the Netherlands were given up to the emperor. Sicily was assigned to the Duke of Savoy, and Sardinia to the elector of Bavaria, both with the title of king. Holland received Namur and other towns in Flanders, restoring Lille to France. On his eastern frontier Louis obtained Orange and Franche Comté from Prussia, in exchange for Upper Gueldres. Spain ceded Gibraltar and Minorca to England, which also obtained from France the colonial possessions of Nova Scotia and St. Christopher, and freedom from disturbance in Newfoundland and the Hudson's Bay territory. Lastly, Louis bound himself, "on the faith, word, and honor of a king," to uphold the Protestant succession in Great Britain, and to cause the Pretender to quit France. On these terms the celebrated PEACE OF UTRECHT was signed, March 31, 1713. The emperor alone held aloof, but made peace with France in the following year at Rastadt. The peace of Utrecht has been censured as unworthy of the victories of Marlborough; and the motives of its authors were doubtless mean enough. But the advantages gained were substantial; and subsequent experience has proved that the chance of excluding the Bourbons from the throne of Spain was not worth the prolongation of a war which had lasted for half a generation, and had cost England almost sixty-nine millions.

The short remainder of Anne's reign was occupied with the intrigues of the Jacobites on behalf of the Pretender, calling himself James III., to whose succession the queen herself was favorable. Sophia, the electress-dowager of Hanover, died June 8, 1714, at the age of eighty-three, and her son, GEORGE LOUIS, became heir under the act of settlement. Bolingbroke, who was in correspondence with James, succeeded in driving Oxford from office, July 27, 1714. But two days after, the queen being seized with a fatal illness, sent for the Duke of Shrewsbury, who took prompt measures, in concert with Argyle and Somerset, to defeat the schemes of Bolingbroke. On July 30 Anne delivered the white staff of lord treasurer to Shrewsbury; and on Sunday, August 1, she expired at Kensington, in the fiftieth year of her age, and the thirteenth of her reign. Her easy temper and her faultless domestic life gained her the epithet of "the good Queen Anne." Her weak and indolent temperament greatly contributed to the progress of that change by which the government of England has come to be directed by responsible ministers, rather than by the wishes of the sovereign. Hers was the first reign undisturbed by rebellion, and unstained by executions for high treason, with the one insignificant exception of Gregg. She showed her attachment to the church by giving up the first-fruits and tenths, and making that provision for the aid of poor livings, which bears the name of "Queen Anne's bounty." Among the new institutions of her reign was the establishment of a *General Post-Office* for all the British dominions (1710).

The time of Anne has been honored with the name of the *Augustan Age* of English literature—a name more truly descriptive than those who first used it were aware; for in England, as at Rome, it marks a period of great excellence indeed, but of decline from a nobler perfection. ALEXANDER POPE stands at the head of the poets; while ADDISON and SWIFT are the greatest masters of prose, not only in this age, but in the whole course of English literature. The periodical essays, of which the *Spectator* is the great example, were the invention of this time. Most of the leading writers belong also to the reign of George I., and some reach into that of George II.

Farthing of Queen Anne. (This coin is highly prized by Collectors.)

Medal of the elder Pretender.

CHAPTER XXXII.

THE HOUSE OF BRUNSWICK, OR HANOVER.—GEORGE I.

A.D. 1714–1727.

GEORGE LOUIS, elector of Hanover (son of Ernest Augustus, duke of Brunswick-Lüneburg and elector of Hanover, and of Sophia, the youngest child of Frederick elector palatine and Elizabeth daughter of James I.), was proclaimed by the title of GEORGE I. immediately upon the death of Queen Anne. His accession was unopposed, not only in England, but also in Scotland and Ireland; and he was acknowledged by Louis XIV. as well as by the other powers of Europe. He landed at Greenwich on Sept. 18, 1714, with his eldest son, afterward George II. He was welcomed by the people as the representative of the great principle of a Protestant succession, though personally he had little to recommend him. The king was fifty-four years old, having been born May 23, 1660. In person and manner he was heavy, coarse, and awkward. His mind was uncultivated by literature or science, though he had, like nearly all his countrymen, a natural taste for music. His other tastes were low, and his society was composed of those who pandered to them. His wife, Sophia Dorothea of Zell, had been doomed to perpetual imprisonment for an alleged intrigue with Count Königsmark; while his mistresses came over to enrich themselves in England. To these repulsive traits he added a total ignorance of the English language, customs, and feelings, which disabled him from presiding in his own council or cultivating the favor of his people. Indeed, he seems to have regarded his reign in England as an experiment, and Hanover as his only true country and secure possession. On the other hand, he was straightforward, diligent, and frugal; and desirous of peace, though he had proved his courage and skill in war. He had the good sense to trust the government to well-chosen ministers. To confirm the hope of stability in the new dynasty his son *George Augustus*, now Prince of Wales, was already thirty years of age, had been a comrade of the British soldiers under Marlborough, and had distinguished himself on the field of Oudenarde; and this prince had a son, *Frederick*, who was seven years old.

Immediately on the death of Anne the Hanoverian minister had produced an instrument, appointing eighteen lords justices, in accordance with the act of regency, nearly all of whom were Whigs; and the king on his arrival identified himself with that party. Lord Townshend, brother-in-law of Walpole, succeeded Bolingbroke as secretary of state, and was in reality prime minister. His principal colleague was General Stanhope, second secretary of state. Shrewsbury resigned the white wand; the office of lord high treasurer was put in commission, and has never since been revived. Steps were taken to punish the late ministers for their intrigues with France and the Pretender. Oxford, Bolingbroke, and Ormond were impeached by the commons for high treason; but the first only remained to answer the charge, which was dropped after he had been detained two years in the Tower. Acts of attainder were passed against Ormond and Bolingbroke. Ormond had escaped to France after Oxford's arrest, and died abroad in 1745. Bolingbroke had taken the alarm still earlier, and fled to the Pretender, who resided in Lorraine under the assumed name of the *Chevalier de St. George*, and became his chief adviser. But they quarreled about the disastrous attempt of 1715; and, after some years, Bolingbroke obtained his pardon and returned to England (1723).

The Chevalier had just published a manifesto of his right to the crown (Aug. 29, 1715), when his hopes of aid from France were crushed by the death of Louis XIV. (Sept. 1), who was succeeded by his infant great-grandson Louis XV. Meanwhile the Jacobites risked a premature rising under the *Earl of Mar* in Scotland, and Mr. Foster and the Earl of Derwentwater in the north of England. Foster advanced as far as Preston, and there surrendered to General Carpenter (Nov. 13), with Lords Derwentwater, Nithisdale, Wintoun, Kenmure, and many members of old families in the north. On the same day Mar was defeated by Argyle at *Sheriffmuir*, near Stirling, and retired to Perth. The Chevalier now risked his person in a cause already lost, landing at Peterhead (Dec. 22). But he only chilled his adherents by his want of cheerful energy. Perth was abandoned on the fatal anniversary of January 30; and James slunk away with Mar from his army at Montrose (Feb. 4), and got back to St. Germain's with his person safe and his honor lost. Derwentwater and Kenmure were beheaded on Tower Hill (Feb. 24), and about twenty-six others were executed. The escape of Lord Nithisdale, by the heroic devotion of his wife, is the sole pleasing incident of this rebellion. It led to the repeal of the Triennial Act of 1694 from fear of a Jacobite parliament, and the enactment of the SEPTENNIAL ACT, which still regulates the legal duration of parliaments. To deprive the Pretender of support from France negotiations were opened with the regent Duke of Orleans, whose interest suggested an alliance with England; since, in the event of the king's death, he would need help to enforce Philip V.'s renunciation of the crown of France. His minister, the celebrated Abbé *Dubois*, negotiated a treaty, which was afterward merged in the *Triple Alliance* between England, France, and Holland (Jan. 4, 1717).

Philip V. of Spain now resolved on war, and seized Sardinia, by the advice of his ambitious minister Cardinal *Alberoni*, who was intriguing with Charles XII. of Sweden and the czar in favor of the Stuarts, and renewing the old Spanish plots in England. Stanhope, who, from causes not worth relating here, had displaced Townshend as prime minister (1717),* hastened to Paris, and formed a new *Quadruple Alliance* between the three former allies and the emperor, to preserve the peace of Europe (1718). He then proceeded to Madrid, but failed to move Alberoni. Meanwhile the Spaniards took Palermo and Messina, but were defeated (Aug. 11) off Cape Passaro by Admiral Byng (afterward Viscount Torrington). The Pretender was received with royal honors at Madrid, and a fleet was equipped at Corunna to convoy him to England (1719). But this new armada (like Philip II.'s) was dashed to pieces by a storm, when it had only just put out to sea. Further reverses led to the disgrace of Alberoni himself (Dec. 4), and Philip V. joined the Quadruple Alliance (Jan., 1720). About the same time Charles XII. died, and the queen of Sweden became the ally of George I.

Stanhope's administration, while thus successful abroad, advanced in a liberal course at home. In spite of the united opposition of the Tories and Walpole, who had resigned with Townshend, they repealed the act against occasional conformity and the Schism Act; and Stanhope himself wished to have repealed the Test Act (1718). But they incurred a serious check in the rejection of the *Peerage Bill*, the object of which was to limit the power of the king to create new peers, and its motive the fear lest the Prince of Wales, on coming to the throne, should use his prerogative to swamp the

* He was created Viscount Stanhope in 1717, and Earl Stanhope in 1718. His descendant, the present earl, is the historian of this period.

Whig majority. Walpole opposed the bill with great eloquence in the House of Commons, and it was rejected by the peers. Walpole also succeeded in healing a quarrel between the king and the Prince of Wales; and, early in 1720, he and Townshend accepted subordinate places in the government.

The autumn of this year brought on a singular commercial crisis. The *South Sea Company* was formed by Harley in 1710, as a means of meeting a deficit of nearly £9,000,000 in the public services. The company took this debt upon itself, in consideration of a large annual payment as interest and the exclusive privilege of trading with the subjects of Spain in the South Seas. In 1719 they paid £7,500,000 for the unredeemable government annuities created during the war, and induced the annuitants to accept South Sea stock on very low terms. The transaction gave rise to a mania for the company's stock, which seemed almost epidemic, for there was just the same rage in Paris for the *Mississippi scheme* of Law; and all manner of bubble companies were launched. In September came the crash. The South Sea stock fell from 1000 to 300. Thousands were ruined. The government were charged with aiding the delusion; and an attack, made on them in the House of Lords by the young Duke of Wharton, was repelled by Stanhope with such heat that the effort caused an apoplexy, of which he died next day (Feb. 5, 1721).

Sir ROBERT WALPOLE now rose to the chief direction of affairs, which he retained for twenty years. His chief colleagues were Lord Townshend, as secretary of state, and Lord Carteret, afterward Earl *Granville.** He took prompt measures to remedy the South Sea disaster, and to punish the directors. In 1722 a new Jacobite conspiracy was detected, and Atterbury, whom Anne had made Bishop of Rochester, was deprived and banished (1723). At the very same time Bolingbroke returned, and became the head of a coalition against Walpole under the name of the "patriot party." He was soon joined by Walpole's former friend, the great orator, *William Pulteney* (1725), who assisted him in editing the "*Craftsman.*"

The year 1724 was marked by party disturbances in Scotland and Ireland; the former arising out of the imposition of a malt-tax, and the latter out of a new copper coinage, called, from the name of the contractor, "Wood's halfpence"—an affair only memorable from the power with which Swift, in his *Drapier's Letters*, turned a perfectly regular business transaction into a weapon against the ministry. To these symptoms of danger to the Whigs was added the threat of a general war, by a new confederacy formed at *Vienna* between Spain and the empire, supported by Russia, against England and France, to oppose which England concluded with France and

* This title became extinct in 1776. The present Earl Granville is the son of the youngest son of the Marquis of Stafford, who was created Earl Granville in 1833.

Prussia the defensive *Treaty of Hanover*, to which Sweden and Holland acceded (Sept. 3, 1725). But after a fruitless attack by Spain upon Gibraltar, and other insignificant hostilities, the French minister, Cardinal *Fleury*, succeeded in restoring peace, the preliminaries of which were signed at Paris, May 31, 1727. It is interesting to trace in this affair the names of what were henceforth the great powers of Europe. Three days afterward (June 3) George I. had started on his usual visit to Hanover. On the journey he was seized with apoplexy, and died in his carriage before he could reach the palace of his brother, the Bishop of Osnabrück (June 11, 1727), in the sixty-eighth year of his age and the thirteenth of his reign. His death is said to have been caused by the shock of receiving a letter from his wife (who had died a few months earlier, after an imprisonment of thirty-two years), in which she summoned him to meet her within a year and a day before the tribunal of God, to answer for his conduct to her.

The reign of George I. completed the system of parliamentary antagonism between the Whig and Tory parties. The former maintained their ascendency during his whole reign; and, contrary to what has since happened, their chief strength was in the House of Lords. The clergy were generally Tories, and many of them Jacobites. The censure which they passed in convocation upon Dr. Hoadley, bishop of Bangor, for a sermon in which he advocated liberty of conscience, led to the suspension of all the powers of convocation. That body was prorogued in 1717, and each new convocation since then has been prorogued at once upon its meeting, till within the last few years.

George I.

Obverse of Medal struck to commemorate the Battle of Dettingen.
(For Reverse, see p. 286.)

CHAPTER XXXIII.

THE HOUSE OF BRUNSWICK (*continued*).—GEORGE II.
A.D. 1727–1760.

George II. was born Oct. 30, 1683. He was therefore in his 31st year when he came over to England with his father, and in his 44th when he mounted the throne. He had learned to speak English fluently, but in other respects he was almost as uncultured as his father. He possessed, however, good natural sense; his habits were regular, though monotonous; and to great personal courage he added some military skill. He was subject to violent bursts of anger, and was most avaricious. His defects were in part supplied by the talents and graces of his wife, Caroline of Anspach, who had always great influence over him, and governed the country during the king's frequent visits to Hanover. They were married in 1705, and had two sons—Frederick prince of Wales, born Jan. 20, 1707, and William Augustus duke of Cumberland, born 1721—besides five daughters. Queen Caroline died Nov. 20, 1736. The Prince of

Wales was only remarkable for his ungovernable temper and his cabals against his father, which were fostered by Bolingbroke; and he died, unregretted by the people, in 1751, leaving his inheritance to his eldest son, afterward George III.

The reign of George II. begins with the great development of the country's internal resources under the peaceful administration of Walpole, and ends with the conquests effected by the military genius of the elder WILLIAM PITT. The middle of it is occupied by the war which was signalized by the victory of DETTINGEN (1743) and the defeat of FONTENOY (1745), and which ended with the treaty of AIX-LA-CHAPELLE (1748), and by the last effort of the Stuarts in the REBELLION OF 1745. This outline must be filled up very briefly, for the minute details of the events are either unimportant or such as to require separate study.

Walpole was continued in office, against the king's inclination, by the influence of Queen Caroline, and he obtained a decided majority in the new parliament (1727). Spain made overtures for peace, and the *treaty of Seville* (Nov. 9, 1729) established a new quadruple alliance of England, France, Spain, and Holland, by which peace was maintained for ten years.

During this period Walpole's skill preserved his power in parliament in face of an opposition growing in numbers and ability, among whom the great WILLIAM PITT the elder made his appearance in 1735. In 1733 Walpole carried some important financial measures, but was obliged to withdraw his *Excise Bill*. He maintained the *Septennial Act* against all the force of the opposition (1734), and his decisive majority in the new elections caused the retirement of Bolingbroke to France (1735). The following year was marked by the *Porteous Riots* in Edinburgh, which have been immortalized by the genius of Scott (1736). In 1738 differences arose with Spain respecting the boundaries of the new American colony of *Georgia*, the right of searching vessels at sea, and the ill-treatment of British subjects. On the second of these grievances it is interesting to see how the right has always been claimed by the chief maritime power for the time being, and resisted by the rest. England now fought against Spain to resist the right of search, and afterward against Europe and America to maintain it. America went to war with England to resist it in 1813, and all but renewed the war to enforce it in 1861.

The king, the opposition, and the people dragged Walpole into the war, which was declared on Oct. 19, 1739. Operations were commenced against the colonies of Spain. Admiral Vernon took *Portobello*, on the Isthmus of Darien (Nov., 1740); but failed in a great combined attack on the strong fortress of *Carthagena* (March 4, 1741). The voyage of Anson round the world (1740–1744) is a romantic episode of these campaigns. The disasters of the war completed the overthrow of Walpole. The elections of 1741 went against him; and repeated defeats in the house compelled his resignation, which was reluctantly accepted by the king, who created him *Earl of Orford.* He died in 1745. His pacific administration had reduced the national debt to £46,000,000. A new government was formed by Pulteney, who was created *Earl of Bath*, with Lord Carteret as secretary of state, and virtually prime minister. Two years later the chief power passed to *Henry Pelham*, who succeeded Lord Wilmington (Spencer Compton) as prime minister. In Nov. 1744 his ministry was strengthened by the addition of Lord Chesterfield as lord-lieutenant of Ireland, and by the support of Pitt in the House of Commons.

Meanwhile a vast change had taken place from the peaceful policy pursued by Walpole and Fleury. The signal for a new series of European wars was given by the death of the Emperor Charles VI. (Oct. 20, 1740), and the almost simultaneous accession to the throne of Prussia by Frederick II., renowned in history as Frederick the Great. The hereditary dominions of Charles VI.—namely, the duchy of Austria and the kingdoms of Hungary and Bohemia—were secured to his daughter Maria Theresa by the *Pragmatic Sanction*, but disputed by several claimants. Frederick of Prussia seized Silesia and gained the battle of *Molwitz.* The elector of Bavaria, assuming the title of Duke of Austria, was carried by a French army to Vienna. He was soon afterward elected emperor by the title of Charles VII. Maria Theresa fled to Hungary with her infant son (afterward the Emperor Joseph II.), and threw herself upon the loyalty of the nobles assembled in their diet, who responded with flashing swords and cries of "*Moriamur pro* Rege *nostro, Maria Theresa!*" They expelled Charles from Bohemia and Austria, and he soon died in poverty at Munich (1745).

England had espoused the cause of Maria Theresa, and voted her a subsidy of £500,000, in addition to a supply of £5,000,000 for the war (1742). The Earl of Stair was placed at the head of an army composed of British, Hessians, and Hanoverians, to co-operate with the Dutch; but nothing was done this year, and Maria Theresa had to cede Silesia to Frederick by the treaty of Breslau. In 1743 George II. joined the army in person, just in time to extricate it from a dangerous blockade in the valley of the Main, by the victory of Dettingen over the French and Bavarians under the Duc de Noailles (June 27, 1743). This battle gained the young Duke of Cumberland high honor for his courage, and it was the last fought by an English king in person. It delivered Germany from the French, but it led to a declaration of war from France (March 20,

1744). Louis XV. took the field in person with Marshal *Saxe* in Flanders, while Frederick, in defiance of the treaty of Breslau, attempted to conquer Bohemia and Moravia, as the ally of Charles VII. At length, by the efforts of England, which had formed a quadruple alliance with Holland, Austria (Jan., 1745), and Saxony, a peace was concluded with Prussia at Dresden. The Austrians kept the French in check upon the Rhine, and covered Frankfort, where Francis duke of Lorraine, the husband of Maria Theresa, was elected emperor by the title of Francis I. (Sept. 15, 1745).

The campaign of this year, in Flanders, was marked by the great battle of FONTENOY. Marshal Saxe had invested Tournay; and the English, Dutch, and Austrians, under the Duke of Cumberland, marched to its relief. The column of guards charged the French centre, broke through two lines of infantry, and were advancing upon the village of Antouing, occupied by Louis XV. and the dauphin in person, when they found themselves abandoned by their allies. They left 9000 men upon the field, and the remnant of the army made good their retreat to Ath (May 11, 1745). This victory gave Flanders to the French. In America the English took Louisbourg, the capital of Cape Breton (June 15).

It was at this juncture that CHARLES EDWARD, son of the pretender James Francis, made his great adventure to recover the crown of Great Britain. James himself had fallen into obscurity ever since the attempt of 1715, and was now sinking into old age; but his son, who was born in 1721, seemed to have all the popular merits that his father wanted. In person he was tall, well formed, and active; his face eminently handsome, his complexion fair; his eyes blue; his hair fell in natural ringlets on his neck. His address, at once dignified and affable, was calculated to win attachment; yet his misfortunes had rendered him somewhat jealous of his dignity. He possessed courage and a romantic sense of honor; he was decisive and resolute, yet without much ability as a leader. His letters breathe both energy and affection, but they are ill spelled and written in the scrawling hand of a school-boy; for his education had been shamefully neglected. In politics and religion he retained all the bigoted notions of the Stuarts; and the end of his life showed that his early promise was not proof against the chill of adversity.

His first attempt was made early in 1744, with the support of a large French fleet and army under Marshal Saxe; but the expedition was totally wrecked by a great storm off Dungeness, and the French government abandoned the enterprise. Deprived of their support, and without even his father's knowledge, Charles Edward pawned his jewels and borrowed from his friends to buy arms and ammunition, which he put on board a French ship of war, the *Eliza*, *beth*, of 65 guns, embarking himself in the *Doutelle*, a fast brig of 18 guns, and sailed from Belleisle July 2, 1745. The *Elizabeth* was disabled by an English cruiser, but the *Doutelle* escaped, and the CHEVALIER, as he was styled, landed on the wilds of Moidart in Inverness-shire with only seven followers. After some hesitation his Highland friends followed the example of chivalrous loyalty which was set by *Cameron of Lochiel*, and mustered their clans in Glenfinnan, whence Charles began his march with 1600 men, on Aug. 20, 1745. The government were totally unprepared. Sir John Cope occupied Stirling with less than 3000 men. His strange plan of marching northward to join the friendly clans opened the road to the Chevalier, who marched to Perth (Sept. 3), where he received £500 from the corporation, and was joined by new adherents. On Sept. 17 he entered Edinburgh, took possession of Holyrood House, and compelled the heralds to proclaim King James VIII. Meanwhile Cope had brought his army back by sea, and landed at Dunbar. Charles marched out from Edinburgh to meet him, and the impetuous charge of the Highlanders won the battle of *Prestonpans*. England seemed now at the mercy of the adventurer, for the Hanoverian dynasty had become unpopular; but France withheld the aid which might have proved decisive, and the Chevalier lost time in recruiting his army and besieging the Castle of Edinburgh. His followers wished him to be content with the conquest of Scotland; but he saw that he must win all or lose all, and began his march southward on Nov. 1. The government had made good use of the delay. Marshal Wade was at Newcastle with 10,000 men; the Duke of Cumberland was assembling an army in the midland counties; and that reserve camp was formed at Finchley which has been immortalized by Hogarth. Charles evaded the royal forces, and advanced as far as Derby. The news created a panic in London, which was long remembered as the *Black Friday*. But his career was run. He had been received with little enthusiasm, and joined by very few adherents. The chieftains insisted on a retreat; and Charles, who had marched gayly on foot, in the Highland dress, at the head of the column, retraced his steps in moody despair. At *Clifton Moor*, near Penrith, he gallantly checked the pursuit of Cumberland. He recrossed the Esk on his birthday (Dec. 20), entered Glasgow on the 26th, and arrived before Stirling Jan. 3, 1746. Repulsed thence, he retreated to Inverness (Feb. 1), deserted by most of the chieftains, who promised to collect a new army of 10,000 men. On April 8 the Duke of Cumberland advanced from Aberdeen, and met the little army of Charles Edward on CULLODEN MOOR. The Highlanders broke the first of the three English lines, but were repulsed by the second and utterly routed. Charles dismissed his few remaining followers; and after adventures more romantic than those of Charles II. after Worcester, embarked in a French vessel (Sept. 20), and landed at Morlaix (Sept. 29, 1746). The Duke of Cumberland obtained the epithet of *the Butcher* by his cruelty to the insurgents. Most of the chieftains escaped; but the Lords Kilmarnock and Balmerino were executed on Tower Hill, with the old intriguer Lord Lovat, who had acted a double part throughout. Many of lesser note suffered all the hideous penalties of high treason. But wiser measures were soon adopted to weaken the system of clanship and to civilize the Highlands. Foremost among these were the military roads, whose excellence has been commemorated in the couplet:

"If you'd seen but these roads *before they were made*,
You'd hold up your hands, and bless General Wade."

No serious effort was again made by the exiled family. James Francis, the "Old Pretender," died at the age of seventy-seven in 1765. His son Charles Edward, the "Young Pretender," sank into sottishness, and died on the fatal anniversary of Jan. 30, 1788, just a century after the revolution. His only brother, *Henry Benedict*, assumed the empty title of HENRY IX.; but lived quietly at Rome as *Cardinal York*, on a pension provided by George III. The ancient and ill-fated line of Stuart died with him in 1807.

After some further successes of the French in Flanders and of the English at sea, the war was ended by the general PEACE OF AIX-LA-CHAPELLE, on the basis of the mutual restitution of conquests; but Frederick was allowed to keep Silesia (Oct., 1748). The peace lasted barely seven years. Besides the disputes in India, to be mentioned presently, serious collisions had occurred between the French and English in America; the French fleet at Brest was suspected to be destined for the St. Lawrence, and Sir Edward Hawke was directed to destroy every French ship between Cape Ortegal and Cape Clear. Even while perpetrating this outrage on national law, the Duke of Newcastle's government were blind to the preparations of the French for attacking Minorca, and Port Mahon was already invested, when Admiral Byng (second son of Lord Torrington) arrived with a badly equipped squadron of 10 ships (May 19, 1756). After a partial action with the French fleet Byng retired to Gibraltar. Fort St. Philip, the key to Port Mahon, surrendered on June 27, and Minorca was lost. The popular indignation demanded a victim. Byng was condemned to death by a court-martial, and shot on the quarter-deck of the Monarque, for not having done his best against the enemy (March 14, 1757).

A great change was now effected in the English ministry. Since the death of Henry Pelham (1754) the government had been conducted by his brother, the Duke of Newcastle, with the aid of HENRY FOX (afterward Lord Holland) and secretary MURRAY; but the resignation of the former, and the elevation of the latter to the chief-justiceship, with the title of Lord MANSFIELD, broke up the government, and the king was obliged to send for William Pitt. Dismissed after a few months, Pitt was borne back to office by the popular voice, and entered on his *first administration*—one of the most glorious periods in British annals. Newcastle held the almost nominal office of first lord of the Treasury, and Fox was paymaster of the forces, but without a seat in the cabinet (June 29, 1757).

Meanwhile the ambition of Frederick II. had provoked a European coalition, of which the mainspring was Baron *Kaunitz*, the prime minister of Maria Theresa. He formed a secret treaty with France at *Versailles* (May 1, 1756), and another with Russia, Poland, Saxony, and Sweden, for the partition of Prussia. The treachery of a clerk revealed the plot to Frederick, who at once seized Dresden, the capital of Saxony, and so began the SEVEN YEARS' WAR. George II. now resolved to support his nephew, though he feared his ambition, and had often been offended by his sarcastic speeches. In the first campaign, however, the Duke of Cumberland was driven out of Hanover by the Duke of Richelieu. The king did not conceal his resentment, and the duke retired from court, and took no conspicuous part in public affairs for the rest of his life. He died in 1765, at the age of forty-five.

While the King of Prussia retrieved his affairs by the victories of *Rossbach* and *Leuthen*, which obtained for him in England a subsidy of £670,000, and the title of the champion of Protestantism, Pitt was planning vast campaigns in Europe, Africa, America, and India (1758). The ports of France were threatened. An attempt on Cherbourg failed at first, but, on its renewal in August, the place was found deserted, and the works were destroyed. Next year (1759) RODNEY bombarded Havre, destroying many of the boats collected for invading England; Boscawen dispersed the Toulon fleet; Brest and Dunkirk were blockaded; and Sir Edward Hawke gained a great victory over the French fleet under De Conflans, off *Quiberon* (Nov. 20). On land, Prince Ferdinand of Brunswick drove the French out of Hanover (1758), pursued them over the Rhine, and gained the victory of *Crefeld* (June 23, 1758), but was obliged to retreat. Next year he was defeated by the Duke of Broglie near Frankfort and driven back to the Weser; and he then gained the decisive battle of MINDEN, where the French were only saved from destruction by the misconduct of Lord George Sackville, who commanded the cavalry, and thrice refused to charge (August, 1759). Pitt dismissed Lord George from all his employments. The campaigns of Frederick himself are too complicated to be narrated here. Lastly, in 1760, Admiral Thurat failed in an attempt to invade Ireland.

In AFRICA, the island of *Goree*, at the mouth of the Senegal, was taken from the French (1758). In AMERICA, an expedition under Admiral Boscawen and Lord Amherst took Cape Breton and the island of *St. John's*, the name of which was changed to *Prince Edward's Island*, in honor of the next brother of the Prince of Wales. In this expedition great credit was gained by a very young general named JAMES WOLFE, whom Pitt had appointed second in command, on his uniform principle of paying regard to merit only. He was now chosen for the most important, though not nominally the highest post in a grand expedition which Pitt had planned for the conquest of Canada. Three armies were to co-operate from the base of the North American colonies and the mouth of the St. Lawrence. On the west a body of colonists and Indians, under General Prideaux and Sir William Johnson, were to advance by Niagara and Lake Ontario upon *Montreal*. In the centre, the main army, under Amherst, was to take Ticonderoga, secure the navigation of Lake Champlain, and proceed along the river Richelieu to join Wolfe, who was meanwhile to ascend the St. Lawrence and lay siege to *Quebec*. His army of 8000 men were conveyed by the fleet of Admiral Saunders to the Isle of Orleans opposite Quebec, where they disembarked on June 27, 1759. Here Wolfe found himself alone; for, though the other armies had been successful, they had not had time to join him. Wolfe saw the city towering above him on the almost inaccessible banks of the St. Lawrence and the St. Charles, and defended by an army of 10,000 men under the Marquis of Montcalm, the governor of Canada, and a general of the highest reputation, who occupied an impregnable position outside of the city. Having in vain attempted an assault (July 31), Wolfe resolved to turn Montcalm's position by ascending the St. Lawrence and scaling the Heights of Abraham. His little force of 3600 men, which was all he could now make available, was conveyed in silence up the river in boats to a place now called *Wolfe's Cove*, on the night of September 13. As they rowed on, Wolfe repeated Gray's *Elegy* to his officers, and, pausing on the line,

"The paths of glory lead but to the grave,"

he added, "Now, gentlemen, I would rather be the author of that poem than to take Quebec." The enterprise succeeded perfectly. Montcalm was forced to abandon his position and fight under the disadvantage of a surprise. The first volley, which the English had reserved till they were within forty yards, made the French waver.

As Wolfe, though already wounded, led on his grenadiers to the charge, two more shots struck him down. He was carried out of the battle; and, as he lay dying, an officer exclaimed, "See how they run!" "Who run?" cried Wolfe. "The enemy," replied the officer. "Then God be praised!" said Wolfe, "I shall die happy;" and with these words he expired at the early age of thirty-three. Montcalm, an antagonist worthy of him, was also killed in the battle. Quebec capitulated on September 18, and the conquest of Canada was finished in the following year (1760).

While these scenes were passing in Europe and America a still more glorious conquest was begun in India by the genius of ROBERT CLIVE. Little is known of Indian history from the invasion of Alexander the Great to the conquest of the Mohammedans of Central Asia. In the second half of the 17th century nearly the whole peninsula was united under the sceptre of Aurungzebe, who had his capital at Delhi (1659–1707). After his death, his empire fell a prey to the reviving power of the warlike Mahrattas and other native princes, and to the incursion of the Persians under Kubli-Khan; and the internal disorders of the peninsula laid it open to European conquest.

The Portuguese, sailing round the Cape of Good Hope, had formed settlements as early as 1498, of which *Goa* became the chief. The Dutch followed them; and, in 1599, the merchants of London formed the *East India Company*, which has been already mentioned several times. Their first permanent settlement was on the Coromandel coast, at *Fort St. George* and *Madras.* Under Charles II. the *Isle of Bombay*, on the Malabar coast, was acquired as the dowry of Catherine of Braganza. In 1698 a territory at the mouth of the Ganges was ceded by the Great Mogul, for an annual tribute; here *Fort William* was erected and named in honor of the king, and the capital of *Calcutta* grew up. Each of these three stations had its *president*, responsible to the company at home; and each was defended by a small force of English soldiers and of natives who were called *Sepoys* from the Indian *sipahi*, a soldier. But as yet there were no thoughts of conquest. The jealousies excited by the Dutch and Portuguese had subsided, when the French appeared in India as rivals. They formed under Louis XIV. the settlements of *Chandernagore* on the Hooghly, near Calcutta, and *Pondicherry*, south of Madras; while the possession of the *Isles of France* (*Mauritius*) and *Bourbon*, in the Indian Ocean, aided their communications. In 1747, *La Bourdonnais*, the governor of these islands, defeated an English fleet and took Madras; but it was wrestled from him by the jealousy of *Dupleix*, the governor of the French possessions on the Coromandel coast, and given back to England by the peace of

Aix-la-Chapelle. Dupleix now devoted his great talents to humble the English and to turn the wars of the native princes to the profit of France. But he found a worthy antagonist in ROBERT CLIVE, who rose from his clerk's desk at Madras to save and renew the British power in India. We can not here follow in detail the course of those events which led to the recall of Dupleix by Louis XV., and to the loss of his conquests by the convention of Madras (1754). In 1756, Surajah-Dowlah, viceroy of Bengal under the Great Mogul, took Fort William, the sole defense of Calcutta, and gave a horrid celebrity to his victory by shutting up 146 English prisoners in a dungeon 18 feet square, with only a small barred-up opening for air, during the night of the summer solstice (June 21, 1756). When the den was opened next morning only twenty-three were found alive. This outrage banished all thought of submission from the other English possessions, which united in an effort to recover Calcutta, under the command of Clive, supported by Admiral Watson. Clive took Calcutta (Dec., 1756), surprised Surajah-Dowlah in his camp, concluded a treaty with him, and then, turning against the French, took Chandernagore. But this step roused the anger of Surajah-Dowlah, who assembled all his forces to crush the English, and was himself crushed by Clive in the decisive battle of PLASSEY, the first of those great victories which have been gained in India by a handful of British soldiers and sepoys against a host of Asiatics (1757). It made the English masters of Bengal, and began that career of conquest which proceeded with scarcely an interruption for exactly a century, to the time of the great mutiny of 1857. The last remnant of Frence power in India was destroyed by Clive's capture of Pondicherry (Jan. 16, 1761).

Such was the glorious close of the reign of George II., who died suddenly from the bursting of the right ventricle of his heart, on Oct. 25, 1760, within a few days of completing his seventy-seventh year, after a reign of more than thirty-three years. Among the acts of his reign we have still to mention the *reform of the Calendar*. This useful measure was introduced by Lord Chesterfield. The Julian year, or *Old Style* as it is called, had been corrected by Pope Gregory XIII. in 1582, and the *New Style* had been adopted by every country on the continent of Europe except Sweden and Russia. The error of the Old Style, which had now grown to eleven days, was universally admitted. In preparing the bill for the reformation of the calendar Chesterfield was assisted by the Earl of Macclesfield and Mr. Bradley, two of the ablest mathematicians in Europe. By this bill the year was to commence on January 1, instead of March 25, and eleven days in September 1752 were to be nominally suppressed, in order to bring the calendar into unison with the actual state of the solar year. The great body of the people, however, regarded the reform as an impious and popish measure, and numbers were of opinion that they had been robbed of eleven days. Sweden followed the example of England in 1753; but Russia and those countries which belong to the Greek church still follow the Old Style.

In *Literature* the age of George II. boasts the poetry of *Young*, *Thomson*, *Gray*, and *Collins*, and the commencement of the vast influence of SAMUEL JOHNSON. The matchless oratory of the elder Pitt can be judged of only by tradition. In *Art* it was distinguished above every other period, before or since, by the rise of the genuine English school of *painting*, in which Sir JOSHUA REYNOLDS, GAINSBOROUGH, and HOGARTH are the great masters; while, in music, the sublime genius of GEORGE FREDERICK HANDEL may be called English by adoption. *Science*, as well as literature, received a new impulse from the foundation of the *British Museum*.

Reverse of Medal struck to commemorate the Battle of Dettingen.

William Pitt the younger.

CHAPTER XXXIV.

THE HOUSE OF BRUNSWICK (*continued*).—GEORGE III. FROM HIS ACCESSION TO THE BREAKING OUT OF THE FRENCH REVOLUTION. A.D. 1760–1789.

When George III., son of the late Frederick prince of Wales, ascended the throne, the people rejoiced in having at length a native king; and he inserted with his own hand in his first speech to parliament the words that "he gloried in the name of Briton." He was twenty-two years old, having been born on June 4, 1738. His person was tall and strong, his countenance open and engaging. His intentions were pure, his habits simple and laborious; and the active part he took in state business was a new element of power for the crown. But the obstinacy with which he clung to his private opinions and personal predilections had fatal consequences for his country. His frequent letters to his ministers prove his clear perceptions, his strong will, and his imperfect education. He married the Princess Charlotte of Mecklenburg-Strelitz (Sept. 8, 1761). She was insignificant in person, and of a narrow understanding. But she shared her husband's sincere piety and simple tastes; and, for the first time since the reign of Charles I., the court gave the example of a pure and happy home.

We saw the last reign close with the complete ascendency of Pitt; but now there was another power behind the throne, in the person of the *Earl of Bute*, who had long been the favorite counselor of the king's mother, and who was made secretary of state without Pitt's being consulted (1761). Meanwhile the English fleets had taken Belleisle, on the coast of Brittany, and Dominica in the West Indies. Pitt seemed in a position to dictate terms of peace, and was resolved to have Minorca. But the negotiations were broken off in consequence of the FAMILY COMPACT, formed by Louis XV. with Charles III. (who succeeded his brother Ferdinand VI. as king of *Spain*, in 1759), and with his son Ferdinand, to whom Charles had resigned the kingdom of *Naples*, in accordance with the treaty of Vienna. These three branches of the house of Bourbon agreed to guarantee each other's dominions, and to regard each other's enemies as their own. Spain engaged to join France against England, on May 1, 1762, if the war still lasted, in which case France would restore Minorca to Spain (Aug. 15, 1761). Pitt felt that the compact demanded instant and decisive hostilities with Spain; but his counsel was rejected, and he resigned. He refused several offers of the royal favor, but accepted for his wife the title of Baroness Chatham, with a pension of £3000 a year for her life, his own, and their eldest son's.

As Pitt had foreseen, Spain only waited the safe return of her West India fleet to declare war (Jan. 4, 1762). The campaign which followed was successful in all quarters. While Frederick and Prince Ferdinand were victorious in Germany, and Burgoyne aided Portugal in repelling the Spaniards, the English fleet and army in the West Indies, under Rodney and Monckton, took the Caribbean islands and Havana, with great booty, and in the east the Philippine islands were captured. Meanwhile Bute, who had become first lord of the treasury, was all for peace; and at length the *Seven Years' War* was ended by the PEACE OF PARIS (Feb. 10, 1763). Minorca was restored to England in exchange for Belleisle. Havana and the Philippines were given back to Spain for Florida and Porto Rico. The West Indian islands of Guadaloupe, Martinico, and St. Lucia were restored, but England retained Tobago, Dominica, St. Vincent, and Grenada. The national debt had risen to £122,600,000. During the last year of the war Sweden had become neutral, and Russia had been converted from an enemy into an ally by the death of the Empress Elizabeth and the accession of Peter III., a devoted admirer of Frederick the Great. But the new czar soon fell a victim to a court revolution, and was succeeded by his wife, a princess of Anhalt-Zest, who has gained "bad eminence" under the title of CATHERINE II. (1762).

The peace was opposed by Pitt and was disliked by the people, who vented their feelings on Lord Bute, already odious on other grounds. In many places he was burnt in the effigy of a *boot-jack* (*John* earl of *Bute*). He was frightened into a resignation (April 8, 1763), and succeeded by GEORGE GRENVILLE. Henry Fox was called to the upper house by the title of Lord Holland.

The new ministry were soon in trouble. JOHN WILKES, a demagogue of great talent but the most profligate character, who had contributed to the fall of Bute by scurrilous attacks in his paper, the *North Briton*, wrote an article against the peace and in reply to the king's speech, in the celebrated No. 45 (April 23). Grenville had Wilkes arrested by a "general warrant"—that is, one not specifying any person by name. A contest ensued, which is now of little interest, except for its having settled the illegality of such warrants. Wilkes was expelled from the House of Commons, found guilty of two libels, and outlawed on his retiring abroad. His return for Middlesex in 1768 renewed the conflict with the ministry and the house; and though he did not gain his seat, he became a popular idol. He was elected an alderman of London, and afterward distinguished himself by his courage in suppressing the Gordon riots (1780).

A far more serious imprudence was committed by George Grenville in *extending the Stamp Act to the North American colonies.* Those settlements now consisted of thirteen states—namely, the four "New England" colonies of *Massachusetts*, *New Hampshire*, *Connecticut*, and *Rhode Island; New York*, *New Jersey*, *Pennsylvania*, *Delaware*, *Maryland*, *Virginia*, *North* and *South Carolina*, and *Georgia*. Each colony had a governor and council appointed by the crown, and a house of assembly elected by the people. They had all made rapid progress in wealth, and they had a population of about two millions of whites, and half a million of colored people. They were not unwilling to contribute to the expenses of the mother country; but they had special objections to a stamp-duty, and they adopted the broad principle of *no taxation without representation.* The alternative which they suggested was that a demand for contributions should be laid in the king's name before the several houses of assembly, who would probably have voted annually at least as much as the £10,000 expected from the Stamp Act. The measure was, however, passed in 1765; and even Benjamin Franklin, who was in England as agent for Pennsylvania, had no expectation of the fierce opposition it excited in America. The ministry of the Marquis of Rockingham, which replaced that of Grenville in 1765, following the advice of Pitt, repealed the Stamp Act, but declared the supreme power of parliament over the colonies, and quiet was restored for a time (1766).

The Rockingham ministry soon fell from internal weakness, and was succeeded by *Pitt's second administration.* Pitt himself was made lord privy seal, and raised to the peerage as *Earl of Chatham* (July 29, 1766). His removal from the House of Commons was followed by his almost complete retirement, in consequence of the prostration of his health by repeated attacks of gout. The chief direction of affairs fell to the chancellor of the exchequer, Charles Townshend, against whom the opposition carried a bill to reduce the land-tax. To raise the petty sum of £40,000 toward repairing this loss, Townshend imposed taxes on tea, glass, paper, and painter's colors, in America (1767). The scenes of 1765 were renewed. Riots broke out in Boston. The assembly of Massachusetts was dissolved for its opposition (July 1, 1768); and associations were formed to forbid the use of the taxed articles. Again the government gave way; but, in an evil hour, the *tea duty* was retained when the others were repealed; and new irritation was roused by the harsh tone in which Lord Hillsborough, the colonial secretary, announced the concession (1769). Meanwhile the ministry had been greatly changed. Charles Townshend died in September 1767, and was succeeded by Frederick lord North (eldest son of the Earl of Guildford), who became prime minister on the resignation of the Duke of Grafton in 1770. At the beginning of that year Chatham, who had resigned in October 1768, appeared in new health, as a violent opponent of the government (Jan., 1770). It was during these years that those celebrated attacks upon the ministers and the king appeared in the *Public Advertiser*, the name of whose author is still concealed under the appellation of Junius (1767–1772).

The Americans appeared to have acquiesced in the tea duty, when the discovery of some letters that had passed between Grenville's private secretary and the government of Massachusetts kindled a new flame, which burst forth on the arrival of some ships laden with tea, on which Lord North had allowed a special drawback for the advantage of the colonies as well as the East India Company. The teas were refused admission, and at Boston the ships were boarded and their cargoes thrown into the water (Dec. 16, 1773). The restriction of the charter of Boston completed the breach between the government and the colonies, whose cause was supported in the English parliament by Chatham, EDMUND BURKE, and CHARLES JAMES FOX, second son of Lord Holland. In spite of their warnings measures of coercion were adopted, and the first blood was shed at LEXINGTON, in a conflict of the Massachusetts militia with the troops of General Gage, who was soon after blockaded in Boston by 20,000 New Englanders. On May 10, 1775, a *Congress* of the states met at Philadelphia, and appointed GEORGE WASHINGTON as their commander-in-chief. He took command of the army before Boston, where the English had now 10,000 men under Generals Burgoyne, Howe, and Clinton, Gage being commander-in-chief. A few days after his arrival a battle was fought at BUNKER'S HILL, where the English only carried the American batteries after suffering enormous loss (June 17). A bloody war now spread over the whole seaboard and even into Canada, where the Americans laid siege to Quebec. Boston was evacuated in March 1776; and on the 4th of July in that year the members of congress signed the DECLARATION OF INDEPENDENCE of the *United States of North America.* We can not here follow the details of the war, which was maintained under Washington with unflinching resolution, though he was often reduced to the greatest straits. Howe took New York (Sept., 1776) and Philadelphia (Sept., 1777); but the capitulation of General Burgoyne at SARATOGA turned the tide of war in favor of the Americans (Oct. 17, 1777), and induced Louis XVI. to declare openly for their cause. Himself imbued with the theories of liberty which the French of all ranks had learned from Voltaire and the Encyclopædists, the young king, who had succeeded his grandfather in 1774, had already permitted the Marquis of LA FAYETTE and other young nobles to enter the American service; and now two treaties of commerce and alliance with the United States were signed at Paris, Feb. 6, 1778.

Lord North had already given way. He carried two bills, renouncing the right of the British parliament to tax America, and appointing commissioners to treat for peace on almost any terms short of independence. Just after they had received the royal assent (March 13, 1778) the French embassador delivered an insulting note announcing the new alliance. North wrote to the king, urgently advising him to send for Chatham; but he could not overcome the resentment justly excited by the great orator's invectives. It was at this juncture that Chatham went down to the house to express that indignation against the dismemberment of the empire which was as strong as his zeal for the rights of the colonies. On the 7th of April the Duke of Richmond moved an address to the crown for peace even if independence must be granted. Chatham, who was so ill that he had been supported into the house by his second son WILLIAM PITT, and his son-in-law Lord Mahon, rose upon his crutches, and opposed the motion in a speech faltering through weakness, but lighted by flashes of his former eloquence. The Duke of Richmond's reply provoked him to rise again to speak, but he fell back in a swoon, was carried out of the house, and, after lingering for a month at his favorite abode at *Hayes* in Kent, he died on May 11, in the seventieth year of his age. He was buried in Westminster Abbey, and an annuity of £4000 was settled on the earldom of Chatham forever. The scene in the House of Lords has been immortalized on canvas by JOHN SINGLETON COPLEY, an American colonist, whose distinguished son, Lord Lyndhurst, having then already been born at Boston (May 21, 1772), a subject of George III., has outlived the disruption of the United States, and seen the fall of three monarchies, two republics, and an empire in France. Such are the strange vicissitudes that may occur in the space of a life protracted to more than 90 years!

In consequence of Chatham's death Lord North retained office, intrusting the great seal to Lord THURLOW. The Americans refused overtures which came too late, and the war lasted another five years. Spain declared war in 1779; the French prepared for an invasion; and the coasts of Scotland were insulted and two men-of-war taken by the renowned *Paul Jones*, a Scotchman by birth, but bearing an American commission. Out of this general war arose a new contest respecting the rights of neutrals. The northern powers, Russia, Sweden, and Denmark, formed an "armed neutrality," to enforce the principles that *free ships make free goods;* that *no goods are contraband of war, unless so declared by treaty;* and that *a blockade must be effective in order to be acknowledged.* Holland had even gone so far as to plan an alliance with America, the discovery of which led to a declaration of war (Dec. 20, 1780).

On the continent of America the English gained great successes, but neither their forces nor their tactics were adequate to subdue a nation in arms for its freedom. At length the Americans gained a decisive success by the capitulation of Lord Cornwallis and his army of 7000 men at Yorktown (Oct., 1781); and the war was virtually ended on the land. One touching episode of these campaigns was the fate of the young and accomplished Major JOHN ANDRÉ, who was employed to arrange with the American traitor, General Arnold, for the surrender of an important post on the river Hudson. Being captured in disguise, André was condemned to the gallows as a spy, and Washington even refused him a soldier's death. His sternness, which forms almost the only blot on his own character, has embalmed the memory of the victim in pity. The name of André lives in American tradition, and a tablet in Westminster Abbey records that he fell a sacrifice to his zeal for his king and country.

The maritime campaign was on a grand scale. Louis XVI., who made the greatest efforts to revive the French navy, sent to the West Indies a fleet of twenty-eight sail of the line, with 4000 troops on board, under the Count DE GRASSE. After an indecisive engagement with the English fleet of nineteen ships under Sir Samuel Hood and Admiral Graves, off the coast of Virginia, De Grasse retired to the Chesapeake. On the other hand, Admiral Sir GEORGE RODNEY, who had distinguished himself by a victory over the Spaniards off cape *St. Vincent* in 1780, took the Dutch island of St. Eustatia, and the Dutch also surrendered Demerara and Essequibo. These places were soon reconquered, with all the Leeward Islands, except Barbadoes and Antigua, by the Marquis DE BOUILLÉ, who then effected his junction with De Grasse, and the combined fleets threatened to extinguish the English power in the American seas by the capture of Jamaica. Rodney at this moment returned from England, where he had been received with enthusiasm. He effected a junction with Hood, and gained a great naval victory over De Grasse, off St. Lucia (April 12, 1782). The battle lasted eleven hours, and ended in the capture of De Grasse's flag-ship, the *Ville de Paris*, and four other first-rates. It is believed that the great manœuvre of "breaking the line" was first practiced in this battle. Rodney returned to England to receive a peerage and a pension from the new Whig ministry, who had sent out to him, on May 1, a contemptuous letter of recall! Hood was raised to an Irish barony.

In the seas of Europe Admiral HYDE PARKER defeated the Dutch off the Doggerbank (1781); but the fleets of France and Spain had the mastery in the Channel and the Mediterranean, and *Minorca* surrendered, after an heroic defense, Feb. 5, 1782. Against this loss was to be set off the splendid defense of *Gibraltar* by General GEORGE ELLIOT. The place was besieged for three years, and twice partially relieved by Darby and Rodney. In the spring of 1781 there was a terrific bombardment; but the casemates afforded effectual shelter, and only 70 men were killed. On the night of Nov. 26 Elliot made a sally and destroyed the works of the Spaniards. The final effort was made early in 1782, when *De Crillon*, the victor of Minorca, took the command, having 33,000 men and 170 heavy guns. The besieged had 7000 men and 80 guns. All Europe watched the result, and the king of Spain's first question every morning was, "Is it taken?" "No! but it will be soon," said the courtiers; while Elliot's guns replied, "Not yet!" At last, on Sept. 13, De Crillon brought up some immense floating batteries within a range of 600 yards, and (in the French phrase) a "fire of hell" was opened from sea and land, nor did it slacken the whole day. But at night the red-hot shot of the fortress set fire to one of the largest floating batteries and to the Spanish flag-ship. The flames gave encouragement as well as light to the besieged, and soon the giant rock glowed with the conflagration of all the batteries in the bay. Lord Howe arrived soon after with 34 ships of the line, and entered the harbor unmolested. The key of the Mediterranean was saved, though the siege was not abandoned till peace was made. General Elliot was rewarded with the title of Lord HEATHFIELD, of Gibraltar. Rodney's and his victories concluded the war with France and Spain.

A separate peace had already been made with America, and the preliminaries signed at Paris Nov. 30, 1782. England recognized the independence of the United States, and gave up to them the vast unsettled territory in the west. The American loyalists were recompensed with £10,000,000 for their losses in property, and with annuities amounting to £120,000 for the ruin of trades and professions. The treaty was negotiated by Dr. BENJAMIN FRANKLIN, the father of electrical science, of whom it has been happily said—

"Eripuit cœlo fulmen, sceptrumque tyrannis;"

but who left for the young a nobler philosophy in his wise precepts and his blameless life. Even such a man, on such a day, was not above the enjoyment of a personal triumph. He had been grossly insulted before the privy council by Solicitor-General *Wedderburn* (afterward Lord Loughborough) for his conduct in the affair of the intercepted letters (p. 290). On returning home he folded up his court suit, vowing never again to wear it till his country was free; and in that same suit he signed the peace of Paris. It is related, too, of George III., that when, after some delay, he received Mr. Adams, the first minister from America, he assured him that, "as he had been the last to consent to a separation, he would be the first to welcome the friendship of the United States as an independent power." England has since learned how good a thing it was thus to part, in order to form anew the ties which unite free peoples. The products of American wealth have supplied English wants and supported English industry; and they are now suffering severely (1862) from the disruption of the Union just eighty years after its recognition.

Two months later peace was concluded with France and Spain at *Versailles* (Jan. 20, 1783). Various exchanges and restitutions were made in the West Indies, Africa, and India. Spain recovered the Floridas and Minorca, and popular feeling alone prevented the abandonment of Gibraltar! Peace was made with the Dutch some months later. The definitive treaties were signed Sept. 3, 1783.

We must now cast back a glance over the domestic politics of England. In 1772 George III., offended at marriages contracted by his brothers the Dukes of Cumberland and Gloucester, obtained the passing of the *Royal Marriage Act*, which prohibits any descendant of George II., except the issue of princesses married abroad, from marrying without the king's consent under the age of twenty-five, and then only with the sanction of parliament and the privy council; and subjects all who aid such marriages to the penalties of *præmunire*. The king marked the opponents of the bill as his personal enemies. Among them was Charles James Fox.

In 1778 the repeal of a cruelly severe act of William III. against the Catholics roused the cry of "No Popery!" especially in Scotland. Protestant associations were formed under the presidency of Lord George Gordon, who seems to have been insane. On June 2, 1780, he assembled a mob in St. George's Fields, which had possession of London for several days, burning Catholic chapels, Newgate and other public buildings, and private houses. Among the latter was the house of Lord Mansfield in Bloomsbury Square, with its priceless collection of materials for the history of his times. The riot was only quelled on the 8th of June. Twenty-one of the rioters were executed; and Lord George Gordon, after renouncing Christianity for Judaism, died in Newgate, 1793.

The new parliament, which met in the autumn of 1780, was adorned by the first appearance of Richard Brinsley Sheridan, William Wilberforce, and, above all, William Pitt, second son of Lord Chatham, whose first speech marked him as a perfect orator, though his age was only twenty-one (Feb. 26, 1781: he was born May 28, 1759). The ministry of Lord North, opposed to nearly all the talent of the house, and now in a minority, was upheld by the king's refusal to dismember his empire. At length, upon the loss of Minorca, General Conway carried a resolution against any further attempt to reduce the insurgent colonies (Feb. 27, 1782), which was followed up by an address to the king, denouncing all who should advise the continuance of the war as public enemies. Finally, on the rejection of a motion of want of confidence by only nine votes, Lord North resigned, after a government of twelve years (March 20). The Marquis of Rockingham, who now became prime minister for the second time, yielded the claim of Ireland for the *legislative independence* of its parliament. The chief advocate of the measure in Ireland was the eloquent Henry Grattan.

The year 1782 may be regarded as the commencement of the great conflict for the supremacy of the popular element in the constitution, which was settled half a century later by the Reform Act of 1832. The cessation of the old conflicts of dynasties on the accession of George III. had restored the Jacobites (now such only in theory) to a political influence which they naturally threw into the scale of the Tories, whose power steadily increased after the fall of Walpole. This revival recalled attention to the old foundations of the constitution, while abstract theories of liberty and human rights were discussed by philosophers in France, and openly declared as the basis of the American republic. To the demand for the *reformation* of abuses was now added a cry for the REFORM of English institutions themselves. From its very first adoption this word has had two distinct meanings. While the *Radical Reformers* have demanded for every citizen the utmost degree of liberty which can be proved to be his right by reasonings from the law of nature, the great *Whig* party have sought for the practical exhibition of that liberty in the rights secured by the ancient constitution, enlarged and amended by new light from age to age. A like distinction must be made in the opposite party, between the extreme *Tories*, who distrust all claims of popular liberty, and those who, regarding the concession of them as a question of time and prudence, prefer to be called *Conservatives.* Eighty years ago, however, the "Radicals" were an insignificant and persecuted minority, of whom WILKES and HORNE TOOKE may serve as examples; and the contest began between the *Whigs* and the "friends of the king." The watchword of the Whigs was the proposition that "*the power of the crown has increased, is increasing, and ought to be diminished;*" that of the Tories was "Church and King." A reform of the system of returning members to parliament was now proposed by William Pitt, whose motion for a committee of inquiry was rejected in the commons by only twenty votes (May 7, 1782, comp. p. 317). At the same time revenue officers were deprived of the franchise; contractors under government were excluded from parliament; and, on the motion of Burke, several sinecures and pensions were expunged from the civil list.

On the death of Lord Rockingham (July 1, 1782) the Earl of SHELBURNE became prime minister, and Pitt was made chancellor of the exchequer; but the secession of Fox, Burke, and Sheridan, with most of the Rockingham party, left the government powerless; and soon after concluding the peace (1783), Shelburne resigned. After much difficulty a *coalition* was formed between Fox and Lord North as secretaries of state, with the Duke of Portland as prime minister. The king and the people were alike disgusted with the coalition; and on the rejection of Fox's *India Bill* by the House of Lords, though he had a majority in the Commons, royal messages were sent to demand the seals (Dec., 1783). PITT now succeeded, as prime minister and chancellor of the exchequer, to the power which he held, with only a short interruption, till his death in 1806. After a bold struggle with an adverse majority, he dissolved parliament. The people rallied round the king and minister, and the new elections gave him a large majority (April, 1784).

After settling the government of India by the creation of the *Board of Control* as a department of the government, Pitt carried a series of great measures for the reform of the finances. His bill for parliamentary reform was rejected by a majority of 74 (1785); and many other great questions, including those of Catholic emancipation and the abolition of slavery, were discussed only to be postponed for a whole generation. Then came the case of WARREN HASTINGS, who, as the first *Governor-General* of India, had carried on the work begun by Clive, reformed the administration, retaken Chandernagore and Pondicherry from the French, rescued the presidency of Madras from HYDER ALI, and, after having vastly extended the power of the company, left the peninsula completely pacified in 1785. But these brilliant services were stained with tyranny and extortion, for which the Whig leaders resolved to bring him to trial. The chief mover was EDMUND BURKE, whose speeches in this case are his master-pieces. With him were joined Fox and Sheridan; and Pitt also supported the impeachment (1787). The trial commenced in the following spring, and was protracted for seven years. In the end Warren Hastings was acquitted, and passed the rest of his life in retirement. He died Aug. 22, 1818.

Clouds had meanwhile gathered about the royal family. The heir apparent, GEORGE, prince of Wales, who was born Aug. 12, 1762, followed the example of his grandfather, Frederick, and his great-grandfather, George II., in quarreling with his father and king. He not only threw himself into the hands of the Whigs, but made his mansion of Carlton House a scene of disgraceful revelry, and incurred enormous debts by reckless extravagance and gambling. To add to his father's resentment, he had been secretly married to Mrs. Fitzherbert, a Roman Catholic lady of sense, virtue, and accomplishments (Dec. 21, 1785). The king refused to help him; but, at length, to avoid an attack from the opposition, he instructed Pitt to move for a vote to discharge the prince's debts, and for an increase of £10,000 a year to his income. In 1788 George III. suffered the first severe attack of that mental derangement, some symptoms of which had already appeared in 1765. The opposition claimed the regency as the Prince of Wales's right. Pitt triumphantly refuted the claim of right, without however opposing the prince's appointment. The dispute was ended by the recovery of the king (Feb., 1789), who became more than ever hostile to the Whigs.

Nelson.

CHAPTER XXXV.

HOUSE OF BRUNSWICK (*continued*).—GEORGE III. FROM THE BEGINNING OF THE FRENCH REVOLUTION TO THE DEATH OF THE KING.

THE year 1789 marks a new epoch, from which the history of England is for a time almost merged in that of Europe. The causes which led to the French revolution, and the vast events which followed it, can only be related in a brief outline, to be filled up by future study. The oppressions and abuses of two centuries of despotic government had reached their climax, and a new school of philosophy had taught men to believe they had a right to perfect freedom, when the benevolent weakness of Louis XVI. encouraged the attempt to reduce these theories to practice. The crisis was brought on by the disorder of the finances, which rendered it necessary to assemble the *states-general*—that is, a general assembly of the three estates of *nobles*, *clergy*, and *commons*, or, as they were called in France, the *third estate* (*tiers état*). They had scarcely met at Versailles (May 5, 1789) when the impending storm burst forth. The commons assumed the title of the NATIONAL ASSEMBLY, and compelled the other two orders to sit with them in one chamber (June). On July 14 the people stormed the Bastile; and a courtier, to whom the king exclaimed, "This is a revolt," announced to him the truth, "*Sire, it is a revolution.*" In one night (Aug. 4) the assembly abolished all the feudal rights and exclusive privileges of the nobility. Those of the clergy soon followed; and the property of the church was declared to belong to the nation. The ancient provinces of France were replaced by a division into eighty-four departments. A new constitution was framed upon the principles of *equality* and *universal suffrage*, though still retaining a king; and it was solemnly sworn to by all orders of the state at the *fête of the Federation* (July 14, 1790). The hopes of that day were shared in England by most of the Whigs; but the frightful excesses of the mob of Paris roused general disgust, and threw a new suspicion upon liberal politics. Party divisions were widened and embittered. EDMUND BURKE, the greatest orator of the Whigs, uttered his mournful predictions of the downfall of law and order in France, in his "*Reflections on the Revolution in France*," to which Sir JAMES MACKINTOSH replied in his "*Vindiciæ Gallicæ*." The result was a separation between Burke and Fox, which was completed by an affecting scene in the house (May 1, 1791). The popular feeling against those who sympathized with the revolution was exhibited by the riot at Birmingham, in which Dr. PRIESTLEY's house was destroyed (July 14, 1791).

Meanwhile, in France, the attempt of Louis XVI. to escape to the frontier, and his capture at *Varennes*, destroyed the little confidence that was left between king and people (June, 1791). The National (or, as it was also called, the Constituent) Assembly was replaced, on October 1, by the LEGISLATIVE ASSEMBLY, which was divided into the three parties of the *Constitutionalists*, the *Girondins* (the pure republicans, so called from the department of the *Gironde*, to which most of them belonged), and the *Jacobins*, who reflected in the assembly the fierce passions of the mob of Paris, and obtained their name from the chief revolutionary club; the last were also called the *Mountain*, from the raised benches which they occupied in the chamber. Among them were the terrible names of *Danton*, *Marat*, and *Robespierre*. The court had the madness to gratify their animosity against the constitutionalists as the authors of the revolution, and against LA FAYETTE personally, by intriguing with the Girondins. Their real reliance, however, was on the European powers. LEOPOLD, emperor of Austria and brother of the Queen Marie Antoinette, and FREDERICK WILLIAM II. king of Prussia, issued a declaration against the revolution, at Pilnitz, August, 1791; and FRANCIS II., who succeeded Leopold in 1792, sent an ultimatum to Paris, which was answered by the formation of a Girondin ministry and a declaration of war (March 20, 1792). A combined army of Austrians and Prussians invaded France under the Duke of Brunswick, and, what was most hateful to the people, attended by a band of emigrants who had fled early in 1790, and among whom was the king's brother, the Count of Artois (afterward Charles X.). The flight of the French armies before them, the threatening manifesto of the Duke of Brunswick, and the dismissal of the Girondin ministry, hastened the fall of Louis. The mob of Paris twice stormed the Tuileries (June 20 and Aug. 10); and on the second occasion the king took refuge in the assembly, which deposed him, declared a republic, and sent him to the fortress of the *Temple*, with the queen, the dauphin, the king's sister (Madame Elizabeth), and his daughter, afterward the Duchess of Angoulême. The rest of the royal family had emigrated, except the Duke of Orleans and his sons, who had joined the revolution. Then followed the horrible *massacres of September*, the repulse of the invaders by DUMOURIEZ at *Valmy* (Sept. 20), the victory of *Jemmapes* (Oct. 20), and the conquest of *Belgium*, which was proclaimed a republic (Nov., 1792).

The NATIONAL CONVENTION of the French republic met on Sept. 21, 1792, and proceeded to the trial of the king, whom the Girondins and Jacobins united to condemn, the Duke of Orleans (or, as he now called himself, *Philippe Egalité*) giving his vote for *death*. The execution of Louis by the guillotine (Jan. 21, 1793) severed all ties with the monarchies of Europe. The convention had already offered their help to all nations who desired to recover their liberty (Nov. 19), and to English republicans in particular (Dec. 31, 1792). Democratic clubs were corresponding with France; and while Pitt, who had been steadily pursuing his financial reforms, hesitated between his desire for peace and the necessity of self-defense, the convention declared war against England and Holland (Feb. 3, 1793).

While, by incredible efforts, the French, amidst the REIGN OF TERROR at home, overran Holland, the banks of the Rhine, Piedmont, and the Spanish side of the Pyrenees, their chief settlements in the East and West Indies surrendered to the English. An army was sent under the king's second son, FREDERICK duke of YORK, to co-operate with the Austrians in Belgium, and Dunkirk was besieged, but without success. A fleet under Lord HOOD took possession of *Toulon*, which had revolted, and the siege of which first displayed the military genius of NAPOLEON BONAPARTE, a young officer of artillery, born in Corsica. In 1794 the French victory at *Fleurus* (June 26) decided the campaign in Belgium. Holland was conquered by Pichegru in the winter, and the English army re-embarked at Bremen in March, 1795. To compensate these disasters on the land Lord HOOD took *Corsica*, where great distinction was gained by HORATIO NELSON; and Lord HOWE defeated the Brest fleet of twenty-six sail of the line off Ushant (June 1, 1794). An attempt to aid the royalist insurgents in Brittany by an expedition to *Quiberon* was defeated by HOCHE (July, 1795). In 1796 Spain joined France in an alliance against England and Portugal; and Napoleon Bonaparte made his splendid campaign in Northern Italy. Lord Malmesbury was sent to Paris to negotiate a peace with the Directory; but the effort failed.

Schemes were now organized for the invasion of Britain. A fruitless descent was attempted on Ireland by Hoche, and another at Fishguard in Pembrokeshire (1796); but the grand effort was to be made by the union of the Dutch, French, and Spanish fleets lying at the Texel, Brest, and Cadiz. By the vigilance of Commodore Nelson the Spanish fleet of twenty-seven sail was brought to action, off cape *St. Vincent*, with the English fleet of fifteen sail under Sir JOHN JERVIS (Feb. 14, 1797). Though the Spanish ships were also vastly superior in size, the English gained a complete victory, for which Jervis was made Earl St. Vincent, with a pension of £3000 a year, and Nelson received promotion and the order of the Bath. Earl St. Vincent was one of the greatest admirals and naval administrators England ever had. Great alarm was caused by the *Mutiny at the Nore* and that at Spithead in April, for which there was too much provocation; and the English sailors regained their character at *Camperdown*, where Duncan defeated the French and Dutch fleet off the Texel, which had sailed under De Winter, with 15,000 men on board, to invade Ireland (Oct. 11). Duncan was rewarded with a peerage and a pension of £3000 a year.

In 1798 General Bonaparte sailed on his celebrated expedition to EGYPT. His object, as he afterward declared, was "to conquer the East, and take Europe in the rear." He escaped the vigilance of Nelson, who only reached the bay of Aboukir after the army had disembarked, but then almost totally destroyed the French fleet in the BATTLE OF THE NILE (Aug. 1, 1798), which gained him a peerage and a pension of £2000, besides presents from the sovereigns of Turkey, Russia, and Sardinia, and that unbounded fame which gratified him most of all. Bonaparte's expedition was foiled in Syria by the defense of Acre under Sir SYDNEY SMITH; and he left Egypt in August, 1799, to accomplish his wonderful destiny in France. After mentioning the failure of an expedition to Holland (in conjunction with the Russians) under Sir Ralph Abercromby and the Duke of York (1799), we must glance at domestic politics.

The government were sufficiently occupied in administering the war, providing for its financial necessities, and combating the growth of principles esteemed revolutionary. Pitt displayed all his splendid powers of debate in defending his policy against the opposition; and his law officers undertook numerous prosecutions for sedition, the most remarkable being those of *Hardy*, *Horne Tooke*, and *Thelwall*, who were acquitted; while in Scotland Watt was hanged, and Muir and Palmer transported (1793–1795). Toward the end of 1795 there were serious riots, and the king was mobbed on his way to parliament. In 1797 the Bank of England was authorized to suspend cash payments, and notes of £1 and £2 were made a legal tender, and remained so till 1819.

Meanwhile IRELAND was in the most dangerous state. In 1791 was formed the society of *United Irishmen*, consisting chiefly of Protestants, who aimed to set up a republic independent of England. Their leader, THEOBALD WOLFE TONE, fled to America, and thence to France, where he contributed to the attempted invasions of 1796 and 1797. In March, 1798, a plan of insurrection was betrayed to the government, who arrested *Emmett*, *Bond*, and other leaders, and soon afterward the chief of the whole plot, Lord EDWARD FITZGERALD. The rebellion was only put down after much bloodshed and cruelty; and the insurgents were finally defeated by General Lake at *Vinegar Hill* near Wexford (June 21, 1798). This outbreak determined Pitt on proposing the long-desired measure of the legislative UNION OF IRELAND WITH GREAT BRITAIN, which passed the English parliament in May, 1800, and was carried through the Irish parliament by the same means as had proved effectual in Scotland. The House of Commons received an addition of 100 Irish members; and 32 Irish peers (including 4 prelates) obtained seats for life in the House of Lords. At the same time the sovereign dropped the title and arms of "King of France." The Union took effect on the first day of the present 19th century (Jan. 1, 1801).*

The 18th century closed in England with scenes of famine and discontent. In France, the power which Bonaparte had usurped on Nov. 9, 1799, was consolidated by the great victories of MARENGO in Italy (June 14, 1800), and HOHENLINDEN in Bavaria (the latter gained by *Moreau*, Dec. 2, 1800), which led to peace with Austria

* The young reader should perhaps be cautioned against the ridiculous blunder of supposing 1800 to be the *first* year of the new century, instead of the *last* year which *completed* the 18th century.

at Luneville (Feb. 9, 1801). Malta was surrendered to the English in Sept., 1800; but a new danger threatened from the north, where the Emperor Paul, a fanatical admirer of Bonaparte, seized British ships and property, and united Russia with Sweden and Denmark in an armed neutrality. At this crisis the king's scruples against the removal of the Catholic disabilities, a measure which Pitt deemed necessary for the settlement of Ireland, combined with that minister's desire to remove an obstacle in the way of peace, led to his resignation (Feb., 1801). He was succeeded by Mr. Addington, with Lord Eldon (John Scott) as chancellor.

In March, 1801, Prussia joined the northern league, and took possession of Hanover, Hamburg having already been seized by Denmark. A British fleet was sent into the Baltic, and Nelson's great victory at Copenhagen (April 2, 1801) detached Christian VII. from the league, which was soon broken up by the assassination of Paul, whose son and successor, Alexander I., made a treaty with Great Britain, Sweden, and Denmark, to regulate the rights of neutrals (June 17, 1801). In the same spring an English army landed in Egypt (March 1, 1801); and after the victory of *Alexandria*, which cost the life of Sir Ralph Abercromby (March 21), the French army capitulated (Aug. 31). Bonaparte had carried with him a body of *savans* to collect manuscripts and monuments, which now became the prize of war, and were presented by George III. to the British Museum as the foundation of a gallery of Egyptian antiquities. Among them was the trilingual inscription known as the *Rosetta Stone*, which forms the key to hieroglyphic writing.

The peace, for which Bonaparte had made overtures when he became First Consul, was at length arranged (Oct. 1, 1801), and signed at Amiens (March 18, 1802). While England ceded nearly all her conquests, France retained Belgium, the left bank of the Rhine, Avignon, Savoy, Geneva, and Nice. Bonaparte, who was elected consul for life on May 9, annexed Piedmont to France on the abdication of Charles Emmanuel (June 4), seized on the duchy of Parma, found a pretext for keeping his troops in Holland, and made great naval preparations in the ports of France and Holland. He complained of the countenance given by England to French emigrants, and of the delay in surrendering Malta to the knights of St. John, and publicly insulted the British embassador, Lord Whitworth, who at length left Paris, May 13, 1803.

The rupture was followed by the seizure of all the English whom the peace had attracted to France, to the number of 10,000. Hanover was overrun by General Mortier (June, 1803), and a great camp was formed at Boulogne for the invasion of England. The menace was met by a most patriotic response, and 300,000 volunteers were enrolled, some of whom have survived to return to their standards at the present day. The British fleet swept the Channel, and recaptured the French and Dutch colonies; and the naval preparations of Spain led to a collision which was followed by a declaration of war on the part of that power (Dec. 12, 1804). Addington had already resigned, and Pitt returned to the helm to conduct the war against NAPOLEON I., who had assumed the title of Emperor of the French (May 15, 1804), and whose murder of the *Duc d'Enghien* (a Bourbon prince), with other outrages, made him the object of the bitterest personal animosity. All the powers of Europe now combined against him except Prussia, which the bait of Hanover kept aloof. His invasion of England was completely organized, and only awaited the junction of the fleets of Toulon, Cadiz, and Brest to sweep the Channel. Nelson blockaded Toulon through the winter of 1804. On his retiring to Barcelona to draw out the enemy the French fleet, under Villeneuve, passed the Straits of Gibraltar, was joined by the fleet of Cadiz, and sailed for the West Indies, pursued by Nelson, who had at first mistaken its destination. The terror of his name chased them back again, but Nelson returned to England without meeting them. To the west of Cape Finisterre, however, Villeneuve fell in with Sir ROBERT CALDER, who gained a victory and took two Spanish ships (July 22, 1805). Calder was brought to a court-martial for not doing more, but was acquitted. Villeneuve got back to Cadiz, where his fleet of 35 sail was blockaded by Lord Cornwallis. NELSON was now called from his retirement at Merton to win his last battle. He hoisted his flag on board the *Victory*, and arrived off Cadiz on his birthday (Sept. 29, 1805). Villeneuve put out from the harbor on Oct. 19; and on the 21st ensued the BATTLE OF TRAFALGAR, memorable alike for Nelson's presentiments of his death—for his thrilling signal, "ENGLAND EXPECTS EVERY MAN WILL DO HIS DUTY"—for his masterly tactics in breaking the double line of Villeneuve by a double column of attack—for the fury of the conflict, the completeness of the victory, and his own glorious death. The "mighty seaman, tender and true," was buried in St. Paul's, amidst a pomp of ceremony and a depth of sorrow which few live to remember, but which can be in part conceived by those who saw the victor of Waterloo laid beside him.

> "Not once or twice, in our rough island story,
> The path of duty was the way to glory."

Not even the victory of Trafalgar and the blood of Nelson could save Europe. Eager to chastise Austria, and doubtful of his success in the attack on England, Napoleon suddenly marched the "Grand Army" from the shores of the Channel to the banks of the Danube

(Aug. 28), forced Mack to surrender at Ulm on the very day before Trafalgar (Oct. 20), occupied Vienna (Nov. 13), pursued the Austrians and Russians into Moravia, and there gained the great victory of AUSTERLITZ on the anniversary of his coronation, a day which became marked in his calendar like the 3d of September in Cromwell's (Dec. 2, 1805). The news was Pitt's death-blow. "Roll up that map of Europe," he said; "it will not be wanted these ten years." His weak constitution, worn out with the cares of office, now gave way, but he worked on to prepare for the opening of parliament up to the very day of its meeting (Jan. 22), and then expired at the age of forty-six (Jan. 23, 1806).* His great rival did not long survive him. Fox, called to the government as foreign secretary under Lord GRENVILLE, finding that Napoleon would only consent to peace on terms dishonorable to England, had resolved to prosecute the war with vigor, when he fell ill from an attack of dropsy. In July he was too unwell to transact business, and he died on Sept. 13, in his fifty-eighth year. On the 10th of October he was buried close to Pitt in Westminster Abbey.

The government of Lord Grenville was called the *Ministry of all the Talents.* It comprised Lord ERSKINE and Lord HOWICK (who, as Earl GREY, carried the Reform Bill of 1832); and one of its subordinate offices was filled by Lord HENRY PETTY, now the Marquis of LANSDOWNE. They had the honor, which Pitt had sought in vain, of abolishing the *African slave-trade*, after an agitation of twenty years, conducted by GRANVILLE SHARP, THOMAS CLARKSON, and WILLIAM WILBERFORCE. In the conduct of the war they had little success. Their income-tax of 10 per cent. was very unpopular; and though the brilliant victory of Sir John Stuart at MAIDA (July 4, 1806) raised the *prestige* of the British arms, the expeditions of Sir John Duckworth to Constantinople and General Frazer to Egypt proved unsuccessful, and caused Turkey to declare war (1807). In March, 1807, a bill brought in by Lord Howick to enable Roman Catholics to serve in the army gave George III. a pretext for dismissing the government. They were succeeded by the ministry of the Duke of Portland, in which GEORGE CANNING was foreign secretary, Lord CASTLEREAGH secretary for war and the colonies, SPENCER PERCEVAL chancellor of the exchequer, and Lord ELDON lord chancellor. Viscount PALMERSTON, then 23 years old (b. 1784), was a junior lord of the Admiralty.

Meanwhile Napoleon was in the full tide of success. After Austerlitz he formed the lesser states of Germany into the Confederation of the Rhine. Mutual provocations led to war with Prussia, which

* It is only this year (1862) that Pitt has found a worthy biographer in Earl STANHOPE.

was laid at his feet by the battle of JENA (Oct. 14, 1806). On the 25th he entered Berlin, whence he dated his first decree against all commercial intercourse with Great Britain. (The second was issued from Milan in 1809.) The victories of EYLAU and FRIEDLAND led to his interview with the Emperor Alexander, with whom he formed a close alliance at TILSIT (July 7, 1807). To prevent the fleets of the northern powers from falling into the hands of Napoleon a powerful force was sent to demand the surrender of the Danish navy, which was only given up after the bombardment of Copenhagen by Admiral Gambier (Sept. 7, 1807).

The same autumn Napoleon began his schemes of conquest in the Spanish peninsula. An army under *Junot* overran Portugal, and entered Lisbon on Nov. 30, the royal family fleeing to Brazil. Napoleon then decoyed the imbecile Charles IV. of Spain, and his worthless son Ferdinand, to Bayonne, and obtained from them a renunciation of the throne of Spain, which he conferred on his brother JOSEPH BONAPARTE, who entered Madrid July 20, 1808. The Spaniards had meanwhile risen and established a "*Junta*" at Seville, which proclaimed Ferdinand VII. king, and Joseph was driven out of Madrid in a fortnight. The British government sent an expedition to Portugal under Sir ARTHUR WELLESLEY, who had earned great distinction in India, where he defeated the Mahrattas at ASSAYE, and had served in the expedition against Copenhagen. He defeated Junot at VIMIERA (Aug. 21, 1808); but was superseded by Sir Harry Burrard and Sir Hew Dalrymple, who, by the shameful *Convention of Cintra*, permitted Junot to evacuate Portugal (Aug. 30). Then came the advance of Sir JOHN MOORE into the north of Spain to co-operate with the Spaniards, and his disastrous retreat to *Corunna*, where he fell in the battle which he fought and gained to secure the embarkation of his troops (Jan. 17, 1809). His burial at night, on the ramparts of Corunna, forms the subject of one of the most touching odes in our language.

Napoleon took part in this campaign; but before its end he was called away (Jan. 1) by danger on the side of Austria, which declared war (March, 1809). With his wonted rapidity he marched upon Vienna, and, after the doubtful battle of *Aspern*, gained a decisive victory at WAGRAM, and dictated terms of peace at *Schönbrunn* (Oct. 14). During this campaign he declared the States of the Church annexed to the French empire, and sent Pope Pius VII. a prisoner, first to Grenoble and then to Fontainebleau. An expedition which the British Government sent to the Scheldt during Napoleon's advance into Austria came to a disastrous end at the island of Walcheren (Nov., 1809). The discussions on this affair in the house led to the committal of Sir FRANCIS BURDETT to the Tower, and to riots in his cause (April, 1810). Disputes arising out of it also caused a duel between Canning and Castlereagh, who had long been at variance, and had both resigned. Spencer Perceval soon afterward became prime minister, the Marquis WELLESLEY foreign secretary, and Lord LIVERPOOL secretary for war, with Lord PALMERSTON as under secretary.

Napoleon was now master of Europe. Russia was his ally; Prussia and Austria almost his vassals; Germany at his feet. The boundaries of France itself reached from the mouth of the Scheldt to the frontiers of Naples, the throne of which kingdom was held by his brother-in-law, JOACHIM MURAT; while his brothers Joseph and Louis reigned in Spain and Holland. The latter country was soon afterward added to France. To perpetuate his dynasty he divorced his loving and beloved wife, JOSEPHINE, and married MARIA LOUISA, daughter of the Emperor Francis II. (April 2, 1810). His hopes were crowned (March 20, 1811) by the birth of an heir, NAPOLEON, whom he named KING OF ROME, and who was afterward called *Duke of Reichstadt*. And here we mark the hand of Divine Providence. While Maria Louisa deserted Napoleon at his fall, and his son died childless at Vienna in 1832, the descendants of Josephine by her first husband, General Beauharnais, are allied to most of the royal families of Europe, and her grandson, CHARLES LOUIS BONAPARTE, the son of her daughter *Hortense* and Louis Bonaparte, reigns in France as NAPOLEON III.

Already, however, the "little cloud" had arisen in the West. The English government, and Canning in particular, had resolved not to abandon the peninsula after the retreat of Sir John Moore. Sir ARTHUR WELLESLEY again landed at Lisbon (April 22, 1809), and, at the head of about 25,000 British and Portuguese, he crossed the Douro in face of Soult's army, whom he drove out of Oporto; and then, advancing into Spain, he defeated Marshals Victor and Sebastiani at TALAVERA (July 28), and gained the title of Viscount WELLINGTON. The utter failure of his Spanish allies, and the vast forces of the French, who had 200,000 men in the peninsula, compelled him to retire to Portugal; while the Spanish junta were shut up in Cadiz, and remained so till August, 1812. Napoleon poured in fresh troops, and sent MASSENA to "drive the English leopards into the sea." Wellington prepared the wonderful lines of TORRES VEDRAS, from the Tagus to the sea, in front of Lisbon, and retired behind them, after checking the pursuit of Massena at BUSACO (Oct., 1810). In the spring he advanced from those lines, before which Massena had worn out his men during the winter, to pursue a course of conquest, slow but sure, and with only one serious check (the retreat from Burgos), till he crossed the Pyrenees. The most salient events of this great *Peninsular War* are the victories of *Fuentes de Oñoro* (May 3, 1811) and *Albuera* (won by Marshal Beresford May 15); the taking of *Ciudad Rodrigo* (Jan. 19, 1812), which made Wellington a Spanish duke and an English earl; the horrible storming of *Badajoz* (April 6); his decisive victory over Marmont at SALAMANCA (July 2), followed by the occupation of Madrid; his advance to Burgos, and retreat thence to Ciudad Rodrigo for the winter; his final advance in the next spring, crowned by the decisive victory over King Joseph and Marshal Jourdan at VITTORIA (June 21, 1813); the occupation of the passes of the Pyrenees (July); the taking of *St. Sebastian* (Aug. 31) and *Pampluna* (Oct. 31); the entrance on French soil, and forcing of the position of the *Nivelle* (Nov. 10), after which Soult, who had bravely defended the frontier, went into winter-quarters at Bayonne.

In England, meanwhile, George III. finally succumbed to his mental malady in 1810, and the Prince of Wales governed as REGENT during the last nine years of his father's reign (Jan., 1811—Jan., 1820). Mr. Perceval was shot in the lobby of the House of Commons by one Bellingham, whose petitions had been rejected (May 11, 1812); and Lord LIVERPOOL became premier, with Lord Castlereagh as foreign secretary, and Mr. VANSITTART (afterward Lord Bexley) as chancellor of the exchequer. Just at this time the United States declared war against Great Britain in consequence of various commercial and maritime disputes. An attack on Canada was repulsed, but over-confidence on the sea led to the capture of several frigates by stronger American cruisers.

It was now that Napoleon undertook his gigantic expedition to chastise Russia for resistance to his Berlin and Milan decrees. He set in motion the vast forces of his empire, with those of Germany and Austria, over a base which stretched from the Baltic to the Alps; and, after gaining the battle of BORODINO, he reached Moscow, Sept. 15, 1812. But Alexander refused to treat; the winter set in early; and finally the conflagration of Moscow forced Napoleon to that awful retreat in which, pursued by winter and the Cossacks, he left nearly HALF A MILLION of men dead upon the route. He himself hurried from Smolensko to Paris to prepare for one last effort; and he fought the campaign of 1813 in Germany, against the combined armies of all Europe, till he lost the decisive BATTLE OF LEIPZIG (Oct. 16–18, 1813). Still he rejected even the offer of the frontier of the Rhine and the Alps; and after a campaign in France, which is reckoned among the most skillful that Napoleon ever made, the vast armies of the allied sovereigns put them in possession of Paris. Napoleon abdicated at Fontainebleau (April 11, 1814), and retired to Elba, retaining his imperial title, while Louis XVIII., brother of Louis XVI., was proclaimed king. His first act was to sign the *Peace of Paris* (May 30), by which England, after all her conquests and expenses, gained little more than Malta, the Cape of Good Hope, Mauritius, Ceylon, and a few islands in the West Indies. Hanover was made a kingdom, with succession in the male line. During these events Lord Wellington had renewed the campaign against Soult (Feb., 1814), who lost the battle of TOULOUSE on Easter Sunday (April 10). A convention was signed on the 18th; and after the conclusion of the Peace of Paris Wellington went to Madrid, and tried to reconcile the Spaniards to their restored king, Ferdinand VII. Thence he returned home to receive fresh honors. He was created DUKE OF WELLINGTON; and, in addition to former grants, £500,000 were voted for the purchase of an estate, which is held by a tenure similar to Blenheim (See p. 265). In the rejoicings which followed the duke divided the applauses of the people with the Prince Regent and his guests, the emperor of Russia and the king of Prussia.

Many of the veterans of the Peninsula were sent to reinforce the armies in America, where two more attempts on Canada had failed (1813 and 1814); and the navy had regained its prestige. One most brilliant action was the capture of the frigate *Chesapeake* by Captain BROKE of the *Shannon* in fifteen minutes, off Boston harbor (June 1, 1813). On Aug. 15, 1814, General Ross took Washington, and barbarously burnt the Capitol and other public buildings, besides the arsenal and dock-yards. He was repulsed and killed in an attack on Baltimore, and a still more disastrous defeat was suffered at New Orleans in December. This unnatural war was concluded by the *Peace of Ghent* (Dec. 24, 1814).

The congress of European powers, which assembled at Vienna in January, 1815, was startled by the news that Napoleon had escaped from Elba and landed at *Cannes* in the south of France (March 1, 1815). They voted him a public enemy, and agreed to put him down with all their forces. In the mean time he advanced on Paris, welcomed by all the troops that were sent to take him, and entered the Tuileries on April 20, whence Louis XVIII. had fled to Lille the night before. His reception was cold, except from the soldiers, and he soon raised six armies to meet the allies, who were advancing on all sides with 1,000,000 of armed men. The post of honor was held in Belgium by the English and Prussians under Wellington and Blücher; and against them Napoleon hastened at the head of his veteran troops. He crossed the frontier on June 14, by Charleroi, and engaged the allies on the 16th, with a view to separate them and advance to Brussels. Blücher was defeated at *Ligny*, and thrown off, as Napoleon supposed, to the right, pursued by Grouchy; but on his left Ney failed to dislodge the English from *Quatre Bras;* and Wellington, after arranging with Blücher for a new junction on the field of the approaching battle, fell back on the 17th to a position which he had long marked and caused to be surveyed, and which is said to have attracted the notice also of Marlborough, on the ridge of *Mont St. Jean*, in front of WATERLOO. Napoleon took up his position on the opposite ridge of *La Belle Alliance;* and here, on Sunday, June 18, 1815, was fought one of the most obstinate and decisive battles of all history. Napoleon had about 78,000 men, and Wellington 72,720; but the emperor was vastly superior in artillery, and he commanded his own veteran troops, while only half of Wellington's were British, most of them raw recruits; and the rest were Hanoverians, Dutch, and Belgians, some disaffected, and some cowards who fled at the first volley. But the Duke's iron will maintained the position against Napoleon's fiercest efforts, while the Prussians strained every nerve to reach the field. Leaving his rear engaged with Grouchy at *Wavre*, Blücher made a cross march against Napoleon's right, which his van began to threaten early in the afternoon, and he arrived in force upon the field just as the column of French guards had reeled back broken from their last attempt to charge, and Wellington had given the signal for the advance of his whole line. It was about seven o'clock when Napoleon exclaimed *Sauve qui peut*, and rode off the field to Charleroi. The Prussians took up the pursuit throughout the night; while Wellington returned, after meeting Blücher, to his quarters at Waterloo, and recorded in one of his letters the conviction that "no amount of glory could compensate for the losses of such a day:" a use of the word *glory* even more significant than its supposed absence from his dispatches. The loss of the French from the 16th to the 18th was about 30,000; and that of the allies 15,000.

Napoleon reached Paris on the 21st; and after a brief struggle with the Chambers he abdicated in favor of his son, Napoleon II., and fled to Rochefort, intending to embark for America (June 29). Thus ended the HUNDRED DAYS of his second empire (March 21—June 29). Louis XVIII. re-entered Paris on July 8; and Napoleon, after writing to the prince regent that "he came, like Themistocles, to throw himself on the hospitality of the British people," embarked for England on board the *Bellerophon* (July 15). By the decision of the allies he was conveyed to the island of *St. Helena*, where he died on May 5, 1821. A new *Peace of Paris* was signed by the allies, Nov. 20. The affairs of Europe were regulated by the *Congress of Vienna*, which parceled out kingdoms regardless of the wishes of their inhabitants; and a second congress, at *Aix-la-Chapelle*, arranged for the withdrawal of the allied troops from France (Sept., 1818). The Duke of Wellington, who had remained as generalissimo, returned home in November. The war had raised the English national debt from a little less than 228 millions to nearly 800 millions, involving an annual charge of 28 millions. In 1816 the piracy of the Algerines was suppressed by Sir Edward Pellew (Lord EXMOUTH), who bombarded Algiers (Aug. 27), and compelled the Dey to release 1083 Christian slaves.

The war was succeeded by much distress and discontent. Trade languished, and the high price of bread was aggravated by the mistaken policy of a corn-law, closing the ports till the price of wheat reached 80*s*. a quarter. The prohibition was afterward modified by a sliding-scale, lowering the duty with the rise of the price (1829). The reform agitation was renewed, with its adjuncts of political clubs, mob orators, and government prosecutions. The Habeas Corpus Act was suspended in 1817, on account of an attack on the prince regent as he returned from opening parliament. A reform meeting at Manchester, in Aug., 1819, at which the yeomanry were called out and some lives lost, was long remembered as "the Peterloo Massacre." Amidst the general alarm the home secretary, Lord Sidmouth (formerly Mr. Addington), carried the "*Six Acts*" for suppressing seditious meetings and writings and the use of arms. A more wholesome measure was the act passed by Mr. Secretary (afterward Sir Robert) PEEL, for the resumption of cash payments and the regulation of the currency (1819).

The unhappy death of Sir SAMUEL ROMILLY, by his own hand, deprived the country of a leader in the reform of the criminal law; but the work of its mitigation was steadily carried on from this time, against much opposition from Lords Eldon and Ellenborough.

The last years of George III. were clouded with mournful events in the royal family in addition to the king's continued illness. The Princess CHARLOTTE, only daughter of the prince regent, formed a marriage of affection with Prince LEOPOLD of Saxe-Coburg, afterward king of the Belgians (May 16, 1816); and, on Nov. 6, 1817, she died in childbirth, amidst a grief even more intense than that England has lately witnessed. Marriages were now contracted by the Dukes of Clarence, Kent, Cumberland, and Cambridge. The Duke of Kent espoused the Princess Victoria of Saxe-Coburg, who gave birth to the present queen, May 24, 1819; but the duke died on Jan. 23, 1820. In less than a week he was followed to the tomb by his father, George III., who expired Jan. 29, 1820, in the 82d year of his age and the 60th of his reign; the longest in British annals. Queen Charlotte had already died in November, 1818.

Windsor.

CHAPTER XXXVI.

THE HOUSE OF BRUNSWICK (*continued*).—GEORGE IV. A.D. 1820–1830.

THE reigns of the first and third sons of George III. may be regarded as a period of transition, during which the great political questions that had been postponed by the war received their solution. The accession of the prince regent to the throne as GEORGE IV. (1820–1830) involved little more than a change of title. He was in his 58th year, having been born August 12, 1762. His accomplished manners had gained him the character of the "first gentleman in Europe," and he was a patron of literature and art. But he was vain, selfish, and insincere. His nature, originally amiable, had been spoiled by a life of dissipation. His domestic relations were most unhappy. In 1795 he was forced, as a condition of the payment of his debts, to abandon Mrs. Fitzherbert, and to marry the Princess CAROLINE of Brunswick, to whom he took a deep disgust. After the birth of the Princess Charlotte (Jan. 7, 1796) they separated, and the Princess of Wales lived abroad, giving color by her imprudence to charges against her chastity. On her return to England (June 6, 1820) to claim her rank as queen, a bill of pains and penalties against her was brought into the House of Lords, and passed its third reading by a majority of only 9. As there was no hope of success in the commons, and the popular agitation was extreme, the bill was abandoned. But the queen's name remained excluded from the liturgy, and she was repulsed from the door of Westminster Abbey at the coronation (July 19, 1821). She died, broken down by her troubles, on Aug. 7, 1821, at the age of 52. Her remains were conveyed to Brunswick for interment, by way of Harwich; and the passage of the funeral cortège through London was attended with serious riots. The trial of Queen Caroline was the death-blow to George IV.'s popularity in England; but Ireland and Scotland were rejoiced at receiving visits from the only king whom they had seen since the Revolution. Meanwhile the Tory government were alarmed by the Radical agitation, and by the *Cato Street Conspiracy* to assassinate the ministers and change the form of government, for which Thistlewood and four others were executed (May 1, 1820).

In 1822 Lord Sidmouth was succeeded as home secretary by Mr. Peel, and the suicide of Lord Londonderry (Lord Castlereagh) called Canning to the post of foreign secretary. He devoted all his energy to resisting the "Holly Alliance," which had been formed, after the Peace of Paris, between France, Russia, Austria, and Prussia, for the maintenance of despotism on the Continent. At the *Congress of Verona* they resolved on an armed intervention against the constitutional party in Spain, which was executed under the Duc d'Angoulême in the following year (1823). Unable to resist this movement Canning formed treaties of commerce with the American colonies which had revolted from Spain, and boasted that he "had called the new world to redress the balance of the old" (1824). In the House of Commons the splendid eloquence of Canning and HENRY BROUGHAM was called forth by these foreign questions, and by debates on parliamentary reform and Catholic emancipation. In 1825 occured a terrible commercial crisis; and the failure of many banks led to new laws to regulate the paper currency. The systematic adoption of emigration as a remedy for distress gave a new impulse to the colonies of Canada and Australia.

Great changes occurred on the thrones of Europe. In France and Russia Louis XVIII. and Alexander I. were succeeded by their brothers CHARLES X. (1824) and NICHOLAS I. (1825). In 1825 John VI. of Portugal erected Brazil into an independent empire under his brother DOM PEDRO, who, on John's death (March, 1826), abdicated the throne of Portugal in favor of his daughter, DONNA MARIA, at the same time giving the people a constitution. The usurpation of the throne by Dom Pedro's brother, *Dom Miguel*, a ferocious tyrant (1827), led to a civil war, which lasted till May, 1832. England declared in favor of Donna Maria, who was ultimately established on the throne; and Commodore Charles Napier distinguished himself as commander of Dom Pedro's fleet. In the east of Europe Russia pursued a course of aggrandizement at the expense of Turkey, and the Greeks took up arms for their independence. The combined fleets of England, France, and Russia, under Sir Edward Codrington, destroyed the Turkish and Egyptian fleet at Navarino (Oct. 20, 1827). This blow decided the war, and Greece was erected into a kingdom, the crown of which was ultimately accepted by Prince Otho of Bavaria.

Meanwhile the Catholic question had become pressing. In 1824 Daniel O'Connell, a barrister of great eloquence, organized the "*Catholic Association*," and collected a "*Rent*" from the Irish people. In 1825 a relief bill, brought in by Sir Francis Burdett, passed the commons, but was lost in the lords, where the Duke of York uttered a solemn oath that, if he came to the throne, he would never consent to the repeal of the Catholic disabilities. The duke, however, died on Jan. 5, 1827, and in February the long administration of Lord Liverpool was ended by his seizure with paralysis. The king, who disliked Canning for his opposition in the affair of Queen Caroline, as well as for his former advocacy of the Catholic claims, felt nevertheless obliged to receive him as premier (April 1, 1827). But Canning had already contracted a mortal disease at the funeral of the Duke of York. He was regarded by the aristocracy as an upstart. He was deserted by the Duke of Wellington, Mr. Peel, Lord Eldon, and the old Tory party. He was harassed by his false position between the opposition, who called on him to redeem his professions in favor of the Catholics, and the king, who declared that he should break his coronation oath if he consented to emancipation. In four short months Canning died (Aug. 8, 1827). He was buried privately in Westminster Abbey, and his widow was made a viscountess. The title descended to his son, who raised it to an earldom by his signal services in India, and has just died, like his father, a martyr to the public service (June, 1862).

The short administration of Viscount Goderich, now Earl of Ripon (Aug., 1827—Jan., 1828) was again succeeded by that of the Duke of Wellington, with Mr. Peel as home secretary. The friends of Mr. Canning—namely, Mr. Huskisson, Mr. Lamb, Mr. Grant, and Lord Palmerston—afterward left the ministry. It was under this Tory government that the disabilities both of the Protestant Dissenters and of the Roman Catholics were removed. Lord John Russell (b. Aug. 18, 1792), the younger son of the Duke of Bedford, and the faithful inheritor of the principles for which Lord William Russell suffered under Charles II., moved the *Repeal of the Test and Cor-*

poration Acts passed under that king (see pp. 230, 231). Mr. Peel was left in a minority, and withdrew his opposition. In the lords the measure was supported by Lord HOLLAND, the nephew of Charles James Fox, and the Duke of SUSSEX, the sixth son of George III., to whom his consistent support of civil and religious liberty had been most distasteful, as it now was to George IV. The passing of this act gave a new stimulus to the agitation for Catholic relief. The crisis was brought on by the election of O'Connell for the county of Clare. The Duke of Wellington was convinced that his choice lay between concession and a civil war, the horrors of which he deprecated with deep feeling; and his ministry announced a measure for the relief of the Catholics in the king's speech (1829). Mr. Peel, who had always opposed the Catholic claims, was rejected by his constituents of the University of Oxford in favor of Sir Robert Harry Inglis, a kind-hearted, simple-minded Tory, who always held that "wherever the king carried his flag, there he should carry his church." Peel came back to the house as member for Westbury, and introduced the bill, which passed the lords on April 10, after earnest opposition. Lord Eldon was moved to tears, and Lord Winchelsea came forward as the champion of religion in a duel with the Duke of Wellington. The act opened parliament and offices of state to the Catholics on their taking a new oath in place of the oath of supremacy; but they were excluded from the offices of regent, viceroy of Ireland, and lord chancellor both in England and Ireland. The exclusion from the crown, and its forfeiture by marriage with a Catholic, remained in force. The words of the new oath, "on the true faith of a Christian," had the effect of excluding the Jews from parliament till 1858, when they were admitted.

The king gave his assent to the bill, but showed a resentment against the ministry, which was shared by the Tory party. Their violent opposition, in concert with the Radicals, was only neutralized by the support of the Whigs, which enabled Peel to carry some valuable measures, among which was the formation of the new police (1830). He had previously mitigated the criminal law; and Mr. Brougham had moved (Feb., 1828), in a speech of surpassing eloquence, for a commission on the state of the law, which led to most important reforms. But the rejection of Lord John Russell's motion to give members to the great manufacturing towns of Birmingham, Manchester, and Leeds, left the question of parliamentary reform to be settled in the next reign. Meanwhile the king was living in peevish seclusion at Windsor, where he died on the 26th of June, 1830, in the 68th year of his age and the 11th of his reign, and was succeeded by his next surviving brother, William Henry duke of Clarence.

William Wilberforce. Medal struck on the abolition of the Slave-trade.

CHAPTER XXXVII.

THE HOUSE OF BRUNSWICK (*continued*).—WILLIAM IV. A.D. 1830–1837.

WILLIAM IV., the third son of George III., was within two months of completing his 65th year when he came to the throne. He was married to the Princess ADELAIDE of Saxe Meiningen (July 11, 1818), by whom he had two daughters, who died in infancy. He had entered the navy at the usual early age, which shut him out from the advantages of education. He never affected statesmanship, but followed at one time the current of popular opinion, and at another the influence of those about him. He gained popularity by his sailor-like frankness and simplicity of manner.

He ascended the throne at a great crisis in Europe as well as England. The continental princes had cast to the winds the liberal professions which had raised the hopes of their people during the last conflict with Napoleon, and relied on their vast armies and the support of Russia. In France the *Charter* had been tolerably observed by Louis XVIII., but Charles X. followed a reactionary policy, which became more decided under the ministry of POLIGNAC (1829). The ordinances against the freedom of the press caused a revolt in Paris, which lasted three days (July 27–29, 1830), and ended in the REVOLUTION OF 1830. Charles X. fled to England, and the Duke of Orleans, son of Philippe-Egalité, was made "king of the

French" by the title of LOUIS-PHILIPPE I. An equally sudden revolution separated *Belgium* from the kingdom of Holland, to which it had been united by the congress of Vienna. Ultimately Prince Leopold became king of the Belgians.

These events had a marked effect on the English elections, which were unfavorable to ministers. The tone of the king's speech, and the declaration of the Duke of Wellington against any change in the representation, produced the greatest ferment. There were rumors of vast bodies of reformers marching up to London from the North, and the king's visit to the city on Nov. 9 was put off. At last, on Nov. 15, the government were defeated on the motion of Sir H. Parnell for an inquiry into the civil list; they resigned next day, and were succeeded by the ministry of EARL GREY, in which BROUGHAM (b. Sep. 9, 1779) was lord chancellor with a peerage, Lord Althorp chancellor of the exchequer and leader of the House of Commons, and the other leading members were Lords Lansdowne, Palmerston, Melbourne, Goderich, and Durham, and Sir James Graham. Their bill for parliamentary reform was brought in by Lord John Russell, who was not in the cabinet, on March 1, 1831. The modest claim of seats for a few great towns was found to be replaced by changes so vast that the announcement was received at first with silent wonder, and then with derisive shouts; and the first reading was only carried by a majority of 1. A dissolution produced a parliament pledged to "the Bill, the whole Bill, and nothing but the Bill." It was carried by large majorities in the commons, after tremendous struggles, but rejected in the lords by a majority of 41 (Oct. 3). Formidable riots ensued. Nottingham Castle, the residence of the Duke of Newcastle, was burnt; and Bristol was in the hands of the mob for several days, and a large part of the city was burnt down. Amidst these commotions England was visited in the autumn by that new plague, the CHOLERA, which had gradually advanced from India across Asia and Europe. A second great outbreak of it occurred in 1849.

The Reform Bill was brought in again on the meeting of parliament in December, and passed the commons in March, 1832. The opposition of the lords was only overcome by the resolution of the ministry to create a body of new peers, a measure forced upon the king by a temporary resignation, which proved the inability of the Tories to form a government. The execution of the threat was avoided by the wisdom of the Duke of Wellington, who advised the king to desire the absence of the great body of opposition peers, and so the bill was carried. It received the royal assent on June 7, 1832, 50 years and a month after Pitt's first motion (p. 296). Its principle was the proportioning of the representation to the importance of the constituency. All boroughs with less than 2000 inhabitants ceased to return members. In the list of them (Schedule A) were places, such as Gatton and Old Sarum, which had ceased to exist at all, but still returned members on the nomination of the owner of the soil; and, absurd as this arrangement seemed, it was strongly defended as a means of introducing into parliament young and unknown men of great ability, of whom several had in fact sat for nomination boroughs. Places whose population was between 2000 and 4000 were restricted to one member. The 143 seats thus gained were given partly to great towns of modern growth, including the suburbs of London, which were divided into four boroughs; and partly to the counties, several of which were divided into districts, and altogether they returned 159 members, instead of 94. The franchise was greatly extended, on the basis of property (as before) and of income, as tested by the occupation of property. The constituency in boroughs was composed of occupiers of houses to the value of £10; but in the city of London the livery retained their votes. In the counties the voters were freeholders to the value of 40*s*., copyholders of £10 per annum, leaseholders of £10 for 60 years or £50 for 20 years, and, lastly, tenants paying a rent of £50. The last (called the "Chandos clause," from its mover) was carried against ministers, who opposed it as likely to create a constituency subservient to the great landlords. There were also important provisions for regulating and shortening elections, and for the registration of voters. Similar bills were passed for Scotland and Ireland, but with some difference in their details, especially as to the amount of the Irish franchise. The parliamentary constitution thus created has remained substantially the same for 30 years; the chief alterations being the extension of the Irish franchise and the abolition of the "property qualification" for members. The two boroughs of *Sudbury* and *St. Albans* have been disfranchised for corruption; and their four seats have been lately (1861) given, one to Birkenhead, one to South Lancashire, and two to the West Riding of Yorkshire,* making the composition of parliament as follows:

	England.	Wales.	Ireland.	Scotland.
COUNTIES	147	15	64	30
UNIVERSITIES	4	0	2	0
CITIES and BOROUGHS	320	14	39	23
Totals	471	29	105	53

Grand Total of Members for the United Kingdom, 658.

The first reformed parliament met on Feb. 5, 1833. The Tory party seemed almost destroyed, but the tactics of Sir Robert Peel

* These two members are not to be elected till after the present parliament (1862).

organized a steady though small opposition, who assumed the name of *Conservatives*. The overwhelming majority for ministers enabled them to carry some great measures, especially the *abolition of negro slavery* in the West Indies and Mauritius, which was effected at a cost of £20,000,000 for compensation to the slaveholders. The motions of the Radical party for vote by ballot, triennial parliaments, and a further extension of the suffrage were unsuccessful. Ireland was a constant source of trouble. Neither Catholic emancipation, nor reform, nor the reduction of the Protestant Church establishment, which was carried by the Irish secretary Mr. STANLEY (now the Earl of Derby), could satisfy the priests and demagogues. O'Connell headed a new agitation for the *Repeal of the Union*, and collected a larger "rent" than ever, while payment of tithe was generally refused. The disorders which thus arose were met by a *Coercion Act*, which produced a schism between the Whigs and Irish Catholics. The proposal to apply Irish Church property to purposes of education led to the secession of Sir James Graham, Lord Stanley, Lord Ripon, and the Duke of Richmond from the ministry (May, 1834); and Earl Grey soon resigned (July). Lord Melbourne, formerly Mr. Lamb, now became premier, and carried an important bill for the amendment of the poor-law. But the ministry were much weakened; and on the removal of Lord Althorp from the House of Commons by the death of his father, Earl Spencer, the king suddenly dismissed them (Nov., 1834), and sent for Sir ROBERT PEEL from Rome, the Duke of Wellington meanwhile holding the seals of several departments.

Sir Robert Peel undertook the government on "liberal conservative" principles, and appealed to the country. But his intentions, since known to be sincere, were distrusted at the time, and, though he gained greatly by the new elections, he was still in a minority, and after several defeats he resigned (April, 1835). Lord Melbourne returned to office, but without Lord Brougham, who, however, helped the government to carry their measure for *municipal reform* (1836). They also passed an act authorizing marriages by dissenting clergymen and by a purely civil form, coupled with a general system for registering births, marriages, and deaths. The support of O'Connell, however, made the Conservatives the more hostile to the ministry, and they were violently attacked by the Radicals. At this juncture the king died, June 20, 1837, in the seventy-second year of his age, and within a week of completing the seventh year of his reign. He was succeeded by his niece, the Princess Victoria of Kent, and in Hanover by his brother Ernest, duke of Cumberland. The joy of the nation at the accession of a young and hopeful princess was not diminished by the loss of a troublesome burden and an unpopular prince.

Sebastopol.

CHAPTER XXXVIII.

THE HOUSE OF BRUNSWICK (*continued*).—VICTORIA I.
A.D. 1837–1862.

VICTORIA I. was proclaimed on June 21, 1837, by her two names of Alexandrina Victoria, but she immediately dropped the former. She was born May 24, 1819. The death of her father (Jan. 23, 1820) left her to the sole care of her mother, Victoria, duchess of Kent and princess of Saxe-Coburg-Gotha, the sister of Prince Leopold; and the charge was fulfilled with a care and wisdom of which the fruit has been shown in every step of her Majesty's life.

She soon displayed a character totally opposite to the selfish indolence of George IV. and the weak good-nature of William IV. She devoted herself to public and private duty with diligence, activity, punctuality, and economy. Having given up the domains of the crown for a very moderate civil list, she speedily paid her father's debts and those contracted by her mother for her education. Her accession was hailed with cheerful hope, based on the knowledge of the training she had received, and with chivalrous devotion to a second virgin queen, who had the advantage over Elizabeth in youth and gentleness. She was wisely guided into the strict path of the constitution by Lord Melbourne, and after him by succeeding ministers, by her lamented consort, and by the Duke of Wellington, whose advice was always sought in great emergencies.

The queen was welcomed with enthusiasm on her first public appearance in the city, Nov. 9, 1837. Lord Melbourne's tottering ministry revived in the sunshine of her favor and in the strength of her liberal principles; but there were clouds around and breakers ahead. They were suspected by the Radicals of receding from liberal principles under shelter of court favor, especially when Lord John Russell announced the "finality" of the Reform Act (Nov., 1837). Offense was given by their resistance to the shortening of the term of "apprenticeship" which preceded the final emancipation of the negroes. Their Irish policy offended the Tories without satisfying the Repealers; and in CANADA they had to meet a formidable rebellion with measures of coercion. This rebellion led to the settlement of the affairs of Canada by Lord Durham in the following year, and the union of the two provinces under a new and popular constitution. There was a marked coolness in the queen's reception on her way to open parliament at the beginning of 1838. The Conservatives under Sir Robert Peel gained strength in the commons, and the government were in a minority in the lords, where they were assailed by the tactics of Lyndhurst and the invectives of Brougham. The Radicals raised a cry for "Peerage Reform," which ministers lost popularity by opposing. The bad harvests of 1837 and 1838 inflamed popular discontent, and a formidable agitation was raised by the *Chartists*, who propounded a new "People's Charter" of *five points*—namely, universal suffrage, vote by ballot, triennial parliaments, equal electoral districts, and salaries for members of parliament. Lastly, the repeal of the corn-laws was demanded by the *Anti-Corn-Law League*, which was formed at Manchester by Mr. RICHARD COBDEN, in September, 1838. At the same time the finances of the country were falling into confusion. In 1839 the ministry were defeated, and resigned; but Sir Robert Peel having been prevented from forming a government by a matter relating to the court, they returned to office. In the autumn there were serious Chartist disturbances in Wales, and blood was shed in an attack on Newport.

On February 10, 1840, her Majesty was married to her cousin, Francis ALBERT Augustus Charles Emanuel, second son of the Duke of Saxe-Coburg-Gotha, who was born Aug. 19, 1819. Parliament voted him an annuity of £30,000, and the queen afterward conferred on him the dignity of PRINCE CONSORT. In this year was formed the *Quadruple Treaty* between England, Austria, Prussia, and Russia, for the protection of the sultan of Turkey against his rebellious vassal, Mehemet Ali, viceroy of Egypt, whose army, under his son Ibrahim Pacha, had overrun Syria. The English fleet, under Sir Robert Stopford and Sir Charles Napier, in concert with Austria and Turkey, bombarded Beyrout, Sidon, and Acre; and Ibrahim Pacha was driven out of Syria. Mehemet Ali was afterward secured in the possession of Egypt as hereditary viceroy; but France, which had favored his designs, for her own ulterior objects in the Levant, resented the conduct of the other four powers, and threatened war. The danger was averted by the removal of M. THIERS from office, and the accession of M. GUIZOT, who established with England the "*entente cordiale*" (Oct. 29, 1840). The English government permitted the removal of the remains of Napoleon from St. Helena; they were deposited in the church of the Invalides (Dec. 15, 1840), under the dome of which they now rest in a magnificent sepulchre.

In 1841 the ministry of Lord Melbourne fell through its own weakness and the growing confidence of the nation in Sir Robert Peel, who came into power with a decided majority in the commons, after the Whigs had tried an appeal to the people and offered to the Corn-Law Reformers the bait of a fixed duty of eight shillings a quarter. Sir Robert grappled at once with the whole question of commercial policy, and with the accumulated deficit of several years. He adopted the principle, which has been since universally accepted, of lightening the weight of taxation on articles of necessary consumption and on the raw materials of our manufactures, and trusting to the impulse thus given to trade for supplying the revenue under other heads. In old times particular branches of industry were encouraged by "bounties;" they were afterward "protected" against foreign competition by import duties; but the free-traders had condemned such protection as an injustice to the consumer, and, in the long-run, an injury to the producer; and Peel now proclaimed that the true commercial policy was "to buy in the cheapest market and sell in the dearest." But he proceeded cautiously at first. He abolished many petty and unproductive duties, and reduced others which were so high as to check consumption or encourage smuggling. For corn he retained the "*sliding scale*," but lowered the "*pivot price*" at which the duty became small enough to admit foreign grain freely in seasons of scarcity. To meet the existing deficit and the temporary loss involved by his reforms he imposed a property and income tax of sevenpence in the pound on all incomes above £150. The tax was limited to three years, in the hope (though *no pledge was given*) that it might then be dispensed with. Those three years bore triumphant witness to the Peel policy. A large annual surplus enabled him to go on reducing taxes, and especially to attack the *excise duties*, which not only raised the price of articles of necessity, but most vexatiously hampered manufacture and invention, such as those on *soap* and *glass*. The latter duty alone would have prevented the erection of the "Crystal Palaces" at Hyde Park and Sydenham. The success of Peel's policy was, in fact, too great for its author. It convinced men, except some farmers and landlords, that "protection" for the growers of corn was no longer tenable. The Anti-Corn-Law League was declared to be "*a great fact*," and the end was hastened by the cold, wet summer of 1845, and the "potato disease," which plunged Ireland into a famine. The league was joined by Lord MORPETH (now the Earl of Carlisle). Lord John Russell, who had become the leader of that party, declared for free-trade in corn, taunting Sir Robert Peel for adhering to protection. But Sir Robert had already made his decision and carried with him the majority of his cabinet. To avoid, however, the apparent inconsistency for which he had once suffered so severely on the Catholic question, he resigned (Dec. 11, 1845), promising his support to any ministry who would repeal the corn-laws. The queen sent for Lord John Russell, who failed to form a government, and Sir Robert returned to office, though with the loss of some of his colleagues, especially Lord Stanley, who became the head of the new "protectionist party." The repeal of the corn-laws (leaving only a duty of one shilling per quarter for the purpose of registering statistics) was accompanied by another sweeping reform of the tariff, to effect which the income-tax was renewed for three years more, and it has since been continued at various rates (1846). This great change involved personal consequences, of which Peel had counted the cost. He was deserted by a large section of the party which he had spent fifteen years in rallying, amidst much bitter resentment, such as was expressed in the invectives of Mr. BENJAMIN DISRAELI (b. 1805). An Irish question was again seized as the occasion for his overthrow. That unhappy country was still the prey of agitation. O'Connell had quarreled with the Whigs before their fall, and roused the nation for repeal by a system of "monster meetings." In 1843 the government had prosecuted him and obtained a verdict, on which he was imprisoned; but the House of Lords reversed the judgment. His influence was, however, declining and his health failing;* but he was succeeded by a more violent party, who, under the name of "Young Ireland," appealed to the memories of 1798 and of the United Irishmen. The scarcity of 1845–6 came to their aid, and a new coercion bill was required. On its proposal the Whigs united with the Protectionists to defeat Sir Robert Peel, who finally retired from office in 1846, leaving, as he truly boasted, a name which will ever be held in honor by the industrious producer—the class from which his own father rose—though exposed to the charge of vacillation and inconsistency.

Like Sir Robert Walpole, whom he resembled in many points, he was a peace minister; but he was more than once in danger of war. A long-standing dispute with the United States about their boundaries on the northeast and northwest was settled by the mission of Lord Ashburton (Alexander Baring) on terms by which strict rights were sacrificed to the desire for peace. The "*entente cordiale*" with France was endangered in 1843 by her seizure of Tahiti and imprisonment of the English consul, Mr. Pritchard, and still more in 1846

* He died at Genoa (May, 1847), on his way to Rome, to ask the blessing of the pope.

by the affair of the Spanish marriages, which needs a brief explanation. In 1833 Ferdinand VII. died, having made a will in favor of his daughter, who succeeded him as Isabella II., and revived the constitution; but Don Carlos, the late king's brother, claimed the crown as the male heir. As in Portugal, the queen's cause was espoused by England and France, and a "British legion" of volunteers went to Spain under a Peninsular veteran, Sir DE LACY EVANS. After a long Carlist war and many internal revolutions Queen Isabella was established on her throne. Louis Philippe now revived the old Bourbon policy of the "family compact;" and, in spite of the successive opposition of Lords Aberdeen and Palmerston, the king of the French arranged the marriage of the queen of Spain with her cousin, Don Francisco of Assisi, while her sister, the Infanta Louisa, was united to Louis Philippe's youngest son, the Duke of Montpensier (Oct. 10, 1846). The result was a coolness between France and England till the revolution of 1848; and at one time there was even an alarm of a French invasion.

Meanwhile the government of Lord John Russell pursued Sir Robert Peel's commercial policy in their settlement of the sugar duties (1847) and of the navigation laws (1849); but the course of prosperity soon received a severe check. In 1847 a bad season and a failure of the potato-crop produced a famine in Ireland and great distress in England. A loan of £10,000,000 was voted for the relief of the Irish; but they found a more effectual refuge in emigration; and, while they began to prosper in America and the colonies, their removal, together with the sale of encumbered estates by a court established by parliament, opened the way for a new race of owners and cultivators and for the influx of capital. A new era of prosperity began with the famine of 1847; but it is already overclouded by the renewal of those agrarian murders which have been a greater curse to Ireland than Celtic indolence, Saxon tyranny, priestly domination, or even professional agitators (1862).

The year 1848 was a great epoch in European politics. Ever since 1816 the restoration of despotism had created profound discontent. The French revolution of 1830 vibrated through the Continent. We have seen its effect in Belgium. The *Poles* struck another blow for independence, but it failed after a fierce conflict, and the kingdom of Poland was absorbed in Russia. The Prussians and Hanoverians asked in vain for their long-promised constitutions, and Germans of every state dreamed of a united Fatherland. But the deepest source of discontent arose from the rule of Austria over Lombardy and Venetia, and virtually, through family alliances and treaties, over the whole of Italy. All resistance was kept down by martial law, and Italian patriots were immured in dungeons such as those described by Silvio Pellico. Tyranny begat conspiracy, and conspiracy was made the pretext for fresh tyranny. At length, in 1846, a new pontiff was elected, Pope PIUS IX., who was believed to be a friend of Italian liberty; and he introduced some reforms in the Papal States. About the same time the Italians found another leader in CHARLES ALBERT king of Sardinia, who granted a constitution to his own states. At this crisis the question of parliamentary reform was agitated in France. The new dynasty had been greatly weakened by the sudden death of the Duke of Orleans, the heir to the throne, a popular and liberal prince (July 13, 1842), and the government had been conducted too much by corruption and intrigue. The prohibition by Guizot of a reform banquet (Feb. 22, 1848) led to an insurrection in Paris, which ended in a revolution and the proclamation of a republic (Feb. 24, 1848). The flame spread over Europe; but this is not the place to write the history of the rising of 1848 and the collapse of 1849. The English Chartists attempted a display of force, which was put down by the mere attitude of precaution (April 10, 1848); and a more serious insurrection of "Young Ireland" had a grotesque end in the capture of Mr. SMITH O'BRIEN in a cabbage-garden. He and several other leaders were found guilty of treason, but their lives were spared, and after some years' transportation they were pardoned.

The half-century ended amidst a profound peace, which suggested to Prince Albert and other philanthropists an exhibition of the industry of all nations in Hyde Park. The genius of Sir JOSEPH PAXTON provided a fit edifice of iron and glass, and Sir Robert Peel was laboring for its success when he was killed by a fall from his horse (May, 1850). The exhibition was opened by the queen on May 1, 1851; and its brilliant success, besides being imitated in other cities and countries, led to the plan of *decennial Exhibitions*, and the second was opened on May 1, 1862. Owing to a breach with Lord Palmerston the ministry of Lord John Russell fell in 1852; and the Earl of DERBY (formerly Lord Stanley, b. 1799), on acceding to power, with Mr. Disraeli, renounced the policy of protection. In the autumn of this year the Duke of Wellington died (Sept.), and was laid by the side of Nelson in St. Paul's (Nov. 18, 1852. By a strange coincidence the dynasty of Napoleon was restored in France just after his conqueror's death. CHARLES LOUIS BONAPARTE, son of Louis Bonaparte king of Holland, and Hortense Beauharnais, having been elected president of the French republic in 1849, overthrew the constitution by a *coup d'état* (Dec. 2, 1851), was elected emperor of the French by the modern invention of universal suffrage, and proclaimed by the title of NAPOLEON III. (Dec. 2, 1852). Before Christmas the government of Lord Derby were defeated on Mr. Disraeli's budget, and a coalition ministry was formed from the friends of Sir Robert Peel, the Whigs, and the Radicals, with the Earl of ABERDEEN as premier. Mr. WILLIAM EWART GLADSTONE (b. 1809), as chancellor of the exchequer, produced his memorable budget of 1853, on the principles of Sir Robert Peel; but some of his calculations were deranged by the war with Russia in defense of Turkey, which broke out early in 1854. The events of that war, and of the INDIAN MUTINY of 1857, which led to the transference of India from the Company to the imperial government, are too recent to need relation here; nor have we thought it necessary to give the details of the Indian wars since 1840, or of those by which CHINA has been brought into commercial intercourse with Europe. The year 1859 witnessed the conquest of Lombardy from Austria by the united arms of France and Sardinia, followed by the wonderful enterprise of *Garibaldi* in Naples, which made Victor Emanuel king of all Italy, except Rome and the Venetian territory (1860).

During the period thus glanced at the country has been governed by Viscount PALMERSTON, who was called to power on the fall of Lord Aberdeen (1855), and has since remained premier, with the short interruption of Lord Derby's second government (1858–1859). On the verge of fourscore, he is still, in cheerful vigor, "our youthful premier." Lord John Russell, called to the House of Peers as EARL RUSSELL, is foreign secretary. The last achievement of this ministry has been the completion, by Mr. Gladstone, of Sir Robert Peel's great scheme of free trade, by means of the budgets of 1860 and 1861, and the commercial treaty with France negotiated by Mr. Cobden. Nor must we omit from this brief review of the last decade the revival of a military spirit, "not for defiance, but defense," which has called 150,000 citizens to arms as volunteers, while the resources of science are taxed to the utmost in the competition between guns such as Milton's angels fought with, and ships which may almost be described in his words as clad with triple folds of "adamantine steel, impregnable." That the time is not yet come to dispense with such engines is proved by the frightful civil war now raging in America, between the northern and southern divisions of the United States, and which for a moment threatened to involve England at the close of 1861.

Twenty-five years are now completed of a reign which more than rivals that of Elizabeth in prosperity and glory. Though by no means a period of unbroken quiet, all its troubles have thus far ended well. The rebellions of Canada, Ireland, and India have led in each case to better relations with the imperial government. Wars have closed in honorable peace, after their disasters had been retrieved; liberties have been extended, laws improved, the penal code mitigated, and imprisonment for debt virtually abolished. Commerce has been set free, and practical force has been given to the new doctrine that the interests of nations are mutual and not opposite. The British colonial empire has been secured and vastly extended, and the gold of Australia and Columbia has given a new impulse to industry. The spirit of enterprise and discovery has unlocked the secrets of the Arctic Seas and of the continent of Africa. Science has made rapid strides; and the discoveries of the power-loom and the steam-engine in the last generation have been crowned by the general use of the railway and the electric telegraph. Famine, pestilence, and other visitations of Providence have called forth abundant springs of private charity, and forced upon the people the study of the laws on which life, health, and welfare depend, under the new names of *Sanitary* and *Social Science.* Among the foremost in this movement was the foremost subject of the queen, her royal consort, Prince ALBERT; and the last great event that we have to record is his untimely death on Saturday, Dec. 14, 1861. He had long been steadily growing in the respect and love of the British people, earned entirely by his merit. When he came to England the popular prejudice against the German connections of the royal family had not died out; and there were some in high places who looked with jealousy upon a prince whose youth had been spent in the cultivation of sound and elegant learning. An extreme party raised the cry of undue influence when it was found that the prince had, with the consent of successive ministers, taken his natural position as the queen's helper in state affairs. But he lived down all these prejudices by abstaining as well from party politics as from the meaner temptations of his lofty place, and devoting himself to the sacred duty of helping the queen and training their children for their exalted station in the fear of God. To have done this and given no offense would have been much; but it is his peculiar praise that, shut out from political activity, he found a new scope for his energy and wisdom in a work which no one else could have done as well, and in which he will long be missed. He was ready to aid every well-planned scheme of social improvement; and his speeches on these occasions are as much marked by freshness of thought and purity of language as by the earnest desire to do good. But his great achievement was the Exhibition of 1851—an untried experiment, which his perseverance carried through popular coolness and powerful opposition to triumphant success. When the new Exhibition was opened on May 1, 1862, the most striking feature of the ceremony was the absence of him who had planned the scheme. Meanwhile her Majesty's profound grief has been shared by a dutiful and affectionate people, and consoled by her children, of whom none have been lost and none have proved unworthy. They are: (1.) *Victoria Adelaide Maria Louisa*, princess royal, born Nov. 21, 1840; (2.) ALBERT EDWARD, prince of Wales, born Nov. 9, 1841; (3.) *Alice Maud Mary*, born April 25, 1843; (4.) *Alfred Ernest Albert*, born Aug. 6, 1844; (5.) *Helena Augusta Victoria*, born May 25, 1846; (6.) *Louisa Caroline Alberta*, born March 18, 1848; (7.) *Arthur William Patrick Albert*, born May 1, 1850; (8.) *Leopold George Duncan Albert*, born April 7, 1853; and (9.) *Beatrice Mary Victoria Feodore*, born April 14, 1857. The princess royal was married Jan. 25, 1858, to Prince *Frederick William*, now crown prince of Prussia. The Prince of Wales, by his father's care, has resided for a time at the Universities of Oxford, Cambridge, and Edinburgh, and traveled through Canada and the United States, where he obtained much popularity; he has visited Rome, Egypt, and Palestine, where he was the first European, since the Crusades, who has been permitted to see the tomb of the patriarchs at Hebron. Prince ALFRED has entered the navy; and on July 1, 1862, the queen, without laying aside her mourning, celebrated at Osborne the marriage of the Princess ALICE, who has been her chief earthly comfort in her deep affliction, to his royal highness Prince Louis of Hesse Darmstadt. The Prince of Wales attained his majority on Nov. 9, 1862, and the year closed with the announcement of his betrothal to the Princess Alexandra of Denmark.

Queen Victoria.

A. Genealogy of the House of Egbert.

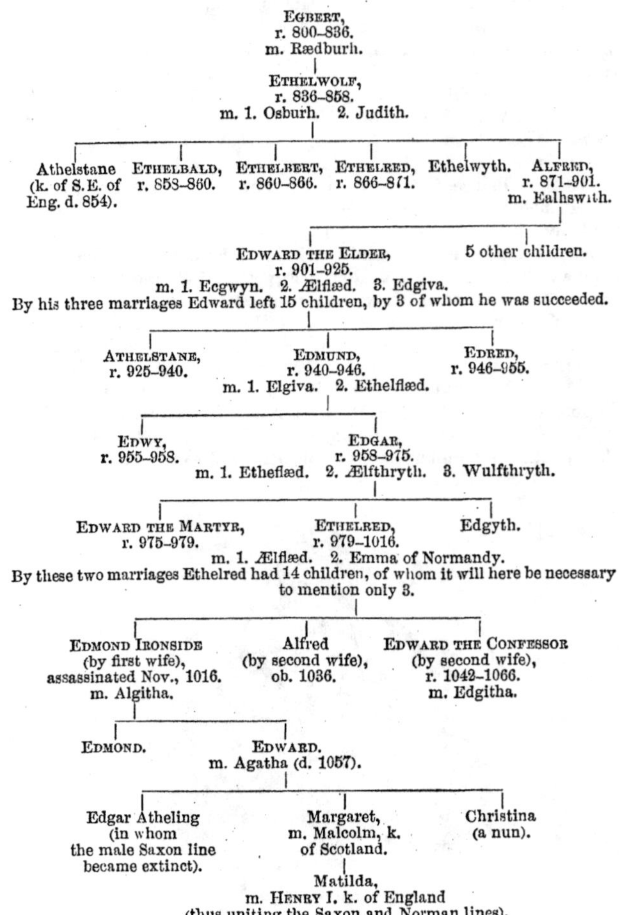

B. Genealogy of the Anglo-Danish Kings of England.

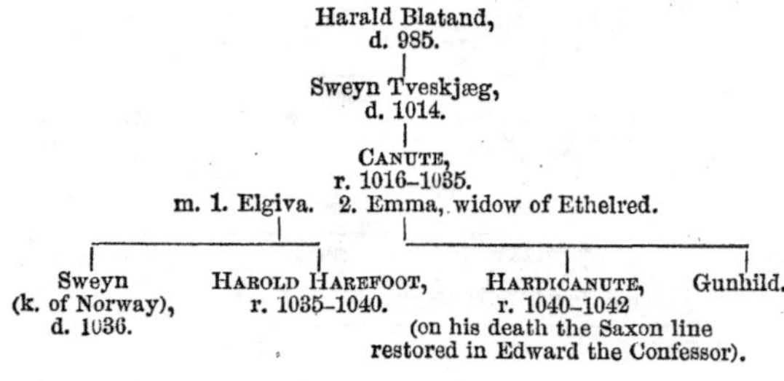

Harald Blatand,
d. 985.

Sweyn Tveskjæg,
d. 1014.

CANUTE,
r. 1016–1035.
m. 1. Elgiva. 2. Emma, widow of Ethelred.

Sweyn (k. of Norway), d. 1036.

HAROLD HAREFOOT, r. 1035–1040.

HARDICANUTE, r. 1040–1042 (on his death the Saxon line restored in Edward the Confessor).

Gunhild.

C. Genealogy of William the Conqueror and his House.

(FROM ROLLO, FIRST DUKE OF NORMANDY.)

Rollo the Ganger, d. 931.

William Longue-épée, d. 942.

Richard I. Sans Peur, d. 996.

Richard II. le Bon, d. 1026. | Emma, m. Ethelred.

Children of Richard II.: Richard III., d. 1028. | Robert the Devil, d. 1035.

Robert the Devil (by Harlotta.)

WILLIAM I.
b. 1027. d. 7 Sept. 1087.
m. Matilda, d. of Baldwin,
count of Flanders.

Robert. | Richard. | WILLIAM II. d. 2 Aug. 1100. | HENRY I. d. 1 Dec. 1135. m. 1. Matilda of Scotland. 2. Adeliza of Louvain (by whom, no children). | 6 daughters. Of whom Adela, the fourth, m. Stephen, count of Blois.

Children of Henry I.: William, d. 1120. m. Matilda, d. of Fulk of Anjou. | Matilda. m. 1. Henry V. of Germany. 2. Geoffrey of Anjou. | Robert (by a concubine). d. 1147. | Several other illegitimate children.

Son of Adela: STEPHEN, d. 1154.

Son of Matilda: HENRY II.

D. Genealogy of the House of Plantagenet.

GEOFFREY PLANTAGENET,
count of Anjou, d. 1151.

HENRY II. b. 1133. d. 1189.
m. Eleanor, countess of Poitou and Aquitaine.

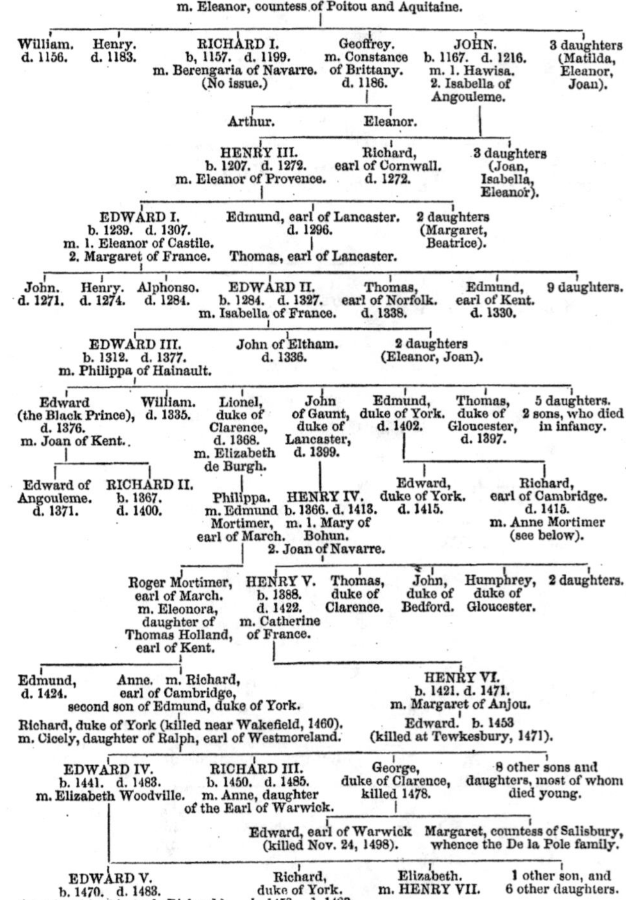

E. Genealogy of the House of Tudor.

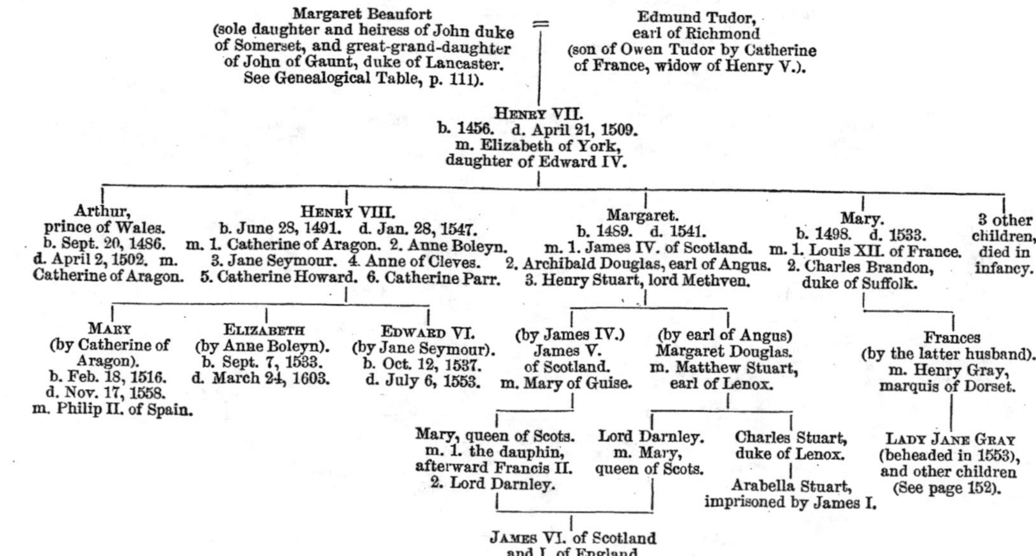

F. Genealogy of the House of Stuart.

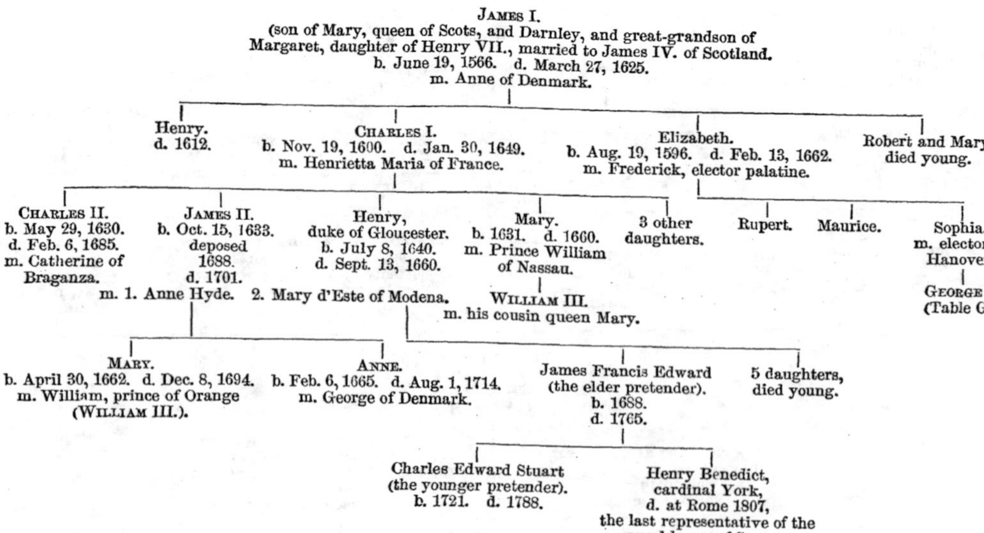

G. Genealogy of the House of Brunswick-Hanover.

GEORGE I. (son of the duke of Brunswick-Luneburg, afterward elector of Hanover, and Sophia, youngest child of the elector Palatine and Elizabeth, eldest daughter of James I.—see p. 333). b. May 23, 1660. d. June 11, 1727. m. Sophia Dorothea of Zell.

- GEORGE II. b. Oct. 30, 1683. d. Oct. 25, 1760. m. Wilhelmina Carolina of Brandenburg-Anspach.
- Sophia Dorothy. m. 1706, Frederick William, afterward king of Prussia.

Children of George II.:

- Frederick, prince of Wales. b. Jan. 20, 1707. d. Jan. 29, 1751. m. Augusta of Saxe Gotha.
- William Augustus, duke of Cumberland. b. 1721. d. 1765. (unm.)
- Anne. m. prince of Orange. d. 1759.
- Amelia. d. 1786. (unm.)
- Elizabeth. d. 1758. (unm.)
- Mary. m. Landgrave of Hesse Cassel. d. 1771 (leaving issue).
- Louisa. m. Frederick V. king of Denmark, d. 1751 (leaving issue).

Children of Frederick, prince of Wales:

- GEORGE III. b. June 4. 1738. d. Jan. 29, 1820. m. Sophia Charlotte of Mecklenburg Strelitz.
- Edward Augustus, duke of York. d. 1767. (unm.)
- William Henry, duke of Gloucester. b. 1743. d. 1805. m. countess Waldegrave.
  - Frederick William, duke of Gloucester. b. 4776. d. 1834. m. princess Mary, daughter of George III. (no issue).
  - Sophia Matilda. b. 1773. d. 1844.
- Henry Frederick, duke of Cumberland. b. 1745. d. 1790. m. lady Luttrell (no issue).
- Augusta. m. duke of Brunswick-Wolfenbuttel.
  - Charles Frederick William, duke of Brunswick, fell at Quatre Bras, June 16, 1815 (leaving issue).
  - Charlotte. m. duke of Wurtemberg. d. 1788.
  - CAROLINE. m. George, prince of Wales (GEORGE IV.). d. Aug. 7, 1821.
- Caroline Matilda. m. Christian VII. king of Denmark (leaving issue).

Children of George III.:

- GEORGE IV. b. Aug. 12, 1762. d. June 26, 1830. m. Caroline of Brunswick.
  - Princess Charlotte. b. Mar. 7, 1796. d. Nov. 6, 1817. m. Leopold of Saxe-Coburg, now king of the Belgians (no surv. issue).
- Frederick, duke of York. b. 1763. d. 1827. m. Frederica of Prussia (no issue).
- WILLIAM IV. duke of Clarence. b. Aug 24, 1765. d. June 20, 1837. m. Adelaide of Saxe Meiningen (no surv. issue).
- Edward, duke of Kent. b. 1767. d. 1820. m. Victoria, of Saxe Coburg Saalfeld.
  - VICTORIA. b. May 24, 1819. m. Feb. 10, 1840, ALBERT, second son of Ernest I. duke of Coburg and Gotha. b. 1819. d. Dec. 14, 1861.
- Ernest, duke of Cumberland and king of Hanover. b. 1771. d. 1851. m. Frederica of Mecklenburg Strelitz.
  - George V. king of Hanover. b. 1819 (has issue).
- Augustus Frederick, duke of Sussex. b. 1773. d. 1843.
- Adolphus Frederick, duke of Cambridge. b. 1774. d. 1850. m. Augusta of Hesse Cassel.
  - George, duke of Cambridge. b. 1819.
  - Augusta. b. 1822. m. duke of Mecklenburg Strelitz (has issue).
  - Mary Adelaide. b. 1833.
- Charlotte. b. 1766. d. 1828. m. king of Wurtemberg (no issue).
- Augusta. b. 1768. d. 1840 (unm.).
- Elizabeth. b. 1770. d. 1840. m. landgrave of Hesse Homburg (no issue).
- Mary. b. 1776. d. 1840. m. her cousin the duke of Gloucester (no issue).
- Sophia. b. 1777. d. 1848 (unm.).
- Amelia. b. 1783. d. 1810 (unm.).

Children of Victoria:

- Albert, prince of Wales. b. Nov. 9, 1841.
- Alfred. b. Aug. 6, 1844.
- Arthur. b. May 1, 1850.
- Leopold. b. Apr. 7, 1853.
- Victoria, princess royal. b. Nov. 21, 1840. m. Frederick, prince of Prussia, 1858 (has issue).
- Alice. b. Apr. 25, 1843. m. Louis, prince of Hesse, July 1, 1862.
- Helena. b. May 25, 1846.
- Louisa. b. Mar. 18, 1848.
- Beatrice. b. Apr. 14, 1857.

H. Descent of Victoria I. from Egbert.

1. Egbert. 2. Ethelwolf. 3. Alfred the Great. 4. Edward the Elder. 5. Edmund. 6. Edgar. 7. Ethelred. 8. Edmund Ironside. 9. Edward (not a king). 10. Margaret, wife of Malcolm king of Scotland. 11. Matilda, wife of Henry I. 12. Matilda or Maud, empress of Germany, and wife of Geoffrey of Anjou. 13. Henry II. 14. John. 15. Henry III. 16. Edward I. 17. Edward II. 18. Edward III.

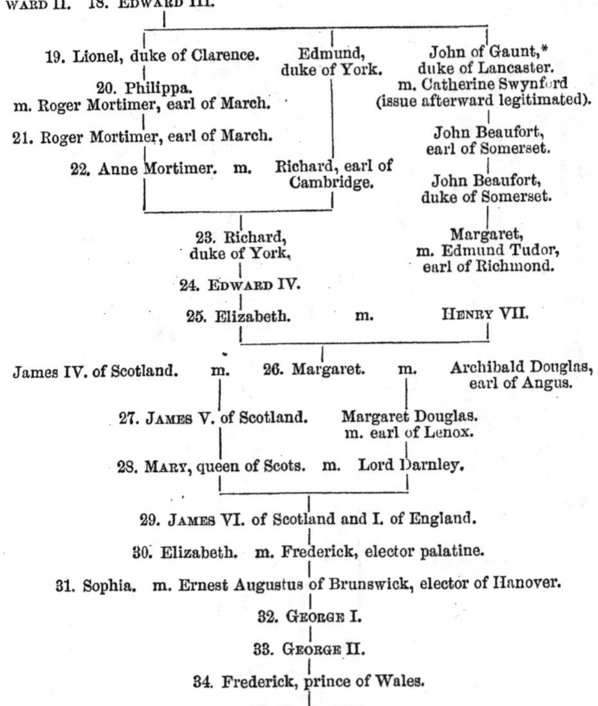

29. James VI. of Scotland and I. of England.

30. Elizabeth. m. Frederick, elector palatine.

31. Sophia. m. Ernest Augustus of Brunswick, elector of Hanover.

32. George I.

33. George II.

34. Frederick, prince of Wales.

35. George III.

36. Edward, duke of Kent.

37. Victoria.

* John of Gaunt was older than Edmund, but the latter is placed second for typographical convenience.

INDEX.

C.

D.

E.

F.

L.

N.

S.

Wolsey's Groat.

THE END.

www.ingramcontent.com/pod-product-compliance
Lightning Source LLC
LaVergne TN
LVHW020119110826
845151LV00001B/214

* 9 7 8 1 4 2 5 5 4 1 9 4 1 *